SABBATH BLOODY SABBATH

SABBATH BLOODY SABBATH

JOEL McIVER

OMNIBUS PRESS

LONDON / NEW YORK / PARIS / SYDNEY / COPENHAGEN / BERLIN / MADRID / TOKYO

Exclusive Distributors
Music Sales Limited,
14-15 Berners Street,
London W1T 3LJ, UK.

Music Sales Corporation,
257 Park Avenue South,
New York, NY 10010, USA.

Macmillan Distribution Services,
53 Park West Drive,
Derrimut, Vic 3030,
Australia.

To the Music Trade only:
Music Sales Limited,
14-15 Berners Street,
London W1T 3LJ, UK.

Every effort has been made to trace the copyright holders of the photographs in this book but one or two were unreachable. We would be grateful if the photographers concerned would contact us.

Printed in the United States of America by Quebecor World.

A catalog record for this book is available from the British Library.

Visit Omnibus Press on the web at www.omnibuspress.com

This book is dedicated to Tom McIver,
Born on June 29, 2006

CONTENTS

ACKNOWLEDGMENTS

Thanks to Carlos Anaia, Geoff Barton, Kat Bjelland, Mark Brend, Chris Charlesworth, Dave Clarke, Mat Croft, Becky Deayton, Karl Demata, Katon W. Depena, Bernard Doe, Malcolm Dome, John Doran, KJ Doughton, Jeff 'Mantas' Dunn, Daryl Easlea, Darren Edwards, Gillian Gaar, Ian Glasper, Dorothy Howe, Glenn Hughes, Mirai Kawashima, Sharon Kelly, Killjoy, Bruce Lamond, Sarah Lees, Joe Matera, Bob Nalbandian, Mike Oldfield, Dennis Pepa, Thomas Pilhatsch, Martin Popoff, Ken Sharp, Garry Sharpe-Young at Rockdetector, Joe Shooman, Jim Simpson, Andy Sneap, Louise Sugrue, Carl Swann, Tommy Udo, Sarah Watson, Barry Winton, Mark Wirtz, the Corky Nips, the staff of *Acoustic, Bass Guitar, Bass Player, Classic Rock, DVD Review, Future Music, Metal Hammer, Record Collector, Total Film* and *Total Guitar* magazines, and the personnel at Universal, EMI, Roadrunner, Century Media, Peaceville, Union Square, Warners and BBC 6 Music who helped out along the way.

Love to Emma, Alice, Robin and Abi, Dad, John and Jen, the Parr, Houston-Miller, Everitt-Bossmann, Sendall and Tominey families, Phil and Kate, Vinay and Ren, Dave and Dawn, Woody and Glynis, Simone, Quinn, Amy and Anden Harrington, Christof and Anja, Big Alice and the Knight family, Frank, Raddion, Ian Salsbury, Wyrd, Dora the Winter Sprite and the Barnes, Ellis, Johnston, Legerton and Maynard warriors of metal.

INTRODUCTION

HEAVY metal is a circus – ridiculous, laughable and garish, but com-
pelling and addictive. The music is loud and angry; the performers
vary from the peeved via the homicidal to the outright deranged; and the
image is ludicrous, picked apart by psychiatrists and mocked by those not
in on the joke. They think it's stupid, old-fashioned, prejudiced, ignorant,
intolerant and, worst of all, unfashionable.

How wrong they are.

Black Sabbath fit all these descriptions, and then some. Labelled by most
as the world's first heavy metal band, pigeonholed by many more into the
hard-rock category, and simply worshipped by millions more who don't
give a toss either way, the ever-changing line-up has bludgeoned its way
through thousands of stage shows on dozens of tours, scooped up an array
of gold discs, headlined over more or less every rock band that has meant
anything since 1970, inspired a legion of Sabbath-indebted metal bands
and – crucially – seen their errant singer transcend his rock roots to
become one of the world's most recognisable celebrities. Although other
rock idols have taken the step out of the dressing-room and onto
prime-time TV – Gene Simmons of Kiss and Steven Tyler of Aerosmith
come to mind – Ozzy Osbourne is the only wild man of metal to merit a
witty aside in a speech by an American president, appear on non-music
TV for years on end, and be lauded (rather than castigated) for his lifelong
struggle with addictive substances. Unbelievably, Ozzy is cool, and
Sabbath with him.

Some readers of this book may not be fully aware of the 30 years as a
musician that Ozzy endured before mainstream success launched him into
a million living rooms. Others may not realise what a vast creative force
Black Sabbath were in the Seventies, how they struggled to find their way
in the Eighties and how they settled at last into a place of simultaneous
respectability and commercial appeal in the Nineties and beyond. *Sabbath
Bloody Sabbath* tells the unique story of the band from Aston, Birmingham,
that shook the world – and somehow survived to tell the tale.

A story as epic, brightly coloured and downright violent as this only
works if the protagonists involved have their say – and so you'll read interviews personally conducted by me over the last few years with Sabbath
band-members Tony Iommi, Geezer Butler, Bill Ward, Glenn Hughes,

1

Ian Gillan, Ronnie James Dio, Bobby Rondinelli and Bob Daisley in this book. Their first manager, Jim Simpson, provided plenty of illuminating insights too. Other musical luminaries who shared their opinions about Sabbath with me include Ritchie Blackmore, Leo Lyons (Ten Years After), Tom Araya and Kerry King (Slayer), John Lydon, Ian 'Lemmy' Kilmister, King Diamond, Nikki Sixx (Mötley Crüe), Bill Gould (Faith No More), Yngwie J Malmsteen, Dave Mustaine (Megadeth), Stephen O'Malley and Greg Anderson (Sunn O)))), Geddy Lee (Rush), Zakk Wylde (Black Label Society/Ozzy Osbourne), Paul Allender (Cradle Of Filth), the late 'Dimebag' Darrell Abbott (Pantera/Damageplan), Ice-T, Joey Jordison and Mick Thompson (Slipknot), Bobby Ellsworth (Overkill), Jeff Becerra (Possessed), Conrad Lant and Jeff Dunn (Venom), John Bush (Armored Saint/Anthrax), Katon W. DePena (Hirax), Mikael Akerfeldt (Opeth), Phil Fasciana (Malevolent Creation), Sean Harris (Diamond Head) and Rob Halford (Judas Priest). Quite a stellar gathering, I'm sure you'll agree: these people give a truly widescreen perspective to the whole Sabbath story.

No Ozzy or Sharon, then? No indeed – penetrating that particular command bunker, with official books crowding the shelves, was impossible. But that's OK with me: as I pointed out in my 2004 book *Justice For All: The Truth About Metallica* (also published by Omnibus), access to the stars often means being handcuffed to being eternally positive about them – and I don't think you, the reader, me as an author, or the band as a subject would be best served by a book that wasn't objective. Where Black Sabbath have strayed from the paths of righteousness or common sense, I've said so, in big letters for all to see.

Also in common with the Metallica biography, I've interrupted the chronological flow of narrative from time to time to discuss various aspects of Sabbath's history that needed investigation. There are some serious questions to be answered, and a whole lot of conclusions to be determined. This is, after all, a one-of-a-kind subject which requires some analysis. If that sounds too serious, just remember that we're dealing with decapitated bats and severed fingertips here – there's a funny side to the story too . . .

But don't be put off by all that. Like Sabbath themselves, we're here to rock. Enjoy the ride, and feel free to drop me a line when you've read it.

Joel McIver, spring 2006
www.joelmciver.co.uk
joel@joelmciver.co.uk

PART ONE

Invoking The Demon: 1948–1978

CHAPTER ONE

Before 1968

O N every level imaginable, the Birmingham suburb of Aston in 1948 was a world away from today.

When John Michael Osbourne was born on December 3 and taken to the home of his parents, Jack and Lillian, who lived at 14 Lodge Road, nothing indicated that he might one day become the area's most famous resident. His parents both worked in the local motor industry, his dad enduring night shifts and his mum employed by the Lucas light company in their wiring factory. Aston itself was slowly recovering from serious bombing during World War II, a mere four years before, and the poverty that most families experienced was easily visible in the back-to-back houses where they lived – mostly grouped around communal courtyards and designated for demolition as soon as the area could regain its post-war feet. Until this could take place, in the Fifties and Sixties, most of Aston's working population was confined to living conditions that would seem Dickensian to modern-day observers. John, his brothers Paul and Tony, his sisters Jean, Iris and Gillian and their parents were forced to live in typically cramped style for the area.

"We only had three bedrooms, and there was six kids . . . My mother and father had the front room, and we used to fucking pile into the back room," recalled John, then and since universally known as 'Ozzy' after his surname. "We had a bucket of piss at the bottom of the bed – a fucking plastic bucket of piss – for months," he added. "We never had clean sheets, we used to have overcoats as fucking bedclothes. This is God's honest truth."

Another Aston family, the Wards, who lived on Witton Lodge Road, had a son William born seven months before Ozzy on May 5, 1948. Bill once described Aston as "a no-frills place. It's a hard-core, very old area of the city that was bombed in the war. When I was growing up, we had gas-lights; the landscape was all bombed out from the Germans. And I've seen tough things, lots of stabbings, men coming out of the pub and literally dropping dead, and things like that. There were a lot of vagrants, but the city had an incredible beauty at the same time. For me, it was all I knew."

The half-destroyed carcass of Aston was showing signs of recovery during Ozzy and Bill's childhood, but it was still a dangerous place to be, as Ward explained: "Birmingham is on a par with Pittsburgh or Detroit. It's full of industry. They make cars, guns, bullets and all kinds of metal stuff. It is a really big industrial place. During the Second World War, the Germans knew what was going on in Aston, so it was blitzed. Growing up in Aston, there were a lot of buildings that were blown up but not demolished. I would walk out of my door and there were all these green fields for two or three blocks that were filled with structures that were left over from the war . . . People from Aston were very strong. They would place a high value on how their homes looked. The front doors of their houses were immaculately polished. On any given Saturday night, however, any Astonion worth his salt would turn around and smack the crap out of you. It was pretty bad, really."

As with any depressed urban area – and especially immediately after the war – career options were limited, but a common solution for young men who couldn't find work in industry was to enter the armed forces. The nearby Butler family, whose youngest son, Terence Michael Joseph, was born on July 17, 1949, saw two sons join the army. This proved to be an eye-opening experience for the Birmingham-bred recruits, who forged friendships with soldiers from as far afield as London. As Terence recalled, "Two of my brothers were in the army, and the regiment they were in had a lot of blokes from London in it – and they used to call everybody a 'geezer'. So when my brothers came home on leave they'd be calling everybody a geezer. Then, of course, I picked it up and when I went to school I'd be calling everybody it."

Terence thus rapidly lost his given name and was nicknamed 'Geezer', permanently. He sighed, "I got cursed with the name from then on."

"He used to call everybody a geezer – he was always pointing at people and saying this geezer or that geezer . . . It just stuck. I won't tell you what we called Bill," sniggered Ozzy, much later.

It wasn't long before the boys began to get into trouble: not yet criminal in nature, but involving escapades that could easily have left them injured or killed. As Ward recalled, "In order to be in a gang when we were kids, one of the initiations was to walk down this sewer. It was absolutely terrifying as a youngster. It was about half an hour long. I was initiated into a gang after I had finished walking through there. The river runs through it very swiftly, as well. It was pretty fucking stupid stuff. It was black down there."

School didn't offer much respite for any of them, least of all Ozzy, who attended the King Edward VI Grammar School on Aston's Frederick Road. As he remembered, "I'm the original clown. When I was a child at school, if people were miserable around me, I'd do some crazy things like jump through fucking doorways, anything to make them amused – hang myself, anything, because I hated to see sad faces."

This reference to hanging himself was no joke. As he explained, he gave it a go in 1962, at the tender age of 14: "I tried to hang myself once. I thought I wanted to find out what it's like to be hung. In England, you get these fucking terraced houses, and you get things they call entries – sort of alleyways – and you get these bars on the entries. I thought, well, I want to hang myself – this is God's honest truth. So I got my mother's washing line, made a noose, put it over the bar in the entry, then fucking jumped off the chair and held the rope. I thought if I'm gonna die, I'll let go of the rope and I'll fucking be OK."

Such behaviour came at a price, paid by Ozzy to his stern father Jack: "My father come out of the house and caught me doing it, and he beat the shit out of me. I thought, fuck, I should have done it for real."

Despite the beatings, Ozzy's parents imparted to him certain skills that he could put to good use later in life, as he recalled: "My father was a fucking gem. I got my front from my father, and my singing voice from my mother . . . he'd come back from the working men's club, a bar that he used to go and drink [at], and they used to throw him off the bus every day. My mother was an amateur sort of singer . . . she used to go to these talent contests."

Like many fathers of his generation, Jack Osbourne believed firmly in discipline and enforcing it physically on his children. Ozzy recalled being beaten "a hell of a lot", but added, "It was a part of life in them days. It was good times, man." In any case, being beaten didn't stop the young Osbourne from notching up a veritable litany of unhinged behaviour, beginning at the age of 11 when he attacked his aunt's cat with a knife. Visiting his family in Sunderland ("That was the first time I ever saw the ocean. I fucking broke apart. I've got an auntie, fuckin' – what's her name? Elsie? Ada? Auntie Ada! She's got a fucking husband who's like a village monk"), Ozzy explained, "I once stabbed her cat, when I was 11, in the backyard when my mother was sunbathing. I got whupped around the fucking house . . ."

He went on: "I set fire to my sister once. I didn't like her. I poured gasoline on her skirt and set fire to her. I got beaten round the fuckin' house, as usual . . . I tried to strangle my younger brother 'cause I hated him . . . One day some friends of mine gave him a used contraceptive and told him it was a balloon . . . He came in the house blowing it. My father washed his mouth with soap."

Ozzy's brief stint at school was equally eventful ("I beat the teacher up one day, with an iron bar . . . He got fired, for picking on me") and was probably most notable in hindsight for his unwilling acquaintance with a surly, quick-fisted boy called Frank Anthony Iommi, eight months older than Ozzy, who had been born on February 19, 1948 and also lived in Aston, on Park Lane. "Tony Iommi used to bully me all the time when I was at school," complained Ozzy later, and well he might – Iommi was a tough individual with the brawn to back up his temper. "It was always Tony who used to be the badass guy, going round beating everybody up. He's totally mellowed out now," sniggered Geezer.

Iommi's aptitude for physical toughness went beyond mere casual presence, as he recalled: "My original ambition when I was small was to try martial arts, boxing, that sort of thing, and I expected to be something in that business. I was always at the gym three or four times a week back then and I was a fanatic. Then I [started] listening to music, and eventually all the physical stuff died off. But I never thought I'd end up playing guitar, ever. I had a lot of dreams when I was young about being onstage, but I never dreamed it would be as a guitarist. I suppose I thought it would be in karate or a field like that."

Sex was an early pleasure – and a burden – for the young Ozzy, who explained in typically graphic detail: "We used to have this next-door neighbour. She was 63 years old, and I used to go and fuck her. It's the God's honest truth. I used to fuck her, as a child. She lived in a house right next to us, and she used to go to work at seven every morning. I used to go and fucking steal from her. The house was like the war had ended yesterday – this was like nineteen-sixty-fucking-four, or something. Her kids got killed in an air raid, and her husband got killed at Dunkirk, or something. Her world had stopped then . . . She'd worked for years and years and years in this factory and still believed that her family was around her. She'd talk to the children that weren't there, and she would take me as being her husband. I think he was Joseph, or something like that. And she was fucking insane."

While Ozzy's sex life may have been unusual, the psychological spin he placed on masturbating – the eternal solace of teenage boys – was weirder still. "I remember one time, I was ill. I was *really* ill . . . I'm lying in bed, masturbating. You know when you're a kid, you think of something to masturbate on – you can close your eyes and think of an object, a person, something to get your rocks off. And the perspective of the object got all out of – it wouldn't be big, it wouldn't be small, it wouldn't be round, it wouldn't be long – it wouldn't be anything. And it used to fucking do my brains in – I used to go fucking crazy. I ripped my Beatles pictures off the wall and started burning them and doing crazy things."

On another occasion he resorted to jerking off to defuse a homicidal urge: "I'm lying on the fucking couch . . . all the rest of the kids have gone to bed, see . . . This thing comes to my head, 'Kill your mother. Get up and kill her – she's evil.' I swear to God, I felt myself come off this fucking couch, and I ran, and I ran. I stopped myself running, went straight back through the kitchen, into the bathroom, and masturbated for about four hours."

Despite his dislike of school – where his fellow pupils coined the nicknames 'Ozzy' or 'Oz-brain' – he showed early signs of performance ability in productions of Gilbert & Sullivan light operas such as *HMS Pinafore, The Mikado* and *The Pirates Of Penzance*. However, Ozzy left school at the first possible opportunity, aged 15. His hair-raising boyhood escapades now began to take on a rather more serious edge as he moved from the playground to the adult world of work. His first job was as a toolmaker's apprentice, and industrial injuries were common, as he lamented: "I left school at 15, went to work and cut my thumb off the first fucking day. Sewed it back on." Moving through a succession of dead-end jobs, including killing livestock in an abattoir, he ended up assembling car horns in a factory. "If you're in a room with 10 guys tuning car horns all day," he explained, "you'll come home like a lunatic."

Years later, Ozzy looked back on Aston with little nostalgia, it seemed. "Birmingham wasn't and isn't a very rich area. It was rather dreadful and everybody in my family worked in factories, really mindless jobs that were physically exhausting. My father, my mother, my sisters, they all worked in factories in Birmingham and my dad thought I should become a tradesman to get a chance and better myself, get away from the factories, you know. So when I finished school I tried to become a plumber. It didn't work out; it wasn't for me. Then I tried to become a bricklayer. It didn't work out. Then I tried to be a construction worker – same story. Everything I tried seemed to be doomed. I hated it, got sick of it really quick."

In 1965 Ozzy tried to join the army, as so many other disillusioned young men from Aston had done before him, in an attempt to escape the factories. "I was 17 and pissed off," he told writer Sylvie Simmons. "I wanted to see the world and shoot as many people as possible – which is not much different from being in a band these days, the rap world anyway.

How far did I get? About three feet across the fucking front door. They just told me to fuck off. He said, 'We want subjects, not objects.' I had long hair, a water-tap on a string around my neck for jewellery, I was wearing a pyjama shirt for a jacket, my arse was hanging out and I hadn't had a bath for months. And my dad would say, 'You've got to learn a trade' – he was a toolmaker. I thought joining the army would please him."

The sequence of soul-destroying jobs was interrupted in 1966 by a stint in prison for breaking and entering, which Ozzy had half-heartedly taken up as an attempt to escape the relentless monotony of his life. Famously, he was an incompetent burglar, once wearing fingerless gloves during a break-in at a clothes shop called Sarah Clarke. Although he was offered the alternative of a £25 fine (the equivalent of a couple of weeks' pay at factory rates), the penniless Osbourne was obliged to serve six weeks of a three-month sentence in Birmingham's Winson Green Prison, a forbidding Victorian institution built in 1849. A second sentence there followed after Ozzy was stupid enough to punch a policeman in the face. He came out determined never to be imprisoned again, although he'd partially alleviated the boredom there by tattooing O-Z-Z-Y across his left knuckles with a sewing needle.

The situation was bleak. The young Osbourne, deprived of criminal income and stimulation, faced a future of slavish labour and poverty – as did all the local teenagers. His aggression ran unchecked, as he later admitted: "Where I came from, it was kill or be killed. I'm a lunatic! I went through a shop window, fighting with three guys. My arm was virtually fucking ripped apart, you know? I was on a glucose drip for 12 hours, had several pints of blood pumped into me. I'd just gotten out of prison . . . burglary."

It was no better for the other young men. As Bill Ward put it, "We were all destined to go to the factories . . . I didn't know if I was gonna kill myself, have a job, go to jail, or anything. And none of us did . . . I left school when I was 15 and I worked for exactly six months in a factory. I left at Christmas time and I got part-time jobs and such. I kept the part-time jobs till I couldn't do them any more."

One thing kept them going: music. When The Beatles released 'Love Me Do' on October 13, 1962, boys like Ozzy, Tony, Geezer and Bill were between 13 and 14 – the perfect age for the new dawn of British beat music to hit them hardest. They had been aware of American and British rock'n'roll before, of course – especially Bill, who had actually started learning to play drums as a pre-teen. As he remembered, "The guiding light for me was Elvis Presley. My brother is four years older than me, so he was the main influence in my life when I was a youngster . . . I listened to Little Richard and Elvis and everyone else. I was also very into my mother and father's music, which was American big band music . . . When I heard 'Jailhouse Rock', something connected with me. I connected to it like some sort of magnet. I knew I wanted to sing and play in a rock'n'roll band."

Growing up in a musical family meant that it wouldn't be long before he was pushed into music-making of his own. "I was already playing drums," he stated. "I started playing drums when I was five years old. My mother played piano and my father sang, so the drummer who lived on the corner would bring his kit over on the weekend and we would have a party."

The blitz spirit which had united so many communities in the previous decades was still alive and well at this time in the early Sixties, as he recalled: "Everyone would get together on Saturday night and have a really good time. There were lots of kegs of booze. They were still celebrating the end of the war. There was a real closeness with families and friends because we had lost so many people. The next day everyone was either still drunk or hung-over, so I would come downstairs early and start learning what drums were. That was really my instruction on the drums. By the time I was eight or nine years old, I was already defined within myself. I knew I was going to be a drummer."

Before the rock'n'roll and beat movements had settled into Ward's consciousness, he had already gained some awareness of the jazz and swing scenes imported from the US – a key indicator of the development of his later drumming style. As he said: "There was some classical music that I enjoyed, but I was born in 1948. So as a child growing up just after the Second World War, my mother and father had been somewhat influenced by what was then called 'GI music' or American music . . . My mother and father had lots of records that they played from the American big bands like Count Basie, Benny Goodman, Glenn Miller . . . That's what influenced me as a child."

But any music appealed to Bill: "There's something inside me that attracts me to music, as a moth would be to a flame, I guess. I don't know what that is, just an instinct. And as far as I can remember, back since I've been a small child, I've been very attracted to music."

It wasn't just Bill. The new beat boom appealed to Ozzy too, who – typically – stole 'Love Me Do' as soon as it appeared. "I used to steal records. I never used to buy them . . . I think it was 'Love Me Do'. I was the classiest fucking shoplifter you ever met in your life. Coat over the arm, "Scuse me, sir' – bong! Gone. I'm a rock'n'roll rebel." The impact on Osbourne of the Liverpool quartet was profound: as he later said, "When I left school I wanted to become a plumber. When I heard The Beatles I wanted to become a Beatle." More tellingly, he revealed: "The Beatles gave me everything. Especially Paul McCartney. I adored him."

The Beatles became a lifelong influence on Ozzy, and he never stopped worshipping at the altar of the Fab Four, even into the later years of his own career: "I was a kid when The Beatles came out and I was just totally fucking blown away. The Beatles were fucking magical . . . Even now, they're timeless records. You can put *Sgt. Pepper* on, 'A Day In The Life', it's fuckin' brilliant. It takes you on a journey. 'Strawberry Fields Forever' is just fucking magic. To this day, I've spent hours trying to figure out how they got those sounds, and how they got this to intertwine with that, and I can't work it out. The Beatles had such an effect on my whole life, my whole structure, my whole being. My room was littered with Beatles stuff; I'd go 20 miles to get a poster of The Beatles."

Far from merely being a fan, Ozzy was obviously aware of how much The Beatles changed the society they lived in: "It was something magical, almost a spiritual experience for me. Of course, my dad hated it. Way back then, The Beatles were revolutionaries and their music was revolutionary music. You know, they were considered to be a bad influence because they gave the kids ideas, the ideas to do something else with their lives rather than waste it in factories or become plumbers. For adults, it was a dangerous thing. But for us, they were heroes."

Elsewhere in Aston, Tony Iommi was also smitten by the pop music bug and poured his efforts into learning the guitar – just as thousands of other teenagers, impressed by the effortless twangs of Hank Marvin and Duane Eddy, were doing at the same time. Iommi later recalled, "My early influences were The Shadows . . . They basically got me into playing and later on I got into blues and jazz players. I liked Clapton when he was with John Mayall. I really liked that period. I went through a period when I started off playing all jazz and blues."

Iommi progressed at a fearsome rate, impressing anyone who saw him play with his deft style – and was soon in demand as a player in the many home-made bands that were springing up in the area. His first band was The Pursuers, which he joined aged just 15 in 1963. Hampered by the prohibitive cost of decent electric guitars in the early Sixties and – as a left-handed player – frustrated by the lack of suitable instruments, Iommi's first instrument was a now long-forgotten Watkins Rapier. "It was very cheap!" he told me, laughing. "I was attracted to it because it was left-handed and in those days you didn't really get lefties. Jesus, did I really buy it over 40 years ago?"

Iommi's next rehearsals came as part of two short-lived acts called The In Crowd and The Birds And The Bees at the tender age of 16. A much more solid act called The Rockin' Chevrolets – comprising Neil Cressin (vocals), Alan Meredith (guitar), Dave Whaddley (bass) and Pat Pegg (drums) as well as Iommi – established a well-received live act, with Brumbeat.net reporting: "The Rockin' Chevrolets played every week at the Bolton Pub in Small Heath and were soon getting many other bookings. Tony Iommi's talent as a guitarist was clearly evident even in those days, as the audiences went wild when he played brilliant renditions of instrumental numbers by groups such as The Shadows and The Dakotas."

By 1965 The Rockin' Chevrolets were doing so well that – like other acts from the North including The Beatles – they were offered gigs in West Germany, where young crowds of music lovers were queueing up every night to see the new beat outfits. Iommi, who worked in a factory – like all his peers – handed in his notice in preparation for the trip abroad and, on his last day, operated his machine press as usual.

"It's funny, really," chuckles Iommi ironically when I ask him about that fateful day. "On the day it happened I was actually leaving that job to go and be a guitarist full-time . . . it's mad when you think about it."

As Iommi operated the enormous machinery, with his mind no doubt on the future of rock'n'roll that awaited him, his hand suddenly became trapped inside it. "I was working on a pressing machine, which pressed sheet metal. I got my middle fingers on my right hand caught in it," he recalls. All might not yet have been lost, it emerges – but he reacted wrongly: "Without thinking, I pulled them out quickly. The weight on them was so great that parts of those fingers stayed behind – down to the first joint on the middle finger and most of the way down to the joint on the ring finger."

In extreme pain, Iommi sought medical help. In hospital doctors stopped the bleeding and even managed to save his fingernails – as he recalls, "The nails were broken off and then surgically re-implanted." But it took weeks for the fingers to heal, and even then they never completely mended. In the intervening years Iommi has investigated many different solutions, without much success, as he says, "To this day it hasn't really healed: there's only a couple of layers of skin over the ends of the bone and if I bend those fingers, they still hurt. Believe me, I've looked into every conceivable way of getting them repaired surgically . . . they want to pull the skin forward from the rest of the finger to make a bigger covering at the fingertip, but I really don't want to do that."

As a left-handed guitar player the disability to Iommi's right hand was potentially disastrous as, unlike conventional right-handers, he used the finger-tips on his right hand to form chords and fret individual notes, and his left hand to hold a pick. Perhaps the injury wouldn't have been important it if had occurred to his picking hand, but the fingertips used for fretting must – as any guitarist knows – have iron-hard callouses on them if they are to be used effectively. "I had to work really hard to get round it," he says. "I had to play more simply: there were certain chords I couldn't play and some extensions I couldn't do. I had to think of ways of playing that were effective but still possible for me."

Needless to say, Iommi's German gig with The Rockin' Chevrolets was out. As Tony added, "The timing couldn't have been worse – not that there's ever a good time to cut off the ends of two of your fingers! It was an awful experience, and I went through a terrible period of depression because I was convinced that my guitar playing days were over for good. I went to dozens of different doctors and hospitals and they all said, forget it. You're not going to be able to play guitar again."

Inspiration came from another guitarist – not a rock or beat player, and in fact, not even a living musician. The 'gypsy jazz' guitarist Django Reinhardt, who had died in 1953 when Tony was five, had evolved a method of playing his instrument without using the third and fourth fingers on his fretting hand, which had been irreparably damaged in a fire. Reinhardt had become known for his mastery of lead and chord playing despite his apparently crippling handicap, and was a revelation to Iommi. As he explained: "While I was down in the dumps, a friend of mine, who happened to be my foreman at work, brought me a record of Django Reinhardt who, at the time, I'd never heard of before. My friend said, 'Listen to this guy play,' and I went, 'No way! Listening to someone play the guitar is the very last thing I want to do right now.' But he kept insisting and he ended up playing the record for me. I told him I thought it was really good and then he said, 'You know, the guy's only playing with two fingers on his fretboard hand because of an injury he sustained in a terrible fire.' I was totally knocked back by this revelation, and was so impressed by what I had just heard that I suddenly became inspired to start trying to play again . . . It was really depressing at first, but after hearing Django, I just wouldn't accept defeat. I was sure there had to be a way around my problem."

14

After a failed attempt to play right-handed, Iommi cast around for other ideas and eventually hit on the strategy of attaching clips to his injured fingers to reduce the pain of holding down a string. Doctors offered more alternatives but, as Iommi explains, "I'm afraid that if I do that, I'll lose the technique which I had to develop to get round it . . . Some of the other suggestions they've made are basically not much different from what I do already, which is wear fibreglass clips on the ends of those fingers. The surface of the clips has to be a perfect balance of gripping the string and not gripping it too much. It's really hard to get it right. I made the first ones myself years ago, but nowadays I get a hospital to do it for me."

The clips were initially fairly ham-fisted. "What I did was this: I melted down a Fairy Liquid bottle, made a couple of blobs of the plastic and then sat there with a hot soldering iron and melted holes in them so they'd fit on the tips of my injured fingers, kind of like thimbles. When I got the caps to fit comfortably, I ended up with these big balls on the ends of my fingers, so I then proceeded to file them down with sandpaper until they were approximately the size of normal fingertips."

The next stages were laborious: "It took me quite a while to get them exactly right because they couldn't be too heavy or thick, but had to be strong enough so they didn't hurt the ends of my fingers when I used them. When I had sculpted my 'thimbles' to the right size and tested them, I realised that the ends weren't gripping the strings, so I cut up a piece of leather and fixed pieces to the ends of them. I then spent ages rubbing the leather pads so they would get shiny and absorb some oils and would help me grip the strings better. I filed down the edges so they wouldn't catch on anything and it worked! Once I had done this it took me quite a while to get used to bending and shaking strings with those two fingers because I obviously couldn't feel anything. It was even difficult to know where my fingers were and where they were going. It was just a matter of practising and persevering with it, using my ears to compensate for my lost tactile sense."

Crucially for the future of rock music, Iommi also made it easier on himself by tuning his guitar down a semitone from standard E tuning to E flat, a semitone lower. This reduced the string tension on his guitar, thus making it easier to fret the notes. The key effect of this was that the chords he played were lower in pitch – and simultaneously darker and what we would now call 'heavier', although in 1965 this meant nothing.

Asked if the injured fingers meant that he had to focus on heaviness rather than technique, Tony laughs and says, "Yes, exactly!" adding that he almost switched to bass to avoid having to think about chords – or indeed his injured fingers: in those days of simple bass-lines, a player could get away with using two fretting fingers quite easily.

Meanwhile, drummer Bill Ward was looking for a band while still at school. After recruiting a singer Chris Smith and bassist Neil Marshall, he needed a guitarist – and Iommi, now out of The Rockin' Chevrolets, was an obvious choice. As he later explained, "We started playing together when we were 15. Tony is only a couple of months older than I." An instant empathy developed between the two teenagers, as he added: "I just connected with Tony Iommi: when Tony hits a chord and I meet him there, in that moment, that's the most relaxed place for me on earth. I only knew how to play drums in one way, really, which was to thrash. I tried to learn some finesse, like eight years before Sabbath, but I couldn't help but to just thrash, that's where I felt most at home." Ward and Iommi christened their band The Rest.

As for Ozzy, it didn't take him long to put the need to entertain – which he had first displayed in school operettas – to use in a band. First, he tested his untrained vocal chords at the tender age of 14 with an outfit called The Prospectors, notable only for their guitarist, Jimmy Philips, with whom he would play again later. Then he moved on to the now-obscure Black Panthers before joining up with Music Machine (who needed a vocalist when their usual singer was ill) and playing gigs for the first time.

Another band, Approach, recruited Ozzy in early 1967 and rehearsed in the cellar of a local church cellar. Rehearsals were as far as the band went, unfortunately, with the small shows they put on for friends. Ozzy duly quit, then placed an ad on the musicians' notice board at Ringway Music Store. This bore his self-chosen stage name and read: "Ozzy Zig requires gig. Owns own PA". Even as early as 1968, Ozzy had developed instincts towards showmanship, it seems. More importantly on the cash-strapped musicians' circuit, he had some gear, having bought his PA (a set of Vox speakers, a microphone and stand) from George Clay's music shop on Broad Street.

One browser at the shop that day noticed the ad. His name was Geezer Butler.

CHAPTER TWO

1968–1969

AND so it all began.

In mid-1968 Terence 'Geezer' Butler was playing rhythm guitar in a band called Rare Breed. Along with singer John Butcher, lead guitarist Roger Hope, Mick Hill on bass and Tony Markham on drums, Butler had built up a set of covers of psychedelic tunes which drew in an enthusiastic local audience. In the summer of '68, however, Butcher became dissatisfied and announced his departure, and promptly secured a better gig elsewhere. So Butler contacted Ozzy and recruited him into Rare Breed. Full of enthusiasm, Ozzy rehearsed with the band but was disappointed when the outfit promptly split up, its members unwilling to continue in the wake of Butcher's departure. Nevertheless, an alliance was formed between Butler and the extrovert Osbourne, who was slightly older than him and much more of a showman. Geezer made a permanent switch from guitar to bass at this point, inspired by his hero, Cream's Jack Bruce. Famously, as he couldn't afford a proper bass, he removed the top two strings from his guitar and tuned the remaining ones down to at least simulate a bass sound.

Although Geezer was a huge fan of Bruce, it took him a while to develop a style anything like the Cream maestro's elaborately melodic approach. As he explained, "I didn't even play bass before we got together. I was a rhythm guitar player first, but we didn't need a rhythm player in this band so I switched to bass. A lot of people think a bass player is supposed to be more melodic, like Paul McCartney, playing all these nice things to give everything more depth. But I couldn't do it that way so I just followed along with Tony's riffs. In addition, when we used to go into the studio, they'd say I couldn't have this much distortion on bass, because bass players don't do that. But that's me, that's my sound. We used to have battles with producers and engineers about distortion and what a bass is supposed to sound like. It was always an argument on every album."

As Iommi added: "In the studio they would always try and separate the guitar and bass sound. They'd get into the control room and listen to our

17

tracks separately and complain that Geezer's bass sounded so distorted. They didn't understand that what we had together was the sound we wanted. You just can't start listening to the parts individually, because together it created our sound."

On the subject of guitar technique, Iommi is often credited with evolving the 'power-chord' style – which has since become ubiquitous – in which the player frets only the root and fifth notes of each chord for a tighter, more focused sound. "I did it purely because I had to," he said. "But to make it sound bigger, I developed a vibrato technique and put it on the whole chord. I was already playing guitar for three years when the accident happened, but I had to completely re-learn. I was playing with two fingers for a long time and that's how the fifth chords came about. I can't feel a thing, so I just have to do it by ear. It is hard and it took a lot of getting used to. Put a sewing thimble on your finger and that would be the equivalent."

As Rare Breed ground to a halt, Ward and Iommi's band, The Rest, was carving out a name for itself on the live circuit. The band had changed its name to Mythology and evolved a blues-based sound with distinct nods towards the pioneering music of Cream and Jimi Hendrix, which – thanks to the new guitar amplification and effects technologies – was getting heavier and louder year by year.

Ward was looking for something new, a direction that would take his band away from the lightweight psychedelia of 1966 and 1967 into a harder, more impressive arena. This change in direction was happening with bands all over the UK, with musicians taking note of the more powerful PA systems that were becoming available and the in-vogue guitar overdrive pedals pioneered by Hendrix and his only real rival, Eric Clapton.

Mythology seemed, at one point at least, to be going places. The band had been founded in early 1967 by Marshall along with Mike Gillan (vocals), Frank Kenyon (lead guitar) and Terry Sims (drums) and toured Europe the same year. Gillan and Kenyon quit at the end of the year, and Iommi joined, bringing Chris Smith, the singer from The Rest, with him. Bill Ward joined up at approximately the same time, after Sims departed.

"Tony came into that band and he was so good," said Bill. "He was one of the best players in Birmingham and he was only 16 . . . We played as many as three gigs a night. We would open up in one ballroom at 6.30 and then we would go open up another ballroom or club at 9.30. We did that all the time. In the end, I couldn't work any more. I was just too tired. A lot of times we didn't get any money for the gigs. Any money we did get, we put into petrol for the van, or we would buy guitar strings or drum sticks."

The British music scene was on the move. As stage volume increased, so the attention of the press was attracted to the bands making the noise. One such band was Deep Purple, who – alongside Led Zeppelin – were poised to make a permanent impact on the British music scene. Their soon-to-be singer Ian Gillan, who was fronting pop band Episode Six at the time, told me: "A whole lot of people were thinking the same way at the same time. You look back at seminal moments and influences, and you'll notice that things were getting heavier and harder, because of Jimi Hendrix and Bob Dylan. You look at the power of those songs that Bob Dylan sang, just with a guitar and a harmonica, and then how powerfully they were interpreted by other artists. And there were other messages from people like The Doors, The Beach Boys, and the John Lennon part of The Beatles. All this was leaning towards a more rebellious stance." Gillan added: "Imagine if Arthur Brown had done an album to the same level as his big hit, 'Fire' – *he'd* have been the one to instigate heavy rock."

Back in Aston, Bill Ward was witnessing the same phenomenon. He felt that there had to be more than the current music scene, which in Britain in 1968 leaned heavily towards pop, singer-songwriter ballads, traditional blues and the odd bit of populist jazz and soul. As he said: "I know all of us – at one time or another in interviews – have quoted the fact that there was a lot of music at the time that didn't represent where we were at. It might have represented where other bands were. I know I would listen to certain stuff and think, 'That's very nice, but it doesn't have any meaning to where I'm really at right now.'"

Shows in the summer of 1968 in northern towns such as Halifax, Chester, Manchester and Salford – as well as tiny communities such as Whitehaven, Cumersdale, Lanercost, Nenthead, Langholm, Cockermouth and Maryport – saw Mythology build a small following. Although this live schedule gained the band some attention, a police raid on their rehearsal room at Compton House in May saw the entire band arrested for possession of cannabis. Iommi, Ward and Smith were given two-year conditional discharges and £15 fines, but the older Marshall was put on probation for two years. This proved to be the end of Mythology, who disbanded in July.

The next steps were, with hindsight, serendipitous – although no one could foresee their impact at the time. Both Iommi and Ward knew Geezer Butler, who had by now developed a rudimentary bass technique, and invited him to join their new, as yet untitled band. Geezer suggested his recent Rare Breed bandmate Ozzy Osbourne, although Iommi was at first reluctant to work alongside the cheeky kid he had so disliked at school. Nonetheless, Ozzy was asked to join, along with a saxophonist called Alan Clarke and a second guitarist, Jim Phillip. Adopting the name The Polka Tulk Blues Band, they began rehearsing, even though one and all were doubtful at Ozzy's recently adopted skinhead haircut, which he was soon persuaded to grow out again. The Polka Tulk name was Ozzy's idea: he either saw it on a tin of talcum powder or took it from the name of a Pakistani clothes shop in Aston, both theories being equally plausible and equally impossible to substantiate, as Ozzy himself appears to have completely forgotten anything about the name's origin.

From the start, Iommi and Ozzy were a fractious couple. "We've had our ups and downs," said Iommi several years later, before recounting, "Actually, we had them at school – because he went to the same school as me. We went to Birchfield Road School and he was a year younger than me. And I couldn't stand him. He used to mix with these other kids and he was a real pain . . . Every time you saw him you used to give him a clip round the ear. It was ironic how we ended up in the same band . . . but me and Bill were in a band and we were looking for a singer. We saw an advert in the music shop: 'Ozzy Zig requires gig'. And I said to Bill, 'I know an Ozzy but it can't be him . . . he can't sing.' Sure enough, we went round the bloody house and his mum comes to the door and says 'John, it's for you' . . . and he comes to the door and I looked at Bill and said, 'Forget it, it's that bloody kid from school' . . . So we said, 'We're just looking for a singer', and then we legged it. A few days later Ozzy came to my house with Geezer, looking for a drummer . . . it was just really strange how it all happened."

Ozzy's version of the events, as later recalled, was slightly different: "I used to play in a band called Rare Breed, but the guitarist really annoyed me. Tony, Bill and Geezer were playing in bands, but they kind of split around the same time and that is how we all came together. It was really funny; I vaguely knew Tony. We went to the same school, but he was older than I am. One day I went into a record store and put up a sign saying 'Ozzy Zig seeks gig' – I used to call myself Ozzy Zig because I thought it sounded cool and I thought everybody would start asking who Ozzy Zig was. Anyway, Tony showed up and I thought he'd think I'm a complete idiot, but he ended up joining our band."

Bill was much impressed by Tony and Geezer, the former with his guitar skills and the latter with his extrovert personality. "I met Tony at his house," he recalled, "we were about 15, I was going on 16 . . . he got his guitar and played 'Johnny B Goode' and a few other things, and I just looked at him and thought, 'Oh my God, this guy really can play!' His fingers were already cut on the guillotine when I first met him. He was quiet, that was the first thing that came into my head. He was joking around all the time. It was obvious that he was studious, he was already a great player when he was 16 – one of the best in Birmingham."

As for Butler, Ward recalled: "I used to see Geezer all the time around Aston. He stood out a mile, like a fuckin' . . . you could see him a mile away coming up the street. He just looked so unusual!"

"We all got together and started playing," recalled Iommi. "And what a noise it was. I didn't even know what Geezer was playing. He'd got a regular Telecaster guitar, trying to play bass on it. I thought, what are we doing here? We had a saxophone player as well . . . and we had a slide guitar player and it just sounded horrible. But we persevered."

Geezer later recalled: "I had never played bass before. In fact, when we did the rehearsals it was on a Fender Telecaster, because I used to play rhythm guitar. It was so easy to pick up 12-bar blues bass-lines. That got me started. Once I was confident doing that I could go on to other things . . . because it was so simple. Then you get bored of that so you go on to some other bits and you can feel yourself progressing all the time. Eventually you've got the background to go and write your own songs."

As time passed, Bill and Geezer became close friends, with the drummer constantly amazed at Butler's antics. As he told me, "There was a period when we first started hanging around together. We were in the dressing-room together, I was lying back on a couch, you know, I was pretty high at the time, and Geezer came in and he was trying to climb up this fuckin' wall! He kept falling down, but he kept running up the wall and falling on his ass. And I'm just watching this repeatedly and thinking, 'I've gotta get to know this guy.' He was laughing, you know, because he kept falling down. I've had so many good times with that man."

Events moved rapidly and it was soon apparent that Clarke and Phillip were not gelling with the rest of the band. Iommi's overdriven blues style left little room for a second guitar, and the saxophone sounded bizarre in context. After two shows in August 1968, one at the Banklands Youth Club in Workington and the other at Carlisle's County Ballroom, Phillip and Clarke were dismissed. Of the slimming-down, Ward later recalled: "I remember playing with them at the ballroom in Carlisle. There was a really bad fight after the gig, but other than that it was great. It was a magical night. We were a six-piece when we went up but we were a four-piece when we came back. We had a slide guitar player and a saxophone. Over the weekend, we let them know that it wasn't working. It was 200 miles up and 200 miles back. At the time, they took the news well. They were like, 'Fuck you' and moved on."

And so, in September 1968, a band consisting of Ozzy Osbourne, Tony Iommi, Geezer Butler and Bill Ward came into being for the first time. Perhaps, at the time, it seemed like just another one of those things?

Renaming themselves Earth and heading off in a heavy blues direction which got darker and louder as time passed, the new group immediately found itself beset by logistical problems, even though their musical collaboration was working out well. Once, the band arrived to play a Birmingham club booking to be told that the crowd were eager to hear their latest single: Ozzy et al. soon realised that they had been mistaken for a much bigger and more successful band of the same name and booked in error. The show was not a success and Earth returned to Aston, unsure about the next step and uncertain if their new band, the latest in a line of short-lived projects, was a viable venture.

On the Birmingham circuit Jim Simpson was a well-known local musician and industry figure who managed two bands called Bakerloo Blues Line and Tea & Symphony. As trumpet player with the pop band Locomotive, he had enjoyed a hit the same year with the song 'Rudi's In Love' and had just launched a live blues club, Henry's Blues House, on the corner of Hill Street and Station Street. Iommi and his bandmates approached Simpson and asked for a gig.

Simpson, still running the Big Bear management company that he started in 1968, recalls: "After Henry's Blues House had been running for two or three weeks, they came up to me and said, 'We've got a band, can we do an audition?' And eventually they did. They struck me as innocent, confused and a bit directionless: they didn't really know what the next step was. They seemed to have a bit of a following in Cumberland, for some reason. But nobody quite knew how or where . . ."

Arranging a support slot for Earth with Ten Years After in November 1968, Simpson was sufficiently taken with the audience's response to start discussing the quartet's future direction with them. "I remember being impressed with the band – so much so that we tried to help them get gigs in London," says Leo Lyons, Ten Years After's bass player. "I don't know how much help we were, but I heard that Geezer Butler mentioned it in a later interview. He was also quoted as saying that he learnt a lot of his bass licks from me. That was kind of him."

Geezer later recalled: "Ten Years After were one of our heroes. Alvin Lee was billed as 'the fastest guitar in Britain'. One of our big breaks was when we did a gig with him. We supported Ten Years After and they really liked what we were doing. Alvin Lee got us a gig at the Marquee in London. That sort of started the ball rolling for us."

At the time the issue of the band name had become crucial, and Simpson spent some days trying to work out a better alternative. "They hadn't got a name," he explains. "They were between names, so I got them a few gigs at Henry's and a relationship developed and I started managing them. There wasn't any great emotion about it, the scales didn't fall from my eyes or anything – we sort of slowly oozed into it, because I'd been offering them support and advice before then anyway. It was a natural progression from having talked to them. The first thing we did was sit down for several days and worry about names, directions and what we were going to do."

In September 1968, shortly after Simpson's enrolment as manager, Earth played shows in Lichfield and Carlisle as well as another at Henry's Blues House. In November they performed at Mother's Club in Erdington, then in Carlisle once more, and in December in Langholm.

Before any more progress could be made, however, in December 1968 Earth underwent a temporary setback when Iommi left to join Jethro Tull, then a blues-rock band of some standing. Although Tony's tenure with Tull lasted a few weeks at most, he was privileged to take part in the recording of The Rolling Stones' *Rock'N'Roll Circus* movie, which took place at Intertel Studios in Wembley on December 11 and 12. As he recalled, "I actually left Earth for a point and went with Jethro Tull. I didn't stay with them that long though. I did the *Rock'N'Roll Circus* and then we got back together again . . . It was done over a period of a couple of weeks, and it was certainly different. Especially for someone like me, coming from not knowing anybody to flying in and meeting John Lennon and people like that. But it was a great experience and of course Eric Clapton was there and it was good fun."

Iommi witnessed at first hand such legendary contemporaries as Lennon, Clapton, Keith Richards, Yoko Ono and Hendrix drummer Mitch Mitchell in a one-off supergroup called The Dirty Mac, as part of the Stones extravaganza: "It was pretty much thrown together," he recalled. "We went through the rehearsals for that as well. But the whole thing, from day one, was a bit of a shambles. They started with this press reception at the hotel and the Stones were playing at it, and then they started arguing at their own reception. While they were playing, they stopped and started arguing. So, it was a bit of an up and down thing altogether, but it was good. It was good to do. It certainly opened my eyes. The Who were very good live. That was actually the first time I had heard them live. We were sharing a dressing room with them. So that was the first time I got to meet them. They were great."

However, Earth was where his true ambition lay. "I wanted to get together with the [Earth] boys . . . I came back with a totally different approach altogether and I thought we should get down to something different." It says much about Iommi's foresight that he soon departed the land of celebrity musicians in which he had found himself, returning to the as yet untested Aston foursome in January.

As Iommi recalled, the experience made him all the more interested in making Earth work: "It seemed to come together more after I left the band to join Jethro Tull. I told the other [Earth] guys that Tull were interested in me, and they said, why don't you have a go? And I thought, oh, that's great, they're trying to get rid of me. I went to London and it was an audition. I thought, sod this, I'm going home. But they said hang about . . . and I got the job.

"I told the other guys and I felt really bad about it. After a few days of rehearsals, I didn't feel comfortable, and told Ian Anderson, but they asked me to stay to do the *Rock'N'Roll Circus* and I did. After coming back from them, I'd learned the way [Tull] worked . . . but not quite so brutal. With Tull it was a bit of a work situation. I wanted it to be, you know, all friends."

"I learned quite a lot from [Tull frontman Ian Anderson], I must say," Iommi added. "I learned that you've got to work at it. You have to rehearse. When I came back and I got [Earth] back together, I made sure that everybody was up early in the morning and rehearsing. I used to go and pick them up. I was the only one at the time that could drive. I used to have to drive the bloody van and get them up at quarter to nine every morning; which was, believe me, early for us then. I said to them, 'This is how we've got to do it because this is how Jethro Tull did it.' They had a schedule and they knew that they were going to work from this time till that time. I tried that with our band, and we got into doing it. It worked. Instead of just strolling in at any hour, it made it more like we were saying, 'Let's do it!' "

In the same month Earth played in support of Jon Hiseman's Colosseum at The Marquee in London and opened elsewhere for John Mayall's Bluesbreakers as well as for Simpson's bands Locomotive, The Bakerloo Blues Band and Tea & Symphony. Their manager was beginning to pull

24

some serious strings for them and, with London dates under their belts, the band's future was starting to look brighter.

By early 1969 Simpson had secured Earth overseas bookings, both as headliners and support acts, although the regular round of local club shows continued. A quick trip to Denmark to play at the Brøndby Pop Klub in Brøndby was followed by gigs in the Marquee in London, the Bay Hotel in Sunderland (where Van Der Graaf Generator and the DJ John Peel also played) and in April, the famous Star-Club in Hamburg, where The Beatles had cut their teeth. The gig included several sets per day – just as for the Fab Four in the early Sixties – but the band didn't mind, as the audiences lapped it up.

As Leo Lyons, of Ten Years After, told me of his own stint at the Star-Club: "The Germans love rock music and that enthusiasm still exists today in many countries in Europe. Hamburg, being a seaport, was exposed to all the 'race records' brought over from the States. Those records were not easily available in other countries. At that time in the UK there was little exposure in the media for rock music and, with a few exceptions, radio played only trite, contrived pop records of the day. Despite that, there were some great bands around playing the clubs and bars. I don't think it's really that different today." A final sojourn at the Star-Club came in late '69, just before the venue closed.

At least two showcase gigs for record company executives took place in the autumn, following the recording of two demo tracks, 'The Rebel' and 'Song For Jim' – now hard to find. The latter was written in honour of Jim Simpson – although he now says, not unkindly, "I hope 'Song For Jim' is impossible to find! It sounds a bit like Charlie Christian. It's very swinging, with some tasteful guitar and everyone playing very well."

Geezer never forgot the band's raw early songs, remembering: "The stuff we had when we first started was all 12-bar blues. We used to do a lot of Willie Dixon songs, Howlin' Wolf, Lightnin' Hopkins, and Muddy Waters. We learned them from listening to the records. They were easy to play. When we first came together we formed in one day and had a gig a week later! We had never played together so we learned 18 12-bar blues numbers in a week."

Tony added: "It was great practice for learning how to play. It was mainly instrumental. We'd do a bit of vocals and then 10 minutes of instrumental. It was good for us to do that. We used to play clubs in Europe and we could play for hours. We did seven 45-minute spots a night, which was good experience for us to be able to play stuff."

Earth returned for an extended Hamburg residency in August, returning with a new band name, which was announced at a show at Banklands Youth Club, Workington, on Tuesday August 26, 1969. It was around this time they decided to adopt the moniker of Black Sabbath, the US and UK title of a horror film from 1963 starring Boris Karloff (and nothing to do with Operation Agatha, the Palestinian arrests of 1946, as has occasionally been speculated). A still-disturbing phrase in the late Sixties, before the horror-movie industry had entered the mainstream, the name was enough to link the band in many people's minds with satanism and other grim associations.

The group and Simpson agreed that Black Sabbath was a more attention-grabbing name than any of the other alternatives, and began to set up a gigging schedule. Jim knew that their live act had to be different from the usual blues-wailing standards of the day, as he says: "See, the world was full of boring blues bands at the time – with people playing 150-hour-long guitar solos and boring the pants off people. Onstage people were wearing boots and raggedy jeans. So we decided we weren't going to have any of that – we had to get Sabbath out of that blues mode into something that was more commercial. So we thrashed around off and on, and meanwhile I booked them gigs with people who trusted me enough to take on a band without knowing much about them."

Being in a band that could finally pay its own way was a welcome relief to all the musicians, in particular Ozzy, who had grown sick of the factory life, especially tuning car horns. "The last job I had was tuning car horns in a soundproof booth. These fucking car horns are coming down a conveyor belt, and you're in this fucking chamber – a box, like something out of fucking *Flash Gordon*. You take a car horn, put it in this clamp, and you tune this fucking thing in to the dial."

One of his co-workers made Ozzy see the light, once and for all, as he remembered: "This guy's been working there for fucking years. He was telling me about the time during the war that it was fucking ack-acked and the fucking German fucking airplanes bombing England, you know? I said to him one day, 'Arry, how long you been doing this? He says, 35 fucking years he's been here. He says, 'I'm retiring soon. Soon I'll get my gold watch.' I just got my fucking tools and I slammed them on the floor. I said, 'Listen, man – if I want a fucking gold watch, I'll go and break a jewellery shop. I'm out. Tell the foreman I've jacked.' And fuck – it was the last time I ever did it."

Money was still a pressing issue, of course, as Bill recalled: "We didn't earn a whole lot of money, but we were able to make enough to buy food and petrol. We lived on the poverty level but we still managed to tour and get gigs. But it was tough. Looking back, I thought, man, we were spunky kids to do that." As Simpson confirms, "In those days they used to get about £25 for going up to Carlisle to play a gig – which is probably about a hundred quid or so today – which would pay the petrol and whatever else. They used to stay with friends and do quite well there."

The issue of who was the band's leader at this stage is key, as a series of decisions were taken at this point which changed everything. Leadership of Black Sabbath has never really been discussed in public, but it's obvious to anyone familiar with their chequered history that Sabbath is Tony's band. Asked by *Classic Rock Revisited* if it was fair to say that as Ian Anderson is to Jethro Tull, Tony Iommi is to Black Sabbath, the guitarist replied: "I've never said that, but everyone else has. I think it's good to have someone for the other members to turn to. I used to tend to be that one. If there was any problem, then they used to come to me. Sometimes, it wasn't a good thing for me because I couldn't go out and get drunk when they did. Somebody had to stay straight to see things happened correctly."

With Iommi watching out for the band's fortunes, the next step up in Sabbath's career came when Jim Simpson showed his new band to the independent producer Tony Hall, who had his own agency, Tony Hall Enterprises. Tony was blown away by Earth's fearsome live energy and determined to get them a deal. "I just thought they were a great little blues band," he said. "Four good players who deserved to make a record. I would have tried to get a deal for them as Earth. Then they went away to Germany and came back as Black Sabbath."

The next stage would clearly be an album. As the band's live schedule extended into the future, Sabbath began writing their own material at last, centred on Iommi's riffs and Butler's bass lines. Geezer, supposedly the most educated member of the band, soon came to the fore in the matter of the lyric-writing, though the others would help out from time to time. "It was a band thing," he says. "It was nice to get a lot of inspiration from one line. Ozzy might come up with a line at the time when we were writing the stuff . . . then I'd write the rest of it." Sometimes the burden was too heavy, as Iommi remarked: "It was a lot of pressure for him because he wrote the lyrics and played the bass. He used to have a moan at the end: 'Oh, I've got to write the lyrics.'"

Musically, the sound evolved through the unique combination of Geezer's melodic bass and Iommi's solid guitar – qualities that are often reversed. But as Tony shrugged, the method was no secret: "It was as simple as it sounds: just turn up. That was it, really. It was a combination of

Geezer and myself, that unique wall of sound we had."

Geezer's bass playing, much influenced by Jack Bruce, was an integral as the huge guitar sound. As he told me, "I don't want to meet him – everyone that I've ever met that I worshipped has been a disappointment, so I want to keep him as my hero. I wouldn't know what to say to him! He was the first bass player I ever saw who was bending the strings and totally being on his own. At the time, when I saw him with The Cream, he was playing a Fender VI, and they're horrendous to play. I tried one once but I couldn't do it, my fingers are too wide to get between the strings." As for the bass he'd finally bought: "It was a thing called a Top 20. I think it was about 50p at a junk shop. I've never heard of them before or since – I think I bought it off one of Ozzy's friends. And then on the way to the first gig, I borrowed my mate's Höfner violin bass, which only had three strings on it, and then eventually I swapped my Fender Telecaster for a Precision."

Jim Simpson approved of the band's musical skills – which at this stage were solid and dependable rather than extravagant. "Geezer? He did the job," he nods. "Bill kept great time and drove well, but he had all the trouble he needed to do the job that he did. I like drummers who do the job well, not overdo it and play too many fills. As for Tony, I knew about his finger injury, of course but it didn't play a large part by then. He was a very meticulous guitar player, he really planned things carefully. There were times when he'd come offstage and he'd played a different solo than usual: I'd say, good solo, Tony, I see you changed that part to that part – and he'd say, no I didn't, I made a mistake! And I'd say, but you played it in time, you played it within the chord, it was still useful? But he'd say, yes, but it wasn't what I intended to play."

In fact, the only member of Sabbath whose talent was unproven was Ozzy. Although his voice was perfect for Black Sabbath's early songs – and in any case, his skills took second place to his onstage act at this point – he himself was in some uncertainty about how well he sang. As Simpson recalls: "Ozzy was the one who had doubts about his ability. He would get very distraught about it. His confidence was very low, he needed reassurance. It's always harder for the singer, because you open your mouth, you make a noise, and you ask yourself if it's any good or not – whereas if you play the trumpet, you play the notes and the scales and the arpeggios and you know you've hit the note. It's more quantifiable. But just because you like someone's voice doesn't mean the next guy's going to like it."

Slowly the band honed a powerful live show, working successfully as a unit. Osbourne, never the most secure of men, was still a little in awe of the tough, silent Iommi, who "really used to intimidate me", as he would later recall. "He was a big guy. He could fight. But you've always got to have that domineering thing. If you didn't have someone who could kick you up the arse and get me out of the fucking pub, you wouldn't do anything, you know?" Simpson dismisses this today, reasoning: "I can't imagine anyone intimidating Ozzy, because his character and his spirit were indomitable. But I think he could feel crushed by words. Ozzy is the sweetest guy on earth, and if you said something hurtful to him he'd be hurt." Did they ever talk about his somewhat violent upbringing? "No, he didn't talk about his family background – we were all besotted with the music."

Once the band were up and running with what looked like a viably commercial future before them – at least for the next few months of bookings – Simpson drew up a management contract for the band to sign. This meant talking to the musicians' parents. Persuading the Osbourne, Iommi, Butler and Ward families that their sons could make a living out of music was no easy task, as he recalls: "I had to push them to get their parents to take it all seriously. I went to meet their parents and I think they all thought that my enthusiasm was misplaced. I knew the band were going to make it. There was no doubt in my mind whatever. But their mums and dads were a bit bemused by it all, I think. What, our little Tony? How can he be a star?"

The band themselves, perhaps a shade disenchanted by their experiences so far, were also short on optimism, as Simpson recalls with some amazement: "Apart from Tony, they all thought my enthusiasm was pretty misplaced anyway, and that they were destined to be what they always had been, i.e. broke! But Tony had a bit of a fixation on becoming a star. He was the one who spoke most readily. Bill didn't get involved much. Ozzy seemed to want to speak a lot, but he was a bit shy in those days."

Iommi certainly sensed that the songs had something special, even if his confidence in the band was a little naive: "When we first got together we were playing sort of bluesy, jazzy stuff and it just seemed to evolve into this sound . . . we knew it was something new when we first started playing the songs – they sounded different from anything anyone else was doing at that time. But we never had any idea where we were going with it. We sort of played [the songs] the way we did because we liked the way we sounded. We enjoyed it."

In late 1969 Black Sabbath recorded sessions for what would ultimately become their debut album at Regent Sound Studios on Tottenham Court

Road in London, with £500 provided by Hall. It was obvious from the first playback that there was a commercial opportunity to be exploited. Despite the relatively primitive sound, the result of the low-budget conditions and inevitable, in spite of the best efforts of producer Roger Bayed, the band had put in an accomplished performance and Simpson knew that the next step was to find a record company to release it.

The scene was set.

CHAPTER THREE

1969–1970

D ID Black Sabbath invent heavy metal, and if so how the hell did they do it?

Heavy metal wasn't planned: it came about thanks to a set of fortuitous coincidences that placed the vital amount of pressure at a key point in musical evolution, and the whole flow of history was altered as a result.

If that sounds portentous, think what it must have been like for the men – and by and large they were men, not women – who made it happen. They didn't suddenly choose to join a band in order to play heavy music: they played heavy music because they wanted to, and because they *needed* to – to be noticed and to let out the pressure they felt inside them. And where did this come from? From their surroundings.

Jim Simpson remembers just what Aston was like in the late Sixties: "You wouldn't wear a flower-power shirt walking down the road in Aston! Flower-power bands were all around us . . . but not in that town. That said, Aston was a lot better then than it is now, they were nicer people than they are now. The problem with Aston now is that it's very racist, which was a problem we didn't have to contend with in those days – it was just poverty we had to deal with. But looking back, poverty's a lot easier to handle than racism."

Ozzy later explained that the hippie ethos couldn't permeate the Sabbath approach, because they were just too poor for idealism: "We came in at the end of the flower-power thing, but we had no dough, no hope of getting any, and we wrote about what we felt, so it wasn't all roses and happy-ever-after. We were militant and spoke with aggressive feelings, and drugs and alcohol became a part of that." Later, he tried cocaine "because it was expensive and not many people could do it in those days. A successful rock star must sniff coke."

Whatever the problems of the era, there was no denying that Black Sabbath's collective background was grim. As Ozzy later explained, much of his desire to join a band was fuelled by fear – the fear of working in a factory for 45 years and then dying broken and penniless, like everyone else he knew. Thus the urge to make it happen was no mere whim: it was driven by genuine need.

Of course, you had to be a certain type of person to live in that environment, feel at home in it, and still manage to defy it. Simpson: "The Sabs were a tough band right from the beginning – they were fairly uncompromising. They were rough, tough and rocking!" This could be summed up less jovially by pointing to the fighting stance that all four men had to take up just to get by in Aston – whether in the pubs on a Saturday night, on the factory floor, or in the street where they lived. Sabbath, and particularly Tony Iommi, would take no prisoners.

Iommi was once told by an interviewer at CNN that Henry Rollins, the hardcore singer, attributed Sabbath's music to the rough environment of Aston. He replied: "I think it's quite right. It's a big part of where we come from. It was either being in a gang or being in a band. I was rough. To be in a band . . . I think a lot of the aggression came out in that, instead of going out and beating the other gang up, you know."

And so this unlikely foursome convened to make music. With the daily grind all around them and the shadow of urban squalor looming over them at all times, there was little wonder that when they set up and switched on, they played loud and heavy.

But a chance factor of immense importance in the evolution of heavy metal was Iommi's industrial accident. Asked by the author in 2004 if it is fair to say that the disfigurement to his fingers shaped the future of the whole of heavy metal, he simply replied, "Yes, I think it is." He added that the detuning he applied to his guitars in order to make the strings less taut, and therefore less painful, would have been even more drastic if the technology had allowed it: "We go down *three* semitones on some of the songs we do nowadays. I use heavy-gauge strings for those, obviously. But in the early days I could only play light-gauge strings, you couldn't get heavy ones. I made my own out of banjo strings."

In fact, the half-step detuning employed in the early days is far from the only tuning arrangement Geezer and Tony employ, as the latter told *Vintage Guitar* magazine: "We've always tuned a semi-tone down, but on the *Paranoid* and *Black Sabbath* albums we tuned to pitch. On *Master Of Reality* we tuned down three steps. We didn't have any rules, because everybody else made the rules up. We just broke them. Onstage we tune down a semi-tone . . . We always experimented with Black Sabbath. That was the greatest thing we'd done. We had always tried things that weren't the norm. We were the first to tune down, and nobody could understand that."

Iommi also tried to make manufacturers understand his needs on many occasions, usually without success in the early days: "I also went to many guitar companies years ago when I wanted light-gauge strings and was told they couldn't make them because they wouldn't work the same. I had to explain that I'd already been using them and that I'd made up the sets myself."

Iommi's detuning kick-started a whole revolution among guitarists, although the unorthodox tuning was already prevalent in other musical genres, notably folk where, for example, the incredibly talented player Davy Graham had invented the DADGAD tuning that enabled him to fingerpick an octave bass line. By the Eighties it was common for metal bands to drop from standard E down to E flat or even D to add heaviness to their riffing – heaviness gained from the extra bass of the lower frequency and the darker, less brittle and bright sound derived from strings under lesser tension. In the following decade this option reached its logical conclusion: once heavy metal subgenres such as death metal had established themselves, it became the norm to tune down as low as C or B. With the advent of seven-string guitars and their extra low B string, tuning went lower and lower until it seems, at the point of writing, that the lowest practicable point has been reached, by a Swedish death metal band called Meshuggah who use eight-string guitars with an extra low F# string – which they then tune down to F, almost an entire octave lower than the standard E. But these instruments and, indeed, excessive down-tuning are both regarded as unnecessary and modish by most of the classic metal generation. Indeed, as Iommi told me, "I've played seven-string guitars, and they're OK, but it doesn't really seem that useful to me."

The industrial environment itself and the effect it had on Iommi's fingers made their mark on the development of Sabbath's heavy sound, but so did the flaws in entertainment technology of the day; specifically in the case of amplification. As bands often failed to make themselves heard at gigs thanks to feeble PA systems, musicians such as Iommi et al. had to play harder and harsher to coax the maximum volume out of the equipment – thus leading to two of heavy metal's most obvious characteristics: high volume and aggressive playing. As Tony remembered, "We found in a lot of blues clubs that everybody's talking away, so they're drowning you out. So we'd just turn up. We basically turned it up louder and louder and came up with this Sabbath thing. It just happened. I mean, it's one of those things where you think it must've been something planned, but it wasn't . . . really, it just came about. It was just one of those things that we liked. It was a nice feeling to turn it up."

Heavy metal, whose name was coined – depending on who you believe – by William Burroughs in his 1961 book *The Soft Machine* (which contained the character Uranian Willy The Heavy Metal Kid), Steppenwolf in their 1968 song 'Born To Be Wild', or music journalist Lester Bangs, who used the term in a '68 review of an MC5 gig in *Creem* magazine – is characterised by a group of recognisable elements, all of which tie in with the Black Sabbath approach. The first is anger, or rebellion, or aggression, or non-conformity – or a unification of all these. From its outset, metal was loud, often ugly, frequently offensive (depending on the sensibilities of those that heard it, of course) and plain vulgar. Punk, usually thought of as the most angry and rebellious of music, merely wore its venom on its sleeve more ostentatiously: it was metal that brought darkness to its rage with most subtlety. Sabbath recognised this fact, and also how unorthodox the approach was in 1968 and 1969. "The whole thing was totally against the book," grinned Iommi in later years, ". . . just everything was so different than what it should've been, which we liked. Because any time someone says you can't do that, it makes you want to do it more."

This didn't square well with the occasional unmoved audience which Sabbath encountered in their early days, especially on the band's first US tour in 1971. By this point they were used to seeing energetic British crowds. As Bill recalled, "I can remember when we started introducing our own material into the show. I can remember the reactions from other shows when we first started doing that. Everybody loved the music. They thought it was incredible, you know, the reaction was electrifying. Like an almost instantaneous amalgamation between the band and the audience!"

This was sadly lacking in America – and despite the band's best efforts, serious action was required to make the crowd react. Following in the footsteps of The Who – one of the progenitors of heavy metal in many ways – the band occasionally destroyed their equipment and threw it into the audience. Ward: "When we played in New York, it was like the third or the fourth gig we ever did on that very first tour of America. The New York audience just sat there. We went on kicking ass, and you know, doing our show [the way we did in] 1970, and the New York audience just sat there and they didn't respond. And after about the third or fourth song, the band became so frustrated with the audience that we actually started throwing things at them!"

He went on, "It was fuckin' great. That was when booze was working, man! Fillmore East was a real New York crowd that didn't quite know what to expect, so it was a little bit of an education for us. They were sitting on their ass, being cool at first, and we were getting more and more angry. I got so angry by the third or fourth song that I tore up my drums and threw them in the audience. Ozzy was screaming at them and Tony was stomping really loud. It went like lightning – the whole crowd fuckin' stood up and took notice, and Ozzy yelled, 'Now, clap your fuckin' hands!' We ended up doing seven encores that night."

The band needed a powerful show, if only so that crowds would remember them. Geezer was quick to realise that his band was up against stiff competition from dozens of other club acts around on the same circuit, all trying to make it. "Back then there were hundreds of bands doing it. That was the way you had a band – you formed a band and you became a blues band and you jammed and then you formed into whatever music you were eventually known for . . . We were up against bands that were just starting, like Ten Years After, Jethro Tull, and Zeppelin. We knew we had to be as good as them to make a go of it. We knew we had to practise every day and rehearse every day to get as good as them, or to be good at all!"

Add the anger of the music to the hands-on approach to audiences and the recipe was potent, especially as none of the band at this point – apart from Iommi – possessed more than adequate skills on their instruments. Butler was still developing his Cream-influenced style, Bill's jazz background was at odds with what was required and Ozzy was, as he remained, an average singer – all of which gave the songs a gritty solidity but little technical brilliance. That would come much later. "I'm not that clever," said Bill. "I just play what feels right for me . . . If Tony's busy, I stay back, but Geezer goes off and does his own thing. I just stay in the hole and do whatever I can."

I asked Bill myself about his drumming skills, and he talked much about his jazz background, saying, "I started taking drumming seriously when I was about 10. Gene Krupa was a major influence. Everything was big bands and jazz – GI music and a bit of Ted Heath! That was what you had in our house – big band music and a bit of swing. I liked jazz a lot, and I played a little bit. If there's ever a jam session going on or a bit of swing, I like to show up and sit in a little bit. Going back to some of the older guys, Buddy Rich, Gene Krupa, I rate all those guys. They were orchestrational, they were wide open, and they left a lot to the imagination. They did the simplest things, but they were incredibly effective – especially Krupa, he had this image of energy and sometimes very simple riffs that he used."

In his later years Ward became recognised as a proficient drummer, but this didn't come until Sabbath had achieved a modicum of success – at the stage we're discussing he stuck to basic, solid grooves that were heavy rather than flashy. This could well come down to the rock'n'roll explosion of his youth, which had taught him and millions like him that raw, loud music with simple arrangements could be as moving as any virtuouso performance: "When Presley and The Ink Spots and The Drifters and Little Richard and Jerry Lee Lewis happened," he explained, "I was *gone*. I was just a kid at the time, no more than six or seven years old, but I felt so drawn to the music. My big brother was four years older than me, so he turned me on to all those bands like the Everly Brothers. Every week there was a new band – I was bathing in this stuff, as we all were at the time. I used to go to the coffee-shops where they had a jukebox. I might have attempted a quiff and failed miserably."

At this point popular music was going through a sea-change. Evolving guitar effects and amplification technology meant that bands could play louder while maintaining a clean sound, and the range of tones a guitarist could call upon – specifically the overdrive pioneered in the mid-Sixties by players such as Link Wray and the Kinks' Ray Davies, before being adopted by Jimi Hendrix and other luminaries – meant that if you wanted to play heavy, you could do so simply by stepping on a pedal.

Ward: "There were some heavy bands around, Cream had established a lot of new ways of playing hard rock music and there were just a couple of bands there . . . But when Zeppelin arrived, it was a whole new bargain. And when the first Black Sabbath album came out about eight months later, it was like there had been a change in popular music."

It took a small group of influential musicians to take the darker, heavier, more profound elements of rock and make them matter. By 1970 Deep Purple, Led Zeppelin and Black Sabbath were recognised as the unholy trio of British heavy rock – a new genre – and Sabbath quickly evolved this into heavy metal when they stepped away from blues and more into riffs. It helped that this small group of individuals were charismatic performers, of course; in any new scene there is a nucleus of creative people driving evolution, and to be commercially viable these people have to make other people interested. Ian Gillan underlines this: "I don't think it's a lot to do with the music, although without the music it wouldn't have happened. If you took three musicians and cloned their style of music and playing – three Ritchie Blackmores or three Steve Morses – you'll find the public will take more to one than the others, even if they've listened to the same music or their ability. People are drawn towards personality, and a lot of that is to do with the make-up of the band – and if you get a bunch of guys who can project what they're doing in a slightly different way to the others, that's probably it. But we didn't realise that, because you are what you are when you're 20. It was quite a while later that we realised that we were part of something bigger, because you're all big-heads at that age! It's a combination of skill and luck."

Although Deep Purple were never a heavy metal band – despite being labelled as such by a slightly confused media in the Eighties, who also applied the label to mainstream rock and AOR bands like Rush, Bryan Adams and AC/DC – they played a role in its development, as did their loftier compatriots Led Zeppelin. Zep drummer John Bonham was often seen in the company of Black Sabbath in the group's early days, recalled Bill Ward: "I had known John Bonham since we were 15 or 16 years old and we would often meet in the clubs. You know, we met a lot of musicians in the clubs. John was busy in the bands he was in and had a lot of work. We would cross each other's path each week. They would just be leaving a club to go to another club to do a gig and we would be coming in to do a gig, whatever band I was in at the time. We all knew each other . . . I had seen John destroy a couple of kits, or pretty much level some kits to the ground, in the early days." The friendship between the musicians even grew to the point where Bonham was Iommi's best man at the guitarist's first wedding.

Ward again: "We honestly respected Zeppelin. We'd known Robert Plant, of course, about the same we knew John Bonham before Zeppelin. He was in a band called The Band Of Joy for a long time. So, you know, it wasn't unusual for us to see Robert around town. But when they first came out, it was just absolutely phenomenal.

"We were going along in Sabbath, thinking that we were doing pretty good and coming along pretty good. We [had] played a concert in Carlisle and somebody who was a fan of ours used to let us sleep overnight at his house. So we were resting there after the concert at his house when he put on the Zeppelin album. We all sat down and listened to it thinking, 'Oh my God! What are these guys doing?' It was just like coming out of nowhere."

The key moment for many – but not all – observers when defining the start of this endlessly controversial genre is the release of Black Sabbath's debut album in 1970 – such a musical and cultural cornerstone that its resonance can be felt through the three decades that follow. If heavy metal can be defined by the characteristics examined above – just as jazz is recognised by syncopation and improvisation, funk by a groove hitting the first beat of the bar and soul by emotional lyrics accompanied by mellow R&B – then which of these does *Black Sabbath* itself have to offer?

The most obviously 'heavy metal' elements of this mighty recording are the lyrics, the heavily occult and even satanic words (mostly penned by Geezer) that give it such a horror-movie thrill. It wasn't long before the band abandoned this admittedly laughable angle, though, after ridiculous claims by an overzealous record company press officer that Butler had "successfully raised a demon in a churchyard".

"Obviously that stuff came along with the band name," Geezer himself told me, "which we took from the first song we wrote together. Thank God it was that one, or we could have been called Fairies Wear Boots . . . we just took it from there and we thought, we like this name, it sounds good, we didn't even think of any black magic connotations. Some of the lyrics are concerned with the occult, of course, but it's not like we came out with this huge black magic image or anything. The record company came up with the artwork for the first album and had that inverted cross on the inside, plus the verse on the inside. That was out of our control, we weren't allowed to have anything to do with mixing or album sleeves or anything like that. The manager we had at the time didn't have a clue about that stuff."

Ward also told me about the importance of the lyrics to the rise of heavy metal: "The difference was lyrical. Had we been playing hard rock and singing, 'Honey I'm gonna meet you tomorrow', or 'Let me fuck you tonight', or whatever, then Sabbath would have been just another also-ran in my book. But we had the riffs that were unusual, we had the grogginess and the awkwardness in the music, and above all we had Ozzy's mono-lithic sound and Geezer's lyrics, which at that time were so different and contradictory. So I would say the first album is a masterpiece which started a new direction that I can still hear to this day."

He's referring to the black metal movement, a subgenre of the heavy metal parent which was pioneered in 1982 by Venom (who released an album of the same name) and was then extended and made commercially workable in the Nineties by mostly Norwegian acts such as Mayhem, Burzum, Immortal, Dimmu Borgir, Emperor, Gorgoroth, 1349 and the biggest of them all, the British band Cradle Of Filth.*

And although Sabbath were an unwitting inspiration to the black metal movement that followed a decade after their debut, where their influence is more directly felt is in the doom metal genre, which has made a practice since the mid-Eighties of emulating Iommi's slow, crushing riffs and the dark, gloomy atmosphere of the songs. Doom metal isn't a huge

---

* See Chapter 7 for more on black metal.

commercial force and probably never will be, but the commercial clout of the relatively small number of bands involved is impressive. The biggest of them all is probably the sporadically active Swedish act Candlemass, whose 1986 album *Epicus Doomicus Metallicus* is the benchmark for the genre, apart from Sabbath's own early albums. An American act called Pentagram also laid down some highly influential semi-doom albums. Then followed a set of three British bands – Paradise Lost, Anathema and My Dying Bride – who pioneered the so-called 'doomdeath' genre, a blend of classic doom with guttural death metal vocals. In the Nineties a whole raft of epic doom, stoner doom and gothic doom metal bands made their presence felt, all of which owe a greater or lesser debt to Sabbath.

Perhaps the ultimate modern doom metal act is the American duo Sunn 0))) (who take their name from a range of classic guitar amps). One of them, Stephen O'Malley, told me how he achieves his earth-shaking sound: "My tuning is A, E, A, D, F, A: my Bean guitar uses a .68 on the bottom and tunes to one half step lower than that." Is there such a thing as too much doom, I asked? "Numbers represent a rate of air movement, not high or low," he added. "Too low is when you start using bass strings on a normal guitar. I love low frequencies around 80–130hz, and the physical vibration caused by this. It's a pleasure to stand in front of the cabinets: it really affects one's physiology. Why be restricted? Darkness knows no boundaries . . ."

Although it might seem set in stone that Black Sabbath were the world's first true heavy metal band, it should be noted that various key personnel – whose word should not be ignored – dispute the fact. Judas Priest, like Sabbath primarily of Birmingham extraction, emerged in 1974 – four years after Sabbath – with a recognisably heavy metal album called *Rocka Rolla*. With this otherwise unremarkable album, Priest staked their claim as a heavy metal band ánd, singer Rob Halford believes, a claim to be the first of their kind. "We were the first ever heavy metal band," he told me in an interview for *Metal Hammer* magazine. "Black Sabbath were before us, but there was always something of a dilemma about whether or not Sabbath were a heavy metal band. Judas Priest have always said that this is what we are, and this is how we're happy to be seen. I have some very primitive demos of Priest and you can hear the metal in the music right from day one."

If you're surprised at this claim, you'll be even more shocked to hear that Geezer Butler himself thinks he's right. As he told me, "I would agree with him. We used to think of ourselves as a heavy rock band. Metal wasn't a term then, and Priest were the first band that I'd heard of who were proud of that label and wore all the leather and studs and stuff . . . I don't know, really. I always thought Led Zeppelin were the world's first metal band. But then Sabbath fans go nuts if you say that. I don't give a toss myself. I suppose the song 'Black Sabbath' did start a whole new movement, musically and lyrically, which took it to the dark side.

There used to be a band called Black Widow, and you'd be amazed how many people used to get us mixed up. They used to do all this fake sacrificing and all this crap onstage, and then musically they were like Status Quo! That was why we steered away from all the black magic thing in the press, because we thought it was corny. I don't get the new black metal stuff at all."

Bill Ward agrees, saying: "I think we were first called [a heavy metal band] by *Rolling Stone*. We thought we were a hard rock band, to be honest with you. It appears people labelled us as a metal band from then on. We just play what we play, it came out of blues and jazz, and we just started to write."

Of all the Sabbath musicians, the one least likely to admit to inventing heavy metal was Ozzy who, even as late as 2000, was telling *Mojo* magazine: "I have a problem with that thing 'heavy metal'. I prefer to call it hard rock. If you take the classic metal albums of the Seventies, Eighties, Nineties and 2000 and play them back to back, you tell me if there is any fucking resemblance. What we were was kind of a cross between blues and jazz mixed, which we played heavy. For me, I go by the spine-curling thing where your hairs stand on end, and the first time I experienced that feeling was when I heard The Kinks' 'You Really Got Me', and Jimi Hendrix, Eric Clapton, the early Fleetwood Mac, and Zeppelin *I* and *II*. Heavy metal now is very aggressive, angry music – which is cool, as long as it's got a melody without getting too fucking happy I like it – but to me the ultimate heavy metal band, and one which has been so underrated, is Motörhead."*

Then again, Priest guitarist KK Downing also told me, "Black Sabbath were the first wave of metal. Then there was us and Scorpions in the second wave. Then Maiden and Accept and Dokken all came out, and then the whole thrash thing started."

So the issue is far from clear. Most people regard Black Sabbath as the first heavy metal band. Others don't. Perhaps we should simply conclude that without them, heavy metal would never have happened.

---

* Motörhead frontman Ian 'Lemmy' Kilmister regards his band as rock'n'roll, not metal.

CHAPTER FOUR

1970

"WE didn't think *Black Sabbath* would ever do anything," said Geezer Butler. "Recording the album was just something we did on the way to Denmark." Pretty casual stuff for an album which kick-started heavy metal, sold in vast quantities and opened the minds of thousands of music fans to a whole new way of thinking.

After the Regent Street recordings were laid down, Jim Simpson started the long trek around the record companies, shopping for a deal. Producer Tony Hall had shown huge enthusiasm already, of course, but what the band really needed was the backing of a major record company.

As has been the case since time immemorial, the preening record label executives of the day failed to see anything of merit in Sabbath's recordings. As Simpson recalls with a bitter laugh over three decades later, he had been through the rounds not once but twice – first with demo tapes and then with the finished masters: "I took them personally round and got straight no's. And after Tony fronted the money, which was £500 as I recall, to go and record at Regent Sound, we took what was the finished master for the first album, and I took that round as well, and got another 14 no's!"

Were any of the execs interested at all? "Oh, some of them listened to as much as three or four minutes of it! I played as much as I could persuade them to listen to. I was madly enthusiastic about it and, generally speaking, they were madly bored. Their eyes were glazed and they were looking in the mirror at their permed hair and their gold medallions and adjusting their purple shirts to make sure their chest hair was on display. But this was par for the course in those days. There were a million times more people in the music industry than there is now, but they weren't too thick on the ground."

But his persistence paid off, and a deal was eventually struck. This pivotal event was made all the more remarkable by the fact that the company Black Sabbath signed to was none other than Vertigo, a renowned stable for progressive rock and the brand-new hard rock scene.

An American deal swiftly followed with the huge Warner Brothers – an ironic move as the Warners corporate behemoth couldn't have been more different from Vertigo, which was set up along the lines of major-label subsidiaries Deram and Harvest to provide a home for the more esoteric acts of the day. Sabbath were delighted to have secured deals with such prestigious entities and could scarcely believe their luck.

In January 1970 the Fontana label did consent to release a one-off Sabbath single, 'Evil Woman', which appeared on the self-titled debut album the following month. A funky, even catchy slice of hard rock characterised by Iommi's warm, bluesy guitar sound and the memorable chorus of "Evil woman, don't you play your games with me" – over a stop-start, slightly Hendrix-like riff – the single was far from heavy metal but a promising indicator of the band's songwriting skills.

The recording of the *Black Sabbath* album itself, produced by Tony Hall Enterprises' producer Roger Bain, was so rapid as to seem ridiculous by modern standards. As Geezer told me, "We did the first album in two days. That's the way it should be. The second album was done in five days and the third one in a week. And those were our biggest-selling albums, and are to this day. We literally went into the studio, set up our equipment and recorded it as a live gig. Tony did a couple of overdubs, solos and things, afterwards, and that was it. We weren't allowed to be in on the mix or anything like that."

The band were ecstatic to be given the opportunity to record, recalled Geezer: "We were probably nervous but we were excited at the same time. We had a chance to make an album. It was what we worked for. We finally had the chance to do it. The only thing I can remember about when we were done with the first album was we played some of the tracks either too slow or too fast because of the excitement; the energy. It was a bit faster than what we normally played."

Bain's presence was a mixed blessing, as Iommi told *Livewire*: "On the first album we had a producer that we brought in who was relatively new to the business. And we didn't know, so it didn't make a difference to us as far as we were concerned. He was a producer and he knew more than we did, so the record company picked him and we were confident that he knew what he was doing. Then in those days we didn't know what we were doing, so we just went in and played. We didn't know any different. We didn't think it took any longer than a day to make an album."

He added: "We were just used to playing a lot, seven days a week – or seven spots a day. When we used to play in Hamburg we used to play a lot, seven three-quarter-of an hour spots. You get pretty used to doing stuff like that. When we walked into the studio, it was a luxury to just be able to play and tape it."

The impressive speed of the recording was enabled, of course, by the fact that Sabbath had been playing the songs live for over a year and grasped the arrangements perfectly. As had been the case for The Beatles and countless other acts, solid work on the road had lent the songs wings when the time came for recording. Butler added: "The songs that you hear on the album, that's how they sounded. Keep in mind that before we recorded that first album, *Black Sabbath*, we'd been playing, I think, most of those songs in the clubs for at least a year to 18 months. So, the very first song that we wrote was 'Wicked World' and we'd been playing that as you hear it . . . whatever we were playing in the clubs, that's how we printed it in the recording studio."

Although Sabbath's expectations for their first album were low – Ozzy once said that he was content just to show his mother that his voice had ended up on vinyl – *Black Sabbath* made an immediate impact on its release on February 13, 1970, surpassing even the predictions of the few faithful such as Jim Simpson by climbing to number eight in the UK charts and number 23 in the US. Vertigo had taken it upon themselves to mix the album and create the artwork (an inverted cross appeared inside the gatefold, to the chagrin of the band), but by and large had done a good job.

Before the buyer even placed the LP on the turntable, *Black Sabbath* made its presence known. Vertigo, which invested much in its sleeve designs, had used a dark, gothic image of a woman standing in a grim countryside setting, all browns and greys. A poem, beginning "Still falls the rain, the veils of darkness shroud the blackened trees, which, contorted by some unseen violence, shed their tired leaves, and bend their boughs toward a gray earth of severed bird wings", sets the scene on the inner gatefold.

The first song is, quite simply, the unholy trinity of metal – 'Black Sabbath' on *Black Sabbath* by Black Sabbath. Starting with the sound of a sinister rainstorm and a tolling, faraway bell – a device copied wholesale by dozens of bands ever since, not least by Metallica with 'For Whom The Bell Tolls' and Slayer with 'Raining Blood' – the song explodes into life with the drone-like riff that anchors it all the way through. For the musically-minded, the riff – E, octave of E, B flat – is based on the tritone or *diabolus in musica*, a sinister interval equating to half an octave, that unnerved church authorities so much in the Middle Ages that it was actually outlawed as the 'devil's interval'. The song itself is nothing more than a repetition of the riff, whether in subtle, almost bass-only form or in a heavier, all-out attack. It's Ozzy's spine-chilling wail of "What is this, that stands before me?" which remains the key moment – not only on this album but in Sabbath's entire catalogue.

Credited as 'Ossie Osbourne' on the gatefold, the singer provides some ascending, slightly uneasy harmonica for the intro and choruses of 'The Wizard', a more lightweight song that showcases Geezer's lightning-fast bass fills inside the main riff and Tony's dexterous, blues-based soloing. The influence of Jimi Hendrix is writ large on this track, although Bill's funk drumming is a marvel too – despite his contemporary claims of only being able to 'thrash' the drums.

'Behind The Wall Of Sleep' is another expert exercise in allowing the space behind a riff to breathe, with the holes in Iommi's simple, catchy figure punctuated only by the slinky drum pattern at times. Occasionally the song breaks step to lapse into a warm, layered chord pattern that evokes an almost West Coast Sixties vibe – not a flavour that would last long, as even at this early stage Sabbath were abandoning their roots to explore a more individual flavour. As the drums fade out at 3' 35", a wonderful bass solo ('Bassically') from Geezer stretches out for the next 40 seconds, aided by a wah pedal and demonstrating that in due course he would become one of British rock's best and most underrated players.

The classic 'N.I.B.' begins with the album's most recognisable riff, other than the arguable exception of 'Black Sabbath' itself. Writer Geezer Butler explained the song's unusual title with the words: "Originally it was [titled] 'Nib', which was Bill's beard, which looked like a pen nib because it was pointy, so we used to call him Nib. When I wrote 'N.I.B.', I couldn't think of a title for the song, so I just called it 'Nib', after Bill's beard. To make it more intriguing I put punctuation marks in there to make it 'N.I.B.'. By the time it got to America, they translated it to 'Nativity In Black'." It's one of the most fully formed songs in the early Sabbath catalogue, switching from the pure Cream rip-off of the main riff to a descending chord sequence and blistering solo that could also have been pilfered from any number of bands, but it's totally Sabbath in tone – unlike 'Evil Woman', which follows and sounds like a different band entirely.

'Sleeping Village' is Sabbath back on form, anchored by a subtle acoustic guitar and Ozzy's atmospheric, reverbed vocal. A slow riff comes in after a minute or two, before suddenly accelerating into a faster, multi-solo section under which Geezer's bass races. The long instrumental section that follows was a high point of the Sabbath live show then and afterwards, allowing the musicians to stretch out – and it's simultaneously one of the most 'metal' parts of the album, with the main riff dragging darkly along. In proto-progressive rock style, the song segues into the 10-minutes-plus of 'The Warning', another grim pontification on fate and the supernatural from Ozzy: "I saw you in a dream and you were with another man," he wails.

The jamming section of the show, which had become an established rock tradition since the late Sixties, was the chance for the musicians to show their mettle, as Geezer explained: "You know, [our] very early shows were quite lengthy back in the early Seventies. I think they were probably an hour and 45 minutes to two-hour shows. At least 30 minutes of that was basically improvisation. We did have a kind of a format that we knew beforehand we would try to adhere to, but often the format would change without any of us really knowing. Tony might just take it somewhere else. It was freeform playing that was pretty popular back in the early Seventies. A lot of it is just spontaneous and total improvisation. And we do that onstage, live in front of everybody. And then it's all the time during soundchecks and things like that. Tony might have written something we would all want to try out, see how that might work . . . We did that too."

Geezer remembered that the jamming had evolved out of necessity rather than self-indulgence, however: "When we first got together there were loads of soul clubs in England, and all anybody wanted to do was dance music, plus there were blues clubs. We used to get these gigs in Germany where we'd have to play eight or nine 45-minute spots every day. And we only knew about 10 songs so we had to make them into 40-minute songs, which is where all the jamming came from, and where the first two albums came from, because we wrote them while we were jamming . . . We just took those blues roots and made them heavier, because we were into Hendrix and Cream, who were the heaviest bands around at that time. We wanted to be heavier than everybody else!"

The original cut of 'The Warning' contained a much longer guitar solo than the edit which appeared on the LP, as Geezer recalled: "[It was] really a live band in the studio. The only difference [was that] Tony did an 18-minute guitar solo on 'The Warning' and that was cut down by the producer . . . we didn't have any control whatsoever over that. We weren't allowed in on the mix . . . We didn't have time to take that song and put it into a five-minute song. We did a gig one night, the next two days we were in the studio and the day after that we were off to Europe. In those days, it was either do it or forget it. You got two days to do it and that's it. Then some other band was in there . . . We didn't know any other way . . . The Beatles took a day to record their first album!"

But this rushed pressure gave the album its genius, as he added: "I thought that was one of the main ingredients of the early records. Because you had two days, all it was is the band playing live in the studio. If we had more time we would have added whatever was hip at the time – a synthesiser or something – which would have totally ruined the sound of the band. Whereas now you can still listen to the first albums and it's just us, as we were playing. There is nothing softening it up; it's just raw in the studio. So it doesn't date."

Perhaps more than any other song, 'The Warning' shows how much Iommi was at the heart of the band, and that he could compete with any other rock guitarist – Ritchie Blackmore and Jimmy Page included – when it came to economic riffing. He masters all idioms on this album, from the blues-wailing style inherited from contemporary idols such as Peter Green, via an early Seventies take on the technoflash shredding that would become ubiquitous in the following decade, to simple one-string riffing – there's an example of this in the eighth minute of the song, when he drops into a 'Roadhouse Blues' shuffle. The song ends with duelling solos between Tony and Geezer and leaves the listener in no doubt as to what they have just witnessed: genius in the making.*

Not everybody took this view, of course: when Ozzy took the record home to show his parents, his father remarked with a comment along the lines of: "Are you sure you were just drinking alcohol? This isn't music, this is weird." Undeterred, the band returned to work.

Geezer looked back at the success of *Black Sabbath* with some surprise, even years later: "On the first LP, we didn't really know what we were doing! . . . 'Black Sabbath' was written on bass: I just walked into the studio and went, 'bah, bah, bah' and everybody joined in and we just did it. However long the song is was how long it took us to write it. So most of the stuff was just done from jams. In those days we didn't have tape recorders or anything and nobody would write stuff at home and bring it to the studio. We just used to go to the studio and jam for two or three hours and see what came out. The first record, we just went in and played it. It was like Sabbath live but in the studio, and the producer just cut out things."

More songs needed to be written, and this time the band knew what

---

* For some unknown reason, the **Warners version** of the album titles the first instrumental section of 'War Pigs' as 'Luke's Wall', **and the end** section of 'Fairies Wear Boots' as 'Jack The Stripper', although the music is identical on all versions.

they were doing — at least, more acutely than they had before. Geezer looked back at those days with recognition that the Sabbath formula at that stage — insofar as there was one — was simply to avoid sounding like anybody else. As he explained, "Back then you had to be totally different from anybody else to get recognised. It still happens now, but it seemed ˙more adventurous then. [For example] we never sounded like The Beatles, but if you did something that sounded like The Beatles, you would immediately drop it because there were so few bands around then. You would know what everybody else was doing. The last thing in the world you wanted to do was sound like everybody else."

One of the more astonishing elements of Black Sabbath's none-more-astonishing story is the awe-inspiring work rate they demonstrated in 1970 and 1971. Although the *Black Sabbath* album had been released a mere eight months before, the foursome wasted no time in unveiling a second album — *Paranoid* — which surpassed its predecessor and, as it happened, has gone down in history as one of the most influential metal albums of all time. It also gained Sabbath a whole new fanbase, including the pre-teen John Lydon, who told the author in 2005, "*Paranoid* was one of the best records ever made, a stonker from start to finish. Every single bit of it is a powerhouse."

Between *Black Sabbath* and *Paranoid*, Sabbath put in some serious road miles. The live schedule had been packed since the start of the year, with a notable March appearance at the Atomic Sunrise Festival at The Round-house in Chalk Farm. The line-up reads today like a who's who of all the prevalent music scenes of the day, not just the rock and nascent metal movements: present on the bill over the week-long event were Alexis Korner, David Bowie (with his band The Hype), Genesis, Brian Auger, Hawkwind, Kevin Ayers & The Whole World and Arthur Brown. The gradual move towards musical heaviness seems to have been a feature of many musical subgenres at the time — witness the psychedelic space-outs of Hawkwind, the extended blues experimentation of Alexis Korner and the first tentative steps towards significance by Bowie. As Ian Gillan pointed out, there was definitely something in the air . . .

By this point Jim Simpson was booking Black Sabbath into larger clubs such as the Marquee in London as well as university venues that could hold a decent-sized crowd. This often meant travelling the country every single day to get from town to town, such as in the second week of April, when the band played gigs in Stoke, Folkestone and Epping in the space of three days. Supported by soon-to-be musical luminaries of the era such as Hardin & York, Van Der Graaf Generator, Caravan and Taste (featuring the young blues guitarist Rory Gallagher), Sabbath slowly carved out a reputation for their fearsome live presence, with Ozzy and Geezer attacking the songs with vigour and Ward a powerhouse on the drums. Only Iommi, by some way the most musical of the group, maintained the still, focused stage presence for which he would become famous.

Although there was the occasional cancelled show – such as a May 3 set at The Castle in Richmond, where Sabbath and support band Yes pulled out for "reasons beyond our control" – the vibe was good for the touring band, with all four musicians at an early peak and demand for their album and live show high.

Their new-found monetary security was a bizarre development for the band, not least for Ozzy, who found it hard to take: "We have a thing in England called the pools. You gamble, and you win a lot of money if you win. Like a fucking lottery over here. When I got successful, my family said, 'Bingo!' . . . I once went to a fortune teller, and she said to me that I would have £1,000 in the bank by the time I was 21, and what else did she say? That I would be a very famous person. At the age of 22 I had £1,000 pounds in the bank – excess of – and I was getting success. It wasn't planned – I don't what the fucking hell's happening to me. It's like death to me, you know? The funniest thing about it all is, when I was born, I weighed 10 pounds and something like 14 ounces. I was one of the biggest children ever – they thought I was twins, you know? . . . Destiny rules me, man."

When Sabbath began to make headway, their relief at being able to escape Aston drove them still harder, as Ozzy explained later: "We wanted to be successful; we wanted to be rich. We wanted to get out of that fucking shithole we were living in." And the modus operandi to achieve this? "We thought, what do people really love to fucking hear? What do people really want – 'Sugar sugar sugar, trying, true true true', and all this fucking lot coming out of your radio? I'm thinking, I've got no shoes on my feet – I'm walking around in fucking rags. I said to the guys, 'Listen, man – there's so many fucking people out there, talking how wonderful the fucking world is, and there's so many of us fuckers that ain't got nothing.'"

The festival circuit welcomed them and among the highlights of the summer was an appearance at the August Bank Holiday Jazz & Blues Festival, an annual event promoted by the Marquee Club which had moved from Richmond to Windsor and ended up at Plumpton Racecourse near Lewes. (It later moved to Reading.) The 1970 event featured acts such as Ginger Baker's Air Force, Richie Havens, King Crimson, Roy Harper and Savoy Brown, but on the night that Sabbath played they were followed by Deep Purple. Purple guitarist Ritchie Blackmore set fire to his stack that night having doused it in lighter fuel, a gesture that sat uneasily with the organisers and prog heroes Yes who were obliged to follow them.

Recording sessions for the new album commenced on June 16, 1970, with the same high-speed recording methods as before very much still in place. Ward told *Beat Instrumental*, "We did the title track in about 10 minutes – virtually a straight run. The whole record only took a few days to produce."

"That's just the way we work," added Iommi. "Everything we do is what we feel at the time, sometimes we can play a song and it will be loud and heavy and yet at other times it could be gentle. With LPs especially, when we have a few songs to record we go into the studio and cut them, then we sit around and think up some more." Ward: "It's not like filling up the record with old crap: it's just that when we have been in the studios for a while, the inspiration seems to be easier, new ideas just flow out."

After dates in Holland, Belgium and the phenomenal Euro Pop A–Z Musik Festival in Munich, Germany alongside Status Quo, Amon Düül II, Atomic Rooster, Free, Traffic, Deep Purple and Black Widow, it emerged that all was not well behind the scenes. Firstly, the American tour was postponed due to recent civil rights disputes at various US universities which had made promoters nervous about booking in rock acts (as they were still labelled) such as Sabbath. Elsewhere clubs were closing their doors permanently in reaction.

Although the *NME* blithely stated that one of the venues was simply unavailable ("San Francisco's Fillmore West is closing for the summer"), Iommi was more specific about what had occurred, telling the *Melody Maker*: "The group was due to go to the States soon, but with the student unrest in the States they have become a victim of many clubs closing down . . . We were hoping to play the Fillmores, but both of them are closed for the summer. So now we have to wait until September when the colleges open again." When the issue had become clearer, the *NME* added: "New York's Fillmore East will restrict its acts to lesser known groups in a bid to avoid any possible trouble [from student action]."

While the band filled in with extra UK dates until the US tour could restart, they were playing small shows that had been booked long in advance of their new-found fame and fortune on the insistence of Simpson. The manager's philosophy was that it would be morally wrong and strategically rash to cancel an agreed booking simply because the band had now become too big for it – although he did attempt to negotiate more money out of the promoters as a result. As Simpson recalls today, "Now, I'd booked Sabbath into many venues I'd known in the past with other bands, and loyalties prevail. If you book the band in and the guy can't pay more than £800, and you decide to accept his £800, if the record goes big you've got to honour these things. You do your best to renegotiate, but the guy deserves some sort of comeback because he booked the band when we needed him to book the band."

This didn't go down well at all with Sabbath, and soon arguments between band and manager broke out. Simpson: "The big fight was really because they thought we should scrap all those bookings and start again. Apart from cancelling all those, you upset lots of fans anyway who are buying your records. It takes you off the map, because if you arrange a date now it ain't going to happen for another 10 or 12 weeks anyway." The key was the sum of money which the band would receive for their evening's work, as he explains: "I was already getting them £800 or £1,000 or £1,200 for them, but once the record [*Black Sabbath*] came out, people were prepared to pay £2,000 or £2,500, and those were going in the book. They weren't going in the book for this week or next week, they were booked for seven to 10 weeks' time. And that was the big problem we had: it was me trying to convince [the band] that they had to show a certain degree of responsibility. I remember saying to them, we need these people on the way up, and we hope they'll be nice to us on the way down! But of course, there *was* no way down . . ."

Jim wasn't blind to the possibility that other managers might try to get into Sabbath's good books and lure them away from him. In fact, approaches had already been made to them by the successful (and much feared) manager Don Arden via one of his signings, The Move's Carl Wayne. Although Sabbath had elected to stay with Simpson, they had met two of Arden's staff, Patrick Meehan and Wilf Pine, who had studied Arden's management methods and in due course broke away to set up their own organisation.

As Simpson remembers, "Wilf Pine and Pat Meehan were Don's enforcers, or whatever the word is. But then Patrick and Wilf walked out on Don. Now, with Donnie, if you work with him and he likes you, he regards you as family. And family do *not* just scurrilously do the dirty on you and walk out on you. They saw what Don did – how he recruited an artist – and thought, let's do this on our own. And the first one they went for was Black Sabbath, who Don had failed to get – through Charlie Wayne, in fact, who made the overtures to the band on Don's behalf."

Without Simpson knowing, the band were being wooed by the newly independent Meehan and Pine, who approached them at the point when Sabbath and their manager were in dispute about playing the low-paying dates which had been booked long before. The end came quickly, says Simpson: "It was resolved by them walking out on me. I got a letter. On the Friday night I heard a knock on the front door and Luke, the road manager, said that the band couldn't go to Liverpool that night because they'd got no money. What had been happening, with my approval, by the way, was that they'd been taking all the fee – you just picked up cash at most gigs – and dividing it in four."

His point was that his cut as manager was not being paid at that time, because the band were keeping the money they made from gigs. This was all above board, he emphasises: "So there was no commission being paid. I didn't care, because all the bookings went in the book, and the next time we'd got a cheque booking I'd have taken that. We'd just turned the corner and all the money was just going to start coming in, so I didn't really care whether I got my commission then or in a month's time."

Mystified by the band's lack of cash, Simpson queried the situation: "So I said, how come you've got no money? You've been taking all the bookings. They said, well, we've spent it all: if you can't give us 200 quid we can't go to the booking tonight. So I raised £200 and gave it to them – and that was a lot more money then than it is now, of course! – and off they went to play in Liverpool."

The blow fell on Saturday, 4 September: "Early the next morning I got a letter from the lawyers saying, we don't want you to contact the band any more, we're handling the band. They want to leave you because you've not been doing your job right."

Simpson laughs with some bitterness about this last statement. "The week they left me, they were number one on the *Music Business Weekly* chart, one of the music industry newspapers at the time along with *Record Retail*. I had a number one album, a number 16 album – because *Black Sabbath* had come back on the chart again – and a number two single. And I hadn't been doing my job right?"

But the die was cast, and professional relations between manager and band had been severed permanently. All that remained to Simpson was to sue for damages against the broken agreement he had with Sabbath – a long and arduous process that dragged out for many years and which was ultimately of little benefit to anyone. As Jim recalls, the only real winners by the time the case came to court were his legal advisors. "The score was Black Sabbath and Jim Simpson 1, the legal profession 321!" he chuckles now. Like so many others, he was the victim of bad advice, as he explains: "My lawyer, James Leckie – who should go down in indelible ink in my book – was confident that we'd get £200,000 from them. Then I was offered £85,000 to be paid before the court case. Two days before the court case I was offered this. If you don't go to court, we'll pay you £85,000, said Patrick Meehan."

This seemed like a reasonable offer to Simpson, who was in favour of accepting Meehan's £85,000 out-of-court settlement. "The argument was, if we don't get it, we go to court; if we do get it, we don't go to court," says Simpson. "Leckie insisted I turn it down. [He said] that we'd get at least £200,000 . . . this was in Lincoln's Inn Gardens, or whatever this poncy place was called. After a day and a half in court he came to me and said, we're going to have to settle for whatever we can get here, they've got no money. I said, is this the same band who can afford to pay us £200,000, and two days later they've got no money? And he said, well, it's the way it's turned out – you can never tell with these things. Arrogant bastard."

The result was disappointing, he remembers: "£35,000 was awarded. £8,000 was paid to us on the day – of which Legal Aid took £6,000, Leckie took £1,000 and I took £1,000. It took 14 years to get the balance. I did what I could: it costs money to enforce a judgment."

Fortunately for Simpson, help came from an unlikely quarter – Pine and Meehan's old employer Don Arden. "It wasn't until Don Arden gave me a lot of support that I actually could [recoup the award]," he says. "He came to me and said, did I want his support on the Wilf Pine and Patrick Meehan situation? And the answer was a resounding yes. Don was really, really great to me. He showed immense support, perhaps partially inspired by his, um . . . lack of love for Patrick Meehan, but he was really good to me."

He adds: "During this whole thing, we used his office in Portland Place. I got burgled once, on a day when I had to go to London and see him, and told him. And he rustled round the office to find things to replace the things I'd lost. I'd had a ReVox tape recorder stolen, and he replaced it with a nearly new one of his, as well as a good hi-fi with speakers. He said, 'I don't know how you're going to get those home, but they're yours.' You have to treat the man with due respect. You wouldn't dream of taking advantage of him, and if you didn't take advantage of him he would treat you with generosity."

Asked if, 37 years later, he still feels resentment about the whole incident – now that Sabbath are a global force, Meehan and Pine are out of the public eye and Arden is elderly and ailing – Simpson explains: "My main resentment is towards the legal profession. As we all know, in this country the legal system is absolutely unjust. If you can afford to pay lawyers – and afford to lose what you pay lawyers – you can get something approaching justice. If you can't, you don't stand a chance."

As for the band-members themselves, he adds: "I liked Ozzy and I still do, I think he's one of humanity's nicer people. He doesn't conform in any way. He's very honest, very loyal, very straightforward, and he was the one who didn't want to leave me when the push came. I've got a lot of time for Ozzy, I think he's a very good man. I've seen him a couple of times and he's been absolutely great. I saw him two or three years ago and he hugged me.

"I've encountered Tony a couple of times and it's been very formal but friendly. We've both been very dignified, polite and pleasant to each other – there's no need to be anything else after all these years. I bumped into Geezer at House Of Fraser in Birmingham and he scuttled away. And I haven't seen Bill. I feel no rancour towards any of them, but I feel real affection for Ozzy still."

How does he look back on it all? "The guys were doing very well when I was with them, and they would at least have had a reliable, honest, vaguely intelligent manager. To give you an idea, I manage a band called King Pleasure & The Biscuit Boys now. We had a contract in our first eight years together, but after that we didn't bother – and I'm now in my nineteenth year of managing them. That says something, doesn't it?"

CHAPTER FIVE

1970–1972

AND so Sabbath's career took a new turn. Armed with a hard-nosed management team who didn't share the old-school traditions of Simpson, and facing a lucrative US tour, the band raised their game. It seemed that some bad blood was hiding beneath the surface between Simpson and Tony Iommi: the former was once alleged to have stated that Iommi's family were better off than those of the rest of the band. Iommi denied it: "Well, that's actually BS [bullshit]. Jim Simpson and myself didn't get along. My family was the same as everybody else's. Maybe they signed for a guitar for me, which is the same as Ozzy's folks signed for a sound system for him. We certainly weren't from a good area, that's for sure . . . it was very rough. Where we lived was probably equivalent to the Bronx . . . I didn't get on with him, no. I didn't like Jim Simpson very much. You see, I don't think anybody else liked him either, it was just me that would tell him! I was the spokesman."

Before the recording of *Paranoid*, Roger Bain, who had been brought into produce again by Tony Hall Enterprises, decided to move the band to Rockfield Studios in south Wales for rehearsals. "The biggest chunk of time was spent in the rehearsing and routining stage," said Bain, "the object being that when you go in to record you're not sort of experimenting in the studio. What you're doing when you go into the studio is transferring it into a recorded version."

As he later added, "The band were cranked up as if they were onstage . . . The building we were in was a fairly old barn. The whole of the roof actually did move. I can remember Ozzy saying, 'Why don't we record here?' Because the atmosphere of the place and the people were so great."

In due course, once pre-production was complete and the songs ready for recording, band and the producing and engineering team of Bain, Tom Allom and Brian Humphries upped sticks to Regent once again.

"We did the backing tracks for *Paranoid* in the same place that we did the first album – Regent, a little four-track [studio] just off Tottenham Court Road in the West End," said Allom. "It was a good-sounding studio; we always got good results in that room. It was an absolute shithole, but it worked."

This time, however, Vertigo were prepared to stump up more cash for facilities thanks to the success of the debut LP, and some of the recording took place at the much more luxurious Island Studios – founded by Island label owner Chris Blackwell in a disused church in Notting Hill. "We started *Paranoid* at Regent Sound," said Ozzy much later, "and then we moved to this magnificent 16-track, Island Studios. That's where we wrote the song 'Paranoid'."

Of the song itself, Iommi laughed: "The actual track, I did when everybody went for a lunch break. I just sat in the studio and came up with this idea." Bill Ward added: "He was just playing it on his own in the studio. Geezer plugged in his bass, I sat behind my drum kit, we automatically grooved with him and Ozzy started singing. We didn't say a word to each other; we just came in the room and started playing. I think it was about 1.30 in the afternoon; Tony had the riffs, and by 2 p.m. we had 'Paranoid' exactly as you hear it on the record."

Bain liked the song, commenting: "It had a very strong beat, a powerful riff. I remember pressing the talkback and saying words to the effect of, 'That's pretty good. What is that?' and sort of getting disbelief. They said, 'You're joking.' I said, 'No, that's really good, that's a really strong riff.' They said, 'We're just pissing around. We just made it up.' I said, 'Well that's great, let's do it!' "

The 'Paranoid' single was released on 29 August 1970, and stormed the charts, peaking at number four and remaining a chart item for 18 weeks. Word was building fast around Sabbath – and audiences were becoming bigger and rowdier at their shows.

The first task on the agenda was the promotion of the *Paranoid* LP, which had originally been titled *War Pigs* after its opening track but was renamed after record company protests. "If you look at the album sleeve, it's got a guy in a pink leotard and a shield and a sword. That was supposed to represent the War Pig," said Ozzy. "A pink pig. They printed the album sleeve and changed it to *Paranoid* at the very last minute."

Released on September 18 – the day that Jimi Hendrix died, just before the management change in the UK – the album was a stronger and more confident work than *Black Sabbath*. With the song 'War Pigs', Sabbath took a political stance against the warmongering leaders of the day, widely presumed (but never specifically confirmed) to include the US administration responsible for executing the final stages of the Vietnam War. The military theme of the album, at least with its initial title, explained the bizarre sleeve art – a blurred, indistinct figure (the 'war pig' himself) emerging from a darkened background wearing a crash helmet.

As Bill Ward said, "I think ['War Pigs'] was a little bit stronger than Country Joe singing about Vietnam – although I love Country Joe . . . it's pretty much in your face. There's a lot of bands – The Beatles, The Byrds – I can probably think of 50 bands off the top of my head who have made political statements, and let's not discount Pink Floyd's 'Dogs Of War', which I think is fuckin' phenomenal. However, at the time when 'War Pigs' came out, it was in your face, and down your throat, and it pulled out your balls. To me, it was just a real heavy fuckin' song."

He was right. 'War Pigs' is an essay in heaviness and precision, with its stop-start riff punctuated by a background hi-hat kick-starting a whole new songwriting method. The pioneering nature of this song is hard to overstate: for example, single-guitar rock bands like Sabbath, Deep Purple and Led Zeppelin were making giant strides in the field of production, beefing up the sound of the solitary axe to maximise the impact of the riff it produced. But it's no mere heads-down simple anthem: as Ward sniggers, "You know, the beginning of that song is in waltz time!", making life hard for more than a few covers bands over the years (although the song was covered expertly by Faith No More and Sacred Reich in the Eighties).

Vocally, Ozzy is about as good as he ever got, more or less mastering the ascending melody on record (live would be a different matter). Lyrically, the song doesn't break many barriers down (famously, Ozzy rhymes "Generals gathered in their masses" with "Just like witches at black masses" . . . no points for invention there), but that's just a part of its naïve, angry charm. At the song's close, Ozzy promises infernal retribution for the war leaders ("Begging mercy for their sins / Satan laughing spreads his wings") – it's little wonder the record company wanted this bit of horror-movie-style political commentary minimised.

Crowds loved 'War Pigs', and still do. As Ward recalled, "Back in the early Seventies, you would see all the Vietnam veterans coming home: whenever you were at the airport, you would see several soldiers coming in travelling. I do know a lot of vets from 'Nam who are friends of mine, like Sib Hashian, who plays drums for Boston. He was a big Sabbath fan, and he did quite a number of tours in Vietnam as well. It was in those early Seventies when we were laying down tracks for 'War Pigs' in America and it was just phenomenal, it was almost like a coming-home anthem."

Ultimately, 'War Pigs' can be seen as a peace anthem, albeit one that threatens a terrible fate for its subjects. In this, Sabbath carried forward the ideals of the peace generation that had slipped away at the end of the previous decade – although, of course, no such ideals existed in everyday life in Aston. Nonetheless, informed by soldiers at a military base gig of the horrors of war, the impulse to record a song about the concept turned out to be a stroke of genius.

The same can be said of 'Paranoid' itself, a Sabbath classic through and through which embodies their early sound as well as any other track. "Finished with my woman 'cause she couldn't help me with my mind . . ." sings Ozzy in his nasal, slightly wobbly tenor, introducing the themes of sociopathy and mental derangement which made the band's image so simultaneously dark and enthralling. Based on a simple riff in E/D with a C/D/E tail – not dissimilar to Led Zeppelin's 'Communication Break-down', released in 1969 – the song straddled the rock/metal divide with ease, not least because Geezer threw in some effortless melodic fills from time to time. While it doesn't have the crushing slowness of, say, 'Black Sabbath', 'Paranoid' (originally titled 'The Paranoid' by Butler) was a rela-tively catchy live anthem that is always a feature of the live set. Ward also recognised this lightness of touch: "I thought 'Paranoid', in comparison to some of the other songs, like 'Hand Of Doom', was a little bit light, to be honest with you. I thought, this is a bit of a pop song. I didn't really pay a whole lot of attention to it."

Ozzy thought it would work as a lead-off single – their last for another seven years – recalling, "I remember going home with the tapes and . . . this was driving me nuts on the train all the way back."

After the heavy warfare of 'War Pigs' and the cunning riffing of 'Paranoid', 'Planet Caravan' is a surprise – a sumptuously layered ballad with loads of starlit atmosphere and even some subtle piano. Demon-strating that a mellower side lay within the Sabbath ranks, 'Planet Caravan' was a fully fledged epic within the confines of its four minutes – even featuring Iommi's jazz and classical influenced soloing, a far cry from the blues exercises elsewhere.

If any doubts remained that Black Sabbath – not yet labelled a heavy metal band, as the term hadn't been adopted – were much harder and heavier than their contemporaries, then 'Iron Man' dispelled any such doubts. Again, it's Iommi's song, with his carved-in-stone riff and Ozzy's vocal melody locked in unison in a way that – like it or not – the listener couldn't ignore. Add its almost comically threatening intro – a sliding wail of a riff and Ozzy's futuristically treated gargle of "I am Iron Man!" and a surprisingly clear production, and 'Iron Man' is a future classic.

'Electric Funeral' is as heavy but denser than 'Iron Man', with Ozzy's gleefully dark vocals and Iommi's modulated layers of rhythm guitar building up to a tempo change at two minutes in that snaps into an almost funky, staccato break and much higher-pitched vocals than before. Matching lead guitar squeals with Ozzy's muttered threat of "Electric funeral!" makes the song too over-the-top for many, but thankfully it reverts back to the grinding, processed riff of before and exits with an extended fade.

The seven minutes of 'Hand Of Doom' allow Sabbath to stretch out, with Ozzy intoning dark, laconic vocals ("You push the needle in . . .") and the song resting on Geezer's understated solo before expanding its horizons with a sudden riff and tempo change. "You're giving death a kiss!" scolds Ozzy over a stamping riff pushed forward by some of Ward's most solid playing yet. After five minutes the atmosphere changes again, with a slight, understated riff-play and an outro of violent weight.

'Rat Salad' is shorter and more fiery, with Iommi and Geezer now showing how perfectly they could lock together in a riff: it's Ward's song this time, with a long drum solo at its heart demonstrating how far his skills had come. Finally, *Paranoid* exits with 'Fairies Wear Boots', written after the band had been set upon in the street by a bunch of aggressive skinheads who took exception to their long-haired hippie look, and presumably their new-found celebrity status. Iommi suffered an injury to his arm during the attack, and the song was the vengeful result. It's a loping, semi-blues full of layered riffing but without extending to the heaviness of 'War Pigs' or 'Iron Man' – and is all the more successful as a result. The usual tempo and key change halfway through is overlaid with a harmony solo from Iommi, among the first occasions that he'd recorded this way. The song and album fade away in a drift of echo.

Astonishingly, *Paranoid* made number one on the UK chart – and elevated Sabbath to a whole new league. Chart action was still a novelty to the band – who had, after all, been an unsigned, unmanaged act with little hope of rising above the club circuit only a year and a half before. The album also made number 12 in the US, a remarkable achievement given the less-progressive culture of the American industry at the time. But the massive backing and promotional muscle of Warners pushed both single and LP through. As Joe Smith, the exec. who signed the Sabs to the company, recalled: "We were looking for a single, and they were hard to get. There was still resistance in Top 40 radio to playing any single by one of these bands. If somebody's going to take a shot, 'Paranoid' was the record to take a shot with. Also, it was a great title for a single at the time."

The *Paranoid* album gives the impression of consistency which the excellent but patchy debut LP doesn't deliver. The band, it seemed, had found their sound at last – as Geezer said, "I think when you write your first album you're influenced by all the stuff that's going on around you, and I think each one of us brought our own particular styles into the music that we did. So, in the beginning all the different influences you've had up until then come together on one album, and from there it gels into this one sound rather than lots of different things. When you realise you've got your own sound then you can just pick up on that and just keep it in one direction . . . I thought it happened on *Paranoid*."

The album (not released until January 1971 in the US) was a smash hit, establishing the Sabbath brand irrevocably. Music fans relished the chance to play it loud, a requirement that was obvious from the opening chords of 'War Pigs'. Asked why volume was so important to the music, Iommi reasoned: "It's just the way we are – heavy music like ours gains a lot of the weight from volume. There's an old barn in Wales where we sometimes go to rehearse; it's a room belonging to Future Sound Studios. We played so loud one night that a lot of the tiles on the roof cracked and fell off."

The 'making music in the country' vibe that had been explored by so many bands of the day – Traffic and Led Zeppelin among them – had clearly worked well for the band, with Ozzy explaining: "I guess it's all part of the system. We record in London, Island and Regent [studios] to be precise. There is no reason why we shouldn't record in Wales – it really is an incredible place to work things out, no hassles, only space – we can go and piss about in the fields if we want to. That's the way it should be everywhere, open and free."

A hippie concept? Perhaps – the normally taciturn Iommi added, almost in a plea for tolerance, "So many people hear little pieces of conversations, shows, news and things, then turn round and retell it all wrong. Did you see *Hair*? Well that's what I mean, everyone goes to see *Hair*, they hear the songs and the music and they see the dancing, but very few actually realise what the whole point and message of the show is."

Live dates followed in the run-up to the American tour, with a jaunt through September taking in venues as luxurious as the Brangwyn Hall in Swansea, the Greyhound Blues Club in Croydon and the King's Head in Romford, Essex. Clearly Sabbath hadn't outgrown their club roots yet, and why not? This was the golden age of the British musical circuit, when top-ranking bands could be seen playing at local clubs on almost any night of the week. And if anyone needs proof of Sabbath's earning their dues, this is where they did it – night after night in every town in the country. A tour through France, Switzerland, Holland, Belgium and Sweden, supported by Manfred Mann Chapter III, was a step up once more, with the line-up powering through the set (now two albums' worth of material) at full steam.

Occasionally the hysteria generated by the band's success spilled over negatively, with one show on October 23 giving Sabbath something of a shock. The inebriated crowd at the Mayfair Ballroom in Newcastle invaded the stage and, unimpressed by a rendition of 'Paranoid' which Sabbath thought would placate them, began stealing equipment from the stage. Ozzy later said, "If it means us having to give up putting out singles, then we will. We want people to listen to us, not try to touch us. I was really terrified, shocked out of my mind."

At this point Sabbath were still fulfilling certain dates booked by Jim Simpson before the management change-over; one of these was a headlining set at the Festival Of Contemporary Music at Newark in Nottinghamshire on 24 October. The story goes that Sabbath – just six days away from their American tour – were reluctant to play the show and pulled out, angering the promoter, who had offered them the sum of £325 (a far cry from the usual £2,000 or more which they were now accustomed to receiving per show). After legal threats, a local band called Cherokee Smith replaced Sabbath and the matter was laid to rest. Two final dates – one at Bournemouth Pavilion and another supporting Emerson Lake & Palmer at London's Royal Festival Hall – were played before the band took off for the States. The second of these was one of Sabbath's most notorious gigs to date: fans inspired by the band's enormously loud and aggressive music behaved badly, and while this probably wouldn't have caused eyebrows to rise at a pub gig in Birmingham, the rather stuffy RFH management weren't accustomed to such unorthodoxy and initially refused to accept a repeat booking for January. Meehan and Pine's representatives were left to negotiate with them while Sabbath toured the US.

The band debuted at Glassboro State College in New Jersey and then moved on to the University of Miami in Florida, Ungano's Ritz Theater on New York's Staten Island (the scene of the apathetic crowd – and subsequent gear-throwing from the band – as recounted earlier by Bill Ward) and included clubs in New York state, Maine (supported by power-poppers Badfinger and good-time vaudeville act Mungo Jerry), Ohio (with Iommi's old buddies Jethro Tull) and California (with Alice Cooper and others). Once on the West Coast, it was as if Sabbath had found their spiritual home: a series of dates at the Whisky A Go Go in Hollywood and the famed Fillmore West in San Francisco were rapturously received by the crowds. With home-grown rock acts such as The Doors, The Grateful Dead and Jefferson Airplane accustomed to performing overblown, high-volume gigs to adoring audiences, Sabbath fitted in perfectly. Even the band's habit of extending their jams into long, experimental solo sessions was the Californian norm.

After finishing off 1970 with dates in Liverpool, Denmark and Germany, Sabbath began rehearsals for a third new album in under two years. This would be the scintillating *Master Of Reality*, which saw them cautiously expanding their musical palette during recording sessions at Island Studios. As Geezer told me, "With *Master Of Reality*, we sort of wanted to change the music a bit because we didn't want to keep playing the same music all the time. So we all bought different instruments, Tony started playing piano. We wanted to expand our musical horizons a bit, so we took our time, plus we could afford to by then."

Was the experimentation – possibly a premature move after barely more than a year in the public eye – a wise decision, in retrospect? "Yes – I think the music was better with more money and more time. We'd done so much touring in such a short time by then, that we were all absolutely knackered anyway, and we needed it – we couldn't just come off the road after six months and go straight into rehearsal. So we took the time out to write new stuff. The first two albums came out of a lot of the jamming we did around the clubs, we had the basics of *Paranoid* done by the time we did the first album. That's why they were only six months apart."

With the album mostly in the can – as with the previous LPs, there would be a lag of some months before actual release – Sabbath took a month's break to continue touring. Life-changing events lay ahead, at least for Ozzy who had by then married his girlfriend, Thelma Mayfair, and become stepfather to her son, Elliot. Not that any of these events interrupted Sabbath's touring schedule, which had been scheduled to kick off on 5 January with the renegotiated booking at the Royal Festival Hall, this time with Freedom and Curved Air. However, the venue management weren't having it, stating that "unruly fans were standing on the chairs and causing damage to the venue" and causing no little resentment between band and RFH staff.

After shows in Hull, Edinburgh, Aberdeen, Newcastle, Nottingham, Manchester and Leeds, Sabbath re-entered the studio to finish off *Master Of Reality*. Playing catchup was the US record company, who released *Paranoid* there in the same month. The next four months were set to be gruelling, as the band were booked to play their first shows in Australia and more in the US. Down under, where demand for Western hard rock – the harder the better – was at its peak in the early Seventies, a whole new set of audiences were waiting to be converted to the Sabbath cause, a fact that band and management were not slow to exploit. On 30 January Sabbath appeared at a press reception for the Myponga Open Air Festival in Sydney – an event at which they (ostensibly the headliners, playing at 11pm) were actually followed by Spectrum. Other acts on the bill included the hardly known Coney Island Jug Band and Sons Of The Vegetal Mother, with Sabbath the only major Northern Hemisphere act to make the trip.

A stopover in Japan was scheduled for February 3, but was cancelled when the band members were denied entry visas due to their criminal records. The same problem occurred the following year – and in fact it wouldn't be until the following decade that Sabbath played in Japan. This must have grated with Meehan and Pine, who were keen to take advantage of the many commercial opportunities that existed for their band in the Far East – more so, in fact, than in Australia.

No matter: another lucrative North American jaunt awaited, kicking off in mid-February in New Jersey and progressing through no fewer than 14 US and Canadian states. Support slots with the phenomenally successful Fleetwood Mac introduced Sabbath to a new audience – the blues and AOR fanbase – and playing over perennially popular home-grown bands such as Mountain kept their profile high, too.

There can be no question that at this point, in early 1971, Black Sabbath had made remarkable progress and their future looked incredibly bright. After tying up April with European dates they took a break and watched *Paranoid* quickly go gold in the USA the following month. The slower-to-catch-on *Black Sabbath* also reached UK gold at this time – and all this with *Master Of Reality* waiting to be unleashed and promoters burning up Meehan and Pine's phone lines to secure Sabbath bookings. Few bands have ever been in this position: and even fewer sustained it for as long as Sabbath's first line-up did in the Seventies.

After two months off the road, Sabbath prepared the ground for the release of *Master* in the US by playing gigs there in July. A headline slot over The Amboy Dukes, The Seigal-Schwall Band, Alex Taylor and Brownsville Station in Detroit was followed by East Coast and Toronto dates with Yes, Black Oak Arkansas and Alice Cooper – before the album appeared on 21 July.

The album made a huge impact. *The Rag* summed it up well later that year when it stated, "Black Sabbath sing lyrics about Satan and death and evil, and attract the most strung-out 16-year-old-reds-users audience of any group around. Well, what should one make of all this? Is it all just another sign of the decadence that seems to be everywhere these days? . . . Sabbath are one hell of a good rock'n'roll band. *Master Of Reality* is a great album . . . If you've ever liked crude rock'n'roll noise, whether the early Kinks and Who or Velvet Underground or Stooges, there is definitely something going on here worth listening to – there's really not that much of a jump from the brilliance of the late great Stooges (or Little Richard for that matter) to what Black Sabbath is doing, after all.''

The timing of the record, Sabbath's most heavily promoted (and backed-up with tours) to date was key. Punk, after all, was only half a decade away, and more than a few reviewers had become sick of the endless country-folk-rock indulgences that American audiences – especially those stuck in the hinterlands, away from the progressive East and West coasts – had been forced to endure for years. The magazine added: "There's absolutely nothing superfluous about Black Sabbath's music, as distinctly opposed to the school of Cream/Jeff Beck/Ten Years After egomania and interchangeable 10-minute jerk-off guitar solos. Black Sabbath grind out riff after riff after unrelenting riff; even the guitar leads are riffs, and there isn't one excessive uncalled-for guitar lead on their whole new album."

Is it going too far to say that the stripped-down aesthetics of Sabbath – who played guitar solos, for sure, but short and succinct ones at this stage – presaged the nihilism of punk? Perhaps. But there's no getting away from the fact that their 'total' riffs, where the vastness of the sound was the point rather than its complexity or beauty, had more than a little in common with the reduce-everything ethos of the punks. No wonder John Lydon liked their music.

The album begins with the fantastic ode to marijuana, 'Sweet Leaf', which caused near-universal controversy thanks to its subject matter. Its main riff kicks in after the sound of a man (reportedly Iommi) taking a hit on a bong and coughing, with the sound taped, looped and panned slowly across the speakers – something of a slap in the face to anyone seeking to hide the song's theme from, say, under-age listeners. Ozzy sings his ode to the weed as if to a lover, musing, "You introduced me to my mind, and left me wanting you and your kind," and adding, most obviously, "Come on now – try it out!" Musically, it's a monster, with a massive riff coming and going with drone-like intensity.

Bill knew the message had been put across to the audiences, recalling later on: "I really believe that a lot of the 'heads' got it immediately – they got 'Sweet Leaf' immediately . . . it didn't go over the heads of the 20 to 40,000 people we played in front of at the open-air gigs – flags were flying, Vets were wheeled down in their wheelchairs holding up their crutches, totally rocking out."

The next song, 'After Forever', was criticised as blasphemy by some clearly confused listeners – some supposedly representing church authorities – who were offended by its subject matter, the warnings of a man contemplating the afterlife. And yet the song seems to be advocating a Christian belief, with lines such as "Perhaps you'll think before you say that God is dead and gone". This song is the most advanced that Sabbath had composed until this point, featuring a warm, very McCartney-esque bass line from Geezer that soared over Iommi's analogue, almost pop-rock riff. The song steps up to a plodding, staccato riff halfway through that is simple and effective, rather than over-complex – signs that Sabbath were realising the value of a less-is-more approach now that they had fully mastered their craft.

The slightly bizarre 'Embryo', a 28-second instrumental, sounds almost like a mediaeval strings and horn quartet, although this must be the result of Bain's in-studio effects trickery. 'Children Of The Grave', a classic Sabbath song if ever there was one, boasts a prime-era Iommi riff – which presages the central, fast-picked riff behind many a future NWOBHM song a decade early – and a spiralling, whole-band riff device between the first and second sections that harks forward directly to early Metallica. Iommi's guitar sound is at its hugest on this song, which on its surface is a paean to youth activism ("Revolution in their minds, the children start to march against the world they live in"). It features vocals from Ozzy that are clearly a stretch and resolves to a weird, almost horror-movie sequence in which Iommi bends his strings into tunelessness.

The utterly beautiful 'Orchid', another short instrumental, lasting just a minute and a half, is spine-chilling. Iommi pulls off a miniature acoustic guitar symphony, backed by bass tones either from Geezer, a keyboard or simply his own recorded and artificially enhanced bottom strings. Listeners were just starting to realise how awe-inspiring Sabbath's musicianship was becoming, thanks to small shifts of emphasis such as this.

'Lord Of This World' rests on another huge, classic Sabbath riff, however, with the master now fully in control of a truly epic guitar sound and intending to use it to its fullest. Geezer's bass is locked in as perfectly as usual, making for a massively fat tone that has been endlessly emulated by the doom-metal and stoner-rock bands of the Nineties without ever quite capturing its vastness or its warmth, probably because modern digital recording equipment doesn't have the necessary analogue characteristics. A slippery bass melody finishes the song, before Geezer crops up again atop the mellow intro of 'Solitude'. Once again Iommi steps off the gas, allowing a distant landscape of echoes to build up behind Ozzy's keening vocals – perhaps his best ever up to this point – and an unexpected flute that drones in the background. The vibe is very much of a Doors-like ethereal ambience, focused on the lyrics of rejection and loneliness ("I've not stopped crying since you went away") and a valuable breathing space in this intense album. The flute provides an almost jazzy interlude before the song spirals to a close.

The vast 'Into The Void' closes *Master Of Reality*, extending beyond six minutes and based on an all-time classic Iommi riff that walks sedately forward, anchored by huge bass (Geezer is on melodic form again) and Ozzy's semi-ecological, semi-devilish vocals. He wails almost science-fiction-based lines such as "Freedom fighters sent out to the sun . . . Leave the earth to Satan and his slaves" with the enjoyable malice that his nasal, often slightly flat voice implies. The riff grinds on past solo after solo, before a truly apocalyptic ending not unlike that of 'War Pigs'.

And so, it seemed, international success was assured. Within a month, *Master Of Reality* went gold in the US. More shows remained for the band to clear up in August, before heading over to the British Rock Meeting on the Rheinhalbinsel in Speyer, Germany the following month. Again, the line-up reads like a who's who of Seventies rock, with Rod Stewart & The Faces, Deep Purple, Family, Fleetwood Mac, Curved Air, Rory Gallagher, East Of Eden, Groundhogs, Hardin & York, Fairport Convention, Osibisa, Juicy Lucy, Mick Abrahams, Gentle Giant, Jerusalem, Beggars Opera, Bullit, Roy Young Band, Ashton Gardner & Dyke and Heaven all on the bill. Gigs in Vienna and Palermo prefaced another US tour which included two shows at which they supported Led Zeppelin for the first and only time.

With the unbeatable one-two-three volley of punches that was *Black Sabbath*, *Paranoid* and *Master Of Reality*, Sabbath had entrenched themselves in the US and Europe as among the leaders of the rock pack. Their relentless darkness and grinding riffs elevated them above most other bands with whom they toured, and a whole different term to describe their music – had 'heavy metal' not been conveniently invented – would have landed on their heads sooner or later.

1971 had been a huge year for Black Sabbath. But more, and still bigger, developments were to come.

CHAPTER SIX

1972–1974

WHILE Black Sabbath were in the critical and commercial ascendant – and from 1969 until the middle of the Seventies, they knew nothing else – their rise to fame and fortune was rarely ostentatious. Once Meehan and Pine had taken over from Jim Simpson, some of the trappings of fame had begun to appear but compared to the excesses of some bands Sabbath were still enjoying fairly moderate lifestyles in 1972. For a long time, no one in the band questioned the situation, but other, wiser eyes were on them.

Extended touring had by now become the norm for Black Sabbath. In the first half of '72 they played a series of shows in the UK that took them the full length and breadth of the country: Birmingham, Oxford, Glasgow, Edinburgh, Carlisle, Liverpool, Leicester, Portsmouth, Manchester, New-castle, Wolverhampton, Bristol, Brighton, Bournemouth, London, Leeds, Sheffield and Bradford within the space of four weeks. And this was only the start of what would be a marathon of almost six months, with the next stage a return to America again. March was taken up with a vast tour through several states with various support bands including Yes, who had by now recruited venerable session keyboardist Rick Wakeman into their line-up and would soon experience significant commercial success of their own.

As the tour wound down and more recording dates for a new album loomed – this time set to be recorded in the USA – a couple of cancelled dates caused some confusion among Sabbath's expanding fanbase. The huge Mar Y Sol Pop Festival in Vega Baja with Alice Cooper, The Allman Brothers, B.B. King, Billy Joel and dozens of others had originally adver-tised an appearance by Sabbath, but the band didn't play – unsubstantiated rumour has it that the Puerto Rican authorities had got wind of songs like 'War Pigs' and 'Sweet Leaf' and vetoed the performance. In April, their second failure to enter Japan due to visa problems left that country's fanbase untapped and the band took a break instead.

By the summer, Sabbath were in the studio at Hollywood's Record

Plant. Journalist Harold Bronson, of the *UCLA Daily Bruin*, visited them on June 30, 1972 amid the aftermath of one of the first of the drug dalliances for which Sabbath would soon become notorious. "For the best coke, just ring three-eight-nine-oh-nine-eight, only one hundred dollars!" laughed Ozzy in the microphone booth, before adding "I'm so stoned." As the singer stumbled through fluffed takes and missed lines, the band watched in amusement. Of Ozzy's headphones, Geezer mocked "Look at 'im . . . He looks like he's in the Guards" – but it seemed that the relatively new father (Ozzy and Thelma had had a daughter, Jessica Starshine Osbourne, on January 20) was still capable of rational thought, explaining to Bronson that his musical education pre-Sabbath had been unremarkable: "I used to like what everybody else did: The Beatles and Rolling Stones. Geezer was into heavier things like the Mothers. We just started playing 12-bar blues about four years ago . . . I used to like anything that was heavy. The Kinks' 'You Really Got Me' did something to me, and I used to dig the early Who and Led Zeppelin. I dig anything that makes the hairs in the middle of my spine stand up. We just started writing our own stuff and our sound just evolved into what it is today – it wasn't planned."

Asked if he saw similarities between his band and the rising US band *du jour*, Grand Funk Railroad, he mused: "I suppose we are similar to Grand Funk Railroad, but I hadn't heard of them until our third tour here. Nobody knew who Grand Funk were in England. We didn't realise how big they really were until we played the Forum with them and they just packed the place – two nights! They turned the crowd on, but musically they didn't do anything for me. I'm not saying they're a bum group, because they've gotta be a good group for people to dig them. Personally, I like to hear music which is considerably different than what we play."

The new album, which, with an uncharacteristic lack of imagination, Sabbath planned to name *Volume Four*, was well underway by the summer of '72 and once again saw some slight changes in the now-trademark Sabbath sound, as Ozzy said with a reasoned approach that would, alas, waver and fade before long: "I think everybody peaks. Not only does the crowd get pissed off of hearing the band, but the band gets tired of gigging. It's not like we're jukeboxes or records that can play for ever. When you're a new band it's like you get a tinge of stardust sprinkled on you. It's born, then accepted, and after levelling off it dies. Our new album still has the Black Sabbath sound, but it's more melodic. Instead of me singing the guitar riff like on 'Iron Man', I'm singing different melodic things and it's all building up. Tony just composed a guitar piece with strings. It's a nice piece of music, and we wanted to write a happy song."

Notably, Sabbath had finally shaken off Roger Bain as producer, although his work on the three preceding albums had been never less than stellar – in fact, the sound of *Master Of Reality* is stunning to this day. But as Ozzy said, all had not been well behind the scenes: "He was someone the record company gave us when we signed with the company. It was really a clash of egos. He got it into his head that he was more responsible for our hit status than we were. He wanted, to a moderate extent, to control our music."

Once the album was in the can, Sabbath took off on another US tour, consolidating their already huge Stateside reputation in large arenas. This was the start of the band's notorious drugs and booze period – or at least, the first time that their experiences with drugs and alcohol began to be publicised – and the attendant tour stories were glossier as a result. Sabbath left a trail of mild destruction behind them from July 1972 as they passed through New Jersey, Pennsylvania (a notable show with Humble Pie, Three Dog Night, Emerson Lake & Palmer, The Faces, J. Geils Band, Badfinger and others), Illinois, Ohio, Georgia, Tennessee (where many Deep South residents reacted unfavourably to them), Virginia, New York, Rhode Island, Kentucky, Michigan, Mississippi and elsewhere until the release of *Volume 4* (actually written as *Vol 4* on the sleeve) on September 25.

More conservative fans shook their heads at the slightly glitzier inner sleeve artwork than had been the case on previous albums – and many an eyebrow was raised at the unsubtle credit for the band's favourite in-studio stimulant, "We wish to thank the great COKE-Cola company of Los Angeles", but thousands of band followers loved the idea that their heroes had embraced the rock'n'roll lifestyle to the full and they bought the LP in droves.

"Long ago I wandered through my mind," warbles Ozzy as 'Wheels Of Confusion' begins, a grinding, brooding riff-fest that isn't as doomily slow as previous work but does feature sterling work from Ward, who is at his best on this song – especially when a tempo change and a complex mid-section pushes it into overdrive. The outright grim misery of the earlier Sabbath albums is absent, with Iommi's incandescent guitar (dual leads and all) more upbeat than ever before: Ozzy hinted at this change of mood when he told Bronson before the album's release: "People call us 'downer rock'. You take the reds [tranquillisers], man, and drink the wine and blow out, get high on the decibels; all that's a lot of rubbish. Whatever people do at our concerts is none of our business as long as they enjoy it. I'm just out to entertain people – a good old showbusiness trip." The last three minutes of the song, a duelling-guitars workout not unlike the last couple of minutes of Eric Clapton's 'Layla', are sometimes referred to by another name entirely – 'The Straightener'. However, when Bill was asked about this some years later, he laughed and said: "You know what that is? That's a publishing trick . . . 'The Straightener', I have no idea where that might come from. Sometimes it comes from the original notes. Like 'Luke's Wall' [on *Black Sabbath*] for instance, I think that was on our original studio engineer notes. Sometimes, I hate to say, but the publishing companies have to come up with a certain amount of songs so they will split the hairs and it's a dupe. I hate it very much . . . There's been so much stuff that has happened with things getting ripped off or being used without permission and things like that."

'Tomorrow's Dream' is less substantial, although the guitar interplay is a thing to behold. Sabbath, proudly proclaiming that the new album had been self-produced, had nonetheless given manager Patrick Meehan a co-production credit on *Volume 4* and perhaps the manager's influence had led them to be more adventurous. This certainly seems to be the case in 'Changes', which was nothing less than a piano and strings ballad. Ozzy had said: "There'll be a lot of gentle things on the new album. One song, 'Changes', about a guy – whether he's with a band or not, I'm not gonna say – who quits with his woman, is the ultimate in the way I feel about things. It's more of a song rather than a frustration-reliever screamer. It's just a pretty, slow ballad."

Having learned something about the fine art of songwriting, Ozzy was quick to pay his respects to those who had taught him: "One thing I learned is that if you've got a good melody, you've got a good song. There are so many bands out there that try to impress other bands with their musical ability, which I respect, but The Beatles had only three chords – but they were such top-line melodies. I mean, Lennon and McCartney were just, for me, the perfect combination. They were sweet and sour. How can you fucking top The Beatles? . . . [although] Mick Jagger was a close second for me. The Beatles were extremely rebellious, but they were a band accepted by the yuppie section as well. Everybody loved The Beatles, from nine to 99. After the 'Love Me Do' period, when they went into flower power, that was their rebellious thing. You know, 'Picture yourself on a boat in a river . . .' When you hear that song it takes me on a journey. It's like a fantasy land."

Meanwhile, 'FX' was a short collection of sounds – tape and pedal effects applied to a guitar signal, hence its title. "This was before samplers and synthesisers," reminisced Geezer in a later interview with *Vintage*

Guitar magazine. "If you wanted anything different or any weird sounds you had to do it yourself from scratch. You had to sit down and work them out and make something that sounded different. Like the track 'FX'. That's Tony standing and playing his guitar in the nude! He took all his clothes off in the studio and he was hitting on his guitar strings with the crosses that he wore around his neck. That's what it was on the whole track."

The core of the album lies in the next two songs, 'Supernaut' and 'Snowblind'. The former is another classic, uptempo rock anthem based on a harmony riff and huge splashing cymbals from Ward. Lyrically, the coke-fuelled confidence that was driving the band led to lines delivered with a barked insouciance that matched up with the frenzied onstage images of Ozzy in the gatefold booklet. This song made an impact in some unexpected quarters, as Ozzy reported years later. "Frank Zappa – who was a very techno guy – invited us to a restaurant once where he was having a party. He said, 'The song "Supernaut" is my favourite track of all time.' I couldn't believe it – I thought, this guy's taking the piss; there's got to be a camera here somewhere . . . we never consciously knew what we were doing: we were just four innocent guys – very awkward and very unorthodox – who played what we were feeling, trying to make ourselves feel good."

Meanwhile, 'Snowblind' was an anthem to cocaine – whether delivered straight or ironically is a moot point. After wailing out an affectionate homage to the drug with lines like "Feeling happy in my pain / Icicles within my brain" in the optimistic-sounding intro, Ozzy descends into a darker mood as the song switches pace to a grim, bleakly arpeggiated extended section with strings and a multilayered guitar solo section of devastating scale. With images to treasure ("Lying snowblind in the sun / Will my ice age ever come?") 'Snowblind' sees Sabbath enter a new era of lyrical attainment, whether assisted by drugs or not. But then Geezer recalled of 'Snowblind', "We were all coked out of our heads in LA. We seemed to be doing more cocaine than playing music, so we wrote it about our exploits . . ."

'Cornucopia', like 'Black Sabbath' and 'War Pigs' is based on a slightly tricky time signature that Ozzy straddles with confidence. As Bill told me, this ability to spot the pocket and stay in it is something that most observers fail to associate with Ozzy: "When we do the song 'Black Sabbath', Ozzy knows where the holes are – whenever we do that song with another singer they sing it in time. And when they sing it in time, it becomes out of time because there *is* no time! They're singing it *properly*.

Ronnie James Dio, for example, sang it properly and in time, but when you sing it in time you'll throw the track out, because it has no rhyme or reason. That song is a great example of that, so with the other singers, things didn't connect." And 'Cornucopia' is one such song – with its layers of fuzz guitar (a little lighter in tone than the previous riffing, and worlds away from all-out crushing heaviness such as, say, 'Electric Funeral') almost obscuring the beat, the singer still manages to stay on top, delivering the lines with effortless panache.

'Laguna Sunrise' is a spectacular instrumental, although many fans disliked its soupy string arrangement, Iommi's slightly winsome acoustic guitar figures and the overall ambience of almost movie soundtrack-like indulgence. However, it works perfectly in context, arriving after three heavy songs and showcasing once more Iommi's many-sided writing talents.

The brief 'St. Vitus' Dance' boasts an almost folk-blues string-bend in Iommi's central riff, beneath the characteristically depressive lyrics. "When you think about the things that she did long ago," intones Ozzy, "it breaks your heart, but deep down, boy you don't want her to go" – and while the song isn't a particularly significant addition to the Sabbath canon, it achieves the desired effect (of leaving the listener slightly perplexed) as it slams abruptly to a halt. In fact, it serves as a perfect intro to 'Under The Sun', which drags into life with a weighty, down-tuned intro that is the heaviest metal that Sabbath have attempted to date. Not one but two tempo accelerations follow in the next two minutes, as well as key changes that lift the song higher – and it's an optimistic note to end on, though once again a two-minute instrumental outro – often given its own independent title, this time 'Every Day Comes And Goes' – finishes the album off.

By this stage Sabbath's recording techniques, if not much more professional, were at least more inventive. As Geezer explained, "In the old days I stood in the same room, as if it was a live gig, especially on the first two albums. We'd mic everything and literally play live in the studio as if it was a gig, because that was all we knew. We had never been in the studio before and we only had 12 hours to do the first album . . . on the third album we started experimenting and that record was made in about 10 days. It wasn't until *Volume Four* that we really took ages, and that took all of six weeks. It seemed like ages for us."

Iommi later looked back in amusement at the efforts to which the band would go to achieve the desired sonic effect on a given song: "We tried different things. We'd spend all day farting about and end up with nothing usable. We'd end up making things, making all these cabinets and coming up with all these brilliant ideas, like trying things going off the piano, into the piano and then miking up the piano strings to hear different sounds. In those days we'd make up ideas and try things. Now you just go buy a box and press a button and you've got that sound . . . Bill threw an anvil into a big barrel of water. He liked to make sounds on the mic . . . We tried violins and cellos, bagpipes – and tried to get sounds out of them, too. We tried all sorts of stuff, but it was just ideas. Sometimes it worked, sometimes it didn't, but it was fun. It used to take a long time, but at least it was original. You wouldn't hear it anywhere else."

Feel, importantly, was integral to the music rather than technical awareness, as Tony explained: "We didn't learn the music side of it – we never learned all the scales and all the stuff they say you're supposed to. We learned by sound and feel. If it sounded good, then it was right for us. We went against the grain in the early days and we always stuck to that. It was a lot of listening to each other. We didn't listen to people telling us that we couldn't do something or that we shouldn't be doing something a particular way. We developed a unique style that worked perfectly together and we played off of each other. We had to make it sound big since there were only two guitar players – a guitar and a bass – to make it sound that way. And that's the way we've always worked it."

Volume Four left a fair few people confused. It was faster, more diffuse and less easy to categorise as a 'Black Sabbath record', just as Ozzy and the others had promised. On the other hand, the musicianship was superior to anything they'd done before and the band had also successfully expanded their lyrical approach. As time has passed, it's become apparent that key *Volume Four* songs such as 'Snowblind' and 'Changes' were B-league setlist perennials in comparison to the massive, all-time great songs such as 'Paranoid' and 'Iron Man', indicating that this album wasn't as immediately gripping as its predecessors. But it's a great LP, make no mistake.

Once again Vertigo exercised a certain degree of control over the release, nixing the band's preferred LP title of *Snowblind* for fear the drug reference was too obvious. Released in September 30, 1972, the LP made number eight in the UK.

Would the band tire of the record/tour/record cycle at some point soon? Not a bit of it, they stated in an interview with Mike Saunders of *Circular* the week before *Volume Four*'s release. As Iommi pointed out with supreme nonchalance, "We play it mainly because we like it, you know. We like what we're doing – the heavy thing. We found it was exciting and really got into it and that was it. We're pretty quick at writing. I think of a riff or melody, and the others write around it usually . . . Geezer writes most of the lyrics. Some of them are very doomy, but they vary from that, to drugs and the bad things that happen sometimes with the band." Butler added: "People feel evil things, but nobody ever sings about what's frightening and evil. I mean the world is a right fucking shambles. Anyway, everybody has sung about all the good things . . . We try to relieve all the tension in the people who listen to us. To get everything out of their bodies – all the evil and everything."

As for critical reviews, Sabbath were long past caring – based on an early experience after the *Black Sabbath* album had come out. Faced with a bevy of bad reviews, the band was speechless: "It really threw us," said Iommi. "What had gone wrong? Were we really as bad as they said? One review of our first album must have been the worst rating ever, and we thought, 'Oh, Christ. This is it.' We were worried that everyone else would think the same."

As if to echo this sequence of events, *Volume Four* went gold in the USA within eight weeks of release. A planned UK tour in November was cancelled due to mass illness: Iommi had flu, Ward cited "total physical and mental exhaustion", and Ozzy was laid low by laryngitis. The singer explained, "I was very ill when we returned from the States. I had a septic throat and a temperature of 105 degrees. I was out of action for a month."

Later on Iommi would look back on those early tours with some resentment. The new science of tour management was still in its infancy – at least on this vast scale – and inevitably, logistical errors occurred. "The reason we haven't been happy about some of our American tours," he said, "was because our organisation hadn't set things up properly. The planning that was needed just wasn't there, and it was all one mad rush so that we drove ourselves to a standstill. Promoters were left in the dark – we were left in the dark. Often we'd have no time to rehearse and it became like trial and error going on the road, at times."

After a Christmas break, Sabbath hit the road for dates in Australia and New Zealand with Fairport Convention and – unusually, with hindsight – local art rock band Split Enz, whose core duo of Neil and Tim Finn later became Crowded House. They spent February and March on an extended European and UK tour.

By July, Sabbath had rehearsed up yet another new set of songs and were recording them in Wales, after an abortive session in the States that had yielded few workable results. The year had been tough on the band-members, with cracks beginning to appear in the Meehan–Pine–Sabbath relationship. Add to this the pressure of touring – which had been near-incessant since 1970 – and the band's relatively new-found interest in drugs, and the tension was mounting. Geezer lamented, "We had been in America trying to write *Sabbath Bloody Sabbath*, but nothing was working at the time. We felt like we were on the verge of breaking up, so we came back to England. After a couple of months we went back to our regular rehearsal place and I think Free were recording there. We had to find an alternative place. They recommended this castle."

Sabbath set up their equipment in Clearwell Castle, an ancient but well-maintained country manor in the Forest Of Dean in Gloucestershire. "We had to rehearse in the dungeon of all places," laughed Geezer, before recalling that the band were visited at one point by an unexpected resident: "We were in the dungeon playing away, and all of a sudden we saw this person walk past the door [with] a big black cloak on. We thought, 'What the hell is going on around here?' Tony and one of the roadies ran after him. They saw him go into this other door at the end of the corridor. They ran after him and they were shouting at him, because they thought he was some lunatic that got into the castle. They went into the room where he had gone into and there was nobody in there; he totally disappeared. We asked the owner of the castle about it and he told us, 'Oh, that's just a ghost.' Apparently, he was the regular castle ghost . . . We all saw it. Tony went after him. You couldn't miss him wearing that big black cloak."

But such occurrences seemed to do the trick. Asked many years later what the high point of his songwriting career was, Geezer replied: "The song 'Sabbath, Bloody Sabbath' itself. It was a whole new era for us. We felt really open on that album. It was a great atmosphere, good time, great coke! Just like a new birth for me. We had done the first four albums and done it that way. *Sabbath Bloody Sabbath* was like Part Two of your life. It was a weird feeling; a good feeling . . . Right before that we were in a terrible slump. We were all exhausted from touring. We weren't getting on very well. Then Tony came up with the riff for 'Sabbath, Bloody Sabbath' and everybody sparked to life. The year while we were doing that was a really good year personally. I'll always remember that album and look back on it with a good feeling."

Iommi agreed, adding: "Some great tracks on that album. It was a great feeling from rehearsals to writing to recording. It was just a great time."

After recording wrapped, Sabbath performed on August 2 at the Alexandria Palace Festival in London alongside Groundhogs, Stray, Uriah Heep, Manfred Mann's Earth Band and The Sensational Alex Harvey

Band as well as putting in a string of dates in Newcastle, Bristol, Birmingham and Leicester. Before the release of the album – *Sabbath Bloody Sabbath*, featuring ambitious artwork and a mysterious 'Direction: Patrick Meehan' credit on the sleeve – in November, the band took some time out to recuperate and get to grips with the unravelling managerial situation, which would come to a head after the New Year.

As all this soul-destroying backstage activity was playing itself out, *Sabbath Bloody Sabbath* was released on December 8, 1973, reaching number eight in the UK. The opener, 'Sabbath Bloody Sabbath', kicked off with a classic walking riff from Iommi, showcasing a lighter sound than earlier but none the worse off for it: in fact, it's a sign of the early versatility of the album that the song devolves after a minute into a mellow, clean section with unexpectedly tender vocals ("Nobody will ever let you know / When you ask the reason why . . ."). Listen carefully for the bridge after this quieter section and you'll hear some decidedly mainstream rock riffs – the band entering radio territory at last?

Ozzy, singing in a higher register than usual, continues on 'A National Acrobat', based on a duelling-guitar riff and double-tracked vocals. A rarely cited song in the Sabbath catalogue, 'Acrobat' is loaded with echo and stop-start riffage that slows it down rather than pushing it forward, and – especially placed just after the title track – doesn't stand up strongly. 'Fluff', however, is another superb acoustic instrumental along the lines of 'Laguna Sunrise', although – like that previous song – it might have been too sensitive for many listeners. Like it or not, it must be noted that Iommi's adventurousness was increasing exponentially – he plays piano and harpsichord on the track as well as acoustic and steel guitars.

The next track is 'Sabbra Cadabra', a slab of rock that eschews most of the heavy metal weight of the day and is based on simple "Lovely lady make love all night long" lyrics improvised from the fact that the studio had another, less romantic function. As Geezer remembered, "I think that was about a girlfriend I was dating at the time. We were just all in the studio and it just came to me . . . Ozzy had made up this whole pornography thing, 'cause we'd been listening to . . . the studio where we were recording it did the voice-overs for German pornography videos, and we were listening to all these voice-overs done in English to these German porno videos, so Ozzy was singing, like, the same thing that the voice-over people were saying. So I changed it to be about the girlfriend I was with at the time."

'Sabbra Cadabra' is a throwback to the melodic, bluesy rock'n'roll approach that had typified so much rock before Sabbath introduced their unique metallic approach into the brew – but that's not to say it doesn't work: it's an all-time Sabbath classic. It slows down at two minutes into the song, later adding some honky-tonk piano over the top and introducing some background organ sounds into the mix.

Would Iommi have intentionally plagiarised the classic riff from Free's 1970s hit 'All Right Now' for the intro of 'Killing Yourself To Live'? Of course not . . . and so the song ploughs into a classic tale of paranoia, the kind that only Ozzy can deliver – lines of "You think that I'm crazy and baby I know it's true" and all. Among the most uptempo songs that Sabbath had delivered to date, it speaks volumes for the band's forward progress and once again, their knack for a spiralling, deftly executed riff.

Fans pricked up their ears in 'Who Are You', which featured an electronic miasma of synthesised noise courtesy of Yes keyboardist and all-round session guru Rick Wakeman, who would eventually become a close friend of the band, as Iommi recalled: "He was great, really great. He was wild back then. We took Yes on tour with us, and brought them to America on their first tour. But Rick used to travel with us, and not Yes for some reason." The song also features expertly sung and layered close harmony vocals from Ozzy, belying the arranging skills of the band, and their self-production skills. Wakeman's piano, space-age synthesiser sounds and ambient washes lend the song an epic (if now essentially dated) atmosphere – it was a shock for followers of the band at the time, but one that promised much change ahead.

If 'Sabbath Bloody Sabbath' and 'Sabbra Cadabra' had been a step towards radio-friendliness, then 'Looking For Today' was a step further still – a funky, descending chorus and picked guitar sound gave the song a catchy air that guaranteed its memorable status. Of course, Ozzy and Geezer were still contributing fairly grim lyrics and vocals to the mix – "Everyone just gets on top of you / The pain begins to eat your pride" and so on – but with Ozzy's expert delivery of the title line, the song could only be a breath of light relief in comparison to, say, 'War Pigs'.

'Spiral Architect' is a tense, grandiose ending to the LP, featuring an ambitious, spiralling string accompaniment – credited to the Phantom Fiddlers – and triple-tracked vocals that keep Ozzy's contribution weighty when juxtaposed against the huge instrumentation that includes some bag-pipes from Tony. There's even the sound of an audience applauding at the song's end, perhaps to underscore the final, unusually optimistic lyrics of "I look upon my earth and feel the warmth and know that it is good".

Multilayered and confident though it was, *Sabbath Bloody Sabbath* was and remains an enigma. Thousands of fans regard it as the high point of the

Ozzy-era Sabbath, but others see it as a confused blend of semi-commercial tunes and a diluted take on the heaviness of old. The truth is somewhere in between, but when taking the whole of the enormous Sabbath story into perspective, it's obvious that the record came at a juncture in which creative and business pressures were reaching seismic proportions.

When the LP was released in the USA in January 1974, it hit number 11 aided by the detailed artwork depicting a dying deity surrounded by angels (or demons, it's not clear which) – perhaps a suitable metaphor for the struggles that Sabbath were enduring in their fight against Patrick Meehan, which had now ended in a severance of the relationship and the start of a long and protracted court battle.

Although Meehan has proved elusive – I would have welcomed his input into this book – it's apparent that he left few friends in the Sabbath camp on the parting of the ways. In his absence, few conclusions can be drawn about the nature of his financial dealings with the band, but all the parties involved point to how completely broke they were afterwards.

Andrew Loog Oldham, former manager and producer of the Rolling Stones, commented on Meehan's business practices in an interview with Dotmusic in June 2001. Talking about the collapse of his record label, Immediate, he said: "From '70 to '75 I was paying off Immediate's debt to EMI, then the liquidator of Immediate Records sold my tapes to Patrick Meehan, an individual whose ethics and integrity could be considered highly suspect and whose business practices have been looked at by the Fraud Squad, and who never paid a cent in royalties from '75 to '96 to anybody. He sold the tapes he'd bought to Castle, who collaborated on this short-changing of artists until they made some payments in 1996. Castle is now owned by Sanctuary, who, it is rumoured, paid The Small Faces . . . £265,000 for past royalties in '95 or '96.

"This they did because Kenny Jones had the muscle to go to court. Ninety-five per cent of Immediate artists and 100 per cent of its producers don't have that wherewithal, are not so fortunate and therefore have never received a post-1970 cent, due to a bizarre, but nevertheless strange arrangement, between Patrick Meehan and the lawyers currently representing Sanctuary, who should know better, but who continue to profit on 95 per cent of these recordings without paying royalties."

As Tony Iommi told Malcolm Dome in *Kerrang!* magazine as late as 1988, "The situation with Patrick was unworkable. We could never find him when bills had to be paid and apart from one girl in the office, there was no one we could talk to about anything. It was a nightmare and eventually I was left with no option but to walk away and try to pick up the pieces. All I wanna do is be left alone to get on with playing music. I just wish all these problems would go away."

Asked by *Metal Sludge* what he'd do differently if he had his time again, Geezer answered: "Consult a lawyer, and an accountant. 'Cause we forged . . . when we made our first album, and we went with our first manager, we were only like 18, 19 years old, and we didn't know anything about the business side of things, and our parents refused – they had to sign a contract for us, we didn't know we had to see a lawyer, and our parents refused to sign the contracts for us. And, so, we all forged our parents' signatures on it. About the worst thing we ever did, 'cause we couldn't prove it in court after."

I asked Geezer in detail about the split with Meehan, and he told me: "It was horrible. We had to pay him off, the way he had us tied up in his contracts, we had to pay him to get away from him. We didn't have lawyers or anything when we signed the contracts, because we didn't know."

This naivety would be almost unthinkable nowadays, I told him, but he explained: "We were clueless about business, we just wanted to play music. When we started out we didn't ever think of making and selling albums anyway. It was just like a hobby to us, anything to avoid the nine to five jobs. We didn't ever once think that it would turn into anything money-making."

Asked when the situation with Meehan became intolerable, Geezer explained: "We started around *Sabbath Bloody Sabbath*, that was when we started the proceedings, but it took ages in the courts. That was why we called the next album *Sabotage*. I think he took all our money and bought a hotel chain. We were potless, absolutely broke. If the band had finished there, we would have been totally destitute, but thankfully we went on and made a few quid back on tour. I think we were totally away from him by the end of the *Sabotage* album."

By January 1974 new management had been secured in the intimidating form of Don Arden, who was connected to both previous management teams – as he had been Meehan and Pine's former employer and later became firm friends with Jim Simpson. Early dealings were notable for an encounter by Ozzy with Arden's then 18-year-old daughter Sharon, who worked as a receptionist in his office (Don's son David was also part of the Arden team at that point). Reportedly, Sharon was scared speechless by Ozzy, who entered the room with the tap around his neck that he customarily wore and sat on the floor, declining a chair. From these inauspicious beginnings a friendship would slowly flourish.

Meehan and Arden were never reconciled, thanks to an explosive confrontation that took place at the Midem festival in Cannes in 1975. Arden, who explained in his 1999 autobiography *Mr Big* that in recent months he had warned Meehan about comments he had made about Sharon (the two had had a brief affair in the early Seventies), wrote: "We were in the casino when we spotted Patrick at one of the tables. Sharon got the hump of course and starting winding me up about it. In the end, just to shut her up as much as anything, I went over there and went off at Patrick again. Then this Italian guy he had with him – who I later found out had just done 14 years for murder – did a flying headbutt at me and knocked me sideways! So I went crazy, my guys jumped in, Sharon jumped in, and the whole thing became like a saloon brawl in a cowboy movie: bottles smashing, chairs flying through the air, the lot." Arden drew a line under the Meehan problem by asking Mafia godfather Joe Pagano to issue him with a warning that one more offence would be his last.

And so the third managerial relationship in Sabbath's career began its course. Meehan vanished into relative obscurity, popping up from time to time as the legal battle progressed, as did Wilf Pine. The latter did score the notable achievement of being – according to writer John Pearson's book, *The Englishman And The Mafia* – one of the few non-Americans to be welcomed into the family fold by the Mafia, and specifically one of the leading godfathers, Joe Pagano.

Don Arden had led a colourful life, and had built a considerable business out of artist management by 1974, when he was 48. Born in Manchester, the young Arden dabbled in show business as an artist in his own right, performing as a singer and comic at the age of 13. As a Yiddish-speaking Jew, he was able to impress Jewish audiences both before and after the war as an entertainer on the variety club scene and sang the popular songs of the day in a fine, untrained tenor. In 1954 he set up an agency, recruiting Gene Vincent six years later, and importing US artists such as Bo Diddley and Chuck Berry for British tours.

Contemporary relevancy post-rock'n'roll came when Arden signed The Small Faces in 1965. He said of the young band, "At that time, on the first hearing, I thought it was the best band in the world." Drummer Kenney Jones said of Arden: "He was kind of a Jewish teddy bear, I suppose. You liked him immediately because he was enthusiastic and he talked about what he could do and what he couldn't do, and whenever he said, 'I'll do this, I'll do that,' he did and it came true."

But an iron hand lurked beneath the teddy-bear exterior and, when another manager, Robert Stigwood, met with The Small Faces in 1966 to discuss a change in management, Arden dealt with him summarily. As legend has it, Arden and a team of "associates" arrived at Stigwood's offices and convinced him that moving in on Arden's band was inappropriate by dangling him from an upstairs window.

However, the band's contract was sold the following year to Andrew Loog Oldham, formerly the manager of the Rolling Stones, payment being made in cash in a brown paper bag, so runs the story. Although The Small Faces were never sure how completely the accounts had been settled, Kenney Jones reminisced later: "I've got good and bad memories, but mainly I think of Don with affection, surprisingly enough . . . without Don, The Small Faces may not have existed, without his sort of vision at that time, be it short-lived or what. The fact is we became known and we got a break through Don. So if you think of it like that, and I think all of us are prepared to swallow what went on, leave it, fine, it's history. We all learned from each other, he gave us our first break, fine, fair enough, you know, leave it."

Arden signed The Move following the departure of original manager Tony Secunda and experienced enjoyed success when Move guitarist Jeff Lynne's later band Electric Light Orchestra and singer Roy Wood's Wizzard landed a sequence of major hits in the Seventies. Once again, it was a mixed blessing for the acts involved. Move drummer Bev Bevan (later heavily involved with Sabbath) said of Arden, "Don has probably got too much ambition for his own good . . . He doesn't just want to make a band successful or make a band or a singer to get a hit record, he wants them to be number one, you know, he wants them to fill football stadiums. He wants everything to be really huge."

As Arden laboured on Black Sabbath's behalf, the band travelled widely in support of *Sabbath Bloody Sabbath*, performing in Sweden, Denmark, Holland, Germany and Switzerland before a vast US tour in February. A Long Island show saw them perform over Bedlam, the band in which a young and supremely talented drummer named Cozy Powell played, before what was undoubtedly the most ambitious live gig of their career to date – the California Jam on April 6, 1974 at Ontario Raceway in California.

This mammoth event has been well documented, largely because it was among the first mega-events of its time, Woodstock in 1969 notwithstanding. The hard rock and nascent heavy metal movements were well underway by '74 and demand for the music, especially in the USA, was such that massive shows such as this could be economically viable. With the expansion in the PA and amplification industries, the events became physically feasible as well.

Headliners Emerson Lake & Palmer, plus Sabbath and Deep Purple, were asked to play (after the largest bands of the day, the Rolling Stones, Led Zeppelin and The Band, had asked for astronomical fees that were unacceptable) over a bill including Earth, Wind & Fire, Rare Earth, Black Oak Arkansas, Seals & Crofts and The Eagles. A staggering 200,000 people arrived, each paying $10 for a ticket, at a venue which had been chosen for its accessibility to LA, San Diego and Orange County and which boasted parking for 50,000 cars. The brainchild of rock manager Lenny Stogel, who secured finance from the giant ABC TV network in exchange for filming rights, the festival was among the first to benefit from large-scale professional events-organisation specialists and went without a hitch, perhaps because Stogel knew that audience unrest had to be avoided at all costs. "When I knew I was putting on a show for 200,000 young people," he said, "I didn't want anything popping off unexpected. I wanted to be in total control and know exactly what was happening that moment and what would be happening in the next few hours. Two hundred thousand kids was a big responsibility. I used to get a funny feeling in my stomach whenever I thought about it. I had to be in control – for the preservation of my sanity."

The first Cal Jam – a second event, Cal Jam II, took place in 1978 but was voted unimpressive by most attendees – set new standards in rock-star excess. This was the gig at which one band insisted that the plates of M&Ms they required backstage contained no yellow sweets – meaning that an employee had to sift through them beforehand – and at which artists were flown in by private helicopter from the Beverly Hills Hotel. But none of this really applied when the music began: the sets, including that of Black Sabbath, ran smoothly – with the exception of Deep Purple, whose guitarist Ritchie Blackmore exploded in anger at a persistent cameraman and smashed his guitar into the offending machinery, causing several thousand dollars of damage. Purple – then in their Mark III line-up with David Coverdale and Glenn Hughes – were also rocked by a pyrotechnic explosion of unexpected violence that knocked the latter off his feet, although no injuries were caused.

The age of corporate rock had begun, and Black Sabbath were at its forefront. Before ascending to the heights occupied by its vanguard, the band had to adapt to the demands of the mainstream fanbase – which meant gradually altering their lyrical stance.

And so, without further ado, a word from our sponsor – Old Nick himself.

CHAPTER SEVEN

1974

THE devil does indeed have all the best tunes.
However, not all of those came from Aston, Birmingham, where the youthful Black Sabbath grew up in conventional Christian homes and, the grinding poverty they suffered aside, lived what would be regarded as normal lives. Why, then, did the band excite such religious fervour in the Seventies?

"You've got to remember the time," said Ozzy with resigned despair, much later on. "It was the end of the Sixties, it was all 'If you're going to San Francisco, be sure to wear a flower in your hair.' What a load of old fucking happy, hippy crap that is. Here's us living 99 million miles away in Aston, Birmingham, industrial city, and the world wasn't happy. We used to rehearse across the road from a movie theatre and Tony Iommi said to us, 'Isn't it weird how people like to go to the movies and get scared? Why don't we start making music that scares people?' And he came up with the heaviest fucking riffs of all time. That first album was just experimental. The most we would do was smoke dope and drink booze – I was always drunk; the whole working-class environment ran around the pub and a packet of No. 6."

It's easy to downplay the satanic element of Sabbath's songs nowadays, after two decades in which the social pendulum has swung into a state of nonchalant permissiveness and nobody gives a damn about blasphemy any more – but at the time, in 1970 and '71 and '72, singing about Satan made you few friends over the age of about 35. Geezer Butler, the culprit behind most of Sabbath's most memorable devilisms ("Begging mercy for their sins / Satan laughing spreads his wings") has spent a portion of every one of the thousands of interviews he has conducted since those early days protesting his innocence. "I was brought up an incredibly strict Catholic, and believed in hell and the devil," he said once. "But though I'd been taught about God and Jesus, no one ever went into what the devil was all about, so when I was 16 or 17, I went about trying to find out. And because I wrote most of Black Sabbath's lyrics, some of that ended up in the songs . . . but it was never advocating satanism. It was warning against evil."

This spin on essentially admitting that the songs were about Satan – that is, that the songs mentioned but did not *support* devil-worshipping, or any of the other associated demonic stuff that gave so many middle English and middle American listeners the vapours – is arguable. Kerry King of Slayer has done the same thing on many occasions, arguing successfully (and rightly, as it happens) that his band's infamous song 'Angel Of Death', about Nazi camp doctor Josef Mengele, merely listed rather than commented upon its subject's crimes.

Even more convincing is Geezer's argument that the devilish themes were a mere vehicle or metaphor for his real target, the establishment: "We hid our real message in the satanic lyrics. The message was very often about the war and the madness of it. We didn't want to be too easy, and no one really bothered to concentrate on our lyrics . . . At one point I was interested in magic, but we were never really correctly understood. If you think about the title 'Children Of The Grave', you may think that it's a really sick song, but it's clearly an anti-war song! . . . The evil in us is in our music . . . if you're playing heavy music, it really has to be heavy."

He added: "Any lyrics that I or Ozzy wrote were actually warnings against satanism, telling people that if you are going to dabble in that, just be careful . . . I had a very strict Catholic upbringing, so I read a lot about Satan. But we never, ever promoted satanism or black magic, we only used it as a reference, and it wasn't our only topic. We wrote a lot of science fiction lyrics, anti-Vietnam war songs, the occult was only dealt with in three or four songs. But people completely misinterpreted them, the way they always do . . . Sabbath even did a blatantly pro-God, Christian hymn type of song, 'After Forever', and people still took it the wrong way. They thought we were taking the piss out of it! . . . Even at the beginning, when everyone was calling us devil worshippers, I didn't think we had a satanic image. It was a dark name, Black Sabbath, but the songs were *never* promoting satanism."

Ozzy, who co-wrote some songs and – as frontman – was responsible for delivering them to the public, was equally vehement on the subject. "Black Sabbath wasn't all black, it wasn't all black magic," he said. "There were a lot of environmental issues that we were talking about years ago. Geezer wrote some pretty interesting stuff, lyrically. We were always trying to do something different. We didn't want to do the 'boy meets girl' stuff. I think we may have done one kind of love song the whole time we were together. We sang about all kinds of things – fiction, political, environmental, occult, every which way you can imagine."

Any interest in the subject of Satan and his associates was strictly limited to entertainment, he stressed – although even then his threshold was fairly conservative: "I must have watched *The Exorcist* eight billion times. When that first came out in the Seventies I can remember going to the movie theatre in Philadelphia with Black Sabbath. And Black Sabbath is, of course, this satanic band of rock'n'roll – and yet we were that scared that we all spent the night in the same room. Up until that point it had been strings and fishing lines when the bat flies out, but that one was so real."

Unfortunately for their protests – but not so for the metal scene – a whole new movement, black metal, evolved in the Eighties. By 1985 three bands, Venom, Bathory and Mercyful Fate, had established a speedy, raw brand of metal and were wailing about Satan – in hindsight, with about as much credibility as an amateur dramatics group – but powerfully by the standards of the time. Venom singer Conrad 'Cronos' Lant told me, "I was a big fan of Black Sabbath – but I always thought they fell a little bit short of going where they should have gone. With perspective, of course, Sabbath went exactly where they should have done, because Ozzy has that comical side to him. He couldn't possibly have stood there and said, 'I'm the fuckin' Prince of Darkness' – because people would have laughed and said, 'Fuck off, you drunk.' It was just that Sabbath were Hammer Horror, and I wanted to be *The Evil Dead* or *Hellraiser*. Sabbath sang lines like 'Oh, the demon's coming', whereas I said 'Fuck that', and sang 'I'm the demon and I'm coming to get you, Ozzy.' Everyone wants to go and see Dracula, but no one wants to *be* Dracula, so I said, 'I'll be Dracula.' "

In the late Eighties the black metal scene had faded from view, replaced by the burgeoning death metal movement from Florida, New York and Sweden. Bands such as Mayhem, Burzum, Immortal, Dimmu Borgir, Dark Funeral, Cradle Of Filth and Gorgoroth established a much more credible and competent template than the pioneers of the previous decade, and the genre is now among Scandinavia's biggest exports.

If proof were required of the enormous power to attract fans which diabolical subject matter possesses, much of this new-found popularity can be attributed to the spate of homicides, church-burnings and grave desecrations that took place in the early to mid-Nineties in Norway. Metal fans were enthralled by the media sensation that accompanied such overblown events, and a commercial future for the movement beckoned, leading older-generation musicians to comment in horror on the turn of events. As Geezer – perhaps in retrospect the man most responsible for the rise of black metal – argued, "I think it's sad that those bands in Norway are trying to get publicity by burning down churches. Music shouldn't ever preach hatred or intolerance, there's already enough of that in the world . . . Some of these new bands are so fake it's unbelievable, they don't even know what they're singing about half the time."

Although he admits he's no expert, he should know what real-life satanism is about, having been obliged to deal with a few of its adherents as the years have passed. In 1970, for example, Sabbath were asked by a group of satanists to play at an event at Stonehenge called 'The Night Of Satan'. The band declined the offer, but were perturbed to say the least when they heard that the head witch, Alec Sanders, was planning to lay a curse on them. It was this, runs the legend, that inspired the four musicians to wear their crucifixes – made up by Ozzy's toolmaker father at Ozzy's request.

Things went from weird to crazy and beyond. A Memphis dressing-room was discovered painted with bloody crosses. Later that same day, a deranged, obviously Satan-worshipping individual ran onstage holding a sacrificial knife. A bevy of witches gathered outside Sabbath's hotel, leading Geezer – so it is said – to threaten to cast a fake spell on them. Death threats came the band's way and during one show the lights failed: Ozzy stood paralysed with fear.

Such was the lot allocated to any band who dared to sing about the devil and play gigs in the Deep South of the US, or indeed the Deep South of the UK, before about 1977, when the spitting, swastika-emblazoned spectre of punk was born and it all started to look rather old hat. But the lineage of black metal was assured, with the bands causing offence to this day. One such is Suffolk's own Cradle Of Filth, who caused enormous protest with T-shirts that carried the slogan 'Jesus Is A Cunt' in large letters on the back. After a few of those wearing it were arrested for public blasphemy or equivalent offences, the band halted manufacture, realising that a line had been crossed. As Paul Allender, Cradle guitarist, told me: "The number of people that got arrested for wearing that shirt was ridiculous. I find it amusing the way that people get so offended so easily. People said, oh, blasphemy! But if you want to be in a successful band, the image has to suit the music" – a sentiment that Geezer had echoed himself on many occasions.

Then again, satanism and Satan are not synonyms, a fact that eludes many and which makes the mention of the old red fellow less threatening when taken on board. The Church Of Satan was founded by Anton Lavey in California and might seem sinister to some – but compared to other, more dedicated philosophies is positively pedestrian. For starters, Lavey didn't believe in Satan, using him merely as a symbol for the satanic lifestyle. In contrast, take a look at the intimidating world-view of Swedish black metal band Dissection, for instance, whose frontman Jon Nodtveidt served seven years in prison for his part in the murder of a fellow Swede in 1997. He passed the time in clink by forming a clique, the Misanthropic Luciferian Organisation, and emerged in 2004 to tell me: "I am definitely a satanist. I base my views on Gnosticism – the perception of the cosmos as a physical, universal prison for the spirit that we must strive to break free from. I identify Satan as a chaotic power, a spiritual formless power that burns inside us all, and as an external power too, counteracting the physical universe. I think satanism is about breaking the chains of the ego, which can be your biggest enemy. For me, music is a way to express myself in a very abstract way. Perhaps this goes for all kinds of creativity. It's a way of expressing something without using words."

Meanwhile, the infamous Norwegian black metal band Gorgoroth have a singer called Gaahl, who was fined 190,000 kronor and sentenced to 14 months in prison in 2004 for beating someone up and threatening to drink his blood. Their guitarist, Roger 'Infernus' Tiegs, was then given a prison sentence for aggravated sexual assault, but while appealing told me: "I think for black metal to be successful it has to have a satanic ethic. We can make a living out of it because we have a satanic fundament for the music. We see ourselves as missionaries . . . to convert as many people as possible to satanism. You can do this through music in a way that you cannot do through Roman Catholic rituals . . . I will define satanism as we see it. I see it as a Gnostic religion. We are removing ourselves from the Church Of Satan and Anton Lavey's humanistic approach. We are in a cosmic war, as we see it, and we are not blabbering on about humanistic things. Basically, Lavey has a far too humane approach. The human element is a part of it, but not the whole thing by any means."

Much more humane is the original stage satanist King Diamond (real name Kim Bendix Petersen), the Danish singer who fronted Mercyful Fate and who has made a living out of looking evil while clutching a cross made of fake human femurs. As he reasons, "People say, are you a satanist? And I say, well, first of all I need to hear *your* definition of a satanist before I can say yes or no. I can relate to the philosophies that Anton LaVey wrote about. When I read his books for the first time, I thought, this is the way I live my life. These are the values I have . . . but at the same time, there's a big void in there – he doesn't say to anyone, listen here, this is the right god and this is the wrong god. There's *nothing* about gods in there. It simply tells you to pick and choose whatever makes you happy, because no one can prove anything anyway. So if people say I'm a satanist if I

BLACK SABBATH IN LONDON IN 1970, LEFT TO RIGHT: TONY IOMMI, OZZY OSBOURNE,
GEEZER BUTLER AND BILL WARD. *(Chris Walter/Photofeatures)*

OZZY IN REGENT SOUND STUDIO, DENMARK STREET, LONDON, 1970,
RECORDING THE *Paranoid* ALBUM. *(Chris Walter/Photofeatures)*

GEEZER AT REGENT SOUND. NOTE HIS NECK-PICKUP FINGERSTYLE TECHNIQUE – A KEY FEATURE OF HIS SIGNATURE BASS SOUND. *(Chris Walter/Photofeatures)*

BILL WARD AT REGENT SOUND, INTRODUCING JAZZ INFLUENCES INTO SABBATH'S CRUSHING SOUND. *(Chris Walter/Photofeatures)*

TONY IOMMI AT REGENT SOUND, TRADEMARK GIBSON SG WELL IN HAND. *(Chris Walter/Photofeatures)*

OZZY AND TONY ON STAGE AT THE STAR-CLUB IN HAMBURG, JUNE 1969. *(K&K/Redferns)*

A POSTER FOR THE MOVIE *Black Sabbath*, WHOSE TITLE INSPIRED EARTH TO CHANGE THEIR NAME TO SOMETHING MORE OMINOUS... *(Rex Features)*

THE YOUTHFUL OZZY AT THE STAR-CLUB.
(K&K/Redferns)

OZZY IN 1973. SOME BANDS USED SILVER SPOONS BUT OZZY MADE DO WITH A PLASTIC ONE.
(Chris Walter/Photofeatures)

TONY WITH A SELECTION OF HIS GUITARS, AT HIS HOME IN LEICESTERSHIRE, 1974. *(Neil Medhurst)*

SABBATH IN COPENHAGEN IN JANUARY 1974. UNUSUALLY, TONY SHAVED OFF HIS MOUSTACHE
AROUND THIS PERIOD, ONLY TO GROW – AND RETAIN – IT AGAIN. *(Jorgen Angel/Redferns)*

SABBATH LIVE IN COPENHAGEN, OCTOBER 1975. THE LESS SAID ABOUT OZZY'S
REVEALING STRIDES THE BETTER. *(Jorgen Angel/Redferns)*

GEEZER AND OZZY LEAVE THE STAGE AFTER A DATE ON THEIR 1978 US TOUR. *(Andrew Kent/Retna)*

BILL, GEEZER, OZZY AND TONY CELEBRATE 10 YEARS TOGETHER, IN NEW YORK, 1979. *(Richie Aaron/Redferns)*

believe in the life philosophy in that book, then sure. But if they're saying, do you believe that baby blood will give you extra energy, and you can conjure demons with it? Then no, I don't believe in that."

He's actually rather tolerant: "I don't have any proof, and no one has any proof, that there is this god or that god. Whatever gets people through the day is great. But religion is everywhere – look at current world events. It's because we don't respect each other. Everyone else's world is as big as yours and mine. Everyone has a different life which creates their values and their views. When I die I hope I'm going to feel the inner persons of the people I loved on this earth. I'll recognise the essence of that being, and I'm totally convinced that that will happen. But I'll never tell people that a certain fact is true, or that there is a certain God."

Now, compare Ozzy, Geezer and their band of merry men with the thoroughly decent King Diamond. There's much in common there. But they look like amateurs in comparison when it comes to proper, scary, goat-sacrificing satanism – and when compared with the actual documented homicide, violence and expertly reasoned philosophy of Gorgoroth and Dissection, there's literally nothing in common. Suddenly Sabbath don't seem so naughty, do they?

But as the decades passed, there was hardly an interview in which Sabbath didn't get asked about devil-worshipping. Even as early as late 1970, Ozzy could see the questions coming a mile off, telling writer Steve Turner, "You're going to ask about black magic. It's rubbish. Geezer wrote a song called 'Black Sabbath' and at the time we were called Earth but were constantly being confused with another group with a similar name and so we changed to Black Sabbath."

Geezer added: "We were trying to get away from traditional boy–girl lyrics. I began to explore the supernatural as a source of subject matter. When I write I want it to be an interesting experience for me as well as, eventually, an interesting experience for those who listen."

Christian magazine *Cornerstone* once asked Ozzy directly about his religious beliefs, and he was unexpectedly willing to be honest. The results were fascinating, as he held his ground stubbornly in the face of the rather gimlet-eyed interlocutors. Asked if the satanic lyrics were for real or all an act, he replied: "It's only a role that I play. I mean, I wouldn't know how to conjure up a Christmas cracker! Anybody who thinks Ozzy Osbourne is into Satan and all that doesn't know what they're talking about . . . I might have mentioned the word 'devil', which I suppose Frank Sinatra has in his day, but they don't picket him saying they don't want him in their town. I write the way I think. It's up to your ears to interpret it the way you want. If you choose to think I'm the Antichrist, that's your problem. I'm not. I'm just Ozzy, and there's only one Ozzy."

Asked about the existence of God, he said: "There are many ways of looking at that. It's like God is within you. God is a nice feeling. He's the flowers and smells and the nice things in life . . . Jesus Christ was the original rock'n'roll star. He gave people reasons to live in the rut they were living in. He was the first man to say, 'You don't have to have human sacrifices, 'cause human sacrifices hurt somebody, you know?' Just believe in the spirit that is within you . . . I'm a Christian person. I mean, do you have to go to church to be a Christian? Do you have to walk around giving out leaflets to people to be a Christian? A Christian man is a man who is within himself, who puts out good vibes. I open the door for old ladies, I help old ladies across the road. I do a show for leukaemia every year, but I don't broadcast that because it's against my image."

Despite all the protestations, Ozzy hinted at a supernatural belief: "When Black Sabbath first got together, we started to read all of these Dennis Wheatley books, and in those books I've seen the most evil forces I've ever heard of. I'd never heard of astral projection until I read those books. It really intrigued me that people can think that deep, you know. I believe that you really can do that if you want to . . . I think if a man can create something like an atom bomb, he can surely create something with his own mind."

Tony Iommi has also mentioned other-worldly experiences, saying: "I know the wavelength Geezer is on – in fact the whole group communicates on a very close level. Like, we have what you could almost call a third eye. We can sense with each other what is going to happen. We've had actual experiences. One I remember – Geezer was asleep and he must have astral travelled. I was stuck in the lift. He dreamt this and when I woke him up he said, 'I'm glad it's you 'cause I just dreamt you were stuck in the lift.' These are quite regular occurrences. They used to frighten me at first till I got used to it."

Perhaps all this satanic expression is just art, as Ozzy mused: "I'm not knocking religion. I don't believe in bad things. I'm not a Satanist. It's just a theatrical role I play. If you want to go on about satanism and suicide, you've got to go right across the board and pick on Shakespeare, too. *Romeo And Juliet* was all about suicide. It didn't start with rock'n'roll. Why do they pick on us? You go into an art gallery and there's pictures of Satan, pictures of nude women . . . In my opinion, we've got just as much right to be artists as a guy who paints on a piece of canvas or writes a poem or a play or movie script."

But in the end it's all only rock'n'roll, as Ozzy explained: "I'm out doing my deal, I'm turning people on. What's wrong with taking people away from their everyday mundane situation and having a good, fun night for an hour and a half at a rock'n'roll scene? That's what it's about. Fun. It's no big deal. I'm not trying to twist people's heads around. I'm not trying to say, 'Believe in me' . . . I'd rather see 20,000 smiling faces than 20,000 crying people. My philosophy is if you're happy being a born-again Christian, if you're happy being a Roman Catholic, if you're happy being a Jew or Muslim . . . great! I'm happy being Ozzy, you know."

The years passed, Sabbath ebbed and flowed and Ozzy jumped off and on the rock'n'roll bandwagon year in, year out. By 1997 he had gained a certain perspective on it all, telling *Guitar World* that, "Black Sabbath was never really a satanic band, although we did touch on topics like satanism and devil worship in certain songs. It was just a different angle. If you think back to the late Sixties and early Seventies, it was all fuckin' flower power and how wonderful the fuckin' world is. That just didn't seem true to us. The world was fucked."

On a more personal note, he complained, "I have been treated like the fucking Antichrist. I've now been sued by about 25 people who claimed their kids committed suicide after listening to my music. That's total crap. It would be a very bad career move on my part, don't you think, if I intentionally put out records that make people commit suicide? If everyone who buys the record is gonna fucking shoot themselves, then the follow-up wouldn't sell many records, would it?"

America, of course, has turned up its fair share of crazies intent on putting the errant Osbourne to rights when it comes to godliness. As he recounted in amazement, "Weird things happen in the name of religion. Years ago, I was on my way to play in a place called Tyler, Texas. And the sheriff told my tour manager he couldn't guarantee my safety because someone from a local quarry had stolen a load of dynamite and they were going to blow the fucking venue up. Of course, I didn't turn up for the gig. I didn't fancy going on in bits and pieces . . . One time, I got on my tour bus after a gig and we drove for seven or eight hours. We stopped at a truck stop in the early hours of the morning for a cup of coffee. We were out in the middle of nowhere. And this guy walks up to me and gives me one of these leaflets: 'Jesus saves'. And I say to the guy, 'Where did you come from? There's nothing for miles and miles around here.' He says, 'I've been following you all night.' I says, 'You been following the bus all night just to give me this fucking piece of paper? You don't want to go a church, my friend. You want to go see a fucking psychiatrist . . .'"

There's a serious side to the mad-groupie phenomenon, though, as he added: "Cardinal O'Connor in New York actually got on the fucking pulpit one day . . . This is a cardinal, next one down from being the Pope, you know? He gets up on his fucking thing and tells the congregation that I am the Antichrist. And that's wrong, that is. Because you're gonna get some wacko out there that's gonna buy a Saturday Night Special and pop me one in the back of the fucking head, thinking that he had a vision from Christ. That is my fear. If it comes from the Church, then it's all right for some of these nutcases. The clergy is in a more dangerously powerful position than you or I will ever be. Because if a cardinal gets on the pulpit and tells his congregation that I, Ozzy Osbourne, am the reason for all the badness in the world, then you're gonna get some nutcase want to wipe me out, you know? I've had threats to my life. Part of the reason I run around so much onstage is because somebody told me a moving target is harder to hit . . . The priorities in America are so fucking weird. I mean, you can't smoke a fucking cigarette in public in California, but you can go buy a machine gun. Just the other night, we were coming out of the studio and some guy got shot five times in the fuckin' head right across the road from us."

All in the name of God, eh? Not Satan, you'll notice. Leave that to the rock'n'rollers . . .

CHAPTER EIGHT

1974–1976

AS 1974 progressed and Sabbath toured in the wake of the management change, the band discovered, to their horror, that few of their worldly possessions – houses in particular – were actually their legal property. When Geezer described the band earlier as 'potless', he did so for good reason: it appeared that Meehan's management strategies had not included making legally binding purchases on the band-members' residences, and their personal fortunes vanished in a puff of smoke.

Luckily, the Arden management team of Don and Sharon, with whom Ozzy was beginning to establish a relationship, and touring income for the year propped up the musicians' drained bank accounts. Gigs were still booked for many months in advance, of course, and major festival dates were sometimes secured years ahead. This guaranteed some revenue and enabled credit after the band had pulled in paying crowds in Bradford, Stoke, London, Liverpool, Manchester, Southampton, Glasgow, Edinburgh, Sheffield, Bournemouth, Newcastle and Coventry by the end of May.

The mood in the camp was low-key as Sabbath approached sessions for yet another album. Legal procedures were now disrupting their professional activities – at one point Ozzy was handed a writ as he walked onstage. One notable show at this time took place at the Summer Rock Festival in Frankfurt alongside Sly & The Family Stone, The Faces, Rory Gallagher, Canned Heat and many others, and was followed by an Australian tour. Meanwhile songwriting sessions provided material for *Sabotage*, due for recording in early 1975 at Morgan Studios in London.

Titled as an angry response to the managerial issues the band were facing, *Sabotage* was the first Sabbath LP to be produced by Iommi (although the overall credit went to Sabbath with Mike Butcher). Fuelled by rage and whatever other stimulants were to hand, the album kicks off with the technicolour 'Hole In The Sky'. Ozzy's vocals are pitched high and prominent in the mix, as he literally shrieks ambitious lines such as "The synonym of all the things that I've said / Are just the riddles that are built in my head", through an epic tale that seems to be a rant against the world in general – and specifically its war-pig paymasters. After invocations such as "I've watched the dogs of war enjoying their feast / I've seen the western world go down in the east", the song cuts off suddenly, followed by a mellow acoustic piece called 'Don't Start (Too Late)'. Once again it's Iommi displaying his classical side, as the layers of pleasant – but hardly cutting-edge – plucked patterns fade away.

The undisputed classic cut on *Sabotage* is 'Symptom Of The Universe', six and a half minutes of intricate riffage, flurries of soloing and expert key and tempo changes underpinning more, almost uncomfortably high-pitched vocals. At 4′ 30″ the song steps sideways into a piano and acoustic shuffle after the overdriven guitars ascend in unison – Iommi showing off with studio technology, perhaps – and becomes arguably the first progressive-metal song. The demanding vocals remained a problem for the rest of Ozzy's career, however, as Geezer told me with a snigger: "We always try to get Ozzy to sing 'Symptom Of The Universe'. But he never will, he says that he can't reach the notes." You could always play the song in a lower key, I suggested: "That's what we say, but he still won't. It's a psychological thing, I think. He won't do it." Perhaps Ozzy's reticence is also something to do with the lyrics – grandiose, image-heavy exercises that are so of their time as to be almost from another age: "Mother moon she's calling me back to her silver womb / Father of creation takes me from my stolen tomb / Seventh hundredth unicorn is waiting in the skies / A symptom of the universe a love that never dies" is a perfect example.

At almost 10 minutes long, the mighty 'Megalomania' is a marathon in which Sabbath exercise all their new-found songwriting and production confidence for the first time. With Ozzy's vocals variously reversed, multi-tracked and drenched in reverb, the song passes through a slow, dignified section in which the singer calls "Why don't you just get out of my life now? / Why doesn't everybody leave me alone now?" before accelerating into a faster, rockier chorus. At 5′ 45″ Iommi unleashes an incandescent solo, one of his best to date, before the almost glam-rock riff underneath Ozzy's call of "How I lied, went to hide / How I tried to get away from you now". The song's last three minutes are a glorious spiral downward into an explosion of orchestra, guitar solos and screams – a totally over-the-top production that reveals Sabbath at the peak of their game.

'Thrill Of It All', in comparison, has largely gone unremarked over the years – a merely competent album track that escapes attention next to huge songs like 'Symptom Of The Universe' and 'Megalomania'. Even

Geezer told *Metal Sludge* some years later that "I can't even remember that one" . . . nonetheless, it's a funky song with a staccato riff that plays out well even if it doesn't make a vast impact. The central piano and synthesiser section is better, even if it's hardly the hard-hitting Sabbath of old.

'Supertzar', an instrumental – but fully formed – riff-plus-orchestra piece that is loaded with soundtrack elements such as choirs, strings, tuned percussion and synthesisers, remained a standard feature of Sabbath's live set for decades, albeit as the intro tape. Even as late as 1987 and the *Eternal Idol* tour, the familiar multi-tracked warbles of the female and male choirs, interspersed with a strange, almost nursery-rhyme lead riff, would introduce the set.

'Am I Going Insane (Radio)' – thought by some to bear its suffix because it was the radio track – is in fact the most commercial song on S*abotage*, with its hummable chorus of "Tell me people, am I going insane?" But this is coincidental, with Bill Ward telling *Shockwaves* that "The term 'radio' was short for 'radio-rental', which is rhyming slang for 'mental'. It's a slang term people in Birmingham used – if you're mentally ill, we would call you 'radio'." And as Ozzy wailed, mental illness was a recurring theme: "If I don't sound very cheerful, I think that I'm a schizophrene". Insane laughter and sinister wails end the song.

Ironically – or perhaps just sadly – mental illness would soon be a real feature of Sabbath's lives. Geezer told me in 2005, "I suffered with depression on and off over the years and it's a hard thing to relate to people. I didn't even know I had it until I had proper tests and got pills to sort it out. People used to think I was just being miserable, but it was actual depression. Originally, and unbeknownst to me, that was what 'Paranoid' was about, the way I was feeling at the time."

There was no talking about clinical depression in post-war Aston, he added: "People just didn't ever talk about it, they thought you were literally a nutcase. I used to get told to cheer up all the time. Ozzy's suffered from it on and off, Bill's suffered from it, it was only Tony who escaped it. You just think that it's part of boozing or whatever, but it's not, it's a clinical thing, something in your brain. The medication really does the trick – I think it was only when Prozac came out that people really opened up to it."

Where does he attribute the cause of this affliction? "I think, with me, I'm the sort of person who doesn't ever switch off thinking about stuff. I have a terrible time trying to sleep, 'cause I'm always thinking about something. Even though there's absolutely nothing bad going on in my life, I just can't stop thinking about things. I think if you don't get the proper sleep, it really messes up your life . . . It's hard to say when you're a kid if you've got depression or if you just get pissed off. I always remember one time that was really bad, and I couldn't explain what the mood was, but there was nobody to talk to about it at the time. They used to tell you to go and take your dog for a walk or something."

Finally, we come to 'The Writ'. "We were getting ripped all over place, and that was a terrible period for us because we were getting bloody law-suits in the studio," said Tony. "People were delivering us writs and stuff. That why there's a song called 'The Writ' on it." And the eight minutes of 'The Writ' are righteously vengeful, spitting out venom at the unnamed prosecutors – Meehan, presumably – who were troubling Sabbath at the time. Musically, the song is unremarkable – at least until the unexpectedly sweet acoustic guitar and percussion section at five minutes in – but the point is the inspired lyrics, which promise retribution ("You're gonna get what is coming to you that's due") and dismiss their target as beyond contempt ("You are a nonentity, you have no destiny / You are a figment of a thing unknown"). The anger is audible in Ozzy's voice, which breaks in emotion from time to time.

It's a truly powerful ending to the LP, made lighter by the final snippet – a joke track called 'Blow On A Jug'. This was Ozzy and Bill fooling around in the studio on a piano song by the Nitty Gritty Dirt Band. In a mock-Elvis whine, Ozzy sings "Everybody come on blow on a jug / Be like me and blow on a jug / I want you to blow on a jug / Everybody dig it, blow on the jug tonight". As Bill laughed, "That's me and Ozzy. It was something that was never supposed to be recorded. We had left the tape running in the studio and Oz and I were having a party . . . it was absolute nonsense."

Their anger expressed, Sabbath hit the road in the interim between recording and release, recruiting a fifth member to help out onstage for the first time. This was Gerald 'Jezz' Woodroffe, a keyboard player whose role was to reproduce the layers of atmospheric synth and piano that Iommi had laid down on the last three albums.

Despite the vast instrumentation of some of the songs on *Sabotage*, Iommi regarded it as a consolidatory step rather than a leap forward: "It's more of a basic rock album, really in the same way that all the albums up to *Master Of Reality* were, but we've taken a lot more care in the way this one is produced. We spent a lot of time on *Volume 4* and *Sabbath, Bloody Sabbath* but they were moving away from a oneness of approach. *Volume 4* was such a complete change we felt we had jumped an album really. It didn't follow suit, because we had tried to go too far, and again *Sabbath,*

Bloody Sabbath was a continuation from it. We could have gone on into more technical things and fulfil a lot [of which] the band is capable of achieving, and which we don't necessarily do onstage either. But we decided we had reached the limit as far as we wanted to go."

But their future work would still be made with one primary objective, he added: "We've always got to be satisfied with what we are doing ourselves. We don't just play for our audience to satisfy them. We play to satisfy ourselves, but we hope that communicates to our audience and that it satisfies them. We haven't held back because we've thought we are getting too involved – you can't put yourself in that kind of position: we felt we wanted to get back to a more basic thing. We'll pick up again and develop from *Sabbath, Bloody Sabbath* – but that will come later when we are more ready for it." Time would tell if this would be the right decision . . .

The line-up planned to hit the US for three short touring jaunts starting in July and extending into the following year – a clever move designed to avoid the aftermath of a single extended, and exhausting, haul – alongside the release of *Sabotage* on September 27. A UK tour came in the winter, with a date in Sheffield supported by a group called Bandy Legs who would rename themselves Quartz and recruit a guitarist, Geoff Nicholls, who would work with Sabbath in the future.

Touring to this extent is hard work for any band, especially one that parties as hard as Sabbath did. At times the strain of being on the road was too much to bear, with Iommi collapsing in exhaustion before a show at the Hollywood Bowl and Bill Ward coming down with hepatitis. The guitarist later explained: "We were just suffering too much strain and worry and we had to stop and sort ourselves out. Touring had become a bit like working in a factory – we lost sight of what we were doing. It got to the point where we were getting bored with our show. At various times the band were ill, as well as just feeling rough and exhausted."

By October '75 the band were beginning to be back on their feet. They had formed their own publishing company and were planning to take more control of the business side of their careers. As Iommi told *Circus* magazine, "We have more control over what is happening and for us as individuals it is another angle to get involved in. We are learning by having to think about sides of the business which we didn't concern ourselves with in the past. It gives us a broader outlook, because we can do whatever we want now. We have a direct channel, so that if we want to arrange a tour or whatever, we don't have to go through our management before it gets to us. It's one and the same. Any decisions are taken by all four of us and we all have to be fully behind them.

"The position we are in now, we don't have to accept anything, and nobody gets fooled and nobody can turn around and call us anything unless they have the right to do so. In the past we have been blamed for things which weren't down to us. There were gigs we didn't turn up to in America where we didn't know there was a gig. We weren't told about them. It happened a few times and eventually it came back to us, because we're the ones people see up there onstage."

All this business acumen was simply an extension of the recovery process that Sabbath had been going through on all levels. Tony explained that a newly relaxed Sabbath had evolved: "We've all been regaining our-selves. A few years ago we wouldn't have dreamed of going down to the pub for a pint and simple things like that . . . By 1973 we were thinking that we could go onstage and, simply because we were Black Sabbath, we couldn't do anything wrong. We were getting away from music because we were working so hard. We weren't really manipulated, but we were just feeling we were."

The road was calling again and Sabbath finished off 1975 with another European and American tour. Business might have been improving, but some observers sensed a slight tension between Ozzy and Iommi. Only time would tell if this might grow to be a problem.

Times were changing and, in 1976, an angrier and more pertinent musical genre would rear its head to challenge heavy metal, by now a fully christened beast in its own right (albeit one which many critics mockingly predicted would be extinct before too long). But punk was still an unknown quantity for most of the audiences who still flocked to see Ozzy and his band on their enormous tours, and that kind of challenge was some months away. Nonetheless, it was there – and the question was how Sabbath and their long-haired ilk would rise to meet it.

One plan of attack was to remind the class of '76 what a formidable force Sabbath had been for the previous six years, and thus a compilation – the slyly titled *We Sold Our Souls For Rock'N'Roll* – was released in January. The tracklisting – 'Black Sabbath', 'The Wizard', 'The Warning', 'Paranoid', 'War Pigs', 'Iron Man', 'Wicked World', 'Tomorrow's Dream', 'Fairies Wear Boots', 'Changes', 'Sweet Leaf', 'Children Of The Grave', 'Sabbath Bloody Sabbath', 'Am I Going Insane (Radio)', 'Laguna Sunrise', 'Snowblind' and 'N.I.B.' – was a pretty thorough run-through of the band's best and best-known songs, and sold respectably if not massively, scoring number 35 on the UK chart.

After finishing off the final US tour leg, Sabbath found themselves at the

High Court in London on 16 March facing Jim Simpson for a final confrontation. As he recounted earlier, neither party benefited hugely from the case, and despite their loss the band roused themselves for more songwriting sessions, this time at Ridge Farm Studios near Horsham in Surrey. Recording and mixing would take place at Criteria Studios in Miami, while mastering would be executed across the nation in California – notably, every stage of the process took place at state-of-the-art facilities, a by-product of the band's enormous stature by this point in their careers. Whether or not this luxury would lead to better songs was a moot point debated even at the time – let alone three decades later, when the albums themselves are the stuff of legend – but fans didn't have long to wait.

On 25 September *Technical Ecstasy* was released, bearing sleeve art designed by the über-cool Hipgnosis design agency – a radical change from previous sleeves, as it depicted two robots passing each other on adjacent escalators, and enjoying what appeared to be a exchange of bodily fluids. The rear sleeve depicted the same stark scene moments after the escalators had moved on, and the inner sleeve was a montage of blueprint-style technical drawings . . . all a long way from the lone woman in her gothic-horror meadow on *Black Sabbath*.

The LP began with 'Back Street Kids', a standard Sabbath riffathon punctuated by a frankly annoying unison guitar and vocal line of "Nobody I know will ever take my rock'n'roll away from me". At 1′ 50″ the song takes a surprising turn, resembling something by The Who – perhaps 'Who Are You', with its over-busy tom fills and buzzing keyboard – rather than the metal of old. Although a blistering solo from Iommi, coupled with a keyboard line played by Woodroffe, could be seen as a sign of Sabbath moving forward, the song's abrupt ending and rather mundane structure in comparison to previous highlights let it down.

Woodroffe makes his presence felt even more clearly on 'You Won't Change Me', a majestic anthem with a church organ-like synth wash placed behind the melodic chords. It's a dark song, with Ozzy's intonation on "I wonder what it's like to be loved / Instead of hiding in myself / Nobody will change me anyway, no no way" painting a dark picture, despite the lead guitar fills from Tony. It's Iommi's song, though, with whole minutes devoted to his by-now scintillating solos. It's at this point that an awareness of how far Sabbath have come crops up: with their first three albums, Sabbath blew a breath of fresh air into the moribund rock scene, overlong guitar solos and all. Now, here they were seven years later, recording those same long solos.

'It's Alright', a pleasant piano-driven pop song (that's right . . . pop) was a first for Sabbath, as it featured vocals from Bill Ward rather than Ozzy. Warners in America liked the song so much that they even recorded a primitive promo video to accompany it, although nothing much was actually done with the footage. As Ward recalled, "I actually saw the video a couple of years ago, and I never recalled seeing that video before. When I saw it I thought, 'Wow, I don't ever remember doing that!' . . . The guys liked the song and I was really shy about doing it, but the guys said, 'Let's put it on the album.' So I was encouraged by the band to do that."

As if to re-establish Bill's metal credentials, 'Gypsy' kicks off with a flurry of complex drums and a driving riff, but the primary influence on this song appears to be Queen, whose expert grasp on a piano break informs the song-shift at two minutes in: it's hard not to hum the words "I see a little silhouetto of a man . . ." at this point. The close-harmonised backing vocals are also pure Mercury and May, although the solo – utterly dramatic – is Iommi at his best. (Ozzy would later say disparagingly of the Queen-derived sound, "Can you imagine me jumping up and down with a pair of pink tights on?")

"All Moving Parts (Stand Still)" is a bizarre song, based on a set of slightly irksome vocal rhymes ("Super animation, turning on a nation", "Since he was elected, adrenaline injected", "What a combination, peace and radiation" and so on) and a strange, almost pointlessly complex set of guitar breakdowns. Meanwhile, Woodroffe's ghostly synth solo is superfluous, and Geezer's dexterous bass-line is too complex for the song. It's at this point that the LP seems to have gone too far.

'Rock'N'Roll Doctor' starts badly, for three reasons. One, the nauseating honky-tonk piano. Two, Bill's terrible cowbells, which come off as a kind of weak pastiche of, say, the Stones' 'Honky Tonk Woman'. Three, the jaunty rock'n'roll guitar riff, which Iommi must have thought was funky – but is in fact horribly dispensable. And added to all those is the puerile lyrical concept, that of a doctor prescribing a happy drug: lines like "If you wanna feel groovy give the doctor a call, yeah / Doctor rock will help you any time at all" were outdated by 1966, never mind 1976.

Later on, Iommi would say, "There are [some] tracks, like 'Solitude', 'Changes', and 'She's Gone', which no one would think of as us. In fact, some of those tracks were being played on the radio and nobody had a clue it was Black Sabbath. At the time it came out, nobody would have guessed 'Changes' was us." He was right, apart from Ozzy's instantly recognisable voice, that 'She's Gone' was a departure from the usual Sabbath style – songs such as this always split the band's fanbase down the middle. Quite simply, the song is a power ballad, loaded with unapologetically James Bond-like strings, suspended acoustic arpeggios (for that heartstring-twanging effect) and Ozzy's ridiculously maudlin lyrics ("And now it's hurting so much, what can I do? / I wanted you to be my wife"; "I sit here waiting but you'll never show / Without you I can't carry on, ooh my baby") which nowadays would have to be delivered with a post-modern tinge of irony to be taken seriously. That's right – he does sing "Ooh my baby" . . .

Technical Ecstasy sinks to its nadir, apart from 'Rock'N'Roll Doctor' that is, with 'Dirty Women', in which – across the course of seven painful minutes – Ozzy sings the praises of prostitutes ("take-away women for sale") who "don't mess around" and who have "got me coming" (this last delivered in a mid-tone, builder's-yard yell). Frankly, it's terrible.

The fanbase knew what was happening and, although the LP reached number 13 in Britain, it remained on the charts for only six weeks before dropping off entirely, a far cry from the 42 and 27 weeks achieved by *Black Sabbath* and *Paranoid* respectively. In September 1976 punk was beginning to make inroads into the charts, thanks to exposure in magazines such as *NME* and *Sounds*, which had championed heavy metal and hard rock in general but which was looking for new music to espouse (it did the same in 1979 with the New Wave Of British Heavy Metal, more of which later). Fans of hard, fast music simply didn't need an overblown, underpowered album like *Technical Ecstasy* to get their kicks: it remains a disappointing mellowing out by a band who had become too comfortable – and much of what followed can be attributed to it.

Black Sabbath, now suffering from too much luxury, too many tours ahead of them and a lack of communication, went out again on yet another huge American tour, for which production rehearsals at Columbia Studios in LA were required. Would this be the straw that broke the camel's back?

CHAPTER NINE

1977–1979

FOR six months from October 1976, Black Sabbath were permanently on the road in America and Europe, starting in Tulsa, Oklahoma. The tour wound its way through Texas, Iowa, Nebraska and Colorado in the first month, featuring support acts Boston and Heart, both of whom had made inroads into melodic heavy rock and both of whom would be erroneously labelled heavy metal acts in the following decade. November brought dates in California, Tennessee, Illinois, Michigan and Ohio, while in December the band hooked up with Ted Nugent – the veteran guitar slinger born in the same month as Ozzy, whose career even pre-dated that of Sabbath – for an intensive trek along the East Coast.

In January 1977, the entourage powered down through Florida, Atlanta and through the Midwestern states once more, almost retracing their previous route as far as the West Coast. Back in the UK, the band devoted March to a countrywide trek – winding up with four London shows – and then hitting Europe with up-and-coming Australian heavy rock band AC/DC and other acts including the Ian Gillan Band and Doctors Of Madness. One Ludwigshafen bill also included prog-rock behemoths John McLaughlin's Shakti and Caravan – at first sight an incongruous coupling, until you remember that by now Sabbath themselves could lay claim to the progressive tag, even though they chose not to. The last few dates were on the tense side after a backstage incident between Geezer Butler and AC/DC's rhythm guitarist and principal songwriter Malcolm Young: the former is alleged to have drawn a knife on Young during a furious drunken argument.

Geezer, superficially the quietest Sabbath member, has never been an alcoholic – but he has done his fair share of crazy things while under the influence of booze. He told me in 2005, "I hate losing control. I like enjoying going for a piss-up, but as soon as it turns to violence . . . there's a line with me, I get really violent if I have too much to drink. One night I got really badly injured and stopped, knocked it on the head. Now I just do it occasionally. I think it was 1992. We were in South America and I was trying to pick a fight with everybody. In the end I nutted this statue! I completely split my eye open, and I was so drunk I didn't even know. I went to bed and I woke up the next day and my head was stuck to the pillow. I couldn't figure out what was going on, I was covered in blood. Apparently I'd phoned my wife and gone nuts at her, having a big argument – but I couldn't remember anything about it. I got a phone bill for 2,000 dollars! It costs like 80 quid a minute or something to phone from South America. And I realised, what the hell am I doing to myself? So that was it, I didn't drink for two or three years. Then I started all over again, not being horrible but just doing it socially. I could have easily killed myself that night, I could have been shot or anything. I totally didn't remember any of it."

Butler's troubles were the least of Sabbath's problems as autumn 1977 approached. Ozzy had been informed that his father, Jack, was seriously ill with cancer – and was likely to die within months. The news shocked him deeply and he was torn as to what he should do. In the end, knowing he should be with his family, he quit the band. The underlying issues which all concerned knew that he had with the other members were not addressed.

The other band-members were shocked and speechless. Ozzy was their singer and their primary live asset, fulfilling the cornerstone role that Tony, the master writer, guitarist, arranger and producer, performed in the studio. As Ozzy headed for the airport and a flight to Birmingham, Iommi, Butler and Ward gathered for an urgent meeting. Geezer in particular was hit hard by Ozzy's announcement, unable to foresee how Sabbath could continue without him. Bill was saddened – he and Ozzy had been as close as brothers.

Tony Iommi proposed the recruitment of a singer called Dave Walker, whom he had had known since his days in Aston and who had been the singer with Savoy Brown. Although Walker and Ozzy could not have been more different in looks or singing style, Geezer and Bill, both still numb with shock, agreed. As Bill recalled: "We all liked Dave Walker as a mate . . . We got to know him when he fronted with Savoy Brown, and earlier when Dave played in the Redcaps, an early Birmingham band, from the Sixties. I liked Dave a lot, and I thought he had a great voice. When it came time to choose another singer, all kinds of names came up, but Dave's stayed."

Iommi duly contacted Walker, who was living in San Francisco at the time. The singer, somewhat surprised by the call, was agreeable to the idea and flew to London in November to meet with the band for rehearsals. As he said in an online forum many years later, "As for Black Sabbath, we were friends from the same city and they felt that I could do the job. While I was with them for a short time, I wrote a large amount of lyrics which were never used . . . the Black Sabbath experience was something that I look back upon with some amazement. I was given the job on a purely friendship basis as Tony Iommi and I were pals."

In December Walker and the Sabs, along with keyboard player Don Airey – who had been asked to step in for sessions – rehearsed new songs for a potential album. The new line-up then appeared on a BBC Midlands TV show, *Look Hear*, hosted by Toyah Willcox, performing a song called 'Junior's Eyes' which would be reworked into a later LP track. The programme was broadcast on 6 January, 1978. Bill later pointed out that 'Junior's Eyes' had been written for Ozzy and his father: " 'Junior's Eyes' was a song very much for Oz and his dad. I mention that only because it was a song we did live at a lunchtime BBC show in Birmingham with Dave Walker . . . of course it didn't work. Not because of Dave, because the song was Ozzy's as far as I was concerned. I felt crap at that time while Oz was away." As Geezer wilted and Iommi ploughed on with his usual steely determination, Ward sank into an alcoholic fug – a state that he would not shake off for some years, until it became absolutely necessary.

On January 20, two weeks after the TV broadcast, Ozzy's father died. In a later interview with writer and author David Gans, the singer revealed how crushed he had been by his dad's death: "The fucking ironical thing about the whole deal was – he was fucked, he had like cancer from his throat, what's this tube down to your stomach? Oesophagus, testicles; he was riddled with it – he died in the same hospital that my daughter was born seven years prior. My daughter was born 11.20 on January 20, and my fucking father died seven years later in the same hospital at 11.23 on the 20th. It was fucking weird, man."

Dignity had not been afforded to Jack, as Ozzy related with obvious bitterness. "They put him in a fucking closet with the fucking mops and buckets, because he was on the death ward and it was too distressing for the rest of the patients so they put him in a cot, sort of a crib thing, a giant crib. They strapped him . . . like a boxer, fucking bandages on his hands, with a glucose drip going into his arm. He was stoned out of his head. You know, the most amazing thing he said to me. I told my father one day, I take drugs. I said to him, before you go, will you take drugs? He says, I promise you I'll take drugs. He was on morphine. Totally out of his mind on morphine, because the pain must have been horrendous. They had the operation on a Tuesday, and he died on Thursday . . . I haven't got over it yet. The twentieth of January, I'll go freaking like a werewolf. I'll cry and I'll laugh all day long, because it's the day my daughter was born and the day my father died. Like a fucking lunatic."

While Ozzy mourned, the 'new' Sabbath were having some problems. Walker either would not or could not fill Ozzy's shoes, and the others may have had difficulty in accepting him, even though his singing and performing abilities were never in doubt. Ward recalled: "These were not the very best of times. I was pretty much numb at that time period. Ozzy's father Jack had died, and we were making, I guess, slow progress on the album." Walker himself noted much later on: "As so often happens, friendship and business do not always go together hand in hand. Towards the end of my short stay with the band it was obvious that there was a clash of styles . . . everything happens for a reason, even though at the time we may not understand it."

In the last week of January, as soon as his father's funeral was past, Ozzy contacted Sabbath and asked if he could rejoin them. The others accepted immediately (Ward: "When Oz started back at rehearsals everything felt normal again . . . even though I was buried in a bottle, with Oz there it was right") and Bill volunteered to tell Walker the bad news. As he said, "Oddly enough, it was me who let Dave know that things were not working out – I felt awkward and uncomfortable telling Dave this, as I liked him as a person very much." Walker duly headed home and retired from the music business for several years.

When Ozzy rejoined Sabbath there was an initial honeymoon period in which the relief was palpable. However, Ozzy wasn't in the most tractable of moods following his father's death, refusing point-blank to sing any of the songs which Walker and Sabbath had written together – and even being fussy about which of Geezer's lyrics he would and would not sing. As Butler later winced, "I used to hate doing it towards the end of the Ozzy era. I used to write these lyrics and give them to Ozzy. He'd say, 'I'm not singing that.' So you'd have to re-think the whole thing again!"

After an LP's worth of songs had been painfully honed, Iommi took his band to Sound Interchange Studios in Toronto, Canada, ostensibly because The Rolling Stones had worked on a live album there the previous year, but perhaps – as Ozzy later stated – for tax reasons: "We go there because The Rolling Stones had mixed their live album, where they're biting each other's arms, or something. Because the Stones had gone there. The fucking studio's a pile of shit . . . The reason we'd gone to Canada was because of the tax-exile thing, because the taxes are so high in England."

In early 1978 the weather in Toronto was horrendously cold, and the band-members were miserable. Forced to shepherd his troops together, Iommi may have taken his eye off the ball when it came to songwriting quality. This may explain why the result, *Never Say Die*, was such a useless album . . .

The title track sounds, from its first few bars, as if the band have been listening exclusively to punk and the lower reaches of the then-rampant glam-rock movement. As if it weren't enough that the album and song title should come from a worn-out English cliché, the lyrics were banal: an example is "Sunday satisfaction, Monday's home and dry / Truth is on the doorstep, welcome in the lie". Underpinned by a surprisingly weak guitar sound – complete with Iommi's unnecessary rockabilly-boogie string-bends – the song ends with a comically baritone "Never say die!" and skids to a halt. Remarkably, Warners chose it as a single – it reached number 21 in June – only Sabbath's third ever 45 release, issued more than seven years after 'Evil Woman' and 'Paranoid'.

After a swirling, miasmic cloud of synthesiser sounds announced the intro of 'Johnny Blade', Ozzy warbles, "Tortured and twisted, he walks the streets alone / People avoid him, they know the street's his home" – and the rest are perhaps the most teeth-grindingly naïve words Sabbath had yet committed to record. The ostensible tale of a young hood who himself is the victim is played out over an uninspiring and very ordinary rock song, although it's livened up by Don Airey's elaborate keyboard solos.

'Junior's Eyes', the song rewritten from the Walker sessions as a tribute to Ozzy's father, is unusual to say the least. It doesn't have any of the musically 'sad' tricks that, say, 'She's Gone' possessed – the maudlin piano, the soupy strings and so on – although with lines such as "With all the pain, I've watched you live within / I'll try my hardest not to cry when it is time to say goodbye" – it's a song of much pathos. Iommi layers on swathes of wah-wah pedal on rhythm and lead guitar but at over six minutes it outstays its welcome somewhat. Collectors should note that the original version with Walker's vocals is available on a bootleg entitled *Archangel Rides Again*.

'A Hard Road' is the sound of Sabbath meeting T. Rex and Fleetwood Mac and writing a loping, catchy pop song. Ozzy's multi-tracked vocal melodies make the song moderately memorable, as he sings "Why make the hard road? / Why can't we befriend? / No need to worry / Let's sing it again" in an almost hands-in-the-air, anthemic style that could have come from any stadium-rock band of the time. The song also sees Iommi and

Geezer sing on a Sabbath song – both men recorded backing vocals, although only Geezer appears to be doing so in the promo video which Warners shot for the song when it was released as a single (it reached number 33 in October). As Tony recalled with a laugh: "I've heard myself sing, and I wouldn't want anybody else to! The only time I've ever sung is when we done 'A Hard Road' . . . They only showed Geezer because I was too embarrassed to get up to the microphone!"

'Shock Wave' continues the album's more commercial approach, with a swinging, very mainstream rock riff that, sadly, could have been plucked from any AOR album released over the previous three or four years. Surprisingly, the band choose to revisit the now-hackneyed horror-movie territory of their first four albums, with Ozzy singing (with a degree of jaded boredom, it seems) "Ghostly shadows from the other world / Evil forces in your mind / Trapped between the wall of life and death / Frozen in the realms of time". The only remarkable thing about the song is Iommi's pyrotechnic lead guitar, loaded with state-of-the-art effects: otherwise, it's a mundane song on an increasingly mundane album.

'Air Dance' commences with a double-tracked harmony guitar line, before settling into a sensitive acoustic guitar and piano groove, with Airey's keyboard flourishes lending a busy, slightly supper-club edge to the sound. There's a saxophone in there too, and the rather sickly effect is to make the song, a paean to an unknown female ("In days of romance, she was the queen of dance / She'd dance the night away"), highly skippable. But the band aren't entirely out of ideas: halfway through a raucous, if safe, riff comes in and the song wanders off into a cloud of synthesised harpsichord.

More unnecessary piano tinkling spoils the otherwise inoffensive 'Over To You' a plodding tale of a character locked in a miserable life ("Travelling endlessly, I'm searching my mind / I'm almost afraid of what I will find"). Unfortunately, there is neither tempo, key nor riff change at any point in the tune, which drifts aimlessly along and is entirely forgettable.

The instrumental 'Breakout' boasts some of the old menace in the loping riff, but loses it immediately thanks to the multiple layers of saxophone – perhaps the most inappropriate instrument yet added to a Sabbath album – and is quickly dispensed with before 'Swinging The Chain', a strange, semi-rock, semi-swing tune with a shuffle beat and harmonica. Bill Ward, who co-wrote it, explained later: "I think we were all blues and jazz-based when we were young. One of Tony's favourite guitarists when he was really young was Django Reinhardt. Since we had those influences, it wasn't that unusual to show up with a little bit of brass, even though it was risqué. The brass section in 'Swinging The Chain' just seemed to fit. I just think it's a nice piece of music." Ward also performs the vocals on this sing, showcasing a medium-range, earthy style that is, like his performance on 'It's Alright', surprisingly versatile – there are even a few falsetto wails at its end.

In retrospect, it's easy to regard *Never Say Die!* as the last, overindulged gasp of a band who had (metaphorically at least) become fat and lazy, although like all Sabbath's LPs the record does have its strengths. Contextually, this was proven beyond reasonable doubt by the band's fatal decision to choose as their support act for the *Never Say Die!* tour Van Halen, the young rock upstarts from Pasadena, California, who were in the process of annihilating their rock contemporaries with their astounding live show.

When the UK tour began in May 1978, Sabbath and Van Halen passed through Sheffield, Southport, Glasgow, Aberdeen, Newcastle, Manchester, London, Portsmouth, Bristol, Ipswich, Coventry, Leicester, Oxford, Southampton, Birmingham, Bradford, Preston, Bridlington, Liverpool and London again. On each and every occasion, Van Halen threatened to unseat the headliners with the showmanship of their singer, Dave Lee Roth, and the antics of shredder extraordinaire Eddie Van Halen and bassist Michael Anthony. Even the drummer, Alex Van Halen, would transcend his seated position on later tours by playing four bass drums.

As writer Sylvie Simmons, who witnessed Van Halen's rise, told me: "Van Halen were almost like a one-off blip. They came out of Pasadena with this thrust of power which absolutely knocked you sideways. It was absolutely fantastic, they were this completely don't-give-a-fuck band. And of course they toured with Sabbath on that last tour they did, and blew them out of the water. The heavy rock scene at that time was incredibly flaccid, it was all Foreigner and that kind of stuff. Kansas, Boston, REO Speedwagon . . . stadium rock was pretty much dead in the water."

If arena-rock was moribund, Van Halen were on a mission to resurrect it. Their appeal was wide: they gained the respect of musicians with their phenomenal musicianship – Eddie's trademark double-tapping technique, evolved from old blues and jazz guitarists but amped up by him with scintillating volleys of neo-classical shred patterns, made even master musicians like Iommi seem reserved and, well, outdated. Van Halen also put on an unmissable show, with Roth straddling a huge inflatable microphone, leaping in the air and sprinting around the stage. Compared with this, the tired and demotivated Ozzy seemed almost introverted: his stage act has, he admits himself, never been the most inventive, restricting himself to invocations of 'Go fuckin' mental!' and a polite jog from side to side of the stage.

Behind the scenes Van Halen consumed groupies and drugs with enormous enthusiasm. Ozzy, no stranger to these activities himself, struck up a backstage friendship with Dave Lee Roth that saw the pair spending whole nights consuming cocaine together. The tour rolled into the USA in August and September, crossing the nation several times and adding other bands to the bill on more than one occasion – these included Sammy Hagar (who would replace Roth in Van Halen in 1985), Richie Lecea and Russia. In October the Sabbath/VH tour covered Europe before returning for the final leg of the States in November.

All went well until November 16, when Ozzy went missing before a show at Nashville's Municipal Auditorium in Tennessee. Roth later recalled in his 1997 book, *Crazy From The Heat*, that he and Ozzy had spent the previous night taking coke "until about nine-thirty in the morning . . . We drove from Memphis to Nashville. Checked into a hotel. It was noontime, and I went right into the bin, fell asleep. Got up, we opened, sold-out show, 10,000 of our closest friends. We're sitting backstage, and suddenly, two of the guys from Black Sabbath and some muscle burst through the door, 'Where is Ozzy? . . . We're not even sure he checked into the hotel. We can't find him anywhere. We can't do the show.'"

Roth was then asked if he could sing the Sabbath songs but explained that he didn't know any of the words. The show was cancelled, the local and national press went into ecstasies and fears arose that Ozzy had been killed, or kidnapped. "Six-thirty in the morning," continues Roth, "Ozzy comes walking out of the elevator. He's back from the dead! No he's not. This character had gone into the new hotel, reached into his pocket, pulled out the key from the last hotel, looked at the number, got into the elevator, went right up to that room. There happens to be a maid cleaning up the room. He says, 'Get out of here!' She runs off in terror, he closes the door and falls asleep."

Ozzy had simply checked into the wrong room, no doubt confused about which hotel (and probably which city) he was in, fallen asleep and thus not been woken for that night's gig. One fan wrote of the event, "I remember when the guy got up onstage to announce the cancellation, the crowd had been waiting for about an hour. When he gave the bad news, the place went berserk and stuff started raining down from above. I was trying to get out of there as quick as possible when an M-80 [firework] went off in the air right above the arena floor. Then, a pint bottle came down out of the nosebleed seats and hit the drum set. I heard later that a bunch of windows were busted out at the Municipal Auditorium as well."

Sabbath and Van Halen played the gig in Memphis three days later, with Ozzy going on local radio beforehand to explain what had happened and to offer his apologies to the fans. The tour went on through December, winding up in New Mexico. The band-members took the opportunity for rest and recuperation.

What happened next is the stuff of legend, and also of much debate.

At this stage in Black Sabbath's career, the band were in a rut. Ozzy was overindulging in alcohol and cocaine, as was Bill. Geezer and Tony have been less forthcoming about their recreational habits, but have hinted on several occasions that they too followed a similar path. After two un-remarkable albums and a fairly radical style change that had pleased no one, the record-tour-record cycle was, after a decade, starting to seem unappetising. A new album, tentatively titled *Heaven And Hell* after one of the songs that Iommi had demoed for it, was on the schedule.

All might have got back on track if it hadn't been for Ozzy, who was heartily sick of life in Sabbath and positively disgusted by their recent music. He is alleged to have said at this point that all he wanted was to drink beer and get fat, and his attendance at rehearsals became sporadic. Something had to give.

In early 1979, he was either fired or voluntarily left for the second time. Or, as he told David Gans, he deliberately got himself fired in order to leave: "I wouldn't fucking put up with their crap any more. I left first, but my lawyer said to me, 'If you leave, you voluntarily fucking leave. But if you fucking get yourself *fired*, you can claim a bit of dough.'"

In order to expedite this, Ozzy hit the bottle: "I got very drunk and very stoned every single day. Plus the fact Tony Iommi was using Sharon Arden as his motivation – he was pretending to be in love with her . . . I can't explain, because it's very complex to try and explain." This reference to a possible relationship between Iommi and Sharon Arden – now firmly Ozzy's wife – has always been shrouded in mystery.

Why was he so sick of life in the band? It seemed that the wealth and status which they had accumulated was too much for him to take: "That was the end of Sabbath and me . . . they went in a fucking macho way, and I never. They went sort of like, 'We ain't gonna do this, we want five towels, we want fuckin' eight bars of soap, we want fucking Courvoisier,' all this shit. It was bollocks to me, because I still remember my roots, where they never." And *Never Say Die!* had killed off his enthusiasm for making music with them: "In the end, it cost us nearly 500 fucking thousand dollars to make that album, and it was the biggest pile of horseshit that I've ever made in my life. I'm embarrassed with that album."

Elsewhere, it has been claimed that the other Sabbath members wanted Ozzy out, and that Iommi was keen on recruiting another singer for *Heaven And Hell*. In April 1979, Bill Ward volunteered to give Ozzy the news of his firing – or at least, the news that he had successfully managed to get himself fired, "I kind of volunteered," he said. "When there are holes and gaps and things like that, I tend to want to go in there and take care of them. It's just my nature. I just thought I'd take it upon myself to tell Ozzy."

Duly told, Ozzy retired to an LA hotel room, without a clue what to do next and with little interest in picking himself up. Worse, he wasn't even sure at first if leaving Sabbath had been the right thing to do. "When I left Sabbath I was in total fucking turmoil in the mind," he said. "I thought I'd blown the biggest thing in my life, the only one crack I'd ever get out of the fucking suburban shithole." For three months he sat in the hotel, ordering endless supplies of pizza, alcohol and cocaine. His sole support was his girlfriend Sharon Arden. Eventually, however, Sharon had an idea.

The young Arden had been watching how her father Don went about his work and – with an inherited eye for business – suggested that she become his manager. This would help him get back on his feet, she suggested, and he could eventually move towards recruiting his own band.

As Ozzy recalled, "I was sitting in the fucking Le Parc Hotel in fucking Los Angeles, sitting there like a sack of shit, and she comes in and says, 'We want to keep you, and we want to fuck them off', because they allowed themselves to [be] got to."

It had been a grim experience, he said, and the time was right for the next move: "I locked myself away for three months . . . I sat in a room and got drunk every day, listening to a guy over the road playing fucking 'Iron Man' every night . . . I was very down, because I was humiliated for the last time . . . [Then I got] a kick up the ass and a smack in the teeth from my management. They said, 'Listen: we believe in you, but you've got to fucking pull yourself together; you've got to show us that you can do it.' "

With renewed enthusiasm, Ozzy got up and, guided by Sharon, began to plan his next move.

While Ozzy plotted, the press speculated and the fans waited anxiously, Tony Iommi had not been idle. Determined to press ahead with Sabbath, under its own name or not, he had been talking to a singer who he thought might fill the considerable gap left by Ozzy.

The name of the new recruit was Ronald Padavona – or, as his existing fan base knew him, Ronnie James Dio.

CHAPTER TEN

1979

AND so the first decade of the world's first heavy metal band came to a close.

Black Sabbath had started their careers in 1969 in a completely different era for rock music. Although the festival scene was well-established, the tradition of well-organised, crowd-controlled mega-gigs would not become professional until the mid-Seventies, after pioneering events such as the California Jam and a select few others. It was shows such as this, and by implication the huge bands who drove them, which allowed the technology and the management behind such events to develop. Accept that point, and it's only a short stretch to understanding that the changes wrought to the fabric of society by Black Sabbath, Deep Purple, Led Zeppelin and the other groundbreaking rock bands of the very early Seventies were far-reaching, extending into further zones than merely music and entertainment.

As Sabbath grew up, so did the rock industry – with the added bonus that Sabbath invented heavy metal along the way. Little wonder that they enjoyed a lifestyle undreamed of by most mere mortals, although by today's standards – when the most intimate details of celebrities' lifestyles are forced down our throats – the luxuries afforded to the rich and famous in the Seventies would seem a little tame, and even mundane.

In fact, there's some doubt to this day about the personal fortunes of the members of Sabbath, at least at the point when Ozzy left them for the second time in April 1979. As he said, "We were potless. Black Sabbath, I'm telling you now, I swear to God . . . at that time, we were fucking penniless. Penniless! We had got ripped off like . . . we got taken for 15 million. By everybody! We didn't know what the fuck it was about! We thought as long as you've got a Rolls-Royce and a fucking toot of cocaine up your nose . . . It's a fucking big syndrome – it's left a scar on my mind – I don't trust many people any more. I trust my management, although a lot of people out there don't trust my management. I trust my management, because I have to, because I do trust them."

The music business, with its corrupt core maintained by untrustworthy people and their personal agendas and vendettas, was at least partly to blame for the split. Ozzy again: "I wanted to sue the fuckin' ass off Warner Brothers, if you want to know my honest opinion. I ain't gonna say it, because I'm not going to be liable . . . I believe at that point, if Black Sabbath had stuck together, that we could have [uncovered] the biggest scandal of the Seventies . . . I'm not mentioning any names, any companies, or anybody, but I do believe that . . . with the strength of a man like Don Arden, who is a strong fucker, and the Arden organisation, we could have burst the whole business open."

It's never been clear what he was referring to with this comment, but after all the shenanigans that Sabbath, as a group and individually, had endured at the hands of management and the usual dishonest promoters who make any touring band's life a misery, there must have been quite a story of exploitation hidden away in the band's history – he mentioned "the horrendous politics involved in Black Sabbath – everybody [agents, promoters, managers] was suing us and we were slogging our balls off just to pay the lawyers". This, as well as the change in songwriting – "All I did with [my band] was took my fucking thing right back to where it started. I said, let's get to basics again, and fucking knock it out" – were the reasons for Ozzy's departure.

It's fascinating to note how, with every step they made in the Seventies, Sabbath laid down a template for future acts to follow. In the intervening decades there have been more than a few acrimonious band splits – often the result of friction between lead singer and lead guitarist, the two most expressive musicians of any band – but they've all seemed to have something of the Sabbath story in them.

The rancour of the departed Ozzy would find an echo in many a musician to follow, especially in the hard rock and metal scenes. Osbourne first expressed his contempt for his ex-colleagues in an interview with *Sounds* magazine on October 13, 1979, in which he mused: "It's like a fucking divorce, that's what it is."

By this stage, six months after the split, things had moved on. Ozzy was looking for a band; Sabbath had recruited Ronnie James Dio; and Sharon Arden had taken up the reins of management over Ozzy, causing no little resentment from her father Don. Interestingly, Geezer Butler had suffered some sort of crisis of confidence after Ozzy's departure and had left Sabbath for a period (although this would prove to be temporary), with his future in the band – or any other – up in the air. *Sounds* also stated that Butler had fallen in love with an unidentified woman ("Geezer Butler left his heart in St Louis and has gone to find romance"), adding weight to his decision to leave, although this too has not been explained further.

One of the first items on the post-split agenda was the actual name of Black Sabbath, which Ozzy stated was owned in equal shares by the four band-members. "I own a quarter of that name and I wasn't notified or anything. And I think they're really robbing the kids – conning them. If you bought a ticket to go and see the Rolling Stones and you get there and it's just Bill Wyman and a bunch of strangers, how would you feel? Let's face it, it's a totally different band." Apparently Bill Ward had told Ozzy that after his departure a new name would be chosen for the band, but Ozzy had found out that this was not to be the case: "I heard from a good source yesterday that they've already started booking a tour out as Black Sabbath. That really got right up my fucking nose, that did . . . I think it's cheap what they're doing – the kids have always been loyal to us. When I found out last night I went nuts – hence one wrecked hotel room. It's over now – finished. It's a funny thing, but to me Sabbath is dead and I don't want no part of it. It's a re-run of the Deep Purple saga* exactly. The kids will only swallow it once . . ."

Revealing that he had invested in a wine bar in England "as a sort of retreat, something to fall back on if it all came crashing down", Ozzy explained that his doubts about his future in Sabbath had been fairly long-established: "I started to get the doubts in the pit of my stomach two years ago – it really ended for me then." A whole list of reasons to leave emerged. Firstly, he was a fast worker – the recording of the first three albums had been rapid and uncomplicated, which had suited him – but the expanded palette of production and composition that Iommi had begun to explore had irked him. "Tony would sit in the studio for days and days just tuning up," he said. "When you consider that our first albums were made in a week or a day or something – there's a lot of difference between a week and a year. The last couple of albums were very trying for me. I would get up early – I'm an early riser – and by the time they got up I was ready to go back to bed again. It was getting on my nerves – all of it. You'd think after this number of years a person would be able to keep his guitar in tune." The *Never Say Die!* tour had been riddled with problems, too, as he explained: "On our last tour it was ridiculous – towards the end

---

* Ozzy is probably referring to the time when Purple's first singer, Rod Evans, formed a band of unknown musicians to tour under the Deep Purple name. Needless to say, Evans was soon obliged by law to cease and desist, and he vanished into obscurity soon after.

there was a lot of trouble with equipment that should never have been allowed to happen."

Add to this the complexity of the newer songs, and the balance was starting to tip Ozzy's way, all right: "I wanted to get back to good basic hard rock, like we were known for. I wouldn't have minded doing the new stuff if it was reproducible onstage, but it wasn't . . . Fucking hell, that took so long to do. It was done in three sections and joined together. No way could you do that onstage. They'd think you were R2D2! Studios drive me up the wall. After a month or two in one of those places I feel like a bat. Fuck this overdubbing and all that mechanical crap, Tony Iommi playing through a jar of Vaseline or something. On the last album, on that track 'Breakout', I couldn't believe it one Sunday morning when 30 guys with trumpets marched in and started playing on a Black Sabbath album. It nearly made my hair fall out. I think Hughie Greene has been approached now for the management of Black Sabbath!"

Perhaps some of Ozzy's righteous anger came from the method of his departure, recounted here – in yet another possible account of events – as a rather backsliding move from Iommi, if indeed it ever happened this way. As he seethed: "When I came off the tour I had a phone call from somebody saying that Tony was going to leave the band, that we'd had an argument or something. So I phoned Tony up and said, 'Have I upset you? Apparently you and I have had a violent row and you never want to work with me again, and I want to know what it's all about.' So he said, 'Well, I'm leaving the band,' by which time he had already met Ronnie Dio out here and made his mind up. So I said, 'If that's what you really want to do, you go ahead and do it, but I'm not going to pack it in.' Then he works it round that he forced me out so he could do what he really wanted to do – because the name Black Sabbath is a hard name to follow with anything else. So it went on and on with them making it more difficult for me to work with them, and it was getting on my tits. I didn't want to know any more . . . What it came down to was, we all agreed it wasn't working. I knew that two years ago."

Asked if he'd discussed the situation with the other band members, he retorted: "Yes, many times, but no matter what I came up with, nobody liked it. So I thought, fucking hell, I'm wasting my time. So I split. I went back home because I couldn't stand the aggravation any more, plus the fact that I was getting drunk every day just to get through the day. So we had a meeting, I said it's over – finished. We'll do a farewell tour, big one, let all the kids say goodbye to Sabbath, do a three hour show and make a live album with all the old favourites right up to the new stuff to remember us by.

"They said, fair enough. But I knew it would never materialise. They were just buying time. I feel really bad about not doing that farewell tour. It would have ended a part of my life that I will never forget, and now it's just fizzled out and everybody's bitter. The kids have been so loyal to Sabbath. I think they deserve for them not to pull that kind of stunt on them. They're like ostriches sticking their heads in the sand waiting for the storm to pass and when it's all rosy again they'll carry on calling themselves Black Sabbath like nothing happened."

The new album, *Heaven And Hell*, was off the agenda for now, he revealed: "It's been scratched. I'm not singing on their new album at all, Geezer's not playing on the album. It's a completely new band – I want that made perfectly clear. They'll probably sound very much like Foreigner – that was the last album they were all into. I couldn't stand where they were going. We were influencing bands at one time, and the bands we were once influencing are now influencing us. It's come full circle. That is the time when you've got to say, hey, what are we doing wrong? The year before, it was Queen."

As he'd left the band before, it was legitimate for the interviewer to wonder if in fact Ozzy might recant and rejoin them for a second time. But Ozzy spat, "This time it's permanent. It's not like I'm going back at the last minute. I definitely don't want to work with them again. They really have been arseholes. After 11 years I think I deserve a better crack at the whip than I did get."

Read between the lines and it's apparent that Iommi, and to a lesser extent Geezer, are the Sabbath members with whom Ozzy was angriest. After a cooling-off period, he would later go on the record, saying, "Billy Ward is like my brother, I'll never say a bad word about Billy Ward," and even at the time he was even charitable about his replacement, Dio: "Ronnie [is] a nice guy and he's got a great voice, but if they do go out as Sabbath I think Ronnie Dio is going to have to have a bullet-proof vest if he ever gets up there singing 'Iron Man' and 'Paranoid'. He's really got his work cut out for him. Replacing the singer in a band is the hardest job of all."

Wise words, and ones not underestimated by the remaining members of Sabbath, who knew that filling the unreliable but enormously charismatic shoes of Ozzy would be tough. Geezer told me that remaining in the band immediately after the split was impossible: "When Ozzy left, everybody was really down. I left just after Ozzy, because I felt I couldn't really go on without him, and I had loads of things to sort out in my own life." This meant that Tony and Bill were left with the tricky task of finding a singer, a bassist and a lyricist.

The situation was bleak. In the modern age, the Ozzy versus Sabbath scenario in late 1979 – in which a unit splits in two and then regroups as two, perhaps inferior, new acts – can be seen in a number of dissolved groups. In the world of heavy metal, Judas Priest – Sabbath's offspring in so many ways – spent a grey Nineties without their singer Rob Halford, who left in 1991 to form a sequence of acts (Fight, Two and finally Halford) in an attempt to find his own sound, before rejoining in 2005 for a comeback album and tour that really should have taken place three or four years earlier. In the interim, Priest recorded a live and studio album with Tim 'Ripper' Owens, a decent singer who couldn't, however, follow Halford. The same happened to Iron Maiden, who replaced their singer Bruce Dickinson with Blaze Bayley for some unspectacular albums – again, before a comeback. All this is true too of the Brazilian thrash metal band Sepultura, whose singer Max Cavalera left after a monumental argument with his bandmates to form Soulfly: neither act is now as good as Sepultura was in the Eighties and early Nineties.

In these situations, no one wins. And the numbers don't usually add up either: should an integral player take the more creatively satisfying route, commercial success is not guaranteed to follow. An example is Deep Purple guitarist Ritchie Blackmore, who left Purple twice – the second time, permanently – to form a Renaissance music outfit called Blackmore's Night, which makes relatively little money in comparison with the megabucks of his old band. It's tough work, as he told me in 2003: "It's difficult to perform this kind of music. People don't understand why a rock performer would want to play to 500 or 1,000 people in a castle when I should be in a rock band playing to 50,000. We've spoken about doing the festival circuit but again, there are a lot of closed doors there and a lot of political stuff with the folkies . . . over here they only really know about rock and jazz and blues, so to find the music you have to go to the back of the record store to the part marked 'throwaway items'!"

Despite all this, the legacy of the 1970s Black Sabbath is supremely powerful, at least if the albums post-*Technical Ecstasy* are ignored. The bands who have covered songs from this era have often had their own identities subsumed as a reault, so powerful are those selfsame songs. As Bill Gould, bass player with Faith No More – who enjoyed massive acclaim for their 1989 cover of 'War Pigs' – explained to me: "At the time we were doing 'War Pigs' and touring with Metallica, and we felt like we were being packaged into something we weren't . . . It was so surreal. You look at it and you think, who the fuck knows why things go as they go?" Strangely enough, recent music history has seen just one departed singer reap the glory that his old band could not. Quite against all the odds, that singer would be Ozzy Osbourne.

PART TWO

Snowblind And Surrounded:
1979–1992

CHAPTER ELEVEN

1979–1980

IN the Sabbath camp, everything was a blur of energetic reorganisation. Tony Iommi regretted Ozzy's departure but was determined to press ahead with the band, seeing no reason why he should call it a day simply because of the falling-out. As we will see, this stubbornness would reach its logical conclusion after a few more years . . .

Of Ozzy, Iommi mused: "I don't think we could have helped him at all, at that time. It had come to an end. He was totally out of control. We weren't that much better, but at least we were still in control. We were all coked out and were doing this and that."

The next album, *Heaven And Hell*, was still on the agenda, as it had been for so long – over a period in which none of the band members could co-operate long enough to write any material. As the guitarist added: "It just kept going on and it got longer and longer between writing sessions; nothing was happening. We went to Los Angeles and we were all living in a house together. I was the only one who used to go to the record company. They were saying, 'We haven't heard any tracks yet. When can we hear them?' I told them, 'They're not quite ready yet . . .' The truth was that we didn't have anything. I was giving them a load of crap. It was very difficult, as I was the only one who would even face the record company. I finally told them, 'We've been here for months and nothing is happening. We're spending money and we're not doing anything.'"

Something had to give for the good of the whole band, and he concluded: "It would have gotten to a stage where we would have broken up and we would have all went our separate ways if we had not told Ozzy at that time."

In the meantime, Ozzy himself was hard at work trying to recruit a new band. He had toyed briefly with the idea of calling the new outfit Son Of Sabbath, but soon realised that this would be inadvisable: "It's not definite that we'll call it Son of Sabbath yet. I might get some of those lunatic Son of Sam people in New York chasing me up. 'Rock Star Gets Shot' . . . It's still copping out on the Sabbath name really though, isn't it. And Sabbath's dead now as far as I'm concerned. Someone suggested the name. I might just call it 'Ozzy'."

That said, he still planned to play some old Sabbath tunes as part of his set ("If I went up there without playing 'Iron Man' they'd go nuts"), but insisted that the point of the solo exercise was to return to the older, more satisfying sound: "It's going to be basically high-energy stuff like the early Sabbath. Hard riffs, which is what it's about."

Ozzy had been working with guitarist Gary Moore, who had recently been a member of the Irish rock band Thin Lizzy, although the partnership was not destined to last. "He's a brilliant guitar player," Ozzy gushed, truthfully. "He was too good for Lizzy – too good for me, actually. To do an album with him would be my privilege, but he's got his own career to worry about. We've just been doing some songs together . . . There's been about two or three hundred people auditioning and I've been gradually reducing it – like 10 drummers, 10 bass guitars. I still think Tony Iommi is one of the greatest guitarists on all the earth, and to find somebody to replace him behind me is going to be very difficult."

He also explained that his new band would be made up of the next generation of rockers: even at the age of 31, Ozzy was demoting himself to the veteran league of musicians. "They're all young guys," he said. "I don't want any old farts! It's bad enough that I have to dust the cobwebs off my tonsils every time I go onstage. It'll give me some new energy. I'm going to have to have rockets fitted to my feet to jump around onstage! Only thing is, I keep coming across guys who are so in awe of seeing me because they've all been Sabbath fanatics, like this drummer who calls himself Loud Lou. He was like, oh my God, Ozzy Osbourne! Once they find out I don't have bat's wings, it's all right."

In late 1979 Ozzy offered the job of guitarist in his as-yet-untitled band to Randy Rhoads, a 24-year-old virtuoso from the glam-metal band Quiet Riot, whose skills as a lead guitarist were almost unparalleled at the time. Together with Eddie Van Halen (in the shadow of whose band Quiet Riot had laboured for some time, finding it impossible to crack the LA glam scene) and the young Yngwie J. Malmsteen, Rhoads pioneered the 'shredding' guitar scene with lead runs of incredible technical dexterity. While players who based their styles on the blues-rock of the Sixties like Ritchie Blackmore, Jimmy Page and to a certain extent Tony Iommi had paved the way for fast lead playing in the Seventies, it was players like Rhoads who brought a speed and finesse to guitar heroics that was entirely modern – and in turn they helped 'older' rockers such as Ozzy update their sound for the Eighties. His audition with Ozzy has become the stuff of urban legend: the young prodigy simply arrived with a Gibson Les Paul and a Fender amp, tuned up, played some riffs for five minutes and was told that he'd got the job. Ozzy has always claimed since then to have a 'feel' for suitable guitarists – a claim borne out here and later on.

As he recalled: "I'd gone to Los Angeles and auditioned so many Tony Iommi lookalikes, it was untrue . . . he was only tuning his guitar when I said, 'You've got the gig.' Phenomenal. His presence! I don't give a fuck about . . . I have a feeling about people. You could be the greatest player in the world, but if you haven't got the feeling that I want to get, I don't go for it."

Meanwhile, Black Sabbath had a new recruit of their own.

Ronnie James Dio was a man with a distinguished pedigree. In his thirties at the time of his negotiations with Sabbath (there has been a career-long dispute over his age, with observers variously concluding that he was born in 1942 or 1949), the Italo-American New York resident had brought his phenomenal tenor vocals to a series of distinguished rock acts for over a decade, although his roots – like those of the other members of Sabbath – lay in Fifties rock'n'roll and rockabilly. He had begun his career as a singer and multi-instrumentalist in 1958[*] with The Vegas Kings, before heading up Ronnie & The Rumblers and Ronnie & The Red Caps, but his first serious success came with Ronnie Dio & The Prophets and then the Electric Elves, whose keyboard player was future Mötley Crüe manager Doug Thaler.

After founding Elf – perhaps named after Dio's diminutive, slightly pixie-like frame – and scoring support slots with Deep Purple, Ronnie's vocal approach was noted by Purple guitarist Ritchie Blackmore, who duly asked him to join Rainbow, the band founded by Blackmore on his first departure from Deep Purple in 1975. Hitting on a blend of progressive rock with metal touches and centring on Blackmore's guitar pyrotechnics and Dio's spiralling vocals, the band – who also included bassist Craig Gruber, drummer Gary Driscoll, and keyboardist Mickey Lee Soule – released the *Ritchie Blackmore's Rainbow* LP in '75 and enjoyed a hit with their 'Man On The Silver Mountain' single.

The band – named after the infamous Rainbow Bar And Grill club in Hollywood, a hangout for rock stars and their entourages – established a heavy metal association with then intriguing, now hackneyed sword-and-sorcery themes that sold hugely in the mid-to-late Seventies which

[*] Which suggests he was born before 1949!

became outmoded by the end of the decade with the arrival of punk, NWOBHM and thrash metal. Still, for a couple of years Rainbow were the rock band *du jour*, and it's little wonder that Dio caught Iommi's eye – especially as Blackmore, always unpredictable, fired all of the band after two more albums. Dio was the last to go but fans were not surprised by the news that this energetic, always outspoken man landed the high-profile post-Ozzy Sabbath slot so soon.

And yet there was a certain incongruity about it all. Black Sabbath had made their name on the raw, unsophisticated music of their first four albums, with Ozzy's trenchant, untrained bark an integral part of their appeal. Dio – who had forged an early Deep Purple association by singing on bassist Roger Glover's *Butterfly Ball* side project in 1974 – possessed an exquisitely honed voice in a completely different range to Ozzy's. What's more, his elaborate vocal style was a planet away from the relatively simple enunciation of his predecessor, and the castles, damsels and dragons who populated his lyrics were in stark contrast to anything Sabbath had attempted before, cod-Satanism notwithstanding.

It remained to be seen whether Dio's arrival into the fold would solve the many problems Sabbath were facing: a needless over-sophistication and dilution of their sound; a divided fanbase; and an uncertain future with Don Arden and his team, whose Jet label was considering releasing Ozzy's first solo LP. All this uncertainty filtered down to the band itself, and the first casualty was Geezer Butler, who couldn't see Sabbath functioning without Ozzy. Recording sessions for *Heaven And Hell* commenced at Criteria Studios in Miami in September 1979, but without Butler, who had left the band. Later recordings took place at Studio Ferber in Paris.

This second splintering of the original line-up might have left a lesser band floundering: however, Iommi exerted an iron will and merely asked Geoff Nicholls, who played in the band Quartz, to step in on bass. Nicholls duly joined the band as a session man, but the new arrangement didn't last long. Geezer apparently regained his senses and returned a few days later. As he told me, two decades after the fact: "Ronnie brought a lot to the band at a time when we needed it. He gave the band a whole lease of life. He gave everybody inspiration!" Of his return to Sabbath, he recalled: "Tony said, 'You've gotta come back and hear the stuff that we're doing,' so I came back and they'd just finished off the song 'Heaven And Hell', which I'd just started with them when I left. I heard it and I said, 'This is brilliant!'" Nicholls was shifted to keyboards and the new, expanded band got down to business.

Iommi looked back on the making of *Heaven And Hell* with a similarly rosy view, recalling to *Classic Rock Revisited*: "I loved that album. It was real challenge for us. We were riding high with Sabbath. We were doing big shows, but then we cut it off and brought somebody else in. It was a risk. It was something we wanted to do. We wanted to make it work with Ronnie James Dio. He was a different voice and he made me write differently. I think it really worked . . . I loved making that album, really. Ronnie was great. He came in really as a professional. We were able to sit down and write the album without any problems . . . he was doing whatever we told him, basically because he wanted the gig. The next album . . . was a little different."

The best people came on board for the new album. The well-known studio hand John 'Dawk' Stilwell, who knew Dio from the Ronnie Dio & The Prophets days, engineered on *Heaven And Hell* and recalled that Iommi was looking for new sounds with the next album. As he recalled, there were some technical problems to solve before any music could be laid down, specifically a broken amp: "The amplifier in question was a new 1959 model 100-watt Marshall amplifier whose tubes were destroyed when it was shipped from England . . . Iommi was unsatisfied with the stock Marshall sound. He was looking for more crunch and distortion."[*]

Additionally, Sabbath's choice of producer was Martin Birch, who had honed his craft by engineering on early Fleetwood Mac and Faces albums. Crucially for Sabbath, Birch had also produced no fewer than five Deep Purple LPs: their groundbreaking *Deep Purple In Rock* (1970), *Stormbringer* ('74), *Come Taste The Band* ('75), *Made In Europe* ('76) and *Last Concert in Japan* ('78). The producer, who would go on to find career-best success with Iron Maiden, had built a reputation for enabling extreme personalities to work together creatively, and the rounded, organic sound for which he was famous put him towards the top of a short list of candidates for the producer's role.

The extra 'crunch and distortion' that Stilwell mentions is in evidence from the first few seconds of *Heaven And Hell*. The LP begins with 'Neon Knights', whose opening – a simple and effective one-chord scrub – is a promising sign that Iommi was back on songwriting form. When Dio's vocals begin, they are a joy – a never overstated but soaring journey through reasonably thrilling lyrics of "Circles and rings, dragons and kings /

---

[*] Stilwell later recruited a young Italo-American bass player named Joey De Maio to work on the pyrotechnics of the *Heaven And Hell* tour: De Maio would later find fame with his band Manowar, who took the Viking-and-loincloth approach to its logical, and utterly ridiculous, conclusion.

Weaving a charm and a spell". Iommi carves out a clean but weighty solo as the song, never overly heavy but sufficiently so to make it listenable for the fans, sprints to a close.

'Children Of The Sea', the first song on which Iommi and Dio had jammed together, is an epic anthem which benefits from Birch's full, modern production. Its intro, a flurry of plucked acoustic guitars, is full of homages – intentional or otherwise – to Led Zeppelin and Rainbow in particular while Ronnie's warbled "In the misty morning, on the edge of time / We've lost the rising sun" could have been lifted wholesale from an unselfconsciously indulgent project such as *The Butterfly Ball*. The song's midsection, a sequence of harmony and single-guitar solos, is drenched in the voices of male and female choirs, marking the ambition of the Iommi/Dio partnership as well as the resources of the ever-inventive Birch.

'Lady Evil' is less impressive, with its juvenile chorus of "Lady Evil, evil / She's a magical mystical woman" providing neither the old-school satanic chills of Sabbath's pre-1976 albums nor the sophistication which latter-day fans had come to expect. There's a riff going on in the background, but it's smooth and polished rather than threatening, and the acres of wah-wah-laden soloing from Iommi are too long and involved to retain much interest.

The seven minutes of 'Heaven And Hell' itself are much better, with the song introduced by a unison riff that recalls the glory days of 'Iron Man'. The verse, which strips down to Geezer's bass and Ward's drums, is all Ronnie's territory, as he pontificates: "Sing me a song, you're a singer / Do me a wrong, you're a bringer of evil". Iommi brings some new sounds to the rock palette, with drones, swells and divebombs laced in reverb by Birch all bringing him up to date. There's a choir in there too, with the pompous conceit fully developed. A temp acceleration at four minutes allows Geezer to stretch out for the first time. Dio yelps "Fool fool, you got to bleed for the dancer / Fool fool, look for the answer" and the song decays, with a minute of mediaeval-sounding classical guitar winding things down. What does it all mean? Who knows?

'Wishing Well' was too politely cheesy for most people, not just because of Ronnie's lyrics ("Throw me a penny and I'll make you a dream"), but because it sounded like an AOR band – Boston or Journey – trying to play fast and heavy. In fairness to Birch and the band, the guitar sound is precise and crisp – but the chirpy, radio-friendly riffs and backing vocals (the band intone "Dreamer" repeatedly in the background) is just, well, *nice*. It's not one of Sabbath's finest moments.

'Die Young', loaded with Nicholls' soupy synth sound, appears to be mostly an excuse for Ronnie to shout "Die young!" over never-ending guitar solos. However, in arranging terms the song does give Iommi the chance to experiment with an ambient intro and a complex riff-salad mid-section and doesn't outstay its welcome. Unfortunately, things don't improve much with 'Walk Away', a lightweight hairspray anthem which, released five years later, might have appeared on MTV with a glossy performance video. As Ronnie warns of a manipulating woman who offers love as "a way to have a child", the band churn out a slick and utterly un-heavy mass of thin riffs. Even Iommi isn't on scintillating form with his solos, the main selling point of the album so far.

'Lonely Is The Word' is a return to form for the close of the album, with a slow, menacing riff underpinning a tale of on-the-road loneliness. "It's a long way to nowhere and I'm leaving very soon / On the way we pass so close to the back side of the moon" beckons Dio, miraculously avoiding a slip into fantasy cliché and allowing Iommi and Nicholls to fill long instrumental sections with strings and echo-laden soloing. It's a mellow way to wind down – almost like 'Solitude' and 'Laguna Sunrise' – and serves a similar purpose to those songs: to present a different side to the band.

Released on April 26, 1980, *Heaven And Hell* did much to restore Sabbath's sagging reputation and reassure the fanbase that remained that the spark still burned within them after the disappointment of the last few albums. Although the overall texture of the LP was polished and meek rather than aggressive and atmospheric, the musical fashions of the day were such that it found a home among millions of record buyers. After all, 1980 was the dawn of a new era in music, with hi-fi technology finally doing justice to the studio techniques used by Martin Birch and his colleagues, and the rise of synthesis and the nascent digital recording industry finding a foothold thanks to the clean, pure sounds that they allowed musicians to make and record. All this made the LP's climb to number nine, followed by a 22-week residency in the charts, explicable, even if it isn't one of Sabbath's best albums.

A vast tour followed the album's release, taking in Germany and Austria before UK dates supported by Angel Witch – one of the stars of the New Wave Of British Heavy Metal (NWOBHM) movement – and Girlschool, the all-female biker-metal group. Shows in London (the Hammersmith Odeon, which was emerging as a major hard rock and metal venue), Glasgow, Edinburgh, Newcastle, Deeside, Manchester, Birmingham and Leicester were followed by more German gigs and then an extensive US tour.

Although the fans welcomed the Dio-led line-up, perhaps understanding that the infusion of blood from the Deep Purple camp (producer Martin Birch included) was a necessary boost for this now-classic British rock band, yet again all was not well behind the scenes. Geezer Butler had overcome his temporary bout of insecurity the previous year, and Iommi was his usual rock-solid self – but Bill Ward, whose parents had both died in recent months, was struggling. Booze had become more than a crutch for him by this stage and the thought of the huge tour ahead was more than he could face.

July 1980 was the last straw for Bill. Jaded, exhausted by travel and the constant damage which alcohol was doing to his brain and body, Ward dragged himself through dates in Dallas, LA, San Antonio, Houston, Spokane, Seattle and Ventura supported by Alice Cooper, Molly Hatchet, Riot and others. There was some good news, however: the second Day On The Green festival at Oakland Stadium, California, was a triumph: Sabbath played alongside Cheap Trick, Molly Hatchet and others beneath the huge-selling AOR act Journey. Moreover, the 'Neon Knights' single hit number 22 that month and NEMS issued a live album from 1975 entitled *Live At Last*, a memento for the fans which kept the profile of the band deservedly high.

It's likely that Ward announced his intention to quit Sabbath after an August 4 show at the Henry Levitt Arena in Wichita, Kansas, but was persuaded to play a few more weeks of the tour so that a replacement could be rehearsed up. However, the defining moment came on August 21, when he left the tour just before a trip to Hawaii. The gig, at the McNichols Sports Arena in Denver, Colorado, was cancelled, with support act Blue Oyster Cult playing an extended set to pacify the fans.

As Ward later recalled, "Speaking for myself, I crossed the line when we were trying to do what became *Heaven And Hell*. I could not curtail my drinking and using at that point. It was just ridiculous at that time. I have no knowledge of recording that album. I was completely and totally gone during that album. I have no memory of making the record. I listen to it and I know it is me drumming but I can't remember anything . . . The only thing I can remember was that Tony would just nod at me. He was really gentle during that album. He would try to get me to where I was going. That is all I remember."

He realises now what was causing him to seek such deep refuge in booze: "It was not a good time at all. I think what enhanced the blackouts during that time was the fact that my mother passed away. Also, Ozzy was not there. I was in grief over Ozzy even though I didn't realise that I was missing him. He was my number one friend. Oz and me were close like brothers. We were broke out of the same mould."

Although many observers believed that his departure from Sabbath on the 1980 summer tour was because he'd realised that it was time to clean up his act, the opposite seems to be the case. As he explained: "I came off the road from the *Heaven And Hell* tour because my addictions were so strong at the time that the most important thing to me was getting high. It had reached such a point that I was just out of it all the time. I didn't know what was going on. I was completely fucked up, period. Booze became the most important thing in my life. It was more important than my children, my wife and even myself. I went on a downward spiral in 1980."

Bill was evidently unable to confine his alcohol intake to a binge from time to time, like most people. He explained: "There's such a thing as heavy drinkers, you know: people who drink heavily but don't become alcoholics. They just drink heavily. It almost gives the impression that they're alcoholics. An alcoholic, basically, is going to need to drink all the time, and there's two types. What we call a periodic alcoholic – who doesn't drink for a while but then drinks continually, hour after hour. And then there's the daily alcoholic, who drinks every single day. An alcoholic will put alcohol before anything and anybody, whereas a heavy drinker will turn around and say, you know what? Fuck this, I'm not gonna drink for another couple of weeks. He or she makes that decision: an alcoholic can't make that decision."

He added: "My addiction had reached the point where all addictions go to eventually. It had reached the point where it had become more important than anything else in my life. The addiction had become more important than me, more important than my wife at the time, more important than my children, more important than my responsibilities, more important than Black Sabbath, more important than anything. The addiction was king . . . What happened was that I went back to southern California with my wife, where I stayed in bed for nearly a year. All I did was drink and use and sleep. I stayed in bed for a year directly from *Heaven And Hell*. I very rarely socialised. I pulled the shades down and . . . That was it. I was dealing with grief. I was dealing with all kind of problems. I didn't know at the time, but today I can look back and go, 'Yes, I was dealing with this and that . . .' But I didn't do that at the time. I didn't realise that I was in the grip of a progressive illness that was going to kill me. I had no idea of what was ahead because it got definitely worse from that point. That was bad enough but it got a lot worse than that."

Ward's replacement was ex-Axis drummer Vinny Appice (pronounced 'a pea see'), whose superior technical skills would bring him much fame and fortune in his later career. Still a relative unknown at the time of his recruitment into Black Sabbath, Appice (whose older brother Carmine is also a well-known rock drummer, having played with Vanilla Fudge and Beck, Bogert & Appice) stepped up for the remaining four months of the 1980 tour with a panache that – sadly – the ailing Ward had been unable to deliver for some time.

Vinny recalled that even at an early meeting with Bill, he had sensed that alcohol and Ward did not make good bedfellows: "I met Bill at the Rainbow in the Eighties – when he was drinking – and I ran out the back door, because when I went over to introduce myself he was all [puts on drunken growl] 'Vinny! Hey!' and he put his arms round me. He was really drunk, and not really a *good* drunk, so I was like, OK, time to get out of here . . . exit stage left!"

How did his recruitment into Sabbath actually take place? "It's a funny story," he recalls, "because before they called me, I'd had a call from Sharon Arden a while before, saying that Ozzy was putting a new band together and would I like to fly out? They'd heard me play with Rick Derringer and Axis – I'd done three albums with Rick by then, and the Axis album had really cool drums on there, so they knew I was capable of playing with Ozzy. I was 21 years old, and I was wow, Ozzy!"

Appice laughs at how naïve he was back then: "But I'd never been to Europe before, and I asked my brother Carmine, isn't Ozzy crazy? Carmine had hung out with Ozzy years before and said, yeah, he's crazy. He's really wild. So I actually turned it down. I was a kid, I didn't know. I just thought, he's a madman, he's crazy, I've never been to England, where's that?

"So I turned down that gig and then, about three months later, I was on my way back from a Ludwig drum convention in Chicago with Carmine. My wife Justine told me that the road manager from Black Sabbath had called and wanted me to go and meet with them at their hotel. So I met Paul Clarke, who was the tour manager at the time, and then Tony came in. He'd heard the Axis album and really liked it, and wanted to know if I wanted to audition with them the next day at SIR Studios on Sunset Boulevard in Hollywood. So I said yeah, went down and played and everything went well. They told me Bill was having problems and had left."

Did Iommi et al. know that Appice had been approached by the Osbourne camp not long before? "No, I don't think they knew I'd been asked to join Ozzy's band before that . . . They were happy with my audition and they went to the pub – then came back and said, 'OK, you're gonna do it: you're in the band!' "

No sooner was the new drummer in place than his work was cut out for him: "So now I gotta learn all these songs, and I've only got four days of rehearsals before a big show at the stadium in Hawaii. For the rehearsal on the first day, Geoff Nicholls and Ronnie helped me through the songs, while Tony and Geezer and some of the crew went over to the pub, you know? The same thing happened the next day – everybody was late . . . it was like, let's play a little bit and then let's go to the pub! But I was like, man, I've got to learn these songs! So I worked with Geoff and Ronnie a lot to learn the songs. What it came down to was that we didn't rehearse much in the four days we had."

Sabbath duly boarded a flight, ready to play a show or not, with Appice frantically trying to learn the songs: "Next thing we know we're in Hawaii – I'm constantly listening to the songs on a Walkman at the time – and we're playing this big festival – a big outdoor show of like 20,000 people. Luckily I know how to read music, and so I'd made these charts indicating 'verse, chorus, verse' and so on – with notes about 6/8 time and accents and all this stuff – for each song. That got me through half the set, until it started raining and the rain made all the ink run on my book! I couldn't read it, but we got through the show."

All seemed to have run smoothly, even if Appice only heard indirectly that the stoically uncommunicative Iommi had been uncertain how it would go: "I later heard from Ronnie that Tony was really, really nervous, because this was the first time they'd played with anybody other than Bill on drums. Tony and Geezer are very . . . to themselves, you know? When they don't know somebody they're very standoffish. But they did come up and say 'Very good, very good,' you know. That was a big thing for them!"

In September Sabbath pushed through the East Coast states, down through Miami and into the American heartlands with their new line-up delivering on all cylinders. Appice slowly settled in, although he never knew when Ward might return to the band and his job would be done: "We continued the tour and it all worked out well. I thought Bill might come back, but the band got along good and the tour went on and on. For a couple of months they thought he might come back, but after that it was obvious that he wasn't going to. Then the tour ended and we were like OK, let's take two months off and go do another record. I just hung out. Actually maybe it was more like a month. We needed a rest, and they needed it even more than me because I hadn't been on the whole tour."

But competition from an unexpected source came on September 20, when Ozzy Osbourne delivered his first solo album, *Blizzard Of Ozz*, credited to 'Ozzy Osbourne's Blizzard Of Ozz' and featuring Randy Rhoads, bassist Bob Daisley and drummer Lee Kerslake. The Jet label had signed him up for a series of solo albums and their press release stated, "Heavy metal fans the world over waited with baited breath for news of their hero, Ozzy Osbourne, ever since his departure from Black Sabbath", as well as revealing details of the Blizzard Of Ozz line-up. "The worst thing was auditioning people. I'd never done it before; I mean, how do you tell a bloke he can't play?" said Ozzy. "Britain was still into punk and I thought that I wouldn't find the right musicians here . . . I'd given up hope of finding anyone when someone suggested Randy to me. He's from LA and played with a band called Quiet Riot. He was a guitar teacher at a local college when I asked him to join the band." As for Kerslake, a veteran of eight years with progressive rockers Uriah Heep, "I'd reached the point when I was going to give up looking and just use session drummers. Lee was going to be positively the last audition."

The album was a moderate success on first release, reaching number seven in the UK and remaining on the chart for eight weeks, but as Ozzy's legend grew it sold steadily. And with good reason: it's a well-crafted LP, even if the production was a little ropey (a remastered CD version was issued in 1995, and a series of Ozzy albums reappeared in 2002) and Ozzy's voice, as always, was straining at times. The first two songs, 'I Don't Know' and 'Crazy Train', are workouts for Rhoads' phenomenal rhythm guitar technique, with the latter a lifetime classic (it was even featured in a 1999 Mitsubishi car commercial). 'Goodbye To Friends', meanwhile, is a ballad of sorts, although its sparse sound and obviously Beatles-influenced melody makes it less durable than the other tunes. 'Dee' is a solo guitar piece composed by Rhoads as a tribute to his mother, showcasing his abilities as an acoustic player as well as a remarkable electric musician.

'Suicide Solution' is an enduring song thanks solely to the cloud of controversy that sprang up about it four years later when certain institutions with nothing better to do with their time interpreted it as advocating suicide. The lines "Wine is fine, but whiskey's quicker / Suicide is slow with liquor / Take a bottle, drown your sorrows / Then it floods away tomorrows" should have made it clear that it was a warning against booze, not a recommendation to kill yourself. Ozzy protested that it was written in the wake of a contemporary's passing: "If these people were to actually read the lyrics to 'Suicide Solution' they would realise it couldn't be further away if it tried," he said. "It was written about [the late AC/DC singer] Bon Scott . . . who drank himself to death. The word 'solution' doesn't mean 'way out', it's 'solution' meaning 'liquid', alcohol. 'Wine is fine but whisky's quicker, suicide is slow with liquor' – and I've lived that life for years, and I know what I'm talking about! Most alcoholics at the end of the day commit suicide because they can't find a way out . . ."

'These people' in the above statement were the representatives of an American family who were suing Ozzy after their teenage son, identified as John M, killed himself, claiming that the song influenced the boy's decision. The case rumbled on for years before finally being dismissed out of court in 1987, but the intervening years were tough for the singer despite his many explanations. As he told one reporter, quite reasonably, "First of all I feel very, very sorry for the boy's death. It was never my intention to write a song to cause anyone harm. But I can't really feel guilty about anything because it's *absurd* – it's like you leaving me now, getting in your car, getting killed in a car wreck and blaming me because you came and visited me to do an interview . . ." He also questioned the reasoning behind the legal action, explaining: "I don't know about you, but if I went home tonight and found my kid lying face down in the bath with a suicide note saying 'Goodbye Dad, I'm off' and a New Kids On The Block album was playing on his stereo, the last thing on my mind would be suing the group – I'd be grief-stricken."

'Mr Crowley' was similarly worrisome for the moral majority, being as it was a song about the eccentric English Satanist Aleister Crowley, whose writings had been the focus of interest for rockers, most notably Led Zeppelin's Jimmy Page who bought Crowley's house on the shore of Loch Ness. In today's liberal environment, 'No Bone Movies' is practically a comedy song, although the anguish with which Ozzy wails its anti-pornography sentiments in lines like "Inspiration that's blue and uncut / Can't kick the habit, obsession of smut / Voyeur straining, in love with his hand / A poison passion, a pulsating gland" seems genuine. The poetry and acoustic guitar of 'Revelation (Mother Earth)' makes it worth visiting: Ozzy sings "Heaven is for heroes / And hell is full of fools" with pathos, while the anger of "Broken chains have fallen all around, yeah / Point my finger at the fools/ Broken chains and broken rules" in 'Steal Away The Night' could well have been directed at Ozzy's former band.

With reviewers mostly positive about *Blizzard Of Ozz* (Geoff Barton at *Sounds* wrote, "Sabs-like to be sure, but faster more furious and updated for the discerning 1980 cranium cracker"), it only remained for Ozzy to see if he could cut it as a live solo act – and, after a couple of shows with the name Law, he embarked on a tour under the Blizzard banner. Both he and Sharon were nervous about how many people would come to his first real show, in Glasgow, but in fact the gig was a great success, with the singer breaking down in tears at one point as he realised that he could in fact make it on his own. Later on he also received the praise of his peers, with Motörhead frontman Lemmy telling me: "I thought Ozzy's first solo album was better than all of Black Sabbath's albums put together."

As both Ozzy and Sabbath toured, it didn't take long for critics and gig-goers to begin to compare and contrast their fortunes and merits and something of a rivalry developed. Stories of crowds drowning out Ronnie James Dio with calls of 'Ozzy! Ozzy!' at Sabbath gigs were rife, and the situation wasn't helped by the occasional barb that the two acts fired at each other via the press, who naturally lapped it all up.

And yet any competition was meaningless. Although Ozzy's pulling power as a live attraction was yet to be tested fully, the two acts were basically playing to the same crowds. Sabbath were still testing the water with a new singer – as Iommi said, "Ozzy had been with us many years. We had a big challenge going out on tour with a new singer. We didn't know if he was going to be accepted by the Sabbath audience" – and, other than the larger venues which Sabbath were booked into, the tours were similar in location, intention and execution.

Both acts, for instance, were immediately welcomed onto the international festival circuit. As Ozzy said, any professional entertainer does his best for the audience irrespective of venue: "If there's one person in the fucking audience that's not getting into it, I will do the whole fucking show for that fucking wanker, because I'm determined that everyone has a good time. But sometimes it doesn't work and there was a time when I'd go tell Tony, 'Tony, get these fuckers out of here, because if they don't like this, they're dead!' It pissed me off, man! It's like you want to stop the show and just go, 'Obviously you're not here to have a good time, so just fuck off.' But I'm not fucking bitter . . . The thing is sometimes I've been out there and it's like, 'Ah, this is fucking great,' and you get offstage and people are asking if you're OK and you're like, 'What?' And then I'll think, 'This is fucking shit,' and people go crazy. There's no telling how you're going to go down."

And so the tours rolled on. Sabbath, with Appice anchoring them, travelled through Chicago, Pittsburgh, Toledo, Detroit, Columbus and Indianapolis in October, with a slight setback occurring in Milwaukee when Geezer Butler was hit in the face onstage by a flying bottle. The aggression of the crowd then accelerated when a member of the band's crew took the microphone and began insulting them, and a minor riot ensued. As the bassist recalled later, "I think I was doing the intro to 'N.I.B.' and I heard something hit a cymbal. Then I was hit in the head. One minute I'm playing 'N.I.B.', the next I'm covered in blood! I backed out and was taken offstage. Unfortunately, this happened while the lights were down so everyone thought we walked off! Our fucking idiot road manager came out and asked the audience if they thought it was 1776 again. Just what you want to say to an American crowd . . . We hated him anyhow because he was a spy for the management that we were going to fire. He continued to say things until the crowd went absolutely nuts. By this time I'm in the hospital and kids in Sabbath shirts started arriving covered in blood. We're all lying there, side by side, as if it was a battle-field. Thankfully, it only made the local news."

Butler recovered in time for the remaining US dates – covering the whole of October and into November 1980 – before Sabbath's first Japanese tour. Four dates in Tokyo, commencing on 16 November, were followed up by shows in Kyoto and Osaka: one show was cancelled halfway through after Iommi, who had escaped most touring mishaps so far, collapsed with food poisoning. "It was something I ate – I just passed out," he remembered. "I remember the needle that went in my arm!"

The entourage then flew on to Australia for dates supported by local rockers Rose Tattoo. Geezer suffered an infected finger for one or more of the Sydney shows, and played in some pain for some of the scheduled dates: other gigs were cancelled as a result. The Sydney shows, captured for posterity on a bootleg LP, were notable for some onstage histrionics by Ronnie James Dio, who asked the audience at one stage to point to an onstage cross in honour of Reverend Fred Nile, the leader of a religious group known as the Festival of Light and later a politician who campaigned against heavy metal music for its supposedly evil qualities, boosting Sabbath's album and ticket sales nicely as a result.

In December, after a mere couple of weeks off, Sabbath – Dio, Iommi, Butler and Appice – retired to Berkshire for the recording of a song for the upcoming *Heavy Metal* movie, specifically to Startling Studios in Tittenhurst Park near Ascot. The studio had been used by many stars of the day, notably its former owner John Lennon, who had recorded his *Imagine* LP there, and subsequently sold the property to Ringo Starr.* The song that Sabbath came up with was called 'The Mob Rules', and it

---

* By sad coincidence, Lennon was murdered just a few days before the band arrived at the studio.

seemed as though more highly successful sessions would follow. After all, Sabbath had always delivered the goods before . . .

But this was an unusual period for British music, and specifically heavy metal. By the end of 1980, the metal-buying public had turned their attention to a new sound – one that threatened to make the mighty Sabbath seem, well, outdated.

CHAPTER TWELVE

1980–1981

BLACK Sabbath, together with Led Zeppelin and Deep Purple, formed the unholy trinity of British hard rock and heavy metal in the early to mid-Seventies. Few music fans doubted the totality of their dominance, although many would also point to the strengths of Rainbow, Motörhead, Uriah Heep, Bad Company, Nazareth, Judas Priest and Thin Lizzy, who formed a strong B-league beneath the three behemoths. Although British music had been infiltrated in the late Seventies by punk and the very early electro scene, it seemed that the big hitters would always be loud, enigmatic and prone to singing about dragons and warlocks.

All this changed in early 1979. *Sounds* magazine, then edited by Alan Lewis and including among its staff the reporter Geoff Barton, identified a new strand of music emerging from the pub and club circuit, much of it focused in London, Newcastle and the Midlands. A series of bands, of which the most notable in '79 was the London quintet Iron Maiden, had taken the heavy metal template established by Sabbath and toughened it up, injecting a dose of punkish attitude into the riffs and the lyrics and playing it faster and harder than their predecessors. Although the venues were small and the bands, if they were signed at all, were releasing their music on small labels with minimal budgets, it was apparent to Lewis and Barton that a label needed to be created for the phenomenon and so Lewis came up with the New Wave Of British Heavy Metal, or the near-unpronounceable NWOBHM.

Although neither journalist expected the term to attain much significance, once the bands concerned started to gain some commercial status it soon became the genre tag *du jour* and has since become deeply entrenched in rock music lore. Fans loved the new bands, who successfully fused the snotty attitude of punk with the musical virtuosity of classic metal (although the latter was, as many of the bands cheerfully admitted, in short supply in the early days) and came up with a new and vitriolic template that made the old guard appear somewhat settled into their comfortable and unchallenging routine.

Several factors helped bring about the success of the NWOBHM, among them the fact that Black Sabbath, Deep Purple and even the mighty Led Zeppelin were all past their peak by 1979. As we've seen, Sabbath's classic line-up had fragmented, with Ozzy gone, Geezer in and out and Ward incapacitated. Purple had split in 1976 and would not regroup until 1984. Zeppelin, meanwhile, had been hit by internal and external upsets that took the wind out of their sails and they would part ways permanently in December 1980, three months after the tragic death of drummer John Bonham. With the three rock behemoths apparently falling apart, or at least failing to match up to earlier glories, the public's unsated desire for heavy music meant that more bands were needed, giving a boost to the hundreds of acts of varying quality which – then as now – filled the clubs.

Secondly, the musicians who formed the vanguard of the NWOBHM had grown up in one of the most fertile eras of British music – the late Sixties and the whole of the Seventies. Surrounded by epoch-shaping sounds, it's little wonder that so many grew up wanting to emulate their heroes and form bands. And the very diversity of the music scene in those years fuelled the fire, too: a perfect example is Iron Maiden's bassist, founder and principal songwriter Steve Harris, whose formative years were spent listening to a combination of progressive rock, from Yes, Uriah Heep and Genesis, and hard rock/heavy metal from Sabbath, Purple and Zeppelin. His band, who exploded out of the NWOBHM to become the biggest-selling metal band ever (at least until the equally startling rise of Metallica), made millions on the back of the dexterous, musicianly riffs of Harris and his colleagues, a perfect blend of driving aggression and complex melodic exploration. As Harris explained: "I used to listen to early Free, early Sabbath, stuff like that. We weren't really aware of this movement that was happening until the press started getting hold of it. There were bands up North like Saxon in Yorkshire, and there was Witchfynde, as well. So, there were all these bands happening all over England during that same time and I don't think anyone was really aware of it until the press started writing about it, and that pretty much started that whole movement."

Maiden, whose line-up would not settle until their second album, *The Number Of The Beast*, released in 1982, expanded on the heaviness in the riffs played by pioneers like Tony Iommi and the pseudo-satanic lyrics of Geezer Butler. Like Sabbath and Ozzy, they experienced pressure from conservative quarters to tone down this element of their work but they refused to do so, only abandoning the devilish themes as they matured and decided the subject was a little passé.

A car accident in which Martin Birch, the producer of *Heaven And Hell*, was involved became the stuff of urban legend. The bill for the damage, incurred shortly after he produced Maiden's *Number Of The Beast* LP, came to £666. "People don't believe this, but he changed it to £667," said Steve Harris. "He's done a lot of work with Black Sabbath, and apparently, they're into that sort of thing. So, I don't know, maybe there's something to it!"

In fact, the lyrical indulgences were just one element that the NWOBHM shared with traditional heavy metal bands, as well as the sometimes ludicrous *Spinal Tap*-style posing that made metal simultaneously so reviled and enthralling. As we saw earlier, the Newcastle band Venom had evolved the faster, less complex sound of the NWOBHM to the point where the category of extreme metal had to be invented to describe it. Frontman Conrad Lant disliked the fake posturing of the NWOBHM acts as much as their predecessors: "The NWOBHM was a case of young kids trying to make their way, rather than some great mastermind telling them what to do and where to go. There were thousands of bands coming out of Newcastle – Raven, Tygers Of Pan Tang, the whole thing. But to me, it was still socks stuffed down spandex trousers – it made me cringe! We couldn't go out and play live with Saxon and Samson and the Tygers Of Pan Tang and Raven, because all these bands were nothing like us. See, I came out of the punk scene as well as the usual rock stuff like the Stones and Deep Purple."

Although Iron Maiden and their contemporaries Def Leppard and Saxon played harder and heavier than Sabbath et al., they still weren't as raw as they could have been. Lant adds: "We put the punk back into metal, which is something that Iron Maiden and so on didn't do. We put the snot and the piss and the shit back into metal, because punk was fucked – it only lasted a year. I was a huge punk fan, I loved the Pistols and Sham 69 and The Exploited. But metal had lost that edge, and heavy metal is supposed to be dirty, horrible devil's music."

Other than Maiden, perhaps the most influential NWOBHM act – albeit one that never enjoyed the commercial success they deserved – was Diamond Head, a four-piece who later inspired Metallica drummer Lars Ulrich to form a band. As singer Sean Harris told me, "We were young then, we thought we were gonna be the biggest band in the world!" – and in 1981 and 1982, it seemed as if this might come to pass, although Diamond Head's progress was hindered by personnel and record company problems for most of their career.

Harris also recalls the glory days of the NWOBHM, when a single review could make all the difference: "We had that great Geoff Barton review in *Sounds*: Fresher than a bucket of Listermint . . . More riffs on one album than on Sabbath's first five albums! That was our white album, the debut album that we made ourselves." Note the revealing Sabbath reference! He went on: "We loved punk, we thought that was the catalyst. If you could play three chords and have an attitude, that was enough. We wanted to be progressive like Purple, but we knew we couldn't be the musicians that they were. We didn't have the Sixties as a background."

Championed by Lewis and Barton at *Sounds* (who set up the long-running *Kerrang!* magazine – initially as a one-off wraparound – in June 1981 to cater for the demand for heavy music), the NWOBHM quickly became defined by a relatively short list of acts, including Angel Witch, Bitches Sin, Blitzkrieg, Budgie, Chateaux, Cloven Hoof, Demon, Fist, Gaskin, Holocaust, Jaguar, Legend, Paralex, Praying Mantis, Raven, Samson, Satan, Savage, Sweet Savage, Tank, Tygers Of Pan Tang, Vardis, Warfare, Witchfinder General and Witchfynde. These bubbled under the major league acts (Maiden, Def Leppard, Venom, Saxon) with a moderate but mostly short-lived degree of success, with a key venue for gigs the Soundhouse club nights held initially at the Prince Of Wales pub in Kingsbury, in north-west London. The Soundhouse – which was held in such affection by fans and musicians that Maiden titled their self-released *Soundhouse Tapes* EP after it – was the province of a rock DJ called Neal Kay, who promoted gigs by NWOBHM acts there. The characters who attended the club nights began to attract attention in their own right, notably Robin Yeatman, who carried a cardboad cut-out of a guitar and, under the nickname Rob Loonhouse, was often pictured careering insanely across the dance floor, frantically 'playing' his guitar and headbanging.

All this lunacy had a time-limit, of course, and the NWOBHM had run its course by 1984, simply because most of the bands involved were unable to establish long-term futures. The movement also had no chance of competing against the brand new – and fearsomely powerful – American thrash metal scene, which was heavily influenced by the NWOBHM bands (especially Venom) and returned the compliment by playing several times faster, heavier and better. Maiden and Leppard went on to arena success, and Saxon and Venom toiled for years at club and festival level with adequate returns, but almost all the rest collapsed by the end of the decade.

But the lessons of the NWOBHM were clear for all to see. Firstly, it was apparent to all, including the promoters and the money-men behind major record labels, that heavy metal still had commercial clout. Bands could, it seemed, wear leather and denim, scream about Satan and still attract paying punters in sufficient numbers to repay investment. Secondly, the success of the NWOBHM gave some legitimacy to the work of older bands such as Black Sabbath, whose music had inspired the scene – as Geezer Butler himself told *The Rocket*, "For years, we went around thinking we were shit, and wondering why we bothered. We knew our fans liked us, but everyone else . . . the press hated us, said we couldn't write, couldn't play . . . other bands hated us, everyone. It wasn't until all the 'new' metal bands like Iron Maiden and Saxon started coming through in the early Eighties that we actually heard anyone say we'd had any impact at all."

Finally, the NWOBHM acts made it clear to their predecessors that the heaviest band of the day would win the game. No longer would half-hearted riffs delivered without maximum confidence do the necessary job: bands like Black Sabbath needed to step up their game, and quickly, if they were to avoid being swept away with the other second-league acts.

In 1981, Sabbath scheduled the recording of a second LP with Ronnie James Dio, this time with Vinny Appice on drums. *The Mob Rules* was scheduled for release in the autumn, after another huge tour in the summer. It's worth noting at this point that Sabbath had settled into the routine of booking themselves into enormous tours as the years rolled by, never crossing a territory once (the lucrative USA in particular) when they could re-cross it another three times. While modern management might counsel their band that too much exposure can damage an act's long-term prospects even if it brings in revenue, the Arden team seemed to have no such qualms. The band toured, and toured, and toured again – with all the soul-destroying pressure that such a regime brings. As we've seen, such a life could be – and was – enough to crack up the most toughened road warrior.

Of the incessant touring – particularly Stateside, which led many observers to accuse Sabbath of neglecting their original fans in favour of the American dollar – Iommi once said, not unreasonably: "I'm totally aware that we must spend more time in Europe. We need to play here much more than has been the case in the past . . . But in all honesty, there was a time when nobody wanted to book Black Sabbath in Europe and that is why the band did so many tours in the States. Lately, there has been a real interest for the band here, but the problem with the States is that the market is so big that you can spend months on the road there before you enter Top 50. Personally I wouldn't mind just dropping America, but it isn't that easy."

Vinny Appice told me how quickly the band snapped back into the recording cycle after the vast *Heaven And Hell* tour. "After a month or two off, they were like, all right, we're gonna start rehearsing for a new album and we're gonna call it *The Mob Rules*. Tony and Geezer live here in California, so that's where we rehearsed it – in LA. So we started jamming in the studio – that's the way the band writes all the time, just set up the studio, Tony or Geezer will start playing, and I'll just play, and I recorded everything. I was in charge of the tapes and I still have tapes of this stuff. We'd come in the next day and listen to some of the riffs; everybody would choose the riffs and we'd start building a song on that. That's how we did it. Then we went into this studio called Can-Am in the San Fernando Valley here to record. They were gonna invest in the studio, but when we went in they didn't like it. So we moved over to the Record Plant in LA and did the rest of the album there."

In the meantime, estranged Sabbath members Ozzy Osbourne and Bill Ward weren't idle. Ozzy was recording another solo LP and Ward, despite his claim of spending a year in bed after jumping ship halfway through the *Heaven And Hell* tour, had jammed sporadically with more than a few pickup bands. One of those was an act called Max Havoc, as he explained: "All of the bands that I kind of went in and out of from the time I left the *Heaven And Hell* tour, nothing ever got recorded because I was really unavailable. I was getting much sicker with the drugs and alcohol so it fell apart. There was no way I could keep anything together. Once I began to stay sober, that's when I was able to make more recordings and so on. But I didn't go back to Patrick [McKeon, vocalist] in Max Havoc, I went on to work with some other musicians."

It didn't matter who he worked with in this period: Bill was seriously sick, and knew himself that a cure had to be found for his addiction or – quite simply – it would kill him. As he told me, booze had been a lifelong enemy, well before this point: "I was pronounced in trouble when I was 22, when I got hepatitis. The doctors told me, 'If you don't quit drinking you're gonna die.' But of course that didn't bother me because I thought I was fuckin' invincible. When I was 27 I got really, *really* ill, and by the time I was 32 I was in big, big trouble. Totally at the end of my life, as I understood it at the time. I was in really bad shape."

Although one of the problems he was facing was sadness over Ozzy's departure – remember, Ozzy himself called Bill his "brother" – it should be stressed that Ward got along fine with Ronnie James Dio: "My relationship with Ronnie was fine. My time with him was good. I missed Ozz, which is why I left. In 1980, when I came off the tour, I went to bed for a year: all I did was do drugs and have sex, and in 1981 I became so ill that I had my first attempt at trying to be sober."

While Bill struggled to stay off the bottle and *Heaven And Hell* shifted units, going gold in the US in January 1981, Sabbath hit the road. Four mid-January dates in London were followed up by a UK tour that took them as far as St Austell in Cornwall the following month. The band then rehearsed for the upcoming tour until July, with the ground regained from the much-lauded LP set to be exploited. Nevertheless, a highly promising early summer gig, the headlining slot at the 'Heavy Metal Holocaust' at Stoke FC's stadium on August 1, was cancelled. This was rumoured to be because a 'mystery support act' on the bill – revealed on the day as none other than Ozzy Osbourne's Blizzard Of Ozz – caused them to pull their slot, despite the obvious PR disaster that this would represent. Although no one has confirmed why Sabbath pulled out of the show – which also featured Motörhead and Triumph – the rumours seem plausible. Mundane commitments such as recording dates (Sabbath were still tying up loose ends on *The Mob Rules* at this point) may have prevented their attendance, but fans were annoyed by the decision and many may have switched allegiance to the Ozzy camp as a result.

The news that Ozzy had – unbelievably – enlivened a 1981 meeting with his new record company, CBS, by biting the head off a live dove to impress the executives, added to his grim allure for most of his fanbase, while parents, teachers and other authorities were quick to censure him. Although many dismissed the story as fiction, one eyewitness was quoted as saying: "I'm ninety-nine and nine-tenths sure it was alive, but now I can't say for sure. I remember I was leaning forward and thinking, 'How cute,' and suddenly he bites its head off. There was blood on the floor. I think he ate the head; he started spitting some feathers out. I was in shock. It's hard to remember too much after that, to tell you the truth. It was horrible." The original plan had been, it seemed, to release two doves as a symbol of unity – but Ozzy chose, spontaneously or otherwise, to alter the plan slightly. The incident marked him for life.

Ozzy followed up on this early notoriety by releasing his second album, *Diary Of A Madman*, on November 7, 1981. It was less effective than *Blizzard Of Ozz*, with Rhoads' incandescent performance toned down a little with perhaps a few too many instrumental flourishes, but his growing fanbase supported it and the ensuing tour, during which Ozzy's reputation as the wild man of rock began to establish itself properly.

'Over The Mountain', with Rhoads' usual expert staccato riffing, is a paean to freedom in vague terms, with Ozzy singing "Don't need no astrology, it's inside of you and me / You don't need a ticket to fly with me, I'm free, yeah!" Once again the pitch seems a bit high for Ozzy to handle, but as usual he flies insouciantly through such hindrances and was, in any case, now so well known for the almost falsetto wails he emitted on so many of his songs that the style was becoming an Osbourne trademark.

The immortal verse of "Daddy thinks I'm lazy he don't understand / Never saw inside my head / People think I'm crazy but I'm in demand" and other surreal sentiments make 'Flying High Again' a drugs song, judging by the repeated intonation of the title. Its layers of guitars and expertly rounded sound make it one of Ozzy's best early songs, as is 'You Can't Kill Rock'N'Roll', which – despite its unsophisticated title – is a sensitive bit of composition. Over Rhoads' expert classical guitar, Ozzy warbles "Rock and roll is my religion and my law / Won't ever change, may think it's strange / You can't kill rock and roll, it's here to stay" – a sentiment that has echoed down the ages from 'Rock Around The Clock' and beyond.

Loquacious as ever, Ozzy later confirmed: "Rock and roll is my religion, and that's the God's honest truth. And it's my law. If I kill myself doing what I do for a living, if people want to fuck me up, say whatever they like, it's their privilege – it's your privilege. But I don't think I do a bad job; I don't think I fucking give people harm. What's more fucking harmful than a simple guy like me that's got an ability to fucking turn people on, to have a good time, to go crazy? What the fuck's wrong with – what's more crazy – giving a young kid a fucking rifle and saying, 'Run over that fucking hill and you're gonna die,' or me getting up there and jumping up and down like a cunt for an hour and a half?"

'Believer', the closest to a standard rock grind that Ozzy approaches on *Diary* – and this is rock, you understand, not metal (at least by modern standards) – features a solid, high-in-the-mix performance from bassist Bob Daisley and a flamboyant Rhoads workout, with feedback and deliberate dissonance to cultivate an air of tension. "You've got to believe in yourself / Or no one will believe in you" sings Ozzy, in another deliberately positive, upbeat lyric that entirely belies his malevolent image – and which a few of those who criticised him would have done well to heed. That said, the next song, 'Little Dolls' – in which Ozzy gleefully recounts the horror-movie tale of an unknown person who dabbles in voodoo curses ("The pins and needles prick the skin of little dolls"), is a simple, demonic tale of the sort that right-wing American politicians would agonise about for decades. Perhaps Ozzy was just having a joke at their expense by writing this kind of deliberately provocative song? Of the songwriting, he explained: "Everyone feeds off everyone else. It's like a rock'n'roll jungle. You know where you're coming from: if it feels for everyone, it feels good for everyone . . . I do the major writing, but if [the band] come up with a thing that we want to use, everyone gets the credit for it. As long as the picture's painted . . . I generally get the idea, the initial push, and we work it out together."

"Am I ever gonna make the grade?" asks Ozzy in 'Tonight', a power ballad that boasts a full house of Rhoadsian guitar harmonies and a fat chorus that worked supremely well live. Fully rounded songs such as this one – always the meat of any rock album, especially once studio technology had reached a certain level in the Eighties – were what made Ozzy and his team (Daisley, Kerslake and Rhoads contributed heavily to the songwriting, it should be noted) such a success on these early LPs. 'S.A.T.O.' (a reduction of 'Sailing Across The Ocean') is less successful, with Ozzy attempting to hit notes that are beyond his reach and Rhoads stepping down his usual apocalyptic riffage in favour of a semi-experimental, atmospheric approach instead. But once again the lyrics are gripping, with Osbourne hinting at hidden obsessions with lines like, "I can't conceal it like I knew I did before / I got to tell you now, the ship is ready / Waiting on the shore".

'Diary Of A Madman' itself is excellent, with Ozzy's comfortably-pitched musings of "A sickened mind and spirit / The mirror tells me lies / Could I mistake myself for someone / Who lives behind my eyes?" over-laying a bleak backing designed to evoke images of insanity – perhaps even the cover artwork itself, which shows Ozzy in vampire make-up and a ludicrously theatrical set. Musically, Rhoads is on top form, with the song's unusual time signature and precise instrumentation the signs of a writer at the top of his game.

Diary Of A Madman, expansive concept and all, went to number 14 in the UK and hung around the charts for 12 weeks, bolstered by the subsequent tour, which rolled out through the following spring and which was characterised by a number of incidents. Bassist Rudy Sarzo, who was asked to replace Daisley for the tour (Tommy Aldridge took Kerslake's place; keyboards were handled by Don Airey, who also played on the LPs) recalled that Ozzy's state of mind was unstable, to say the least: "Few people know this, but he was treated at St John's Hospital outside London. He had a nervous breakdown . . . We were rehearsing – Tommy Aldridge, Don Airey, Randy and myself. We were in England for the

Diary Of A Madman tour, and our singer was in a mental institution. We'd go visit him with Sharon. She was a major instigator and would call us up: 'Come on, let's visit Ozzy!' . . . We'd visit him, and this hospital was like something out of *The Elephant Man*. There's Ozzy in one room with an iron headboard above his bed with a little curtain for him to change and a piss bucket and pitcher of water . . . We'd walk in the room and he'd be so happy to see us. He'd cry and laugh, cry and laugh – back and forth. Total mood swings. Then he finally got released. The doctor told Sharon there was nothing they could do for him."

Ozzy confirmed this later, recalling: "I eventually ended up in the fucking nuthouse. I was hung up on cocaine for years. I took LSD, me and Bill Ward took LSD for two years every day. I ended up a screwball. I got to this lunatic asylum and this guy says to me, first question: 'Do you masturbate?' I turned to this guy and I says, 'Listen, asshole, I'm here for my head, not my cock.' But I've read about it since . . . apparently masturbation for guys is a very big sign of insecurity, which I am – I'm very insecure. Within myself. It's true."

Of his lunatic worldview, he added: "I'm crazy – totally crazy, and the fact is accepting my craziness. I'm totally fucking freaked by every man, your universe, and everybody, because everyone's gone fucking mad. I'm the madman that looks out there and says, 'You say I'm fucking mad! Look at you cunts!' They say I'm crazy – I *am* crazy, OK? But I don't fucking build bombs, I don't build fucking means of killing people. All I do when I get to a concert is try and give them my best shot. Sometimes it works, sometimes it don't. A lot of times, it don't."

He has a philosophical view which is both endearing and challenging: "The funniest thing about death is, you're never gonna go. Death to me is the next step. I don't believe we stop – I don't believe that mankind stops at death. I don't know, 'cause I ain't dead yet. There's many ways of dying, you know?"

Of Aldridge's recruitment, Ozzy later said: "The way I met Tommy was so ironical. An old friend of mine who used to be a roadie was working for Pat Travers, and Pat Travers was looking for a new drummer. I told this guy Dave that I wanted to get Tommy in a band. Tommy was just leaving Black Oak . . . he eventually went with Pat Travers. When I did leave Sabbath finally, I mentioned Tommy's name to everybody. I said I wanted to play with Tommy. I said he was the greatest rock'n'roll drummer in the world, and I really sincerely meant it. It's hard to try and explain, but the way things happened in this band – it was like things were meant to happen, as if we were all meant to meet. Tommy and I have been doing the same circuit since '72, '73, when he was with Black Oak and I was with Sabbath. I think he's the greatest fucking drummer in the world."

With the *Madman* theme echoing worryingly into reality, Ozzy's tour passed through Europe with NWOBHM stalwarts Saxon in support. It became known as the 'Night Of The Living Dead' tour by certain observers, thanks to misfortunes such as a collapsing crane (which destroyed thousands of dollars' worth of keyboards), trucks breaking down and other, deliberate tactics such as Ozzy's decision to throw handfuls of raw meat into the audience. After a few dates at which he doused the crowd with calves' liver and pigs' intestines, audience members began to bring their own supplies to throw back at him. This rapidly escalated until the point where Ozzy was being showered with frogs, snakes and even cats on occasion. The band – and the dwarf who would emerge from a hole in the stage (a castle with smoke machines) to give Ozzy water and towels – were soon treading carefully to avoid slipping on a stage covered in meat, blood and dead animals.

But sometimes not carefully enough. Ozzy's reputation as a madman tripled overnight after an infamous show in Des Moines, Iowa, on January 20 the following year. After a fan threw a live bat on the stage, the frontman picked it up – and assuming it was made of rubber, as it was lying still, presumably stunned by the lights – bit off its head. He was immediately rushed to hospital, where he endured a series of anti-rabies injections in his buttocks, arms and legs for a whole week. Animal rights groups protested against his actions and the world began to take notice. As if the dove decapitation the previous year hadn't been enough . . .

After recovery, Ozzy caused even more serious headlines during a February 19 stopover in San Antonio, Texas, when he went out looking for a drink dressed in his wife's clothing. "What Sharon would do to try to stop me drinking," Ozzy explained later, "was take my clothes. So if I wanted to get a drink I'd have to dress up in hers. I was alone in my hotel room in San Antonio and I wanted the hair of the dog, so I put one of her dresses on. I'm walking around the town with this green evening gown on, slurping from a bottle of Courvoisier, drunk as an idiot, and I want to take a piss, so I see this old wall and I think, 'This'll do.' "

Unfortunately the wall he chose to urinate on was a cenotaph in front of the Alamo, an 18th century fort designated a National Historic Landmark. It was the focus of the 1836 Battle Of The Alamo, a conflict between Texan and Mexican forces, where the celebrated frontiersmen Davy Crocket and Jim Bowie lost their lives, as depicted in the celebrated movie starring John Wayne. It is of enormous sentimental importance to many San Antonio residents, so it's not surprising that the local police didn't take kindly to Ozzy's action when they caught him in the act, telling him, "If you piss on the Alamo, boy, you're pissing on the State of Texas." He was charged with being drunk in public and "urinating on a shrine", fined and banned from the city of San Antonio for 10 years. Later that week he went into a coffee shop with a bodyguard (a Vietnam veteran) and was confronted by a local resident, as Ozzy recalled in horror: "Someone in a suit and tie started screaming 'Put Jesus in front of you' and all the other people in the restaurant turned out to be with him, so they all joined in. Then this Rambo guy who's with me goes into kill mode and starts throwing them all through the window. I had to crawl out of there literally on my hands and knees."

Later on, when LA glam-rockers Mötley Crüe – themselves no strangers to drugs, booze and rock'n'roll irresponsibility – toured with Ozzy's band, they found him exceeding even these antics. As Crüe bassist and songwriter Nikki Sixx reported in the band's 2001 autobiography *The Dirt*, Ozzy once snorted a line of ants off the ground next to a hotel swimmingpool, urinated on the ground and licked it up – and then, after demanding that Sixx do the same, licked up the Crüe man's urine too. No wonder Ozzy was confined to a mental hospital at one point: at this stage in his career, he seems to have been a man constantly on the edge of actual derangement.

Perhaps some of Ozzy's real or apparent insanity might be attributed to his background, and specifically his family. As he once explained, there was a hereditary streak of mental illness in the Osbourne gene pool: "My sister [Gillian] went nuts one day and cut all the heads off the photographs, all we ever had of the family when I was a kid. She went fucking over the top, and all the photos have no heads. She got institutionalised; she's tried to kill herself a couple of times . . . the only person I have any time for is my sister, Jean, who's the oldest, and my grandmother, who's ninety."

With all this focus on Ozzy, Black Sabbath needed to deliver some seriously worthy product to maintain the ground they had clawed back with *Heaven And Hell*. Expectations were high when, on October 11, 1981, *The Mob Rules* was released: after a few spins most fans concluded that while Sabbath hadn't broken down many barriers with the second Ronnie James Dio album, they'd done a decent job of continuing the themes and music first explored on *Heaven And Hell*. The sleeve art – a pack of faceless creatures with cowls and whips toting a strange, bloodstained parchment –

inspired a little controversy, as all the best sleeve covers do. In the foreground of the picture are some stains on the floor: viewed with enough gullibility, they seem to resemble some or all of the word 'Ozzy'. This has been much discussed but never confirmed or denied, adding to the folklore which has grown up around the band over the decades.

The opener, 'Turn Up The Night' – like 'Neon Knights' – a fast, slick slab of heavy rock of the type that many bands were doing at this time: it may have been some way from the chunks of heavy metal that Sabbath had recorded before 1976, but it sounded good and was deftly performed, with Vinny Appice's powerful drums lending the songs a certain weight. Iommi was on great form, as usual, ripping out solo after solo, relying heavily on his wah pedal. Only Dio's lyrics leave something to be desired: with lines like "A rumble of thunder, I'm suddenly under your spell / No rhyme or reason, or time of the season, but oh well", it's not really apparent what he's singing about.

The mystical themes of *Heaven And Hell* were well and good across the course of an album, but when Dio continued along the same lines in 'Voodoo' – and used sixth-form lines like "You were a fool, but that's cool", one or two listeners began to feel impatient. In fact, the song is a standard rock workout, and best skipped across for the mighty 'The Sign Of The Southern Cross', a slow and epic anthem like the Sabbath of old. After a classical acoustic intro, the song evolves into a huge, slow-riffing beast on which Ronnie gets to show off his full range and even Geezer gets to throw in a low-register trill on bass. Iommi's soloing is at its best here – highly melodic and dazzlingly fast – and across the song's near-eight minute duration, all the band-members are at their peak. 'Sign' is followed by an instrumental track, 'E5150', attributed to Geezer playing his bass through an effects unit but probably also given some treatment at the desk (there are slowed-down vocals) for a suitably spooky effect.

As with most Sabbath albums, the title track is among the best: 'The Mob Rules' is fast but still heavy and melodic, with a chorus and solos that show how well the new line-up was gelling as a songwriting and performing unit. "It's over, it's done / The end, the big death / If you listen to fools, the mob rules . . ." sings Ronnie, although it isn't clear what else he's singing about. The song went on to feature on the soundtrack for the 1981 Canadian production *Heavy Metal*, an animated film that featured plenty of gory violence and nudity and which was dismissed by the critics as adolescent trash. Nowadays, however, *HM* is regarded as a cult movie, with all the attendant culture of such a thing, even though a sequel bombed in 2000. As Vinny Appice told me, "During the *Heaven And Hell* tour Warner Brothers wanted a song for *Heavy Metal*, which was a cool thing because we had a couple of days off in England, so we went down to Ascot to this house that John Lennon owned, wrote the song together – I didn't get credited on it, but I was there. We didn't have the song written already, it was like, that's a cool riff, let's play. Everybody had a little say in it. And we put the song together, recorded it there and sent it to Warners. They loved it, and that was a good introduction to us all making the album together. It had been really smooth."

The next two songs, 'Country Girl' and 'Slipping Away', are less impressive, with the former a standard heavy rock grind on the subject of a demonic female ("She was up from a nether world, just to bust another soul / Her eyes were an endless flame, unholy lady . . .") and the latter a dispensable four minutes of riffage that was neither original nor particularly rousing, despite some solo interludes from Appice that amply demonstrate his skills.

'Falling Off The Edge Of The World's violin and treated-guitar intro, laced with choir and strings, suits Ronnie's subtly intoned tenor, even if some of the keyboards are a little gloopy at points. But as Iommi said, "I think what Black Sabbath was all about was expanding. We just didn't stay in one bag. I brought in the complete London Choir . . . for one instrumental tune I'd done. That's what we were about. We were about expanding and trying things. Everybody liked it in the end, so none of the others were complaining. They thought it was a great idea. I mean, I just didn't do it on my own power. I said to everybody, 'What about this?' and they'd say, 'Oh yeah, let's try it.'" In this case the intro gives way to a riff-soup of effective intricacy that lends weight to Dio's musings of "I should be at the table round / A servant of the crown / The keeper of the sign / To sparkle and to shine". The LP ends with 'Over And Over', whose harmony-guitar intro would be stolen wholesale by a host of bands who were emerging at this time, notably Metallica (who would be demoing their own material within a year of the release of *The Mob Rules*). Ronnie signs off with sentiments such as 'Life's only made of paper / Oh how I need to be free of this pain" and some warbled backing vocals, while Iommi turns in the most frenzied solo he has committed to record yet.

The album may have been moderately good rather than scintillating, but Sabbath were rejuvenated – perhaps thanks to the hard-working Appice pushing them along – and as a tour approached, the band laid plans for a live album to be recorded and released in 1982. The new show would have 'E5150' as its intro tape – previous jaunts had used 'Supertzar'

– to lull the crowd into the right mood before the band launched into their opening song.

Although *The Mob Rules* was released soon after Ozzy's *Diary Of A Madman* – and wasn't quite as stunning as that LP – it reached number 12 in the UK and the tour was a success, with Canadian and US dates through November and December attracting capacity crowds. A New Year's Eve date at London's Hammersmith Odeon was a triumphant signing-off to 1981 and the future, uncertain though it might have been, at least looked bright. January 1982 saw the band head through the UK before yet more dates in the lucrative USA in February and March, although some dates were postponed due to the death of Iommi's father.

And so Sabbath came back, all guns blazing. The career of their only reasonable equivalent on the rock scene, meanwhile – Ozzy himself – was about to be struck with tragedy.

On March 19, 1982, Ozzy and his band were en route to a show in Orlando, Florida, from Knoxville, Tennessee. The tour bus needed some repairs, and so the driver, Andrew Aycock, stopped in the Florida town of Leesburg, where he happened to have a house. While repairs were under-way Ozzy went for a sleep in the bus and Aycock invited keyboardist Don Airey and tour manager Hake Duncan for a spin in the small Beechcraft Bonanza aeroplane which he kept at his home. On their return, he took Randy Rhoads and Ozzy's tour seamstress, Rachael Youngblood, for a short flight.

Aycock – who was later found to have traces of cocaine in his blood-stream – attempted a low dive over the tour bus (it has been suggested that he was trying to scare his ex-wife, who was standing near it) but misjudged the distance and clipped the vehicle with his wing. The plane spun out of control and flew directly into a nearby farmhouse, exploding on impact and killing everyone on board immediately.

Ozzy was deeply shocked, and said later: "I think there is such a thing as luck. I also think there is such a thing as destiny. When Randy Rhoads got killed in the plane. I know, without a shadow of doubt, that if I was awake at the time I would've gone on the plane with him, but I was still asleep." Much later he added: "I lost a very dear friend and a wonderful person . . . He was the first guy to come along and give me a purpose, because he would patiently sit there with me and try to work out songs with me. I will always remember him . . . Life, you know, it's gone like a flash."

Sharon Arden knew that Ozzy needed to continue his tour or he would collapse utterly, and within days ex-Gillan guitarist Bernie Torme was recruited. As Torme recalled later, "Quite a few other people auditioned prior to my standing in. I had to go through an audition for two days in LA with four other guitarists, which, shall I say, was not what I was expecting, and not what I had been told by Ozzy's UK management! . . . but if it hadn't been so tragic, I could honestly say it was a great experience. And Ozzy is a great guy."

However, Torme only remained with Ozzy's band for seven gigs, for reasons which have not been fully resolved. Some said that he found the jump from mid-sized venues with Gillan to 20,000-seater arenas with Ozzy too much to handle. Either way, he informed Ozzy that he was unable to continue and another axeman, Brad Gillis of Night Ranger, stepped in. Torme recalled: "In the last few days when I told Ozzy that I did not want to carry on, a few other people, including Brad, were auditioned at soundchecks while I did the gigs. So there were quite a lot of people who wanted to jump in."

Ozzy, with Sarzo, Aldridge and Gillis, went on to complete his tour in a state of suppressed shock and grief, which would pay miserable dividends later.

Meanwhile Sabbath were winding up a stupendous tour in the wake of *The Mob Rules*, which crossed the US and Canada once again through April, May and June. Rumour had it that at some stage in the summer the singer David Coverdale – once of Deep Purple's Mark III line-up, and in 1981 in the middle of a successful 13-year run with Whitesnake – was asked to join Sabbath. He told me that this was never a possibility, saying "I could never see myself singing Ozzy's songs."

Live recordings were made at Sabbath's tour dates for a concert album, and Iommi, Dio, Butler and Appice spent time sorting through the tapes and assembling it. At the same time, Ozzy – who had finished his own tour – was assembling a live album of his own. It certainly seems as if his intention was to compete against Sabbath's own LP; worse, the album Ozzy intended to release was a collection not of his own songs but of old Black Sabbath material. As the obvious questions flew at him, he defended himself with mischievous glee, saying: "It wasn't a thing to 'get at' Sabbath on. I just did it. I understand that Sabbath had an idea of putting a live album out themselves . . ."

As the two teams worked in the studio, Ozzy took time out to record backing vocals with Was (Not Was), the soul/dance act centring on producer Don Was. An unlikely enough partnership as it was, it seemed even more unlikely when it was revealed some years later that none other than

152

the then 24-year-old Madonna also contributed backing vocals to the track alongside him. The song, 'Shake Your Head (Let's Go To Bed)', wasn't a chart hit until 1992, when it was reissued as part of a WNW greatest hits album. For the latter release, Madonna asked for her vocals not to be used: they were re-recorded by actress Kim Basinger.

Of the unlikely partnership, Ozzy later explained: "I'd never heard of Was (Not Was). What happened was, the original singer didn't show up for some session. I don't even know who the original singer was, but Don and I were both staying at the same hotel in New York at the time, and I volunteered. I go down to this studio and it was called 'Shake Your Head'. A couple of months later, they decided to do a different version of it, so I did two versions. Then, later, I saw Don in LA, and he said, 'You'll never guess who the chick singer was on the first version: it was Madonna! Ozzy and Madonna: it's got to be a winner.' He must have gotten in touch with Madonna and she gave him a point-blank refusal, because he got somebody else to do Madonna's bit. Kim Basinger replaced Madonna. I never met her. But it was a huge, huge hit in England and Europe, because that's what they're into – all this techno stuff. I just said to Don, 'That would be great: Ozzy and Madonna,' but the Kim Basinger one did just as well."

Back in the summer of 1982, Ozzy was clearly hitting a commercial and critical peak, with all that was hindering his progress; his mental instability in the wake of Rhoads' death, and his addictions. On the subject of drugs, he mused: "As low as you feel is as high as you feel. It's like taking the first sniff of cocaine: you get up there, you think it's great. But everyone fails to remember that when you get up there as high as a kite, the day's gonna come when you're going to have to come down. The basic's in reality. And that's why people are addicts. I'm an addict in liquor . . . But I have management that fucking gets my shit together. I'm a guy that can't take a fucking pill – I've got to take 15. I've got to go everything to the fucking end. I can't have a drink, I've got to get bombed. I've got to take everything to the end. Everything. Life! . . . I fuck like crazy for about three months, then I stop and I get very miserable . . . my biggest dread is getting a disease I can't get rid of, and there's a lot of diseases that you can't get rid of. I don't want to do that any more. I choose not to do it, so like – I choose to fucking keep myself to myself. It may sound a little bizarre, but I choose to keep myself to myself. I'm a moody bastard, because I want people around me, but I don't."

He added: "I know I ain't going to fucking live to be an old man. I know that. I'm not planning to fucking top myself. But something's going to happen to me soon. What the fuck? I'd rather look good in my coffin than bad in my coffin. Fucking go for it. Can you imagine me at the age of 65 or fucking 70, singing, 'I once was fucking vaudeville, remember him?' That's not my fucking style, man. Burn out with a flash. I don't give a flying fuck about myself any more."

Some of his sadness may be attributed to the divorce he had just finalised with his first wife, Thelma Mayfair, and the arrangements that needed to be made regarding access to his children. As he said: "I'm just getting over the fucking trauma of my first divorce, but yet I still have a love for my ex-wife. When you get a divorce, there are fucking mind-games going, you know? Crazy mind-games; crazy fucking craziness."

He was obviously happy to be free once again: after all, he and Sharon Arden were now a solid couple, with plans to marry. Of Thelma, Ozzy told reporter David Gans: "I met her at Halloween, when she fell off her broomstick, in 1971. Now she's got a part-time job swimming up and down Loch Ness while the monster has his holidays. She's fucking mad – she's like Mrs Fucking Monster . . . I once had a dream about getting a marriage, house in the country, and at the end of the day we'd retire, but I'm never going to retire. My ex-wife said to me one day, 'What are you going to do when you're 57?' I said, 'Listen, you cunt, there's never been a fucking 57-year-old rock star – I'm going to fucking be the first.'"

With age this bitterness passed. Ozzy later told *Launch* magazine, "I was married to a woman before, but because of my alcohol and drug abuse, I screwed up the marriage and it affects the kids the most. They're the silent sufferers. They don't understand why Daddy's not coming home any more. It always affects the kids. The one thing about America that's weird is, like, you'll get married, I'll get married; we'll go out to dinner, we get divorced, I'll marry your wife, you marry my wife . . . why not just swap for a night? If I wanted to be friends with my wife, I would have divorced her, you know? Marriage is so flippantly taken on here: 'Oh I'm bored, let's get married this week.' When I got married, I didn't understand what it was about. But the marriage contract is one of the heaviest contracts you'll ever sign in your life. And when there are kids involved . . . they automatically come first. I did a good job of screwing up my first marriage."

And so Sharon Arden comes fully into the picture. Just 30 in 1982 (Ozzy was 34), she had already shown her mettle as a manager by pulling Ozzy back onto his feet twice – once after he left Black Sabbath and sank into an alcoholic fug for three months back in 1979, and again after Rhoads' tragic death in March '82. Moreover, she had recently endured an acrimonious split from her father, Don Arden. He had been infuriated by her taking on Ozzy's management and, other than on a business level, father and daughter ceased communications entirely. Ozzy and Sharon were said to have paid Don £1.5 million for the rights to Ozzy's contract at this time. (Remember Jim Simpson's words: "With Donnie, if you work with him and he likes you, he regards you as family. And family do *not* just scurrilously do the dirty on you and walk out on you . . .")

The situation turned to tragedy when, on a visit to her father's house, his dogs attacked her: as she told *The Guardian* in 2001, she was pregnant and lost the baby as a result. "It was horrific," she said.

But Sharon was made of tough stuff and took a committed stance over Ozzy, pushing his career as far as it would go. Like her lover, she liked a drink and had once been arrested in LA for drink-driving. Bailed out of prison by her friend Britt Ekland and informed the next morning what had happened, she had no memory of the day's events. Soon after, she quit drinking, as she and Ozzy were becoming notorious for their alcohol-fuelled fights: "Our fights were legendary. We'd beat the shit out of each other. At a gig, Ozzy would run offstage during a guitar solo to fight with me, then run back on to finish the song! We were in the gutter, morally, and I realised that if we both carried on, we'd wind up a washed-up pair of old drunks living in a hovel somewhere. So I stopped drinking."

Such cool-headed strategies towards success led to a little resentment in this most resentful of industries, with Sharon branded with insults over her abrasive management style. She explained: "People would openly say, 'You and Ozzy won't last.' They expected him to have a big-titted blonde trophy wife and he'd got me, a short, fat, hairy half-Jew. I had a lot to fight against . . . If I were a man, I'd just be seen as a great toughie businessman. I'm a woman, so men say, 'Oh, she's a bitch, a whore, a cunt.' I'm afraid it's just what you men do. Plus, I work with my husband, and every woman protects their family."

As for Ozzy, it was clear that he was ready to settle down, at least relatively speaking. After all, he'd certainly done his fair share – and more – of working through the apparently endless line of groupies that surround any band of moderate standing, let alone a behemoth such as Sabbath. He once explained, in typically graphic detail: "At first, when I first come to the States, I fucked everything in sight. I've had the clap more times than fucking God. But suddenly I realised, what am I telling these chicks 'I love you' for when you don't mean it? All you want to do is get their ass in bed and fuck the twat off 'em. I remember one occasion, we did Virginia Beach. The door knocks. I've just spoken to my ex-wife – put the phone down and the door knocks. This beautiful chick comes in, and 'Fuck, I'm happening tonight!' I get her on the bed and I fuck the ass off her. She goes. Knock-knock-knock on the door comes. I think she's forgotten something . . . it's a different chick at the door. Beautiful as fucking God! I swear she looked like an angel. And I fuck the ass off this one. She goes. Knock-knock-knock, and I'm thinking, 'I can't believe this.' Three – five chicks come in, and I fucked five different – where are these chicks coming from? Where are these chicks coming from? I start walking the corridors and thinking, 'What the fuck?'. . ."

He rationalised, "When you're a kid of fucking 24 or 25 and you come from Aston to the States and you see all these fucking cunts wanting to be fucked, you go like a bull at the gate. You're like a fucking lunatic – I was having perverted scenes, fucking . . . all kinds of crap was going on with my sexual life. It's bizarre, it was wild."

Wild or not, on July 4, 1982 Ozzy and Sharon were married on a beach in Hawaii. Ozzy's live album of Sabbath songs, entitled *Speak Of The Devil*, was ready to go – it completed Ozzy's deal with Don Arden, both as manager and with Arden's Jet label – and all seemed to be running smoothly.

If only the same could be said of Black Sabbath. Completing their US and Canada tour in August – on which support was provided on some dates by the Canadian act Exciter, one of the first thrash metal bands to support Sabbath – the band retired to the studio for the final mix of their own live LP – *Live Evil* (coincidentally *Live-Evil* was the title of a 1970 LP by cool jazz trumpeter Miles Davis).

Relationships with Ronnie James Dio and the Iommi-Butler team had cooled slightly in recent months, with the singer apparently trying to take more control of the band than the others were happy with. As Geezer told me, "We just saw it as he was trying to take over the band, and we didn't like that."

Vinny Appice witnessed the breakdown at first hand. As he says, "I don't think anything really started to go downhill until the live album. I mean, I got along with everybody. I love Tony. He's a practical joker and so am I, and Geezer was cool. But the only problem was towards the end when we were recording the live album – the relationships between Tony and Ronnie, and Geezer and Ronnie, were starting to go downhill. It became like the Americans and the British. But I tried not to let that happen. We always had two limos, for example, and rather than always get in the limo with Ronnie I would get in the limo with Geezer! I had no problems with anybody – I was having a good time – and Tony and

Geezer had no problems with me, it was just with Ronnie. You know, it was a lot of egos!"

The tension escalated into actual verbal conflict from time to time, as the drummer remembered: "There were a couple of fights backstage with Tony and Ronnie screaming at each other. Two hot-headed Italians! I don't know what they were arguing about – I would just say, whoa, and not get involved with any of it. So by the end of the tour you could feel the vibe between them – Tony and Geezer would get in one car and Ronnie would get in the other. I tried to keep it going by getting in all the different cars . . ."

Worse, it seems that Dio may have been in the habit of entering the studio to adjust the mix without telling the rest of the band. As Iommi told *Classic Rock Revisited*: "We were going in and mixing the album. Over a period of weeks, I was seeing the engineer beginning to look worse and worse. He was getting more drunk all the time. I wondered what was going on. I asked him one day if he was all right. He said, 'I can't stand it any more. I've got to tell you what's going on.' I told him, 'Go on.' He said, 'You guys are going home after doing a mix and then Ronnie is wanting to come in and do his own mix. I don't know what to do.' Basically, that's what happened – that is the crunch of it. We tried to ban him from the studio. It got pretty bad."

Appice counters Iommi's statement, however, saying: "That's not what happened. I was there. What happened was, during the mix of the live album, they booked the studio for two o'clock. But they wouldn't get there until four or five o'clock, and this was an expensive studio. Me and Ronnie would be there at two. You tell me two, I'm there. So are we gonna sit around for three or four hours? So, we'd start working on the stuff and then they'd show up and it caused a problem because we'd say, we've worked on the drum sound a little bit. And I guess Tony and Geezer didn't want to do it that way.

"They don't communicate: when there's a problem, there's no confrontation. Tony doesn't like confrontation, he goes through someone else. When Tony doesn't talk to you, you know there's a problem. You can't go to Tony unless you really sit down and talk. He'd talk to me once in a while. You know, I never had a problem with these guys – I love these guys. They had a problem with Ronnie. I had no say in this, I just came in when they wanted me in. But Ronnie wanted to do some work, so he would start doing whatever needed to be done, and they took that as Ronnie sneaking in the studio and doing stuff behind their back. And they might have left and went to the pub, or went early . . . well, Ronnie's there, he's a workaholic. Yeah, I'm an innocent party. I'm not gonna say, well, I'm not going in until they go in! I was just a little kid going hey, I'm having a good time – stop fighting, guys!"

The breakdown in relationships was rapidly heading towards a confrontation, and when the end came, it came quick. Appice: "Eventually they accused us of going in the studio and doing stuff behind their back. Yes, it was a little unjust, because I didn't really have any say in the mixing. Maybe I'd say to Martin Birch that the drums needed a little more bottom end here and there, but I wasn't gonna say that the guitars were too low or whatever. So if Ronnie said, let's go in at five today, I'd say OK, because we were driving into the studio from the same area anyway.

"But then Ronnie said, 'I'm leaving the band and I'm going to start my own band – do you want to do it with me?' I said, yeah. I thought, I can relate to Ronnie at that point a little bit more than with Tony and Geezer, and I thought it would be cool to be in a new band, having had a lot of success with Sabbath. It would be fun to build something up from the beginning. But I think they still wanted me to play with them."

Dio and Appice left Sabbath in October 1982: the pair went on to form the very successful Dio, in which the singer was presumably at liberty to execute whichever mixes he liked.

And so Black Sabbath came to the end of another highly troubled era in their often troubled history. Two singers and two drummers had left them; their bass player had left and returned. At the end of 1982, only Tony Iommi and Geezer Butler remained.

CHAPTER THIRTEEN

1982–1984

AS Sabbath floundered, Ozzy released his controversial LP of covers by his old band on November 27, 1982. *Speak Of The Devil* featured Brad Gillis on guitar, doing a reasonable job with Iommi's riffs in place of the late Randy Rhoads. The album was recorded at the Ritz in New York on September 26 and 27, but shortly afterwards Gillis was himself replaced by Jake E Lee (real name Jakey Lou Williams), another super-technical and classically influenced player.

It was difficult to know how to take *Speak Of The Devil* at the time, and equally so today. Sabbath's original versions of the songs on the LP – which ran through 'Symptom Of The Universe', 'Snowblind', 'Black Sabbath', 'Fairies Wear Boots', 'War Pigs', 'The Wizard', 'N.I.B.', 'Sweet Leaf', 'Never Say Die', 'Sabbath Bloody Sabbath', 'Iron Man/Children Of The Grave' and 'Paranoid' – had been as much about Iommi's ferocious riffing and the heavy Ward/Butler rhythm section as Ozzy's voice. In their new incarnations, the vocals – which seemed to have been treated and given extra weight – were the predominant presence, with the other instruments – Gillis' scintillating solos aside – relatively low in the mix. As a result, and perhaps because of metal fans' reluctance to endorse Ozzy's hijacking of his old band, the album stalled at number 21 in the UK charts and fell out altogether after only six weeks. "I don't think Ozzy does the songs justice," Geezer told *Circus* magazine.

Nonetheless, the album contributed to rock'n'roll mythology in its own right thanks to its cover artwork – a vision of Ozzy with werewolf fangs and what looked like pieces of raw meat in his mouth, snarling out of a window frame covered in runes of some kind. Much debate ensued about the meaning of the runes until it was revealed that they translated as: 'Howdy! Dial-A-Demon Productions, in conjunction with Graveyard Graphics, proudly presents the madman of rock dumping into El Satano's toiletto': clearly a laugh at the expense of those who took his devilish image too seriously.

Black Sabbath revealed their own live album on January 22, 1983, finally polished by Iommi after Dio and Appice had departed and – in contrast with *Speak Of The Devil* – a highly professional affair. Offering the listener between-song chat by the very confident (some might say a touch arrogant) singer Ronnie James Dio reveals much about the live presence of the band at the time. So does the audience-participation moment, in which Dio commands the onlookers to shout "Heaven and hell!" and smugly grins, "That's really good!"

The band sweep through a set of Ozzy and Dio-era standards (the intro tape of 'E5150', followed by 'Neon Knights', 'N.I.B.', 'Children Of the Sea', 'Voodoo', 'Black Sabbath', 'War Pigs', 'Iron Man', 'The Mob Rules', 'Heaven And Hell', 'The Sign Of The Southern Cross', 'Paranoid', 'Children Of The Grave' and the excellent instrumental 'Fluff'), and you can't help but wonder why the release wasn't postponed in the wake of Ozzy's own LP, at least until the time when the fanbase might be ready for another collection featuring so many of the same songs.

After watching the LP do respectably well – it made number 11 and stayed on the chart for 13 weeks – Iommi and Butler set their sights on the future. If the band were to continue, they would need a new drummer and singer – and suitable candidates were added to a short list.

One night in early 1983, Tony and Geezer went to meet an old friend in the pub. A night of drinking later, at least half their problem had been solved . . .

Ian Gillan is a reasonable man. He answers questions intelligently and is quite aware of what his past career means to music history.

For example, he had written a series of groundbreaking hits with one of his old bands, Deep Purple, which stand up to this day – all without knowing how important they would be at the time: "I don't know any more how I conceived 'Speed King'," he ponders, "any more than I know how Ian Paice started playing it or how Ritchie Blackmore started playing it. It's an accumulation. I see a lot of young stars on chat shows denying any knowledge of having any formative years or any influences in their early life, and I think we all did. What you got with Deep Purple was a mish-mash of everything we ever listened to – I think Ian is Buddy Rich personified, for instance. You bring all that together, with Jon Lord and his classical and Jimmy Smith background, and you're gonna come up with something unique. If you took one of us away it wouldn't be the same. In my case the influences were Elvis Presley and Little Richard, Chuck Berry, Fats Domino, Ella Fitzgerald, Jerry Lee Lewis. Rock music to me was an attitude."

He is also surprisingly honest about the pressures that lie behind fronting a rock band: "We all have our areas of fragility. But there's a bombast, you know, which later in life would be called arrogance – but at an early time of life, is expected, up to a point, and it gets you through a lot of things."

In this case, it got him through being asked to sing for Black Sabbath after he, Tony and Geezer had all had too much to drink in that pub that fateful evening. He had his reservations at first, as he told *Recension* magazine: "At first I didn't want to know. I never really liked their image at all and I may have looked upon the people in the band in a negative way as well. My manager thought that I could at least meet them [Geezer Butler and Tony Iommi] and discuss it, so we met at this pub and I was really taken with how nice they were. We had the same humour and we shared a lot of views in general. Geezer went under the table first that night and I felt that maybe this was something to think about after all."

When the news broke that Gillan, fresh from the break-up of his own, eponymous band, would be working with Black Sabbath – the equivalent in heavy rock terms to Mick Jagger joining the Beatles – both Sabbath and Deep Purple fans were intrigued. Some were aghast, although there was reason for optimism: the Purple and Sabbath bloodlines had crossed before thanks to the recruitment of Ronnie James Dio (for so long a Rainbow member alongside Purple mainstay Blackmore) and the use of Martin Birch as producer. Both pairings had yielded excellent results.

It should be stressed, however, that the idea was that Gillan would be 'working with' rather than 'joining' Black Sabbath – a subtle but crucial difference. As Geezer told me, "We'd finished with the Ronnie version of the band and I said to Tony, 'It's getting to be a bit of a joke calling it Sabbath, isn't it?' And he totally agreed. I think the management at the time suggested getting Ian and calling it a Gillan/Iommi/Butler/Ward album, not a Black Sabbath album, which was the way we and Gillan felt. We just thought it would be an interesting thing to do as a one-off."

However, Gillan – as the voice of Deep Purple's most respected line-up to date, Mark II, and several line-ups in the Eighties, Nineties and beyond – seemed so essentially 'Purple' that it was hard to see him taking the downwards step away from the eloquent rock of Purple into the heavy metal swamp inhabited by Sabbath (even if the latter band had cleaned up their act in recent years). He noted this point, telling *Recension*: "I write in my own style, and I didn't want to sing a lot of drivel just because others have done it before me in the band. The lyrics are just day-to-day observations, just like in Gillan where a lot of the songs were quite dark and serious by nature . . . To be honest, you can only make it really big in the States today if you make music that the radio can pick up. It has to be hit oriented, radio friendly. Not too much energy – you can't get played if you're too aggressive. In fact, I saw Journey in San Francisco a few weeks ago. They were nice to watch, and little computers [stopped] them from making a single mistake. The audience loved it but they missed out on the experience that provides goosebumps all over your body – that raw energy. To me, that is real power. In America it's more about the show."

He explained that neither the recent split of Gillan due to voice problems he had experienced, nor a possible Deep Purple reunion ("Jon Lord and Ian Paice were ready to do it. But somebody changed their mind so it fell through") would stand in the way of Sabbath, largely because the workload with his new band was much lighter than he was used to: "In my own band we did upwards of 200 shows per year for six years, so to me Black Sabbath is like a holiday. Sabbath has a system that guarantees a day off regularly."

Before rehearsals could begin in earnest, of course, there was the small matter of finding a drummer. Enter – or rather re-enter – Bill Ward, who had begun to manage successfully short periods of sobriety by the end of 1982 and was willing to try his hand on a new Sabbath album.

"Before 1983," as Bill told *Sabbathlive*, "my drinking and using got worse and worse and worse, until I finally started to go to a hospital for treatment. There was one particular instance where I was able to get some sobriety. The guys [Tony and Geezer] had learned at that time that I was trying to get sober. They were very happy about that. They were really supportive.

"I was invited to come over and see if I could do a record. And that, of course, was *Born Again* with Ian Gillan in 1983. I did that album sober. I'm completely clean and sober on that album. In 1980, when we did *Heaven And Hell*, I was completely oblivious. I was totally loaded and I had no comprehension of ever recording *Heaven And Hell*. It's really a vague memory."

Of his new-found mental clarity, Ward explained: "I was concentrating on [doing] a really good job . . . but at the same time feeling very fragile and very scared. That was kind of the atmosphere that I was feeling at the time. I was scared because I didn't want to drink again and screw things up. And so for me it was a very challenging year doing *Born Again*. But I totally enjoyed being with Tony, Geezer and Ian. It was great. Just doing it, playing and recording, was just fantastic. And I thought that everybody was great. I don't really have any bad memories of the *Born Again* album.

"The only thing that I had going on were my own issues which had nothing to do with the band or with the album. The things that were going on that were problematic to me, because I was very, very new in my recovery. I was trying to do a good job and had screwed up righteously by walking away during the *Heaven And Hell* tour. And I'm very ashamed of that. I know I'd let a lot of people down. So when it was time to make *Born Again*, I didn't want to go through and repeat that again."

In fact, the sobriety Ward achieved for the – at least in his case – aptly titled *Born Again* LP was not his first attempt at kicking the habit. As he told me, "By the time we did *Born Again*, I was in my tenth or twelfth attempt at being sober, so when we did it I was completely stark staring sober." He is to be congratulated for pulling himself out of his self-imposed misery, of course – but unfortunately Ward's journey into sobriety had to get worse before it could get better.

"It was personally the most challenging album I ever did," Bill told writer Jeb Wright. "That was in 1983. As soon as the album was finished, I wanted to reward myself. I also had anticipatory fear about touring. I didn't tell anybody about it. I chose to drink at that time as a reward and because of the fear. I was asked to go back with Sabbath in 1984 but I already knew that it wasn't going to work for me. It didn't work with me with Ronnie James Dio and it didn't work with Ian Gillan – even though I have a great relationship with both of those men. Something different happened. When I left in 1983, I was full of shame."

Ward, who provided perfectly good drums for the recording of *Born Again*, fell off the wagon promptly when it was finished and knew that he couldn't do the subsequent tour. But as he explained, it was a complex issue: he drank to stave off the fear of touring – especially sober – and the feeling that Sabbath wasn't Sabbath without Ozzy (a point that fans have debated endlessly since 1979), but chose to let Iommi and Butler believe that he was physically unable to do the tour rather than explain that, in fact, he didn't want to do it sober.

For four months, Bill sank into the bottom of a bottle. As he told me, alcoholism can be likened to a fatal sickness: "It's a physical illness. It's a killer, there's no doubt about that. There's a dependency, but it's a mental illness; a spiritual malady, and then there's the physical illness that comes along with it. It's not a question of saying, oh fuck it, I'm gonna turn my life around and start over, I'm gonna pull my socks up here and fight this thing called alcoholism. Every time you try to fight it, it wins. It's very powerful and an absolutely deadly illness."

Bill was also suffering from clinical depression, just to make things even worse: "I didn't know at the time that I was in maudlin depression. I didn't know at the time that I was feeling so sorry for myself, which is a shit place to be. At that time it was mental depression: there was probably some clinical depression as well, but there was no medication at the time. I'd already tried and failed to be sober, and I couldn't stand drinking any more, so there was no place to live any more."

At the bottom of his personal hell, Ward arrived at the solution: suicide. He picked up a gun and pointed it at his head . . . but couldn't bring himself to take the next step. "I couldn't pull the trigger," he said. "I tried to kill myself three times. And I didn't have the balls to pull the trigger, so I had no choice. I had to get sober. And I didn't want to be sober: I wanted to be dead. And of course I failed miserably, thank God, and I couldn't do the booze any more. I just couldn't do it. So I chose to be sober, and it wasn't easy. It wasn't easy at all."

In early 1984, Ward checked himself into a rehabilitation facility, determined to get his life back.

In the meantime, Sabbath asked drummer Bev Bevan, of the Electric Light Orchestra, to step in for the *Born Again* tour. Bevan, an old friend of Tony and Geezer from the Aston days, was happy to help out and the new band gelled immediately.

On September 24, 1983 *Born Again* was released and went to number four in the UK – an impressive achievement, attributable perhaps to the presence of Gillan, whose profile was high at the time. Somewhat bizarrely, the album came out under the name Black Sabbath, although this clearly had not been the band's intention. Geezer told me: "*Born Again* wasn't supposed to be a Sabbath album. That's where the record company [Vertigo] betrayed us again . . . we finished it and gave it to the record company, who said, we've paid for a Sabbath album and that's what we're putting it out as. There was nothing we could do about it. There's some good songs on it, but the production's really bad. We were still trying to do the mixing ourselves instead of getting a good mixing person in."

He has a point: *Born Again* suffers from a strangely one-sided mix that does the songs no favours whatsoever. The guitars aren't heavy enough, although the bass is over-prominent and the vocals don't have much presence. As Geezer said in response to one interviewer's observation that Gillan had allegedly accused him of tampering with the mix: "That's a load of crap. I'm the one who was saying that it sounded awful. Gillan went on holiday, so he wasn't even there. Gillan came and did his vocals, then left on holiday for about six months so he doesn't know what he's talking about. I was saying the bottom end was too heavy and that it was too bassy. I got sick of telling everyone that it didn't sound right. When I was proved right, Gillan came back and said, 'What the hell is wrong with this?' A lot of people blamed me because I was the one who wasn't there at the time."

Along with the weird production, fans were slightly unnerved by the sleeve art, an utterly malevolent portrait of a newborn baby with added fangs, horns and claws. Bizarrely, the image was identical to the one used on the cover of synth-pop quartet Depeche Mode's June 1981 single 'New Life', albeit with a different line and colour treatment. As Gillan himself later wrote: "The artwork for the cover was a startlingly tasteless imitation of a bright red, newborn baby with long yellow fingernails and two yellow horns on its head," although he, like many others, didn't spot the Mode coincidence.

All in all *Born Again* hardly resembled a standard Black Sabbath album. But what of the music?

Funnily enough, there were similarities in mood, tempo and lyrics between the Purple classic 'Speed King' and the opener, 'Trashed', a high-speed romp with Gillan screaming his way through lines such as "I was going down the track about a hundred and five / They had the stop-watch rolling / Had the headlights blazing I was really alive / And yet my mind was blowing". A tale of tequila, whiskey and, um, oily patches and canals, the song is a blast from start to finish. It's followed by 'Stonehenge', a two-minute keyboard instrumental that is highly atmospheric, even if it's slightly like a self-indulgent horror-movie soundtrack.

Of 'Disturbing The Priest' Geezer later told *Metal Sludge*: "We were recording at Richard Branson's studio, and right next to it was a monastery. We were so loud in the studio that the priests started complaining about it, so we ended up calling the song 'Disturbing The Priest'." It's a great song, with Gillan on almost unhinged form – he shrieks and cackles throughout the song, hollering vague lines such as "The force of the devil is the darkness the priest has to face / The force of the night will destroy him but will not disgrace" and adding some weird, almost spoken harmony vocals to lend distinction from the barrage of wails. Geezer is on top form on this song, throwing in some elaborate fills.

'The Dark' is 45 seconds of electronic keyboard coughs, and quite disposable, leading into the seven-minutes-plus of 'Zero The Hero', a majestic, multilayered riffathon. With a fistful of excellent, ominous riffs, the song is one of the high points of *Born Again*, aided by judiciously applied keyboard sounds. Although Gillan's vocals are too forward in the mix – sounding incongruous against the slightly distant mass of riffs – he delivers lines such as "Your head is firmly nailed to your TV channel / But someone else's finger's on the control panel" with absolute conviction, Geezer's bass part is rock solid (sounding more crunchy than usual) and Ward, no matter what he was going through, plays flawlessly. Iommi's solos are both endless and endlessly inventive.

'Digital Bitch' hasn't aged well, with the concept – threatening computers and the people who make money from them – rather old hat by this stage. "There ain't one thing she can't afford to buy / She's the richest bitch in town / Her big fat daddy was a money machine / He made a fortune from computers" is all very well in context, but the chirpy, ascending chorus is just odd and the riffs rather too stock to stand out.

The six minutes of 'Born Again' itself are worth investing in: with a barrage of studio treatment applied to both guitar and bass, the sound is intriguing. Lyrically, Gillan has stepped back into dragons'n'Dio territory, yelling earnest lines like "The thrust of my challenge is aimed at the hearts of mutant gods who think we're all the same", which must have meant something profound at the time. Still, the sentiments fit the slow, epic nature of the song, and the lengthy outro – Iommi ascending into the stratosphere in a haze of reverb – works perfectly.

"Take me to the river baby drink my wine / When I'm going down won't you throw me a line?" suggests Gillan in 'Hot Line', a respectable if unremarkable rock outing with a meaty riff and some slightly intrusive keyboard effects. Occasionally the regular screams that the singer throws into the mix sounds a little strained, however: perhaps another few takes might have ironed this out.

The album ends with 'Keep It Warm', the tale of a man torn by his commitment to a woman: "D'ya hear the rumour that's going around? / Say I'm ruined 'cos I've settled down / It's not true, well maybe half and half / You know I love you but I still like a laugh!" explains Gillan. Iommi's solos spiral effortlessly throughout, Ward executes a tempo change with panache and the song sprawls downwards until the final fade.

For all its flaws, mainly sonic and lyrical in nature, *Born Again* was immensely popular despite the gut feeling of so many Sabbath followers that Gillan was basically a stranger in the camp. Ian himself enjoyed the experience mightily, telling me: "It was great fun. It was definitely a short-term thing. It came about in a most bizarre fashion, we just got drunk and that was it and I was in the band before I knew it – quite happily and without any regrets too, I might say. We had to complete the whole album, and we had to rehearse, and as usual I had to do a lot of catch-up writing. I didn't see a lot of the band because they were night people and I was really a day person. They'd be coming home from the clubs in Birmingham as I was getting up and cooking my breakfast."

How had the LP turned out so well, I asked him? "Anyone can produce the most amazing heavy rock sounds with today's machines, but it's not the chords – it's how you play them. It's the person that counts. That was very important. If you ever talk about tracing things back to their roots – if ever I could see a direct line from Seattle to Birmingham, it would be Tony Iommi, right back at the birth of it. I never saw anyone else play like him back in those days. No, not better than Ritchie: how could he be better? It's like the rock Olympics: who can play or shout or drum faster or louder? It's a ludicrous concept in my book. They are what they are – neither is better than the other."

The ensuing tour became the stuff of legend thanks to Don Arden, who came up with the idea of an extravagant stage set to suit the anthemic songs, and the *Spinal Tap* movie, which lampooned it mercilessly the following year. As Geezer later told Jeb Wright: "It had nothing to do with me! In fact, I was the one who thought it was really corny. We had Sharon Osbourne's dad, Don Arden, managing us. He came up with the idea of having the stage set being Stonehenge. He wrote the dimensions down and gave it to our tour manager."

So far, so good – but Arden had made a crucial error. "He wrote it down in metres, but he meant to write it down in feet. The people who made it saw 15 metres instead of 15 feet. It was 45 feet high and it wouldn't fit on any stage anywhere, so we just had to leave it in the storage area. It cost a fortune to make but there was not a building on earth that you could fit it into!"

Iommi added: "In fact we didn't know just how huge it would turn out in real life, and in the end we only performed with the full stage set on one single gig, in Reading at the festival there. I mean, we couldn't even get it into the big halls in America. We didn't know when we saw little models of it that it would turn out bigger than a fucking hotel. *Spinal Tap* stole the idea but they turned it around in the movie!"

Gillan later wrote of the massive set: "This was all broken down into sections which sat inside each other, packed into containers and shipped to Canada where we were to open the tour at the Maple Leaf Gardens, an ice hockey arena in Toronto. Most of it stayed in the containers as, with great difficulty, we were only able to erect three of the monoliths, with two cross pieces, reaching some 30 feet in the air."

The lunacy went even further. It was arranged that in the intro to the show, a dwarf dressed as the diabolical baby from the *Born Again* LP sleeve would sit atop the fake Stonehenge and mime to the hideous sound of a baby crying. He would then 'fall' off the back of the 'stone' onto a mattress to cushion his fall. Then a parade of roadies (Gillan: "dressed as druids with cowls pulled over their faces and Reeboks barely showing under their robes") would walk across the stage, attempting to give the impression of demonically possessed monks.

There was only one way all this theatrical foolishness could go, and it came at an early show. Although drummer Bevan and Gillan had raised concerns about the possible pitfalls of such an elaborate (not to say pretentious) production, Arden had apparently said, "Don't worry, the kids will love it," and the show went on. Unfortunately, Gillan had still to learn the words of some of the songs, taping a lyric sheet to the stage for safe keeping, and when a huge cloud of dry ice wafted across the stage, it obscured his view entirely. As he wrote: "For some reason the one element missing from the production rehearsal was the dry ice; and now a chest-high white cloud was billowing at a fearsome rate towards the front of the stage . . . I set off on a hopeless race for my words. I ducked into the cloud and started vainly swatting the mist for a clue to the first line. At this point the footlights came on, increasing my difficulties. On cue, I stood up, not entirely, just my head above the dry ice, and sang some lines of total gibberish . . . as the dry ice was beginning to lower and thin so my flapping and crouching became more bizarre and I was reduced, along with the audience, to a hopeless giggling wreck."

And so Black Sabbath – Gillan, Iommi, Butler, keyboard player Geoff Nicholls and Bevan – hit the road. Europe was calling and the sound of cash-registers ringing must have been deafening.

Passing through Norway, Sweden, Finland and Denmark, the band gave the usual round of interviews. At one point Geezer somewhat tactlessly explained Bevan's presence with the words: "Bill Ward was totally messed up with alcohol and drugs. He had to go to a hospital, otherwise he would have died. When we started to record *Born Again*, Bill was just sober enough to come to the studio and play. But he wasn't able to join us on tour. He has to get his medical treatment constantly, so he [has to] stay near his own doctor. Besides, on tours you usually drink so much, that he would not have survived . . ."

The festival circuit included a notable set at Reading with a host of prog-rock and even punk (or punkish) bands on the bill – including the Stranglers, Marillion, Steve Harley & Cockney Rebel – as well as a Dublin date with Motörhead and Twisted Sister. The full 'Henge set travelled across Europe in September and into Canada and the USA in October and November, incurring vast transport costs but mostly enthralling the crowds – at least after the initial teething problems had been ironed out. To many fans' amazement, Sabbath would often encore with a rendition of Deep Purple's 'Smoke On The Water', a signature song of Gillan's old band.

Rock activity was frenetic elsewhere, too. On December 10, 1983, Ozzy Osbourne released a new album, *Bark At The Moon*. His band – Jake E Lee, Aldridge and Airey resuming their old places on guitars, drums and keyboards with Bob Daisley returning on bass in place of Rudy Sarzo – had produced a fully rounded work, and one which has (like all his Eighties albums) earned its place in history.

The opener, 'Bark At The Moon', is the trademark semi-horror schtick which Ozzy was still peddling some years after Sabbath had dropped that particular angle. "Years spent in torment / Buried in a nameless grave" he wails over Lee's very Rhoadsian staccato riff, as if telling the tale of the creature on the album sleeve – Ozzy dressed up in a werewolf's outfit and draped, rather camply, over a branch. Still, the fans loved all this devilish nonsense: as they did 'You're No Different', in which Ozzy questioned, "Everything that I say and do / In your eyes is always wrong / Tell me where do I belong / In this sick society". The backing – a limp, synthesised soft-rock wash – lets his otherwise competent lyrics down, however, and the song isn't a classic.

'Now You See It (Now You Don't)' is Osbourne at his most obscure, referring to an 'overbearing woman' and asking if she can take it like a man. He adds: "Everybody's feeling everything you've got to feel / I've got something that you can conceal" over a loping riff to moderate success. 'Rock'N'Roll Rebel' is also an average rock song, with Ozzy's vague accusations ("The ministry of truth that deals with pretence / The ministry of peace that sits in defence") neither his best nor his most memorable.

'Centre Of Eternity' is much better, thanks to a completely Sabbath-like organ sound from Airey and suitably epic lyrics such as the commendably honest "There's no present / There's no future / I don't even know about the past'. 'So Tired' is another Beatles homage, with 'Eleanor Rigby'-style strings and all, and – although it's a little sugary – does give the 'madman of rock' the chance to show off his influences. "I stayed at home remaining true / While you were out with you know who", he sings, an unlikely scenario indeed.

'Slow Down', with the descending keyboard motif after every shout of the title phrase, is too poppy to take seriously, as is the message – a warning from Ozzy (of all people) to an unknown subject that life is a marathon, not a sprint: "I tried to tell you time and time again / You know you'll have to pay the consequence / Now you're obsessed with such a pace / Now slow and steady wins the race".

Don Airey lays a load of cheesy keys all over 'Waiting For Darkness', too, which – although it was a favoured technique of so much Eighties pop-rock, from Journey and Bryan Adams onwards – sounds very plastic today. But Ozzy's on good form, executing a memorable chorus melody that helped the tune stand out. At least 'Spiders In The Night', a suitably creepy closer, leaves the listener feeling involved: as Ozzy warbles "Spiders in the night / Creeping round the walls / Now you'll feel them crawling over you" over a clean-picked guitar backing of horror-movie quality, he taps into the right vein at last.

'Bark At The Moon' and 'So Tired' were released as singles, making numbers 20 and 21 respectively, each coming with a memorable video as the MTV phenomenon took off, with Ozzy appearing as a mad scientist in the former. For 'So Tired', a special effect involving a breaking mirror saw Osbourne showered with broken glass, although he wasn't injured.

The album caused some controversy when a young Canadian named James Jollimore stabbed a mother and her two sons in the city of Halifax on New Year's Eve 1983. The Canadian Press Wire Service quoted a friend of the killer as saying: "Jimmy said that every time he listened to the song he felt strange inside . . . He said when he heard it on New Year's Eve he went out and stabbed someone." Another meaningless tragedy, the incident served to fuel the fire under the Ozzy legend.

Bark At The Moon wasn't a huge success – it reached number 24 on the album chart – but at least it maintained Ozzy's momentum, in a time when traditional heavy metal was facing serious competition. Although the NWOBHM – apart from Maiden, Leppard and a couple of other club-level stalwarts – had more or less faded by 1984, metal fans could get their fix from the huge wave of thrash metal bands which were coming out of the San Francisco Bay Area and the US East Coast. Such bands – led into the mid-Eighties by the Big Four Of Thrash (Metallica, Megadeth, Anthrax and Slayer) – were phenomenally powerful in comparison with the old guard, converting legions of ex-Sabbath and Purple followers with their extreme speed and technical precision.

Both Ozzy and Sabbath now had the threat of competition by a second new wave of metal, which at least gave them something in common as they faced each other across the no-man's-land of the press. Although there was still a rivalry between the two camps ("Leaving that band was the best amputation I ever had in my life," sneered Ozzy to *Circus*), the two sides were beginning to mellow towards each other, perhaps encouraged by the success of both new bands. "It's hard to keep a relationship going with new people," said Geezer, adding: "With Ozzy it's different, I mean, we grew up together. Yeah, we might end up back together in a few years." Ozzy said: "It's competition, I suppose. But the whole music business is a game like Monopoly: I turn a card over and I find out I'll be playing with guy X, who last week was playing with the guy I fired three weeks ago. In about the year three billion and four I'll probably wind up playing with Sabbath again. But I haven't got any firm plans for that one." Ozzy was happy, it seemed, to recruit session musicians on an ad hoc basis, under the watchful eye of Sharon. "The people who work with me aren't there on a permanent basis," he said. "They're working with me when I'm working, and if they want to work elsewhere when I'm not working, they're free to."

As well as coming out of the line-up problems into a period of semi-security, Iommi and Geezer had also locked down a new management agreement with Don Arden: "We didn't know what to do next," Butler explained. "We just didn't want to go on with the band the way it was. Don told me and Tony to keep it together, to keep positive thoughts. As long as we are together, he said, we should be able to keep the two of us going. He helped us out with a lot of things at a bad time."

It was encouraging to learn that Ozzy and Geezer had actually spent quality time together in late 1982 when Ozzy, sporting a new skinhead haircut, paid a surprise visit to his old bandmate. "It was three in the morning," said the bassist. "There was a bald-headed lunatic outside the door. I didn't have a clue who he was with his head shaved. . . . We got along fine. We talked about old times. Ozzy and I go back forever, and he just can't get away from the people who were in the original band."

Cheerful as this anecdote undoubtedly was, Butler was – as in 1979 – experiencing some doubts about his future with Sabbath. As he told one Finnish magazine as the exhausting *Born Again* tour wound on, "Sometimes I get tired. I've been in Black Sabbath for almost 15 years, and there are moments when it's not that exciting any more. But I wouldn't want to play in any other band either. And we've noticed that you can't let things [fall] from your hands, you have try all the time and be aware of everything."

It wasn't easy for anyone to be in Black Sabbath at this stage of the band's career, it seemed. As the tour snaked its way around the world into

1984, both Ian Gillan and Bev Bevan made it clear that their time in the band would terminate with the tour.

1983 had been a year of rebirths: but three months into 1984, only Iommi and Geezer remained. They had no idea how much turmoil would follow, and this time, only one man would be left standing . . .

CHAPTER FOURTEEN

1984–1985

WHILE Sabbath wound down their tour with Ian Gillan, ex-drummer Bill Ward finally found the strength to enter rehab for his alcoholism – and stick to the regime it prescribed. This time his recovery would be for real, and when Gillan and Bev Bevan left Sabbath in March 1984, he was asked to rejoin the old band. Clear-headed but physically weaker than he had been in previous years, he threw himself back into preparations for a new album.

Iommi and Butler, meanwhile, were wading through hundreds of tapes sent to the Sabbath office from singers who hoped to replace Gillan. After listening to hundreds of hours of vocals (as Iommi later explained, the only good point about the exercise was that the applicants all knew the Sabbath catalogue), in May 1984 they selected an American called David Donato, who had sung in the glam-metal band White Tiger and other acts. Donato, a former model, had worked with Keith Relf of the Yardbirds and other respected musicians and brought some glamour back into the, by now, slightly ageing band.

The band – Iommi, Butler and Ward – were confident enough in their new recruit to execute some press interviews with him. Although their recorded work together would not in fact extend beyond a few demo tracks, the quartet came across with quiet assurance in a notorious *Kerrang!* feature published at the time, which carried glossy shots of the pouting, hairsprayed Donato and the bearded Ward, who launched into a barrage of self-analysis which the writer barely refrained from mocking.

"I sit on the beach and meditate," said the ursine drummer, "and then I find out what a complete waste of time it all was, then I get down and kick ass, that's the bottom line, anyway! I went through a stage last year when I didn't want to play any more, and it was the most depressing time of my life. I went through this self-pity bullshit thing for months where I didn't feel anything at all . . . [But then] I started to write and play, and then Tony and Geezer called me up around February or March, and I was starting to feel good about me again. I'd come out of that depression or whatever it was I'd gone into. I haven't had a drink for quite a long time now, which is good for me."

Donato and Iommi didn't have much to say, although the former was confident enough to say, perhaps inadvisably, "It all seems to be going very smoothly. I always had a picture of what the right singer in Sabbath should be – and it was me!" Iommi, meanwhile, had learned his lesson in the wake of three departed singers to date, not saying much more than, "I'm not going to say anything, because every time I say something, that we're going in a new direction, I put my foot in it," and adding of Gillan, "Personally, I think Ian's a very nice chap, but I don't think it worked out onstage."

It was left to Geezer to fill in the details. It emerged that there had been some bad blood about Gillan's departure, as he explained, "The first part of the American tour was great. The second part wasn't happening at all. Ian just didn't seem to be interested. Then we heard about halfway through that Deep Purple were getting back together. Ian hadn't told us anything. In fact, he never did tell us he was leaving."

In fact, Gillan did go on to re-form Purple after leaving Sabbath, although subsequent reports have all indicated that the parting of the ways with Butler et al. was nothing but amicable.

Butler also attempted to reassure readers with an indirect reference to a return to the glory days of Ozzy, saying: "We're trying to get back to the old sort of lyrical ideas, because before, when Ozzy was with us, I used to write all the lyrics for him, and a few of our fans have criticised our lyrics since Ronnie and Ian came on the scene."

Iommi added of the Gillan tour: "The entire *Born Again* tour turned out a bit disappointing. And prior to that, we had been shocked about how poor the album pressing was. We were already out on the road by then so we couldn't stop that from coming out. It didn't take very long until we heard that things were going on with Deep Purple, but Ian didn't know that we knew. We heard about it about six months before it happened . . . we played well, but to me Ian Gillan is better off singing with Deep Purple. It may have suffered because we were four stars entering the stage. I like Ian though. He was good on the album and I like him."

Within weeks, Donato was out of the band, to nobody's surprise. Since then, his role has rarely been discussed, although Bill did once tell *Sabbathlive*: "Yes, I knew David. He is a very nice gentleman. I liked the guy a lot."

After the dust had settled on the Donato fiasco, Iommi passed the blame – plausibly – to the record company, saying: "The record company were in a hurry to show that the band would continue. David was there but nothing was really set in stone . . . the Donato thing was done in haste, it never should have gone that far. We went public before we were sure about it. This is typical, we've made so many mistakes like this in our career. In the old days everybody used to come to me, I used to handle everything. I picked up the lads to get them to the rehearsals and so on. I was a little older and they were always asking me for my opinion. I was like the father in the band and I think we needed that at the time. The period of the first three records were like that, they always came to me and asked for my thoughts on things, but I really didn't want it to be like that. I just wanted to be a guy in the band. I wanted everybody to be involved. Once that finally happened, everything turned into chaos. No decisions were being made and it was past the point were I could have the final say because now we were a band."

The madness continued with singer Ron Keel, who had impressed many observers with his vocal performance alongside the guitar virtuoso Yngwie J Malmsteen in Steeler. As Keel later explained, "I had been doing the Keel demos at Pasha in Hollywood, which was owned by Quiet Riot producer Spencer Proffer. Quiet Riot had just sold 10 million records and Spencer was the hot producer, and he was set to do the next Sabbath album. Ian Gillan had just quit and Spencer heard the Keel demos, hooked me up with Tony and Geezer, and I demoed some of the material that Spencer wanted them to record and we hung out for a few days plotting the future (basically Tony and Geezer wishing they could get Ozzy back). MTV, radio, everybody announced that Ron Keel was the new singer in Sabbath, but something went sour in their deal with Spencer Proffer and I went with it. They went through a bunch of other singers, but all they really wanted was Ozzy. I know for a fact that no singer, including me, was ever 'in' Black Sabbath except Ozzy Osbourne." At least Keel, unlike Donato, had the luxury of going on to a successful career: while Donato vanished shortly after, Ron's band Keel went on to become a respected B-league metal act until the effective end of their career in the early Nineties.

Despite all the assurances that the band (with the exception of the wisely reticent Iommi) had given *Kerrang!*, the U-turn was made complete by the departure for a second time of Bill Ward in summer 1984. Although he was maintaining his sobriety, it was by no means an easy task to stay off the booze in the Sabbath environment. What's more, he had finally admitted to himself and his bandmates that as he saw it, Sabbath without Ozzy was not Sabbath at all.

"The biggest thing that was going on for me during this period," he said, "was that I was fighting for my life at that time. After *Born Again*, I had got drunk again and went through a horrible period which lasted for about four months . . . I finally came back into reality. I think it was January 2 or 3, 1984. When I got sober in 1984, sobriety became my absolute number one focus. It had to be. I knew it was life or death, so I knew that's where my focus had to be. I know that it can sound pretty selfish and in a way it is selfish, but as I said, I was fighting for my life at the time . . . My sobriety felt different in the sense that I knew that I had to be ruthlessly honest with the guys, which is something that I had failed to do in 1983. I had a very bitter experience in 1983, even though I loved doing the album. I knew that I needed to be honest with myself and everybody around me.

"During the rehearsals with David Donato, I knew that one of the reasons why I'd been unhappy and why I couldn't allow myself to be fully immersed in the band, was because Ozz wasn't there . . . and it was a nagging truth. It was something I had to come to terms with that and in very early 1984 I came to terms with that truth. I was honest enough to admit that to myself, and admit that to Tony and Geezer at that time. So, very very sadly, I left Black Sabbath. And this time, I didn't drink. I didn't do what I had done in 1983, and stayed sober. And I left with some honour and dignity."

He added when I interviewed him: "I had the same feelings that I'd had when Ronnie and Ian were in the band, which was basically that it didn't feel the same as it had with Ozzy. I would have loved to have continued on, but it felt that I was being dishonest with myself. So I said my goodbyes. After that I basically knew that there was no way back. And it was at that time that I decided – by my own truths – that I couldn't do Sabbath without Ozz."

How did the others react? "They were really supportive. They knew. I said, I just can't do it. There were so many times after that I wanted to go back and play with them, I just felt terrible. I just wanted to play music with the guys that I'd been playing with all my life, but the reason I couldn't go back was that I knew that things wouldn't be the same again, with someone else."

As Iommi considered the band's future without a singer and without Ward, he was rocked shortly after by the news that Geezer, too, had decided to leave. The Gillan tour, with all the mock-theatrics and the disinterest that he perceived in the singer, had disgusted him, as had the farcical recruitments and embarrassing climbdowns with both David Donato

176

and Ron Keel. He quit to form his own outfit, The Geezer Butler Band, although they didn't record seriously. As he later said, "It was a fun group that played around in England with a bunch of songs I'd had in my pocket for 14 years."

However, he had other motivations than simply performing new music. As he said, "It was great because I hadn't seen much of my kids. My second one was born in 1984 and he had a lot of problems. I wanted to stay with him and take time out."

And so Tony Iommi was the last man in Black Sabbath. For the latter part of 1984, silence reigned from the Sabbath camp.

In the Seventies, while heavy metal suffered its birth pains and disco, glam-rock and punk ran wild, much of America's population – as in any country – ignored all of it, simply consuming easy-on-the-ear music from performers who looked good and didn't offer many challenges. If you were in New York at more or less any part of the decade, you might have visited a show on Broadway, where the most successful shows took on charmed lives, enduring for hundreds, and sometimes thousands, of performances. In 1971, a production of *Jesus Christ Superstar* caught the public's attention and was staged an astonishing 718 times.

The singer in the title role was an Ohio native called Jeff Fenholt, who – with his long locks and operatic voice – was perfect for the part. The production was so successful that its reputation spread to the most unlikely quarters, with the interest of those of more rock'n'roll persuasion piqued by the rumoured drugs and booze in which the stars, including Fenholt, indulged. The singer later found employment in the rock band Bible Black, with members of Rainbow, although the band didn't record.

Recordings took place in early 1985. From what Fenholt says, it seems that he was initially brought on board with the expectation of joining Sabbath the group, but this swiftly mutated into demo-ing material for a solo album by Iommi plus session men – drummer Eric Singer and bassist Gordon Copley from the Lita Ford Band (Iommi and Ford were an item at this point). As Singer later wrote: "Jeff Fenholt sang on some demos for Tony Iommi in 1985 in LA. He was never in Black Sabbath. Tony was looking for a singer for what was supposed to be his 'solo' album. Jeff came down and sang some ideas in the studio for what were simply demos . . . that's pretty much all there is to the story. Jeff had a great voice but it just didn't work out."

And so Black Sabbath, effectively just Tony Iommi at this point, ground to a halt again. By May 1985 Fenholt was gone, Geezer was gone, Ward was gone and Gordon Copley had returned to Lita Ford's band. Drummer Eric Singer had elected to remain on board, and Iommi still had his manager Don Arden and girlfriend – and briefly fiancée – Lita on his side.

In fact, the band were about to surprise everyone with an unexpected move – albeit one that might mark them out permanently as a band who were living in the past. At the unseasonably early time of 10am on July 13, 1985, 20,000 music fans were astounded to a man by the arrival onstage of Ozzy Osbourne, Tony Iommi, Geezer Butler and Bill Ward, who tore into a rendition of 'Children Of The Grave'. This being the mid-Eighties, Geezer and Tony were wearing crotch-hugging spandex, while Geezer toted a very of-its-era BC Rich Ironbird bass – bright scarlet and ludicrously jagged in shape – and Iommi peered out behind mirrored shades. Ozzy, meanwhile, had bulked up in previous years and, with his bleached-blonde highlights, nocturnally pale skin and a long silver coat, didn't look his best. Only Bill, in sedate black, seemed not to be playing the overdressed star role.

The band, reunited after so long, were off again almost as soon as they began, adhering to the Live Aid organisers' rule of only 15 minutes per act, although they did deliver crushing versions of 'Iron Man' and 'Paranoid' before their exit. Metal fans were left in shock by the event itself and by Ozzy's wasted, over-the-top look, and immediately asked if a more permanent re-formation – the obvious thing to do in the wake of Sabbath's disastrous last couple of years – was on the cards.

In fact, negotiations for such a reunion were taking place behind the scenes, but were soon scuppered when management logistics got in the way. Geezer once explained that the legal issues between Don Arden and his daughter Sharon were still causing hindrances: "Ozzy was served with lawsuit papers from his father-in-law. He took it personally from Tony even though Tony didn't have anything to do with it." Nonetheless, fans never dropped the idea of a classic line-up reunion, making it rather difficult for Sabbath to make credible headway without Ozzy at least rumoured to be coming back on board.

Regardless of all the hearsay, Tony Iommi returned to the grindstone of assembling a new Sabbath line-up and recording another new album. Basic bass and drum tracks had been laid down in the Fenholt sessions: what he really needed was a singer. He explained: "We had had a meeting with the original band after Gillan and we had decided to reunite within 12 months. Nine months later we're doing Live Aid together in Philadelphia and suddenly it was all too clear that the problems on the business side were just too big for us, [so] that was the end of that. Geezer had been writing stuff that didn't sound like Sabbath at all and he was just fed up and wanted to try that stuff out somewhere else. I immediately decided to carry on as Sabbath then, with or without the other guys, and get my solo LP out with that name on it. All the music was written for it."

Enter Glenn Hughes, the journeyman singer and bassist whose remarkable vocals had graced albums by Trapeze, Deep Purple and a host of other heavy rock projects since the late Sixties, earning him the sobriquet 'The Voice Of Rock'. An old friend of Iommi's since the early days, Hughes added instant panache to the lyrics written by Tony (and rejected by Fenholt) during recording sessions at Cherokee Studios and elsewhere in July and August. Other lyrics came from Geoff Nicholls, producer Jeff Glixman and Hughes himself. Iommi, who still retained the services of drummer Eric Singer, added a bassist, Dave Spitz (nicknamed 'The Beast' for his bouffant hair), brother of Anthrax guitarist Dan, to complete the line-up.

"Glenn has been a friend for years," said Iommi. "I used to know him when he was in Trapeze, way before Deep Purple. In fact, when Ozzy left we considered Glenn for Sabbath at the time. We jammed but for different reasons the timing just wasn't right. But now, as I asked him to contribute with his voice, and later when I told him that I wanted to call it Black Sabbath, he was very eager to give it a shot."

Eric Singer said in an interview at the time, "Black Sabbath was sort of on a hiatus, and Tony asked [Gordon Copley] and I if we'd like to work on some demos with him. We got to be friends, and then he asked me to play on the album. Eventually, he got Glenn Hughes to sing on it and then decided to put it out as a Black Sabbath album . . . I never knew Tony before, but everyone who did tells me that he's real excited about the new line-up. He's a very quiet and shy person. He keeps things pretty much to himself . . . I guess he's happy 'cos he's got younger guys in the band now. He calls it new blood. He says we're hungry, and that gives him new energy . . . It's funny, I remember going to see [Sabbath] at the Coliseum in '76 when Boston opened for them. I would've never thought that I'd end up playing in this band."

As the new album was recorded, mixed and mastered in late 1985, it seemed – as it had done so many times before – that Iommi might at last have found a working band that could last the course. He and Hughes were veterans, although both men were still in their thirties, and their rhythm section was composed of young, hungry musicians with energy to spare.

And yet, when *Seventh Star* was released on March 1, 1986, it received the usual criticism by comparison to the early Ozzy era. Some of this might have been due to its dubious billing – 'Black Sabbath Featuring Tony Iommi' – rather than the more honest option of releasing the LP under his own name. Even the cover art was simply a solo portrait of the guitarist. As Glenn Hughes later recalled, "For me, the album, when we recorded it, was called *Tony Iommi*, period! But when it was all mixed his manager said, 'Let's call it Black Sabbath!' To make more money. So if you listen to it as a Tony Iommi album it's great. If you listen to it as a Black Sabbath album it's not very good. Let's just say that I don't belong in Black Sabbath. I have said that all along."

Revealingly, Iommi said that an actual solo album would sound "exactly like *Seventh Star*. I have always tried to do exactly what I feel like on the Sabbath albums, like jazz stuff for instance. Like the stuff on *Never Say Die!* We also did guitar–based stuff with the London Philharmonic on *Sabotage*. I have written stuff for the next LP that sounds more like typical Sabbath. I have quite a lot of songs ready to go and the only reason that I. haven't recorded them yet is lack of time."

Lyric writing was a new step for Iommi, as he later explained: "That was a new experience for me. Glenn and Geoff helped me out with that. When Ozzy was in the band, everything was written by Geezer and after that we had Dio and Gillan doing most of it. My main job has always been the music. The main theme comes from a Nostradamus prediction that says that there will be a rebirth when the seven planets line up in the sky. Things like that have always interested me. The idea for the cover goes back to the title track, there's nothing there. I'm looking at nothing, a rebirth."

This extended as far as the guitarist considering whether a second guitar should be used onstage. After all, in metal circles of the time, a twin guitar setup was both necessary for heaviness and soloing versatility. As he said, "You know, Geoff has been a member of the band since 1980 and I've been thinking about letting him onstage playing a guitar synth. He is a very good guitar player. But I don't know, maybe people will think that it looks strange with two guitar players? I want him to be seen now."

The opening song, 'In For The Kill', says it all. It's a melodic hard rock song, laced with Geoff Nicholls' keyboards, that doesn't do much for guitar lovers – apart from Iommi's usual blistering solos – as the mix is focused on Hughes' soaring melodies. With lines such as "Raging with fury, the king has come", the band is back squarely in Ronnie James Dio territory – this, however, is preferable to the slick arena ballad of 'No Stranger To Love', which is a soft, slippery tune loaded with synth washes and guitars a long, long way off. Hughes wails "Living on the streets, I'm no stranger to love", an approach which hair-rockers like Bon Jovi were doing more adeptly by 1986 and which was rapidly becoming outmoded.

On 'Turn To Stone', Sabbath (or at least Iommi) attempt a tougher, Motörhead-like blast through biker-style rock, managing not to overdo the keyboard elements or the vocal melodies. Spitz's bass parts are solid and the layers of riffage reveal the fact that, on peak, the new band could deliver an approximation of heavy metal in the era of Metallica and Slayer. 'Sphinx (The Guardian)' is a reasonably effective ambient synth instrumental and sets the scene for 'Seventh Star' itself, a trademark Sabbath epic with pyramids and pharoahs all over it: Iommi's Egyptology-focused lyrics avoided being ridiculous by not overdoing the imagery, merely mentioning the icons while Nicholls swathes the songs with Eastern melodies.

The lightweight hair-rock continues with 'Danger Zone', in which Hughes is required to utter vaguely macho sentiments such as "I'm gonna take a chance in the danger zone" over a barrage of expertly layered guitar lines. So far, *Seventh Star* is suffering from the post-Ozzy phenomenon that has plagued all Sabbath's albums since *Never Say Die!* – musical excellence let down by poor, or clichéd, lyrics. 'Heart Like A Wheel' is better, with a spacious, bluesy sound that allows Hughes to exercise a lower range than usual and a lyric that complains of a capricious lover. At over six minutes it's a little overindulgent, but fans of Iommi relished the chance to listen to him indulge his creative whims on a series of solos, while hints of the crushing Sabbath of old were revealed in some of the main riffs.

The record ends with 'Angry Heart', which segues into 'In Memory . . .': the former is a generic rock song of little note compared to 'Seventh Star' and 'Heart Like A Wheel', but the latter – thought by some to be about Iommi's late father – is a sensitive, partly acoustic tune of some weight. "It's still haunting me . . ." sings Hughes, using all the vocal tricks he can muster to wind the song down.

Seventh Star reached number 27 in March 1986 and dropped out of the charts after only five weeks, a B-league release in the rock environment of the day. The subsequent tour looked set to bolster the LP's performance, however, but more problems awaited the band: the most significant of these was Glenn Hughes himself, who was recovering at this time from a drug addiction that was both well-known and well-documented. After only six dates, Hughes was fired.

The story behind the expulsion of Hughes is one of the more sordid tales of both his and Sabbath's career. After all, Iommi himself had told one reporter that Glenn had mastered his addiction: "He is in control now. He has had problems, but that is true for all of us really. He had a bad period in his life when he was ill and gained weight, but he is in a new phase in his life now where he wants to focus on his life and his career again. It's hard to stop somebody that has made a real commitment and he knows that we are all there for him."

The *Seventh Star* tour was all set to be a career high point, if you believed the band's press spiel at the time: "It will still be a nice show. I think it will look great," said Iommi. "On the left side of the stage there will be like a city, with chimneys and stuff, and then there will be like a bridge that goes by the drums to the other side of the stage, that will represent the future with lasers and stuff. So we are looking at a bridge into the future. A time machine. The idea is to present Black Sabbath entering the future. We have rehearsed for three months. We'll do 'Zero The Hero' from the last album, the rest will be classic stuff and songs from the new album. But Glenn doesn't want to do any Purple songs, I don't think he wants to even think about that period to be honest. It's nice to see him enjoy himself now.

"I don't want to repeat old mistakes again," he added, "and the last band was so false. I want to do it right this time. The guys I'm working with now are very eager to prove themselves. A lot of well-known people were in touch with me but I wanted hungry guys with me, people with no past. Glenn has a reputation, but he still has the hunger that I'm looking for. He has something to prove on his own."

So what caused the disaster? Glenn told me himself what happened . . .

"What happened was, three days before pre-production, we were in this massive studio where everybody plays showcases. The night before, my girlfriend's mother had flown in – I'd never met her before and she turned out to be Satan's child from hell. She was a nightmare. We had a big argument and she pulled a gun and everything. This was the kind of person I used to hang out with before I got sober. We were pretty drunk and this guy [Sabbath's tour manager] John Downey, who is now deceased, got into a bit of a thing with me. He did strike me."

Why did he hit you? Did you hit him first?

"No, no, no. I probably provoked him verbally. He took it on himself to hit the lead singer of a band that was going on tour tomorrow. Even Don Arden said, couldn't you have hit him in the back or something? He really, really hit me so hard that the bottom part of my eye socket was fractured, not known to me, and it went into my nose, which caused a clot – like, clots of blood – to gather on my actual larynx. So over a period of days it kept building up and closed the air . . . so I was making kind of a

THE ORIGINAL BLACK SABBATH REFORM FOR LIVE AID'S PHILADELPHIA LEG IN 1985.
THE NEWLY SOBER BILL FOUND THE GIG A STRUGGLE, BUT THE BAND WERE HAPPY ENOUGH WITH
THEIR PERFORMANCE TO CONSIDER A PERMANENT REUNION – AT LEAST, BRIEFLY. *(LFI)*

RONNIE JAMES DIO (FOREGROUND) JOINS THE BAND, 1982: NOTE THE NOW-UBIQUITOUS
DEVIL-HORNS SIGN WHICH HE INTRODUCED TO THE HEAVY METAL SCENE. *(Fin Costello/Redferns)*

BLACK SABBATH IN 1983 WITH IAN GILLAN, TONY IOMMI, A BEARDED GEEZER BUTLER
AND (SEATED) TEMPORARY DRUMMER BEV BEVAN. *(LFI)*

SABBATH – OR AT LEAST TONY IOMMI – WITH (FROM LEFT) BASSIST NEIL MURRAY, SINGER TONY MARTIN AND THE LEGENDARY DRUMMER COZY POWELL. *(LFI)*

ANOTHER SHORT-LIVED (AND REGRETTABLY-STYLED) SABBATH LINE-UP IN 1986: BASSIST DAVE 'THE BEAST' SPITZ, DRUMMER ERIC SINGER, EX-DEEP PURPLE SINGER GLENN HUGHES, IOMMI AND KEYBOARD MAINSTAY GEOFF NICHOLLS. *(Richie Aaron/Redferns)*

OZZY BITES THE HEAD OFF A WHITE DOVE AT A PRESS CONFERENCE TO PROMOTE *Blizzard Of Ozz*, NEW YORK, APRIL 1981. THE INDUSTRY AND PRESS WERE REPELLED AND ATTRACTED IN EQUAL MEASURE. *(Jeffrey Mayer)*

BOB DAISLEY, OZZY AND RANDY RHOADS RECORDING *Blizzard Of Ozz* AT RIDGE FARM STUDIOS, SURREY, MAY 1980. DRUMS WERE RECORDED BY LEE KERSLAKE. *(Fin Costello/Redferns)*

OZZY AND RANDY RHOADS ON STAGE AT THE HEAVY METAL HOLOCAUST FESTIVAL AT PORT VALE FOOTBALL GROUND, AUGUST 1981, AFTER SABBATH PULLED OUT AT THE LAST MINUTE. *(Alan David Perry)*

OZZY, LOOKING REMARKABLY HEALTHY AFTER BEING SHORN
OF HIS LONG HAIR, NEW YORK 1983. *(Ebet Roberts/Redferns)*

OZZY'S POLICE MUG SHOTS AFTER HIS ARREST FOR 'STAGGERING DRUNK DOWN BEALE ST, MEMPHIS TENNESSEE', IN MAY 1984. *(Rex Features)*

OZZY MARRIES SHARON, DAUGHTER OF MANAGER DON ARDEN (SECOND FROM LEFT), HAWAII, JULY 4, 1982. THE WEDDING TOOK PLACE AMID A MAELSTROM OF BUSINESS PROBLEMS FOR THE NEW COUPLE. *(Neal Preston/Retna)*

OZZY IN 1989, IN ONE OF THE LAST 'MADMAN' – THEMED PHOTO SHOOTS HE PERFORMED. AFTER THIS HIS CAREER WOULD TAKE A MORE SOBER AND SERIOUS TURN… *(Rex Features)*

reedy sound. On my fifth gig with Sabbath – in Worcester, Massachusetts – I couldn't sing, even after a month of rehearsals with Tony and the guys where I sounded great."

To Glenn's horror, he couldn't sing the notes required: "I couldn't physically sing because of the injury. I'd never been onstage before – in my whole career – and not been able to sing. And I didn't know what the problem was. I knew I'd been hit in the face, but can you imagine being this great, talented Voice Of Rock and not being able to sing? It was the worst nightmare for me."

Iommi's reaction was swift. Glenn was ousted – in typical non-confrontational fashion: "You know what he did?" laughs Glenn, not at all bitter after all these years. "He was so upset – infuriated, but still upset at the same time – he slid an aeroplane ticket under the door!"

Hughes is rational about the incident today, after having been fit and drug-free since 1991. "I wasn't kicked out, or asked to leave the band because I was getting high: it was just an unfortunate thing that happened, and it was God's intervention as well. I wasn't supposed to be onstage doing those things, and I was clearly not well. I did make an attempt, but you know, it's such a long time ago and I wasn't firing on all cylinders. I wasn't as well as I should have been. The fact of the matter is that I couldn't have sung it anyway . . . I know these things make great reading, but you know, the worst things that happen in a person's life turn out to be great. Everyone in life that I've met has had a dark period, and this was mine."

Iommi looked back on the Hughes affair regretfully, although the two men ultimately managed to salvage their long-standing friendship. As he explained, "*Seventh Star* was not supposed to be a Black Sabbath album. Glenn thought, and I thought, that he was singing the vocals for what was supposed to be my first solo album. When the record company insisted I release it as a Black Sabbath album, we had to go on tour as Black Sabbath, and that's not something Glenn wanted to do or even thought he'd have to do. He's a great singer, but he's not a Black Sabbath singer, as those few gigs we did with him proved. It also didn't help that Glenn was in a very bad place personally at that time. He was heavily into drugs and alcohol, and he was constantly surrounded by drug dealers and all sorts of shady characters. I actually hired someone to watch over Glenn – this person went on to become Guns N' Roses' tour manager – and I told Glenn that this guy was his bodyguard! I'd actually hired this fellow to keep an eye on Glenn and keep the drug dealers away from him. I mean, every time I turned around there were all these drug dealers just hanging around him. I was like 'Glenn, what the bloody hell is all this?' "

Iommi then recruited his ninth singer in seven years (Ozzy, Dio, Gillan, Donato, Keel, Donato, Fenholt, Hughes) in the shape of Ray Gillen, a 25-year-old New Jersey-born unknown who had been singing in bar bands up until this point. His biggest exposure before that point came with Rondinelli, the project of ex-Rainbow drummer Bobby Rondinelli, his brother Teddy on guitars and bassist James Lomenzo, who would later play with Ozzy's future guitarist, Zakk Wylde. As it happened, Gillen was a friend of Dave 'The Beast' Spitz – and so he was duly summoned.

After a couple of days ("they gave me an ear-nose and throat scrape"), Hughes was put on a plane – but not before discovering that a replacement was already on the scene. "I didn't notice old Ray Gillen snooping around," he says. "He was a sweetheart." This confirms the rumour that Gillen was brought in before Hughes' departure: in order to learn the Sabbath back catalogue, Gillen had to spend a couple of days with the band. However, "I didn't have time [to prepare]" said Gillen. "They told me that I had two days to learn everything!"

A show at the Glens Falls Civic Center in New York State was cancelled on March 28 thanks to Christian protesters (Iommi said, "I think it's ridiculous that certain pressure groups are interested in censoring freedom of speech"), but the band used the opportunity to rehearse with Gillen, who debuted the following day in New Haven after learning the songs in just a couple of days. The show went well – although Gillen resorted to cue cards on a few occasions – and the crowd, slightly mystified by the personnel shuffle, seemed to accept the new recruit.

As Gillen later said: "I came in during the height of the response to *Seventh Star*. Everything was all Glenn, Glenn, Glenn. He left and it stirred a lot of controversy. Nobody knew who the hell I was! The shows I did helped spread the word about me. The band started to regain some lost confidence . . . I wasn't intimidated by the Sabbath name or crowd – although the crowd made me wonder! I sang like I've been a part of that band all my life. That's the kind of attitude I had to take and I had to show them that it's the way I'm going to be. I'm going to deliver the goods whether you like it or not. Singing all of the Ozzy and Ronnie songs are fun, but I can't wait to get my own stuff out there."

He added: "I'm from the old school of rock'n'roll. That will never die. It's in everybody, but it comes back in cycles where the bands just get up there and play without giving a damn for the image. You either got it or you don't with the music. You ain't gonna get it with clothes or make-up. It's from inside and below the belt. Live, I'd rather stand still and sing than run and jump like an idiot."

The tour passed through April without further hindrance, but – interpreted by many as something of a death-knell for the band – some further dates were cancelled without notice, leading *Kerrang!* to print snootily: "Black Sabbath have cancelled their US tour, apparently due to disappointing ticket sales. And one result of this is that *Kerrang!* cannot now take a lucky reader to the States to see the band perform live. If you remember, we announced an exclusive competition in Issue 117, the prize for which was the chance to go to a Black Sabbath date in Texas during late April. A veritable deluge of entries has arrived at our offices and we hope that all entrants will understand that the decision to cancel the Sabs' American concerts was obviously both out of our hands and also those of the band's record company Vertigo, who were going to finance the trip."

However, the new line-up executed a string of shows in the UK in May and June, with audiences at healthy levels despite some local confusion about exactly who was in the band (the similarity of the names Gillen and Gillan was the cause). Gillen was relieved by his positive reception: "I thought they'd react negatively at first because Sabbath is from Birmingham, England, and I thought that they'd be Ozzy and Ronnie fanatics. They weren't like that at all. If you prove to them that you're capable of singing the songs and that you're a good person with talent, you're going to convince them. They try to intimidate you. The audience is very dedicated. Black Sabbath are like the home-town boys. Even though it wasn't the original line-up, the people make you work. If you're in that band, they expect you to be what the band has been for all these years. They want the band to be heavy . . . A few times I had people coming up to me saying, 'Glenn, what's up?' They didn't know. All they did was hear Glenn Hughes and they saw me instead. They thought I was him. American audiences are the best . . . I'm not saying that because I'm an American. They are just very cool. The girls and the guys are friendly. They are really horny for the music. They come to the shows wanting it. You walk out onstage and you see these people salivating for loud, hard, and heavy music. They want it. And you have to deliver it to them. If you don't deliver it, they can turn on you. They'll let you know if you're good or not. If the American audience likes you, it's the best."

Once the tour rolled to a halt, the new-look Sabbath signed into Air Studios in Monserrat for pre-production on yet another new album. Jeff Glixman was scheduled to produce, and – in a switch-around which has never been fully explained – bassist Spitz was replaced by the stalwart four-string Bob Daisley, even though Spitz was credited on the subsequent album.

Of the bassist situation, Gillen explained: "Dave had to leave. He had some difficulties with his personal life at the time. It was affecting him mentally. Tony felt that he should clear up what he had to do. He had to get away from the music because it was making everything worse for him. Sometimes it happens and you have to take a step back and look at what is in front of you. That's what Dave had to do. He had to think about what his priorities are . . . He'll definitely get back into it. When something like that happens, you really start getting an attitude, a fire. It's a revenge type of feeling. You want to fight back. That's where you get that fire from. He didn't have that fire before. Dave Spitz will be back with a vengeance . . . Bob [Daisley] is great. He's like Tony, he's been around for all those years. He used to play with Gary Moore and Ozzy . . . We thought we'd really get some shit from it. Bob likes the music a lot and he wants to stick with the band. I'm happy because I'm working with these legends that I used to see on TV and everywhere else and now I'm working alongside them."

Asked about Iommi's working methods, Gillen said: "He makes you work hard, yet he's lenient in letting you go at your own pace. You have to have things done. When he's ready to go into the studio, you have to have your homework done. He doesn't tell me how to sing. He just lets me know whether it's good or bad. He doesn't pressure you. He lets you flow along with everything . . . He's got that look to him that is very domineering and intense. I watch kids sit there and look at him. They get paralysed. He can give you a look that will put you in your seat. I feed off of Tony. He's without a doubt the main source of energy in the band. Everybody sort of plugs into his energy and we all fire up . . . He's been around for so long that all the experience just oozes out of him. When he sits down next to you and tells you something, you know he's been through it. He's steered me in musical ways that help me look at the music a little differently and he helped my approach. He would sit down and talk it over with me and describe what he felt about the feeling of the song and not necessarily what it was about. He would describe the essence of the song and make it very visual for me."

Recording of the basic tracks on what would become an LP entitled *The Eternal Idol* was completed in September 1986, with lyrics and solos added the following month. The album was finished off towards the end of the year. As Ray told Sydelle Schofield at *Metal Mania*, the results were promising. "The final result is wonderful! When I listen to the tape, I like it more and more. It's good to know that it's my first album. I didn't want to do anything that I would regret. I want to look back on this in a couple of years and feel good about it. And I think I will. But, like anyone would say, I'd probably feel that I should have done some things differently. That always happens when you look back. I am confident about it. Listening to the album at first, it took me awhile to get used to it and I was being a bad critic of myself. It's my first appearance on vinyl, so I guess that's natural. I can't wait until the recordings are over and it's out."

Readers will spot the youthful optimism in statements such as this, given the parade of singers that had passed through Sabbath's ranks in recent years. Gillen went on to discuss *Seventh Star*. "Tony was just getting back to heavy songs. The last album, *Seventh Star*, he kind of got away from that . . . This album, he got back into the metal. He's the Tony Iommi everyone knows and loves . . . I agree that it should be Black Sabbath. It's Tony's thing, though, and if that's what he wants to call it, that's what it's going to be and people should just accept it."

He also waxed lyrical about the press and their vision of Sabbath: "The band, no matter who it is or who's in it, should be previewed on what they're doing at the time. Black Sabbath is a legendary name and people are going to pick on it. After this album is out, people don't have to pick on it any more. It will stand on its own and will change a lot of minds. I believe that the album is great. There's great material, and Tony's playing well . . . I think that Ronnie will listen to it, and appreciate it for what it is. As far as Ozzy is concerned, he can say all he wants. I wouldn't even defend what he would have to say. It doesn't matter to me, and I really don't care. If he wants to say stuff to get himself some press, fine."

You had to admire Gillen's optimism. However, by March 1987, he was out of the band.

CHAPTER FIFTEEN

1986–1987

MEANWHILE, it had been a busy couple of years on Planet Ozzy. As Black Sabbath worked their way through a sequence of singers and readied for the release of *The Eternal Idol*, Ozzy had been on the receiving end of critical plaudits thanks to two successful LPs, *The Ultimate Sin* (released on February 22, 1986) and *Tribute* (issued on May 23, '87). The former had re-established the Ozzy brand after the moderately successful post-Rhoads album *Bark At The Moon* three years before it. Although Sabbath's Live Aid show had done Ozzy few favours, the vast *Ultimate Sin* tour – spanning March to August 1986, and crucially featuring Metallica in support – had grossed vast sums and brought him back to the top of the metal tree in commercial terms. He had now, like Sabbath, achieved 'classic metal' status, although he had only been touring in his own right for six years (the Sabs were approaching their 20th anniversary as a live act). Hooking up with Metallica, then at a critical if not commercial peak with their career-best *Master Of Puppets* album, was an expert move – thrash metal fans came to his shows, to be converted to the Ozzy cause, while older fans were persuaded that he and Sharon still had their fingers on the commercial button.

Perhaps too commercial for some: *The Ultimate Sin* was a radio-friendly album, despite the caricature of Ozzy on its cover as a demon from the pit, accompanied by a raven-haired pin-up. His band – Jake E Lee on guitar plus a new rhythm section of Phil Soussan on bass and Randy Castillo on drums, as well as keyboard player Mike Moran – did their usual virtuoso thing on a set of pleasantly rocking songs that, rather like *Seventh Star*, did little for headbangers but much for fans of airbrushed melodic rock. 'The Ultimate Sin' itself is a prime example of this tendency, all polite riffing and Ozzy's uncertain melodies, while 'Secret Loser' is a classic fists-aloft anthem, as Ozzy wails "Underneath the surface is a wound that cannot heal" and Lee knocks out an expertly dexterous riff.

'Never Know Why' is a low point on this inconsistent album, as Ozzy lowers himself as far as singing, "We rock, rock, rock" in a spirit of rebellion that must have seemed utterly obsolete onstage in '86 after the polished, malevolent social commentary of Metallica. 'Thank God For The Bomb' is almost as bad, with the frontman taking a tongue-in-cheek approach to the same subject he was addressing in the title track, although 'Over And Over' at least adds some singable lyrics to the rather sickly mix of stomping rock beat and technoflash guitar. 'Lightning Strikes' and 'Fool Like You' are semi-heavy, semi-memorable filler tracks, but between them is 'Killer Of Giants', an excellent anti-nukes lament over Rhoads' superb, acoustic suspended chords. The obvious highlight of the LP, however, is 'Shot In The Dark', a number 20 single in February 1986: the song is memorable for its repeated chorus line and the keyboard wash that made it an FM radio smash.

The video for 'Shot In The Dark' is still an Eighties time-piece, causing an equal mix of hilarity and nostalgia among fans to this day. Thanks to Ozzy's ludicrous garb, ham-acting and out-of-shape physique, it's impossible to take it seriously, as he admitted himself. As he said to MTV much later, "I didn't like the *Ultimate Sin* period, at all, because it was like, well, camp. Me wearing sequins and walking around like a walking lampshade wasn't my idea of fun, you know. It was like a lead suit, you know? In England, it's really funny because I just did a couple of TV shows, and they go, 'Yes, Ozzy Osbourne,' and they always show that video of 'Shot In The Dark', or whatever it is . . . it doesn't even look like me. I'm a bloated pig. I look like Elvis on a bad night, you know. That was when I was drinking and getting stoned all the time, which I don't do any more, you know. It's like a different life. I mean, I went through the Seventies when it was cool, man, to get stoned. I went through the Eighties when it was part of it, like you buy a sequined suit, a bottle of hairspray, have your hair frosted and a bag of white powder and a case of whatever you're drinking, that was the Eighties."

More serious events awaited Ozzy in 1986. His old song 'Suicide Solution', which had allegedly caused more than a few troubled teenagers to attempt suicide, was in the news again: a trial was even underway in which the family of the deceased youth John M hired an organisation called the Institute for Bio-Acoustics Research (IBAR) to assess the song. IBAR claimed to have located subliminal lyrics in the song, recorded 50 per cent faster than the normal rate of speech and "audible enough that their meaning and true intent becomes clear after being listened to over and over again." The lyrics were "Why try, why try? Get the gun and try it! Shoot, shoot, shoot", followed by laughter. All this nonsense was dismissed from court, but led to much press attention on the subject.

As Ozzy told *Spin* the same year, "To be Ozzy Osbourne, you got to be special. Because they hit you with so much. If you were soft, you'd be dead."

Despite this, Ozzy had finally given up booze and drugs – 'finally' being open to interpretation, as the following years would show – and was looking much better, having shed some weight. "I started jogging a lot," he said. "At one point I was jogging three miles a day . . . I know this guy who was a bone bender – what do you call it? – a chiropractor! He's also got a sort of a clinic where he does hydro. Hydro! You know, they sort of suck all the shit out of your body, clean your whole system out. He says red meat is fucking disgusting shit. It stays in there forever."

He added: "I'm not sober. I still drink. Not as heavily. When I was on drugs, I always tried never to go onstage stoned. I used to get my highs after the show. The reason I quit taking drugs was I was bored. I was bored of being bored, sick and tired of being sick and tired. I should try and quit the booze, but I've got to have some release. I don't drink as much hard liquor as I used to. I drink a bit of wine and a few beers. It's not as bad as it was. I shouldn't be doing that. I should be totally sober. I can't get to grips with it. It's a hard thing to do."

He described his average day as follows: "I live at night more than the day. I travel through the night. It keeps me out of trouble. If we stay in the town after the gig, it's crazy. A photographer from your magazine came to the show last night, and he was white with fear at the end of the show. The audiences tend to get sort of very, uh . . . I don't know why this last tour . . . I've noticed a hell of a lot of violence and destructiveness from the people. I don't know if it's the changing of time or what. When we did the Meadowlands, there was $172,000 worth of damage to the hall. I remember different tours from different incidents. But there seems to be a hell of a lot of tension in the people now."

He added that his career had taken an unexpected turn: "I'm doing a part in a movie on Wednesday. The movie's called *Trick Or Treat*. It's quite interesting. I'm looking forward to it. I play a vicar, a priest. One of these Bible punchers who puts down heavy metal. I go on a chat show. The story is about a kid who has found this secret thing in a record and has become possessed by the demon in a heavy metal record. And he can do things."

Trick Or Treat came out in October 1987 and was gloriously cheesy: pulling in the then-contemporary theme of subliminal influences, the producers pulled off a coup by getting Ozzy involved.

Asked if he took the accusations of the subliminal lyrics at all seriously, he replied: "You can make whatever you want out of whatever you want. They're trying to sue me in California about this kid who shot himself. It says in this one line, 'Breaking laws, locking doors, but there's no one at home / Make your bed, rest your head, but you lie there and moan / Where to hide? / Suicide is the only way out', or something. But that's one paragraph in the song, and the song is about alcoholism. The danger of alcohol. A certain percentage of alcoholics can't stand it any more, and they jump off a fucking building. They can't live with it any more. But the press picks up on one line in a song and keeps shoving it down people's throats. They're saying this fucking song forced this kid to shoot himself. The kid was fucking well sick in the mind long before he ever heard an Ozzy Osbourne record . . . And I cannot no way take responsibility for some guy who puts a gun to his head. A guy in New York a few months ago got a big tax demand, and he couldn't pay it, and he jumped out the window of a 50-storey apartment. What does his wife do? Sue the government!

"These people are so ignorant. They've never listened to the band. They look at the album cover and think it's shit. They ought to stop and listen to the lyrics. I write so much positive stuff! Food for thought. Like 'Killer Of Giants', 'Revelation Mother Earth', 'War Pigs' – I could go on for years. If anybody thinks for one minute that I am a negative person, then they're fucked. Because I am not a negative person. I am a very truthful person, true to what I believe. I can only do what I believe in. If I was a fake at what I was doing, I couldn't do it."

Ozzy's 1987 album *Tribute*, a live LP of the Randy Rhoads line-up recorded at their peak in 1981, was much better, consisting of the songs from *Blizzard Of Ozz*, some from *Diary Of A Madman* and some Sabbath classics – 'Children Of The Grave' and the inevitable 'Paranoid' and 'Iron Man' among them. The LP was dedicated to the late guitarist, and struck a chord in many of Ozzy's fanbase even four years after the event. Rhoads is, obviously, represented fully on the album, with his unique technique high in the mix, and the album remains one of Ozzy's best: the singer himself is also on excellent form throughout.

Ozzy told Sylvie Simmons at *Creem* that his new band was a great asset: "I think the band has got a revitalised sort of energy from somewhere. Phil and Randy are very positive people. When I had Don Airey it was always like, 'Oh, we're not going to pull it off, it's shaky,' and you don't want a situation where people are forever putting a downer on things. Because if they say something like that long enough, you think maybe they're right. The funny thing is, if you think positive, positive things start to happen.

I'm actually smiling onstage for a change. I'm enjoying this tour for the first time in a long time, because towards the end of the *Bark At The Moon* tour I was really miserable."

Of his band's revolving-door personnel policy, he said: "We're a very good team – today. You never know how things are going to change in the future, so I don't like to look on anyone or anything as permanent except me. Because if the worst happens and you break up, you get shocked. So I sort of have to take it with an open mind: anyone can come, anyone can go . . . Black Sabbath had the same members all the time and that was boring. That was the thing with Sabbath – we all wanted to split, but we didn't know where to split, how to split. I certainly didn't know how to audition people. What do I know about good guitar players or drummers or whatever? I just sing. All I want in this band is a certain amount of technique and a certain attitude. I don't want cocky people, egoed-out people. I don't want 'rock stars'. I want a bit of spark."

He felt that the Live Aid reunion had served him well as a reminder of why he didn't need to do Sabbath any more: "Sabbath is like someone coming up and going, 'Remember me? We were in school together when we were 14 . . .' Nothing came of it. You're fighting a never-ending battle even before you get out the door. In fact the Live Aid thing was really good in the respect that it settled a few little unanswered questions in my head. I thought, 'Well, I am different and my attitude to it is totally different to what it was. I'm miles up the road.'"

Of the last Sabbath album, *Seventh Star*, he said: "I think it's so sad they're calling it Black Sabbath, because it's not remotely like Black Sabbath. It's a damn good album as a Tony Iommi solo project; he should have had the courage to just use his name and salvage what was left of the Sabbath memory. Maybe one day when I feel like it's all gone, everybody'll come back and do an album or whatever. But at the present time it's totally out of the question."

As Ozzy relished his huge international success as well as a new band, a new figure and a newly clear head, in the Sabbath camp things were going from bad to worse.

At the start of 1987 the band, without a bassist – Dave Spitz was sorting out personal problems and Bib Daisley had completed his sessions – also lost their drummer, Eric Singer, who left after deciding that the band had no future, post-*Seventh Star*. Shockingly, Ray Gillen – who had been overflowing with enthusiasm just months before – departed in March, supposedly because he shared Singer's view, although this seems too simple an explanation. Unfortunately Gillen is not available for comment: he went on to a successful career with Jake E Lee in Badlands after Lee eventually left Ozzy's band, but this was cut short by his tragic death from AIDS in 1993, when he was only 33 years old. Bootlegs of Sabbath's half-completed new LP – *The Eternal Idol* – leaked out and are available featuring his demo vocals to this day.

Tony Iommi, again left with only his long-term session man Geoff Nicholls (who, despite his 'session' status, was now the longest-serving band member outside of the original quartet), was obliged to recruit a whole new band to complete the album. He began with singer Tony Martin, whose manager had worked with Sabbath in previous years, but who – as he later revealed – was a little apprehensive at the thought of becoming the latest in a long line of easy-come, easy-go singers: "They were really in a difficult time when I joined, because they had gone through a number of vocalists already and it was beginning to become a joke here and in a few other places. So I joined at a time that wasn't an easy one!"

Iommi then recalled Bev Bevan and Dave Spitz to the band, the former now a reliable session man with many projects on the go, and the latter now recovered from whichever problems had caused his departure some months before. A summer tour was booked and arrangements were made for new vocal tracks to be laid down on the tapes of *The Eternal Idol* by Martin, who stepped swiftly up to the place vacated so mysteriously by Gillen.

Recording was interrupted temporarily when Sabbath flew to Greece and then to South Africa for shows. The former – a festival slot – remains Sabbath's only show in the country to date. The latter, six concerts across each day of three weekends, were highly lucrative for the band (Iommi received a Rolls-Royce as part of the deal) but – of course – enormously controversial. At the time, with apartheid in full swing, agreeing to perform at the Sun City resort – a playground for rich tourists that features gambling, strip shows and the like – was deemed by many as tantamount to endorsing South Africa's policy of racial separation. Status Quo and Queen had both played at the resort's 6,000-capacity Super Bowl and were castigated for it on all sides, but this didn't stop Iommi, who took his band there (minus Bevan, who refused to go). The new drummer was Terry Chimes, who had been an original member of the Clash as well as executing sessions with Johnny Thunders & The Heartbreakers and Hanoi Rocks.

After returning from South Africa, Iommi and Martin finished off the

Eternal Idol LP, aiming for a release date towards the end of the year. The songs had already been sung by Ray Gillen, of course, meaning that Martin merely had to replicate them, as he said, "The words and melody for *Eternal Idol* were already written and I was expected to sing those songs as they were."

When the album was released on November 28, 1987, interviewers were keen to grill Iommi about the South African dates. He was apologetic but resolute, implying that he had been ill-informed: "Lots of artists have played there so I didn't think it would be a problem if we did, but I was wrong. Personally, I don't think that politics and music belongs together at all. We've fans in South Africa as well and we played for them and not for the politicians or anybody's politics."

The Eternal Idol improved on *The Seventh Star*'s mournful cover portrait of Iommi by portraying an image of the Rodin sculpture of the same name, as Iommi explained: "It's named after a famous sculpture that I found at an exhibition in London. Originally, I had another work by the same artist [Auguste Rodin] called The Gates of Hell in mind, but that one would have been tricky to get down for a good album cover, so we did *Eternal Idol* instead. I'm very interested in the arts."

The album starts well, with 'The Shining' – a subtle, clean-picked piece with suitably epic overtones. Although Eric Singer's drum tracks suffer from the clipped, noise-gated snare that is so typical of the mid to late Eighties and Tony's riffs, when they kick in, are processed to the point of inoffensiveness, the song is better than anything on *Seventh Star*, simply because it has good ideas, lyrical and musical. Tony Martin's vocals are clear and tuneful, rather like those of Glenn Hughes or Ronnie James Dio, but without the slightly exaggerated vibrato of both.

'Ancient Warrior' is less impressive, anchored by that intrusive drum sound and some slightly off-sounding vocals. It's also covered in a gloopy keyboard wash, although the chorus harmonies and the solos are, as always, impressive. Listen out for Iommi's slightly Arabic-sounding scale, too. However, 'Hard Life To Love' is a return to form of sorts, with the catchy, slightly funky central riff holding it together expertly. It's a little lightweight, perhaps, but that's been the case since *Never Say Die!*, after all . . .

"Dressed to kill where eagles dare" and similar 'very metal' lines don't do 'Glory Ride' any favours, and nor do the weedy keyboard fills that hobble the song. A falsetto chorus and whole verses in which guitars are virtually absent let the song down, although the inclusion of acoustic picking gives it a slight boost. 'Born To Lose', although it sounds like a

Motörhead title, isn't anything quite so hard-hitting, and is more album filler. The vocal harmonies are pure AOR and – like all latterday Sabbath LPs – the pop-rock vibe is actually quite hard to listen to.

'Nightmare', with its *Tubular Bells*-style horror keyboards intro and the demonic laugh at its end – Ray Gillen's sole recorded contribution to the *Eternal Idol* album – is notable solely for an excellent guitar solo and a tempo change that enlivens the song no end. The mandatory instrumental comes with 'Scarlet Pimpernel', a track added to the LP after the 1986 Ray Gillen sessions, based on more superb clean picking and a keyboard backing that avoids being nauseating by only sticking around for two minutes.

The gallows anthem of 'Lost Forever' is a fast rock song along traditional lines ("As you look the hangman in the eye / Now around your neck you feel the noose") but has the feel of having been knocked together in a quick 10-minute session, even if Tony's solo is expertly varied and the riff itself is simple and effective. Finally, 'Eternal Idol' is a pretty fair stab at a 'Sabbath Bloody Sabbath'-style slab of heaviness – the song this LP has been waiting for. Although it comes too late to redeem this incoherent record, the song shows that Iommi still had the vision to compose a song of serious depth. Perhaps when he's aided by a team whose personalities mesh efficiently with his own – like the Osbourne/ Ward/Butler line-up, for example, but in this case, singer Martin – everything comes together.

Whatever its merits, *The Eternal Idol* was a complete flop, making only number 66 in the UK and staying on the chart for one measly week. The band shot a video for 'The Shining', but no single was released from the record. The tour, it was hoped, would help limit the damage done by the mass apathy towards the LP shown by Sabbath's ever-dwindling fanbase, who by this stage had the brand-new death metal scene to enjoy as well as the now-peaking thrash scene.

Iommi remained solidly unmoved as always, reasoning during one interview that the tour would be a moderately expansive spectacle ("We'll trim it down a little, there's no reason to go crazy with that. That was a lesson that we learnt on the *Born Again* tour. We could only use the entire set for one show on that entire tour") and that, yes, a full-blown reunion might well happen one day ("Geezer actually rehearsed with us for three weeks about a month ago, but decided not to do it in the end . . . I don't have any problems with Geezer and the others"). Tony Martin was also courageously optimistic, bearing in mind that he was the one who would be expected to carry the live show: As he told www.black-sabbath.com's

Joe Siegler, "The majority of the album had been recorded in Monserrat, and they were running out of money to finish it . . . they gave me eight days to finish the whole vocal thing! . . . I joined at a time when not many people were interested in working with the band. By that time a few singers had joined and left . . . To take on an unknown young singer was an uncertain move for them."

And so the *Eternal Idol* tour, a short jaunt through Germany, Italy and Holland in November and December 1987, got rolling. Dave Spitz left the band for good during the run-up to the tour, and Iommi recruited session man Jo Burt (who had worked alongside Freddy Mercury on the Queen frontman's solo recordings) for the tour. Terry Chimes stayed aboard as drummer, too. The tour went well enough, but some British fans were let down on December 28 when Sabbath cancelled a London Hammersmith Odeon show with no notice. *Kerrang!* wrote: "Black Sabbath are once again courting controversy following the cancellation of their sole British date at Hammersmith Odeon on December 28. People turning up at the gig only to be met with 'cancelled' signs included a coach load all the way from Scotland and fans from as far afield as Southend. The official line from Black Sabbath's management is that Tony Iommi returned from Europe suffering from Singapore flu and was ordered by doctors to rest until at least mid-January. The gig will be rescheduled as soon as a suitable date can be found, and full refunds are available.

"The management apologises to everyone who turned up needlessly, but explain that the show was not pulled until Christmas Eve, by which time it was too late to notify anyone of the cancellation. The management also categorically denies rumours currently circulating that the remaining Sab members besides Iommi are nothing more than hired hands and that they refused to play the Odeon show because they have not been paid. They also insisted that poor ticket sales did not force a cancellation."

The rumour mill was in full swing, with questions flying around the ether about the state of the band's finances, the stability of the line-up, the veracity of the band being Sabbath at all . . . reporter Malcolm Dome cornered Iommi about these issues on January 2, 1988 in the same magazine, eliciting the response: "Our equipment had to be impounded and I was suffering from a bout of what was thought to be tennis elbow, but on top of this I came down with Singapore flu while in Europe and got really ill. I couldn't shake it off and felt horrible. Even now, the after-effects haven't completely worn off. It's awful. The last thing I wanted to do was to cancel the Hammersmith show. I was really looking forward to it. But we had no choice and all I can do is to apologise to the fans. But we do intend to reschedule this date as soon as possible, plus hopefully slotting in a couple of other British gigs."

1987 had been, in critical and commercial terms, Black Sabbath's worst year yet, despite Tony Iommi's dogged attempts to keep the band alive. Could it get any worse before it got better?

CHAPTER SIXTEEN

1988–1989

A S *Kerrang!* writer Malcolm Dome wrote in January 1988, "Cancelled shows. Sun City controversy. Management disasters. Financial problems. The past few months seem to have been nothing but a nightmare for Tony Iommi and his shock troops. So is there a future for one of metal's founding fathers?"

A salient question, but one that Iommi – only a month short of his fortieth birthday – met with typical nonchalance. Despite the grim fact that Sabbath was at that time in rehearsals for a possible US tour that would never materialise, he saw no reason for pessimism – the same attitude that had kept his band afloat, even in highly diluted form, since 1979. Of rumours that the newly recruited Tony Martin might fly the coop so soon after his arrival, Iommi replied: "He was offered a job by [Thin Lizzy/Whitesnake/Blue Murder guitarist] John Sykes and was all ready to take it, but he was talked into staying with us and, contrary to other reports, never officially left Sabbath."

But Tony, now being labelled with nostalgic tags such as Godfather Of Metal and other backwards-looking nicknames, needed to produce the goods to back up his confidence. Unfortunately, these were not forthcoming. Sabbath even ended their deal with the Vertigo label in the wake of the dismally performing *Eternal Idol*, signing with IRS Records, the American company founded by Police and Sting manager Miles Copeland in 1979 that boasted R.E.M., Buzzcocks, The Go-Gos and other influential acts on its roster. The severance of the 18-year relationship with Vertigo, which was swallowed up by Polygram and then the vast Universal Music the following decade, was not a promising step.

In fact, Sabbath was then almost completely inactive until August, apart from a one-off charity gig on May 29 executed by the Iommi/Martin/Chimes/Nicholls line-up (Nicholls played bass in this instance). Martin worked for a while with John Sykes, co-writing a song called 'Valley Of The Kings' with him, but he remained a member of Sabbath while the band prepared to regroup for another album. The link with Sykes was notable for Ray Gillen having auditioned for him (he was rejected), as well as Blue Murder's drummer, Cozy Powell, who was asked shortly afterwards if he would join Sabbath.

The recruitment of Powell was a key development. The 41-year-old British drummer, whose real name was Colin Flooks, had gained an impressive reputation for his stunning percussion skills, reflected in the calibre of the artists with whom he had worked – Jeff Beck, Rainbow, Whitesnake, Michael Schenker and the Keith Emerson/Greg Lake team. Along with Ian Paice and Carl Palmer, Powell was one of Britain's best and most powerful drummers ever: he even entered the *Guinness Book Of Records* for the speed of his playing after a televised demonstration in the Eighties.

Powell and the two Tonys, plus the stalwart Nicholls and a session bassist, Laurence Cottle (who had paid his dues with Eric Clapton, Brian Eno and Cozy himself as well as innumerable others) convened in August 1988 to rehearse for a new album, titled *Headless Cross*. Plans for the future included the possible return to the fold of Geezer Butler, whose wife and manager, Gloria, apparently contacted Iommi about it around this time. Recording sessions – with Cottle laying down bass tracks – took Sabbath through until December, when a tour was booked for the following year.

On 22 October, Ozzy Osbourne released *No Rest For The Wicked*, featuring a new line-up after the singer had fallen out with guitarist Jake E Lee. Lee's replacement was the remarkable Zakk Wylde (whose real name is Jeffrey Wielandt, or a variant depending on who spells it), a 21-year-old prodigy whose expert grasp of Randy Rhoads-like rhythm and lead playing got him the job, as well as his explosive personality.

Ozzy, who had recently been through the AA recovery programme and seemed to be well on the way to permanent sobriety alongside his ex-bandmate Bill Ward, was still an unpredictable guy to be around, as Wylde said: "Put it this way, when he used to drink he was out of control. There's something insane going on every day with him. Nothing is normal with him. Every day when you're around him something wacked is going on, which is awesome. Now that he's sober, crazy things still happen all the time."

While Randy Rhoads and Jake E Lee were always willing to let Ozzy do most of the talking, Wylde has actively created a super-macho, uncompromising persona, especially since the formation and promotion of his own band, Black Label Society. As he said, "I gotta keep it simple, like a caveman. All I do in my life is make sure I have massive sex with my wife, take care of my kids, practise guitar, write songs, lift weights and clean up Rottweiler dog shit. If anything gets beyond that, it gets confusing . . . That's why for Zakk Wylde's Black Label Society the colours are black and white. There are no grey issues. Life is black and it's white. There's no in-between. You're either an asshole or an all-right guy. I got no time for drama."

He has always paid enormous respect to Ozzy and Iommi, saying: "Ozzy told me the day I met him and auditioned. He said, 'Zakk, just be yourself and play with your heart and do what you do.' I'll take that beyond the grave. You can't fake being something you're not. Jimi Hendrix and Jimmy Page can't fake what they are and the beautiful thing about those two guys is they are void of bullshit. Ozzy can't fake what he is. He's the real deal."

Wylde spent half an hour with the author in 2003, blowing off steam in a fantastically over-the-top interview for *Total Guitar*. "The first riff I learned on the guitar was either 'Iron Man' by Black Sabbath or 'Smoke On The Water' by Deep Purple. I was eight years old and I had this shitty acoustic with the action a mile high. Later on, when I moved to electric guitar, I got a Gibson L6-S, like the one Carlos Santana plays. A copy, not the real thing – my parents didn't have that kind of fuckin' money. And I've played Gibsons ever since. People bitch about them not staying in tune – you're in New York when you hit the whammy bar and you're in Cleveland when you come back up, know what I'm saying? But that's the charm of it. I like the shitty whammy and no locking nut, the whole fuckin' thing. It always makes me laugh when I see these guys with 15 fuckin' endorsements who say, 'Hey, I'm playing this guitar now, not that guitar!' Well I got news for you. I'm a Les Paul guy and I always will be. I bleed fuckin' Gibsons. Someone says, you know what, fuck the Les Paul, the G-string always goes out of tune, I'm playing a Strat now. Well I got news for you, cunt – they *all* go outta tune! Pick one and fuckin' stick with it."

Citing his lifelong admiration for Tony Iommi, Zakk ranted: "I was always a Sabbath freak. The way those guys have lasted is just incredible. They're living proof that quality endures. Back in the Seventies the Bay City Rollers sold more records than Sabbath ever did, but where are they now? It's the same today. If I signed to Interscope, would that mean I had to wear a fuckin' baseball cap like Fred Durst? Limp Bizkit fuckin' suck ass! Where the fuck are they now? Maybe I should get a tit job and show my midriff off and be the next fuckin' Britney Spears too. That would sell records, right?"

Alongside the reliable Bob Daisley and Randy Castillo on bass and drums, Ozzy and Zakk made a formidable team, with their presence stamped firmly on the *No Rest* album. On 'Miracle Man', the tale of a busted televangelist, Zakk pulls off some squealing pinch harmonics – his trademark – while Ozzy wags his finger in evident delight at the demise of "our little Jimmy sinner on the screen" (a reference to Jimmy Swaggart, presumably, who had confessed to a prostitution scandal eight months previously). It's a standard Ozzy opener – rapid-fire riffing with plenty of opportunity for Wylde to drop in fills – at a healthy tempo, and much more invigorating than pretty much anything that Sabbath had produced in recent years.

'Devil's Daughter' is more of the same, with Ozzy warning against a "holy war" while Zakk wails away, and 'Crazy Babies' is an Aerosmith-like blues-inflected anthem, featuring Ozzy's deadpan command to "Walk that walk/ Talk that talk". 'Breaking All The Rules' also doesn't push the Ozzy envelope much, although Wylde's solo is enjoyably exaggerated, and 'Bloodbath In Paradise' – lyrically interesting, with its references to the Charles Manson-directed Tate-LaBianca murders in 1969 – isn't anything special musically, despite the fuel it added to the fire of controversy around Ozzy, now waning as music fans became a little more inured to 'shocking' subjects as the Eighties moved on.

"The introduction to his heartache began as a child" begins Ozzy in the sparse 'Fire In The Sky', a tale of a man doomed by early experiences: Wylde takes full advantage of the sparse arrangement, resisting the opportunity to show off with acrobatics. 'Tattooed Dancer' is – lyrically at least – another of the 'Evil Woman' songs that neither Sabbath nor Ozzy ever succeeded in making more than mundane, although the precision of Zakk's tremolo picking on the high-speed rhythm guitar track has to be heard to be believed.

It's 'Demon Alcohol' which stands out most on *No Rest . . .*, however. "Although that one's too much/ You know 10's not enough" says Ozzy on this anti-booze anthem, which could only have been written by a man fresh out of rehab who had not yet succumbed to a relapse. As he told the press, news of his recent stay at the Betty Ford Center – the prime rehab facility for many a rock star, then as now – had been met with support by his fans: "I go onstage now and the kids throw those sobriety tokens that you can only get in a recovery program . . . [the fans are] still there, even though I'm different now. Now that's what I call loyalty." He recalled that the decision to quit the booze came after the realisation that, "I woke up in a jail cell at least once a week for the past 10 years," and a wasted weekend where he missed his daughter's birthday, waking up "on some grungy drug dealer's floor – I don't know how I got there. So, naturally, I went out drinking, got on a plane for London and to this day, I have no idea what happened on that flight. I was so frightened that someone could come up to me and say, 'That's the man who ran my child over,' or, 'That's the man who stabbed my husband,' I cancelled my entire tour and checked myself in."

Although he might have worried that listeners would mock him as a hypocrite thanks to songs such as 'Demon Alcohol', he staunchly defended it with the words – slightly earnest in retrospect – "If I can stop any poor sucker out there from going through even one second of the agony I've been through, I'll stand on top of the Empire State Building and shout it."

He concluded with the novel words (for him, at least): "All these good things are happening to me now that I'm not drinking. I haven't been arrested, and I haven't had any major problems either. I feel tremendous . . . I've been fighting for my life for a long, long time and, you know, I think I've still got a little bit of it left."

Meanwhile, Sabbath and Ozzy came together – in a fashion – when Jake E Lee, Ray Gillen and Eric Singer (along with a bassist called Greg Chaisson) formed Badlands, a rock band which received quite a bit of attention from the off, thanks to the main protagonists' pedigrees. Lee was obviously pleased to be out of Ozzy's band, although he wasn't keen to reveal the reasons why beyond a few stock excuses. "I'm a lot happier," he said. "I love playing guitar, I love music, but I hate everything that has to do with the business end of it. It was more than I wanted to handle. The motivation factor had to kick in. Besides, I wanted a break after leaving Ozzy's band. I read some interviews of his where he was less than kind towards me. That sort of disenchanted me more from the whole mess. I thought he was a friend."

Asked why he had left Ozzy's band, he replied: "Because he asked me to. He fired me. He's changing the story about it so much that I don't know. He told me basically that it was time for me to go on my own. The thing is, I found out about it through friends, and I called him up and he confirmed it." Why had Ozzy fired him? Apparently because the singer found Lee "hard to work with": "He's over-dramatising the whole thing. I'm always late, but he knows that. I told Ozzy a lot of times that he was an asshole and to shut up. I don't change my words. I don't screw around with people's heads. If I don't like something I say it. I am always late. I was late for my audition. On the first date of the American tour, right after that, I missed the plane because I was late. He's using that as an excuse to get rid of me, but I was late from day one. That's one of the things about him that upset me. He made it sound like it was something I developed over the course of time I was with him. I try being on time but it never works out that way."

Gillen also had some hints to drop about his previous employment, observing: "The last guitar player I worked with was a little weird, the band wasn't weird, but they had their own thing about how they wanted to work and they didn't open up to new things, ideas." He said of being in his own band that: "With Sabbath and Ozzy, Jake and I had to fill certain shoes and you can't really project your inner feelings of what you want to do, you go by the guidelines of the band. Now it's more coming off singing my own melodies and writing my own lyrics and doing what I want to do. It's not that I want it to go this way or that way. The style of the band is like that."

Into 1989, and Ozzy's career was in the ascendant once again – as in fact it had been since 1982, while Sabbath's slid irrevocably in the other direction. He scored a coup over his old band – and confounded their expectations entirely – by recruiting none other than Geezer Butler to play with him on the *No Rest For The Wicked* tour later that year. Iommi, Nicholls, Chimes and Martin had been expecting Geezer to join them after the previous year's conversation with Gloria Butler, and were presumably taken somewhat aback – and so began the search for another player.

In March, while Geezer took off with Ozzy (as he said: "My kids would play with Ozzy's [kids] and he kept asking me to do an album with him. Eventually I did the *No Rest For The Wicked* tour with him and had a lot of fun"), Iommi asked the respected session musician Neil Murray to stand in for the *Headless Cross* tour that summer. Murray, who had played bass with Whitesnake, Gary Moore and many other British bands, was another excellent choice for the position, even if recent Sabbath line-ups had resembled a trawl through the cream of the session crop for several years now.

Headless Cross, released on April 29, 1989, benefited from a glistening production: the guitars were big enough for most of the metal-deprived Sabbath fanbase, even if Cottle's stolid fingerstyle bass was the epitome of the session-man style in the late Eighties and the dreaded noise gate was all over Cozy Powell's rather restrained drums. Quality will out, as they say, and the calibre of musicians on the album – the golden-larynxed Tony Martin included – helped make the album a genuine improvement on the last two or three.

"There's been no escape from the power of Satan" sings Martin on the title track, a slow-burning jaunt powered by the rhythm section and loaded with Iommi's clean guitar riffs. It's not a patch on the early, supposedly satanic music of the Seventies, of course, but on the other hand only the harshest critic would dismiss it as of the same quality as, say, *Seventh Star* or *The Eternal Idol*. However, when released as a single the song only managed a paltry number 62.

'Devil And Daughter' is more polite occult stuff ("Satan never listens, to the words that they send") and stands up perfectly well as mainstream radio rock, even if it doesn't contain a shred of malevolence. The seven minutes of 'When Death Calls' are much more considered, with Nicholls' keyboards complementing rather than smothering the epic riffage: the backing vocals also push the song along until its suitably pomp-and-circumstance conclusion.

'Kill In The Spirit World' is too slick and insignificant for all but the most dedicated fans, oscillating between an almost poppy verse that is a little sickly after the first minute and a better, complex bit of prog-rock riffing that sees the band play with supreme tightness. The song is also the most ambitious in structure that Iommi has attempted for some time, with a middle section that decays almost to silence before a searing guitar solo and a swathe of atmospherics. 'Call Of The Wild' is more inoffensive anthemic stuff, although a more aggressive production might have lent the song some welcome balls.

'Black Moon' has some stirring riffing, driven by Powell's rock-solid groove and the excellent histrionics of Martin, who is by this point earning his dues as the best post-Dio Sabbath vocalist by far. Once again, however, the song is shackled by a super-crisp production that does nobody any favours apart from the occasional hi-fi salesman (remember, the era of the CD had recently begun, and consumers were focused on audio clarity as much as actual musical content).

The album finishes with 'Nightwing' – later the name of a gothic black metal band who adopted it in tribute – which begins with Iommi's masterful acoustic guitars and some classic Eighties fretless bass soloing from Cottle, who – along with Pino Palladino and others – made this period in British music a particularly popular one for the instrument. The song continues as an epic ballad, and works excellently, even if Martin's spiralling lyrics may be a tad over-the-top at points.

The album – while no *Paranoid* in commercial terms – did a little to alleviate the damage done to Sabbath's reputation by the feebly performing *Eternal Idol*, reaching number 32. However, the band alleged that it could have done better had the IRS label done more to promote it, with Iommi saying: "I know it's always blaming somebody else but it definitely is IRS – they're just very weak . . . although they tried their best. If nobody knows you've got an album out, what's the point of doing one? That's what I can never understand. They get this album then just leave it, don't put any promotion out . . . Cozy and myself went into record stores in Toronto, Canada, where we are pretty big – nobody could get the record, it wasn't in the shops, nobody could get it – unbelievable. We had such a fight with the local rep – I really came close to chinning him! It really was that bad. At the end of the day it's us that suffer: they say, 'Oh, it didn't sell.' How can it sell if you haven't got the record in the shops?"

Tony Martin added, some time into the subsequent tour: "The record company did nothing, and that is important if you're on the road. People didn't know that we're out there. You know, it's a bit strange because America used to be Sabbath's strongest market and now that is not the case any more. We're getting the big support in Europe now, and *Headless Cross* has sold over 100,000 copies in West Germany alone. The priority now is simple, we have to establish the name Black Sabbath again and make it as great as it was before all the hassle started. So we just have to work our asses off now."

He went on, fairly reasonably: "*Headless Cross* is the most important record that Black Sabbath has released since *Heaven And Hell*. That one was also made during a pretty critical time for the band and I have to say that Ronnie James Dio did an excellent job back then, especially if you consider the pressure that he must have felt. I mean, he was the first guy to replace Ozzy . . . the great thing with Black Sabbath at the moment is that this really is a fresh start. We've even realised that we have a brand new audience out there that supports us, and they weren't even born, most of them, when this band started, or even when *Heaven And Hell* came out. We're proud that we've fans that care deeply for the band in spite of all the changes in the line-up, the problems with managers and record companies and all the bad stuff that has been negative for the name. We had fans in England that travelled with us from city to city to catch as many shows as possible. Rock fans are a lot more faithful to their music than disco fans. A rock fan will sell the shirt off his back to catch a show. He'll support his band for many years, come hell or high water."

Sabbath duly hit the road, full of enthusiasm tempered by the experi-ence which Iommi, Powell and Murray all possessed after decades in the business. American dates in May and June saw Led Zeppelin clones Kingdom Come in support – how the wheel turns – and were followed by a much longer jaunt through the UK and Europe into the autumn. Finally, a string of shows promoting *Headless Cross* in Japan and – highly unusually – a long residency (almost two weeks) in Moscow, Leningrad and other cities in Russia (splintering under *glasnost* at that very time) saw the band, inspired by their slight return to form, expanding rather than merely maintaining their international fanbase.

None other than Bill Ward was making his way back towards music at this stage, having jammed with Blue Thunder, a loose group of musicians including Walter Trout and Tim Bogert. "We just got together," he told *Sabbathlive*, "and that was just a jam thing that we did. It didn't last all that long actually. I was still having some problems in my sobriety – not that I was drinking any more, these were just living problems. So, we got together for fun and for free. We just jammed out and, you know, we had a good time. There was a couple of gigs that I did have to miss but yes, I'm the same guy that played with Blue Thunder."

Asked to recap his post-Sabbath career to date, he revealed that – apart from Live Aid in 1985 – he had spent most of his time out of the limelight, mastering his recovery: "What happened to me from 1984? Well, I got invited for Live Aid. I came in and I played that gig sober. I was a bit out of shape. I was about a year and a half, or maybe 14 months sober at the time, so Live Aid was a pretty big deal. Keep in mind that it was a big deal for me just to get on a plane and go to Philadelphia to meet up with the band. It was a big deal, because in my drinking years an aircraft had always been a floating bar – a flying bar – to me. And now I was going to get on an aircraft totally sober and go to Philadelphia and play a gig. I had never experienced that before. Live Aid was my first sober gig. And that was the gig that I had always been afraid of. I was afraid of it when I was doing *Born Again*. I drank over that kind of stuff. But this time, I didn't drink again and Live Aid was my very first sober concert that I ever played. What happened after that? Well, I tried to make a living for myself and I started to try to write my own music. That's what I was doing and that's what I've continued to do until right now . . ."

Ozzy, of course, was not idle, and coincidentally was also making enormous waves in Russia with Zakk Wylde, Geezer Butler and Randy Castillo. On August 12 and 13, the band played at the vast Moscow Music Peace Festival alongside Bon Jovi, Scorpions, Mötley Crüe and many others, receiving a rapturous reception.

However, a turning point in the supposedly sober Osbourne's life came about on his return from the gig. At home in his Buckinghamshire mansion, the singer worked his way through what has been reported to be as much as four bottles of vodka in a single marathon session, before walking up to his wife Sharon and saying, "I've decided you have to go." He then attempted to strangle her. Breaking free, Sharon called the local police, who arrived, arrested the singer and threw him into the nearby Amersham police station for the night.

Years later, Sharon looked back at the incident with wry humour. "I called the police, and they locked him up," she said. "I didn't press charges, but he went into rehab for three months. He was totally insane from all the drink and drugs he was doing, and well, these things happen."

Indeed, these things did happen. But something had to change. The parallel careers of Ozzy – for so long on the climb – and Sabbath, whose fortunes had progressively worsened, appeared to have reached a watershed. From now on, things would be different in both camps.

It might even be time to join forces once again . . .

CHAPTER SEVENTEEN

1990–1991

AFTER the relative success of *Headless Cross*, bloodless in parts though it was, the future looked brighter for Black Sabbath than it had in some time. Crucially, the relationship between Tony Iommi and Tony Martin had flourished (as Martin later remarked, "Maybe I was just the least hassle!") and the backing musicians – the ever-faithful Geoff Nicholls and the rock-solid and professional rhythm section of Neil Murray and Cozy Powell – were a tight, cohesive but above all co-operative unit. Despite the huge talent they possessed between them, none of the quintet seemed to have the kind of intrusive ego that would rock the boat.

Iommi and IRS wasted no time and recording sessions took place in February 1990, at Rockfield in Wales again and at Woodcray Studios in Berkshire. A summer tour was booked and the band readied themselves for an extended jaunt that was predicted to reap full advantage of their return to a position of moderate respectability.

The following month Ozzy released a live EP of recordings from his vast tour of the previous year, entitled *Just Say Ozzy*. If Sabbath wanted to match up to their former singer, they would have some serious work to do: the six-song mini-album was excellent, capturing a phenomenal live band at their peak. Mixed with Geezer Butler's bass well to the front – and showcasing his excellent, melodic fills, which he executed with more eagerness than on studio recordings – the record also demonstrated just how perfectly Zakk Wylde's style (relentless pinch harmonics and all) suited not only the old Sabbath riffs but also the newer, Randy Rhoads and Jake E Lee-era material. The tracklisting – 'Miracle Man', 'Bloodbath In Paradise', 'Shot In The Dark', 'Tattooed Dancer', 'Sweet Leaf' (an unusual but welcome choice) and the inevitable 'War Pigs' – suited pretty much everybody, from Sabbath and Ozzy fans and beyond.

Ozzy was hugely enthusiastic about the enormous Moscow festival that he had played, despite certain logistical hassles which Sharon explained to the press afterwards: "We were promised a certain place on the bill, and when we got there, of course, it wasn't that way. And it was very bad for

Ozzy because we'd pulled out a week before. We knew we weren't going a week before, because what had been promised to us we found out wasn't reality. People who were setting up the show in Moscow were calling us and saying, this isn't what we'd been promised, and this and this and this is what has been going down. So I called [organiser and sometime Mötley Crüe manager] Doc McGhee and I said, 'Doc, it's nothing to us. We really wanted to go to Russia, but this is your trip. This is the Doc McGhee show. So we're bailing out. God bless, we love you, bye!' And he literally begged us to come, and he said he would give Ozzy the original spot that he'd been promised.

"We pulled everybody into place and within 10 hours we were there at the airport. And of course when we got to Russia he hadn't changed anything. Then, Ozzy said he wasn't going on again, and it was only because of the crowd and the way the people were that Ozzy said, 'OK, I'll do it, because I can't disappoint everybody.' So he went onstage and did his show.

"But for us it was very humiliating because basically we were lied to, to get there. And we didn't realize how big Ozzy was in Russia. We had no idea how big he was! Doc knew how big Ozzy was in Russia – you see, he'd had several trips over there. He did turn around and say to us, 'I knew all along how big Ozzy was there . . .' Which we all laugh about now, but it wasn't as fun as it could've been because it was on-off, on-off all the way, it was like two weeks of sheer hell."

She added: "When we were coming home, we got a call from Varig Airlines and they said that the head of Varig was coming in. He was only going to be there for one day and they asked him what he wanted to do – and he wanted to meet Ozzy Osbourne. Would we please take out half an hour of our day and come over and meet him? And we did, we went over and met him in the offices at Varig. And he was very, very nice and he said to us, 'Any time you want to come to Russia, just call and I'll send an airplane for you. Just for you. You can fill the plane full of your own family and guests and whoever you want. You come to Russia and you'll never pay for an airline ticket and I'll take you everywhere.' And I know that it wasn't the typical English or American bullshit. It wasn't bullshit; they don't bullshit. We were touched by the way everybody was."

After leaving Ozzy's band, Geezer Butler spent some downtime in the summer of 1990 with his family. While visiting his in-laws in Minneapolis, he was surprised to receive a phone call from none other than Ronnie James Dio, whose band, Dio – now a seriously successful act in their own right – were playing at The Forum. As Geezer recalled, "I didn't know what to expect since we hadn't spoken in eight years. I didn't know if I'd be greeted warmly or if he'd have a hit man do me in. We got on great. I had a few Guinness from his well-stocked dressing room while he was onstage, and he dragged me on to play." After guesting on an encore, Butler considered the beginnings of an idea – that even if the first Sabbath line-up couldn't work together, perhaps its second might.

On September 1 the new Sabbath album, *Tyr* (pronounced 'tire') was released by IRS. Wrapped in a classic mythologically influenced sleeve adorned with rune-like lettering, the album looked intriguing, and so it proved to be, beginning with a clean guitar arpeggio and a Latin choir (actually Tony Martin's multi-tracked vocals). The song – 'Anno Mundi (The Vision)' – which begins with "Spirito sanctus, anno anno mundi", goes on to feature a heavy raft of layered guitars and keyboards, over which Martin's soaring vocals peak expertly. At four minutes the song sinks quietly back into the ethereal opening figure, before relaunching into the epic, almost power-metal style that had preceded it.

'The Law Maker' is more conventional, beginning with an expert flurry of drum rolls from Powell. "He's evil and mysterious. People fear his name" warbles Martin in droll over-exaggeration, over a standard rock riff that doesn't really offer much new. An extended solo section sees Iommi pull out his usual bag of tricks in deft style, as he does on 'Jerusalem', a slow anthemic song with rather too much soupy synth wash for its own good. Still, the musicians are all on solid form – Murray, however, is buried deep within the huge guitar and keyboard layers – and it's all a decided improvement on previous albums.

'The Sabbath Stones' at almost seven minutes long, is the heart of *Tyr* in the grand Sabbath tradition of including a massive dinosaur of a song a few tracks into any given album. Referring to the concept of a bespoke Ten Commandments, the song stretches out with definite grandeur, allowing Martin to exercise his full range over several quiet sections where Iommi et al. back off to create space. A tempo acceleration after the halfway point gives the song a certain classic atmosphere.

Also in the Sabbath tradition, 'The Battle Of Tyr' – composed, presumably, in the frame of mind which Iommi had arrived at with the album's concept – is a suitably ethereal keyboard instrumental. Tyr, as the guitarist explained in later interviews, was a Norse god, the son of Odin, whose legend raised various questions about supernatural belief, the nature of combat and war and other 'metal' subjects. The Norse idea was explored more deeply in 'Odin's Court' and 'Valhalla', the first a highly impressive acoustic ballad and the latter a more conventional rock anthem. In both songs Martin wails at length about misty horizons, raven's eyes, longships' and other appropriately fantastical phenomena in an overblown style that might seem outdated today but which still invites the necessary suspension of disbelief, if only because it all sounds so good.

'Feels Good To Me' is more prosaic, with lines such as "You're wrong if you think that I'm afraid to love" making it a lament worthy of the most hairsprayed glam-rock band. Still, the atmospherics are excellent, and the closer – 'Heaven In Black' – is a deft way to bow out, all grinding riffage and an iron groove from Murray and Powell. "Don't be afraid, you will never lose your love" promises Martin, and *Tyr* ends in a blaze of pyrotechnics.

The ensuing tour – executed by the same line-up – was a success, too, with UK and European dates taking Sabbath into the heartlands right through until November. The fans were there for Sabbath, without a doubt. As the Nineties dawned, a new breed of metal fan was emerging, for whom extreme metal's aggression was simply too much. Preferring the epic nature of the best traditional heavy metal and the precision of thrash, this demographic – concentrated in the German-speaking countries and to a lesser extent in Scandinavia – relished the fast, but melodic, work of bands such as Helloween, who pioneered the power metal genre. This was Sabbath's new fanbase, who would later claim 'true metal' bands such as Hammerfall for their own in the mid to late Nineties.

Highlights of the tour included special guest appearances at some Sabbath shows by related and unrelated musicians such as Ian Gillan and Brian May, not to mention Geezer Butler, whose presence fuelled rumours that a classic line-up reunion might be on the cards, yet again. In fact, Butler took over the bass spot once more in December, displacing Murray, who continued with the successful sessions career that he had forged before joining Sabbath. For a month or so the band, now Iommi and Butler plus Martin, Nicholls and Powell, debated their next move, but reunion fever was definitely in the air – and the announcement came in January 1991 that Ronnie James Dio would be replacing Tony Martin.

Martin, somewhat blindsided by the move – he had, after all, just led Sabbath out of the dismal pit they had been in at the time of *Seventh Star* and *The Eternal Idol* – wasted no time in setting up his own solo-album deal with a European label. As he later said, "While Ronnie was in the band, I was doing a solo album. I still have, at the moment, a deal with Polydor in Germany. It's a Tony Martin solo album called *Back Where I Belong*. There were 32 musicians on the album, including Brian May from Queen, and Ringo Starr's son Zak played the drums. I had a gospel choir on a track." He looked back on his time with Sabbath with mixed feelings, it seemed, especially towards the industry itself: "We had a problem with the record company at that time. They weren't advertising the shows or the record properly. We could have had a lot more success if we'd had help from the record company. Many of the problems in Sabbath's history were not of the band's making, a lot of it had to do with contracts and company bullshit."

Iommi echoed this, saying once again: "For me, that was very difficult. [IRS] weren't getting the albums in the stores. It wasn't what I expected it would be. Miles Copeland personally wanted to take it on. [He's] why I signed with them in the first place, because all the other record companies that were interested wanted artistic involvement. I didn't want that. I wanted to do my own thing. Miles saw that. He said, 'Look, you know how Black Sabbath stuff's got to be. You write it; I'll put it out.' And I liked the way he approached that. Once I signed with them, Miles, as much as he wanted to be involved, wasn't. It went to somebody else – and it was somebody else who didn't like us. So it was difficult." And yet recent times had yielded results, with Iommi concluding: "*Headless Cross* was the biggest album I ever had in Europe. Bigger than any of the other Sabbath albums."

Clearly fortunes were on the up – at last – in the Sabbath camp – and it was to be expected that the re-recruited Dio would only build on this trend. However, once he was back in the band, very little happened for the rest of 1991 other than occasional writing sessions: the initial excitement about the new line-up died down and fans' attention shifted to Ozzy, who had a new album on the way.

One rather unfortunate incident did puncture the Sabbath silence on September 1991, when drummer Powell was sidelined after a horse-riding accident. The horse he was riding suffered a heart attack and collapsed, injuring the drummer fairly severely in doing so. As Geezer recalled, the incident prompted the idea of a full-scale reunion of the *Mob Rules* band of 1981: "Ronnie suggested the reunion of the *Mob Rules* line-up when Cozy Powell broke his pelvis in an equestrian accident." This meant the re-recruitment of Vinny Appice, who flew in shortly afterwards.

Powell was unhappy about this chain of events, saying: "I was kicked out of the band because a horse fell on top of me and I couldn't play for six months. Also a few dirty tricks were played and Tony suddenly ran off with an American version of Black Sabbath. Ronnie James Dio was hired as a singer, and he demanded that Vinny Appice was hired as drummer. I didn't agree with Dio's choice because I already worked with him in

Rainbow. I was disappointed in Tony's choices and especially because he didn't want to wait for me to recover. Whether I wanted to play with Dio remains to be seen, but I thought Tony was my friend. I was too naïve, of course, I ought to know better in this business. You learn faster by making mistakes. If I took all disappointments in the music business personally, I wouldn't be in it any more. You just have to remain professional and don't think that you can make friends. They need you or they don't."

As Vinny told me himself, the story was more complex than this: there were some currents of resentment running deep, as usual. "I met Ronnie at some show here and we talked, and then Cozy fell off the horse and broke his pelvis. Then I ran into them and they said, why don't we get Vinny? They called me, asked me if I wanted to do it and I said yeah. Cozy was a big player in that band, another ego in the band, and they were spending a lot of money and not getting very far with it. They were trying to work here in the US, but they didn't want to be here – they wanted to be in England. There were a lot of different things making it complicated with Cozy, so when I got in the band it was all smooth."

Ronnie looked back with wry amusement to the early Eighties, when he had first joined the band. As he told me: "The reason why my part of it was successful was because I brought musicality to that band. Before, what they did was great, but that band now had to move ahead, and what it did was, it moved itself into the Eighties. It became very important in that genre because the music was approachable now. It wasn't something that had died 10 years ago, which is what had happened before. Tony could not have been happier when I brought that musicality, and he was the person I was writing with, because early on Geezer left. He was there for about two days when I first joined the band, when they were living in Beverly Hills. Two days later, Geezer was gone: he wasn't in the band any more. He'd left. So the writing burden went to Tony and myself, which was fine for me – I'd rather work with a guitar player and not have too many minds involved in it, too many fingers in the pie, so we were able to cement this wonderful writing ability together."

He went on: "It's so wonderful when you can do that – the singer and the guitarist aren't necessarily the most important members of a band, but they are the most visible, and so we became very good at that. I think I infused in Tony more of a place where he could go to be a better player, which he couldn't do before – play changes he couldn't do before, hear a melody that he didn't hear before that he would have to play to. So that was my part in it. Enthusiastic? Yeah, I was enthusiastic, simply because I go into every project enthusiastically: if I don't, what the hell am I there for? I wanna be there going, this is great. That's really what leaders do – I'm not saying I was the leader of that band, I'm not saying that at all – but if there was one, it was probably me at that time."

He paid his respects, too, saying: "And if it wasn't me, it was Bill Ward. Which sounds strange, I know, but Billy took the bull by the horns and he wanted it to succeed. It was important that we all felt that way. Geezer didn't come back until we'd done a couple of tracks already. The way I saw it was, they had a chance to be as good as they really were, and I think on *Heaven And Hell* you really heard how good Tony and Geezer and Billy really were. You heard that, and that made me more proud than anything. That band got a chance to be successful again, because they deserved that success. That was a great time for me, knowing that I was there to help Black Sabbath be Black Sabbath again and it not be, oh, they're a bunch of losers."

The same had applied on *Mob Rules* – and would again: "When we got together for *Mob Rules*, we had a process ready, so we could write songs. It doesn't mean that the songs were as good as they were on *Heaven And Hell*, but they were songs. It was more comfortable, but you know, that can sometimes be counter-productive as well. Sometimes you're really hungry when you do your best work. We'd had a big blockbuster success with *Heaven And Hell* and the next album was slightly difficult to make because the success kinda got in the way now."

What had caused the split around the *Live Evil* era? "Everybody was successful again and was like, well, I gotta think about this . . . what, you're getting more than I am? Wait a minute there, pal . . . all those things, those paranoia things that go on inside that band, came about, and it made it a lot more difficult. We had a drummer change, and the guys didn't like change a lot. Tony didn't mind so much, but Geezer really minded a lot. I think he always wanted it to be he, Ozzy, Tony and Bill. And I understand that, that's fine, that's what got them there. But that wasn't reality, it wasn't going to happen. If Tony wasn't happy playing with Ozzy, then that was it, he was not gonna be there any more. At the end of the day, it's Tony who propelled that whole thing. My joy was really working with Tony from a writing perspective."

And so yet another line-up got down to work, hoping that history would repeat itself.

Ozzy, meanwhile, had been largely successful with his own battle with alcohol. Since trying to kill his wife in a drunken frenzy he had endured several months of rehab therapy and had pulled himself together well enough to record another new album, appropriately titled *No More Tears*. With its aptly sober cover art – a face portrait in sepia, with his eyes shielded by a sensible dyed-brunette haircut and a reassuringly slender jawline – it was apparent that a new period of common sense had been brokered. Ozzy added that it was time to re-establish himself away from the clichés of the past, explaining: "I really don't understand why people have a negative image of me. Part of me is happy, because rock'n'roll is a sensationalist business. If you haven't got controversy, you haven't really got rock'n'roll, you've got fucking Phil Collins."

The album, recorded with longtime cohorts Zakk Wylde and Randy Castillo, and both Bob Daisley and new bassist Mike Inez (who would later join Alice In Chains, Zakk's Black Label Society and other bands), was a fresh start to the decade, even if it was a long way from being heavy metal. As its creator said, he wanted to explore a new approach now he was finally sober – hence the non-garish title ("I don't want to call it *Return Of The Madman* or *Black Death* or anything like that. That's all gotten kinda boring to me") – and to this end had asked Motörhead's Ian 'Lemmy' Kilmister to assist with songwriting. The angle obviously worked, despite the painstaking 18 months of writing, pre-production, recording and mixing that *No More Tears* required from the band and Mötley Crüe and LA Guns producers John Purdell and Duane Baron. One of the songs, 'I Don't Want To Change The World', won a Grammy award the following January.

Of the lengthy production cycle, he laughed: "I remember doing this interview with a guy from San Francisco. He was a real Metallica fan and he said they just go into the studio and play and it's done real fast. And I said, 'Just wait until they've been at it for a while.' My first album took 12 hours to make. I wish I could do a fucking album now in 12 hours! With success, you have to try different machines and try stereophonic things and the like, because it's there for you to use. It makes you feel good. You gotta put your finger in the pie. You gotta taste different things. It's like a kid in a candy shop. Just because it's there." (He was right: in 1990 and 1991, almost as he said these words, Metallica had spent an entire 12 months recording their fifth, self-titled studio album.)

No More Tears begins with 'Mr Tinkertrain', a creepy tale of a child molester who intones in appropriately unnerving tones, "Would you like some sweeties, little girl?" An oddly bombastic riff – considering the subject – accompanies the song, making it weird but memorable.

The Grammy-winning 'I Don't Want To Change The World' is next, in which Ozzy sings, "I don't want to change the world, and I don't want the world to change me". It's highly catchy, which might explain its mainstream appeal, as well as boasting scintillating guitar work from Wylde. The next track, a radio-friendly ballad co-written by Lemmy called 'Mama, I'm Coming Home', remains one of Ozzy's biggest career songs, with its sympathetic acoustic backing. "I could be right, I could be wrong, hurts so bad, it's been so long" may not be the most original line ever, but it was a moderate success as a single nonetheless, ensuring royalties for Lemmy for decades to come.

'Desire', a simple rock song on which Zakk is admirably restrained, is a defiant anti-trend warning to anyone who might have been mocking Ozzy's relatively advanced age – a moderate 43 at this point – with the line "Who wants to be cool? Life's amazing".

'No More Tears', another single made unusual by Ozzy's falsetto break and a slide guitar performance, isn't as listenable as 'Mama . . .' or the other 'big' songs, and neither is 'S.I.N.', which possesses a strange, slightly poppy descending chorus. The band are all on top form, of course, but every Ozzy (and Sabbath) album has filler tracks, and here they are. Of the ballad-heavy quotient of *No More Tears*, Ozzy said: "I just read in a review, 'Ozzy Osbourne has never had a ballad.' Bullshit. For 20 years I've been singing ballads. I've done ballads on quite a few albums, you know, and they've never picked up on it. I like Seventies music. Music in the Seventies was much more musical than before. The techniques for recording were wild. In the Seventies there was a variety of music. Music wasn't categorised."

'Hellraiser' is better, written obviously to fill the audience-participation moments in the typical Ozzy show, and boasts a singalong chorus tailor-made for the early Nineties. 'Time After Time', meanwhile, may have slightly sickly lyrics ("It was written in your eyes/ I guess it's no surprise"), but as ballads go it's a crafted one. 'Zombie Stomp' is much better, a musical hangover in which Ozzy discusses the "demons in my brain" which torture him after a boozing session. Zakk and the rhythm section do an excellent job of building atmospheric tension, too, and it all has the sense of reality – from a man who knew what he was singing about.

'A.V.H.', a highly melodic rocker of the sort that Ozzy and his band could knock out in their sleep, is an unremarkable prelude to the album's real classic, 'Road To Nowhere', in which our hero looks back on his life. "The wreckage of my past keeps haunting me," he complains, but concludes in cheerful therapy-speak, "The road to nowhere leads to me".

Ozzy still had no idea if his album was any good, complaining: "With Black Sabbath, I had no fucking idea that we had impressed anybody. We never did any radio, we never did any press, we never did any tricks. It's now 11 years since my split from Black Sabbath and I've just begun to realise . . . Because when you're involved with it you haven't got the time for a second thought. You just do it. I've always been a self-critical person. I suppose that's what's kept me striving in a lot of ways because I always want to try and better myself.

"Every record I've ever made, I've got something I've gotta write; I want to lock myself in the room with a bottle of vodka. I go crazy, you know. It's not so bad on me, but what I've put my wife through is unbelievable. 'You bitch,' and I moan all night. I don't understand why I feel this way. I don't like how I feel, so I have to find something to justify why I'm feeling that way. Most of the time, the closest things are my bottles. I've gotta calm down. It's not my wife's fault that I can't cope with the fucking sun. It's not my wife's fault that I'm losing confidence in myself in this period, because it's tough, you know. It's not my wife's fault it didn't sell, or it did sell, or whatever . . . She's my manager and my wife. I'm thinking, as time goes on as I'm going through this phase, 'It's gotta be good, it hasn't gotta be fucking incredible. Is it incredible? Have I got an incredible album?' And I'm thinking, 'Maybe not, maybe so.' But now I'm thinking, 'You've got no excuse, you've gotta come up with a fucking dynamite album!' I'm constantly walking around tearing my album apart and I haven't even recorded it yet."

Was it rock? Was it metal? Ozzy didn't care, saying: "It's fucking ridiculous because you're stuck in one bag. In the Seventies you identified yourself as an individual, rather than having a thousand bands like this and a thousand bands like Ozzy Osbourne and a thousand bands like whatever. It was individuality. I did a bill with the Eagles, Lynyrd Skynyrd and Black Sabbath. I've played lots of bills with Jethro Tull!"

A number 17 UK hit, *No More Tears* was a respectable success in the new era, all the more remarkable considering just how rapidly musical fashions were changing at this time. In 1991, grunge was the new music, and heavy metal had been forced to reinvent itself – or be swept away. It remained to be seen if Ozzy and Sabbath could weather the oncoming storm.

CHAPTER EIGHTEEN

1992

DESPITE the popularity of *No More Tears* and the luxury of having a supremely talented band that was also a stable unit, Ozzy Osbourne – even though he was newly sober and physically fit in 1992 – was beginning to feel the strain of the touring musician's lifestyle. After all, he had been fronting a rock band for almost a quarter of a century, not to mention taking full advantage of the various substances, entertainments and distractions that membership of a huge rock band confers.

The same year the family – Ozzy, his wife Sharon and his six children (Jessica, Elliot and Louis by his first wife Thelma and Aimee, Kelly and Jack by Sharon) – were rocked by the news that he might have multiple sclerosis. Although the disease's onset is usually fairly slow, he decided that retirement was the best move and that a farewell tour should be organised, an appropriate decision in the wake of the new-beginning *No More Tears* in any case. The 'No More Tours' tour was duly set up for the summer and autumn.

The final dates would, he announced, feature some special guests.

Meanwhile, Black Sabbath – Dio, Iommi, Butler, Appice and Nicholls – were preparing for the release of the *Mob Rules*' line-up's new album, *Dehumanizer*. As Geezer said, "Musically, it's back to the original sound of Sabbath; that's what we all wanted. Lyrically, I think Ronnie has advanced. So it's a bit of both. Going back to the roots, yet moving forward . . . it's really good, because after all the years of slagging from the critics and everything, the bands are naming us as the major influence on them. It's especially good because it keeps our sound sort of fresh and current."

As Vinny Appice recalled: "I flew to England, we started writing and the same thing happened. I set up a little studio recording thing – in charge of the tapes again! – and by the time I got there they had three or four songs already written. We did the rest of the writing in about two weeks; everything was smooth again. We went in the studio and for the first six weeks Ronnie and me had a house in Stafford: we rehearsed in the living room, with little amps – it was pretty funny! We demoed it at Monnow Valley, came back home for a couple of weeks and then went back and recorded it at Rockfield. So it took two groups of six weeks to record."

The lyrics would move away from the old-style fantasy approach in line with current, more realist musical trends. Said Geezer: "Ronnie and myself sat down to discuss lyrical directions, and he didn't want to do all the dungeons and dragons and rainbow stuff, and neither did I. So we said, 'Let's deal with what's going in the world now.' There was loads of material to delve into and write about."

The Cozy Powell line-up, it seemed, hadn't really gelled when it came to songwriting: "After the first six months we didn't really think the sessions were working," said Butler. "It wasn't until Vinny came back into the band that we really sat down and jammed for about eight hours every day. It sort of took off from there, really. The first six months was a bit of a waste of time, just feeling each other out and being a bit too polite with each other . . . What we have learned is that if you keep polishing the work, you lose the soul of the band. Plus, we knew that we weren't going to be played on radio, so we didn't have to try to be commercial."

Asked how Tony Iommi and his old sparring partner Ritchie Blackmore differed as writing partners, Dio said: "Well, Ritchie was a lot more committed to what he wrote for a riff, or the changes inside a song. You know – I want it *this* way. He knew what he was, I guess, and he knew what he wanted. The great difference is, I think, that Tony was a lot more open to everything. Y'know, can we go here? What d'you think about that? Yeah, let's try that. He was learning my Rainbow method, to tell you the truth, because I had to survive within that and write things over riffs, which Ritchie likes to do a lot. It's hard for a singer, but that's how you get good at it. Ritchie was a great training ground for me to get into the Sabbath thing where, as I say, Tony had a real open mind and was very enthusiastic about the things that we wrote. Musicians don't regard singers as real musicians, so when you show them that you understand their instrument and in fact maybe know more about it than they do themsleves, then you've got respect. I didn't think that Sabbath needed to get into the sometimes semi-classical region that Ritchie got into: that wouldn't have been Sabbath."

Although Geezer and Iommi had been hinting at a return to the classic Sabbath style for several albums now, the songwriting connection that they now had could not be denied: "We don't even talk about writing songs, we know what's going to happen," he said. "There's no explanations, no monotony. It's incredible. Tony can riff forever – we have to make him stop sometimes. He was a great jazz player when we first met. He covers all styles. This band actually limits his abilities."

Of the forthcoming tour, Geezer reasoned: "You can't beat live gigs. You can be as clever as you want in the studio, but nothing beats the atmosphere of a good crowd. When we play . . . it's all Sabbath people. Our last show was a small audience of three thousand people, but they know us back to front. Some gigs the crowds don't really have a clue." However, he wouldn't be drawn on the post-*Dehumanizer* future for Sabbath, saying: "I've learned not to predict anything with this band. I've done it too many times only to have it read back to myself three years later!"

When the album was released on July 4, 1992, it made an impact, thanks to its nods towards the vintage sound that Geezer had been promising and Dio's powerful vocals. The sleeve bore the rather grim image of a robot Grim Reaper, resembling a kind of heavy metal Terminator, 'dehumanizing' a hapless long-haired rocker by shooting lightning bolts into his chest, while a malevolent altar bore a computer. Cheesy, of course, especially looking back from the internet era, but at the time many bands were making much of the potential ill-effects of the rise of computer technology, and no doubt it all seemed highly cutting-edge at the time.

'Computer God' says it all, with Dio's surprisingly low-pitched vocals ("Man's a mistake so we'll fix it, yeah") encapsulating the sci-fi theme. A couple of tempo changes lend weight to Iommi's masterful shredding, which had now approached the speed and technical expertise of genre leaders like Steve Vai and Joe Satriani. But as 'After All (The Dead)' demonstrated, Iommi was no mindless speed freak, churning out a pure 1972-era riff that was, probably deliberately, a look-back across two decades of musical progression, fast 'War Pigs' hammer-ons and all.

The fast doom metal (if there can be such a thing) of 'TV Crimes' is a high point of *Dehumanizer*, with Dio not overdoing the vocal arabesques and the super-tight technical riff shared by Geezer and Iommi a thing to behold. The song was released as a single, making a respectable number 33. 'Letters From Earth' is also a slow, heavy song that harks back to the glory days, with Dio's tale of alienation ("What if I send you confusion?") a highly workable churn through a series of treated guitar wails and moans that sound at least 15 years older than their actual age.

The six minutes of 'Master Of Insanity', beginning with Geezer's complex guitar riff, are worth investment: the band stroll forward through a layered, semi-arpeggiated guitar storm that paces itself perfectly, even if

Dio's lyrics never reach true sophistication ("You've got to hold on, open your eyes" and so on). 'Time Machine', which appeared on the sound-track for the part *Spinal Tap*, part *Bill And Ted's Excellent Adventure* movie *Wayne's World* the same year, doesn't have much to recommend it other than its relentless pace and the strength of the production.

When 'Sins Of The Father' begins with the lines "I am the crazy man who lives inside your head", it's like a return to the early Seventies again: the song's pitch would have been perfect for Ozzy's untrained bark, while the simple, echoing riff is Iommi at his peak. It's a classic, unlike the seven-minute 'Too Late' – which bears the requisite mellow atmospherics and epic structure that we've seen on every Sabs album to date, but which fails to deliver a truly memorable impact. Dio's vocals are excellent, though, despite the fairly mundane instrumentation.

Dehumanizer winds down with 'I', an unremarkable, slightly experi-mental track with varying acoustic and electric moods, and 'Buried Alive' – a much more impressive song for which preparations could have been made by listening to a contemporary Pantera album such as *Cowboys From Hell*. The staccato riff, with its rolling, unison guitar and bass downstrokes, sounds heavily influenced by the metal scene of the day, from Metallica on downwards.

For Sabbath fans who wanted to hear the band invoke some of their older sounds, *Dehumanizer* was manna from heaven. Just the sound of Iommi's brutal, unrefined riffing on some of the songs was enough to get significant numbers of reviewers drooling over the album, and the metal-buying public were interested enough to take it to number 28, a fair achievement in the age of Nirvana.

Vinny Appice is proud of *Dehumanizer*, telling me: "I love that album, it had a lot of fire in it. It has a lot of aggression and a great sound. Also, the drums are real loud on that album! Which is funny, because after we finished it we started mixing. It was pretty boring at Rockfield, so I said, you know, why don't I just fly home? You guys are pretty capable of mixing this. And then, with me not being there, they were worried that the drums might not be loud enough! That's why the drums are so loud: if I'd been there I would have suggested that they'd been a little lower. When Ronnie and I played it afterwards, we were like holy shit, the drums are *loud*!"

The band-members were mostly delighted with the quality of *Dehumanizer*, with Ronnie James Dio telling me much later: "I think *Dehumanizer* is an highly underrated record. After we re-formed I'm sure the media were thinking, now we're gonna get another *Heaven And Hell*.

And the reaction was exactly the opposite, because that's not what we wanted to do. In going so dark, we alienated ourselves right away just a little bit to the people who were expecting that. It was probably way, way too heavy for its time: the world was changing then, with boy bands and all that sort of stuff, and grunge. So it probably became a dinosaur right away, because it was out of its time. But most of the albums I've been involved with – and I hope it always goes this way – kind of become timeless, because of the songs' structure and the way they are, and because they're so unique and so different most of the time. You can listen to it 20 years later and think, wow, that's a good album – not wow, is that dated. Maybe in 20 years' time it will be dated, but maybe by then we'll be playing bricks, and that'll be the new sound. But I think most of my albums have stood the test of time, and that's probably the one thing I'm most proud of. You always get consistency with the things I've been involved with."

The subsequent tour, which had started rolling through South America in the month before the album release, gained momentum as *Dehumanizer* took off and passed successfully through the USA. The metal/blues hybrid Danzig supported, as did the remarkably cheesy Love/Hate, a hair-metal band who had somehow escaped being washed away by the grunge wave. In August more US dates demonstrated the pulling power of Sabbath, as support acts varied from rap-metal (Prong), power metal (Helloween), vintage thrash (Slayer, Testament), sub-Ozzy shock-rock (WASP) and, bizarrely, Iron Maiden, whose commercial fortunes were plateauing at the time.

A UK and European tour in September was punctuated by a slot on the bill at Italy's prestigious Festa Nazionale Dell' Unita, which also featured Pantera and Megadeth. This was the peak of commercial extreme metal (excluding the smaller but more intense Scandinavian death/black metal wave of the next century), and bands such as Sabbath were being exposed to a whole new fanbase by playing alongside these acts. "We went on to do a smaller tour – 2,000 to 3,000 seaters – and we were filling them up," recalls Appice. "Then we did a couple of shows with 10,000 people, and at that time music was changing – we were going through the grunge thing – so this band was doing good."

The next leg of the 1992 US tour continued in October and November, and was set to culminate in a once-in-a-lifetime event – Ozzy Osbourne's final show at Costa Mesa, in California, after which he promised he would retire from touring for good. The idea that he and Sharon came up with was that he would begin and end his live career as a member of Black Sabbath: the original foursome would play together to close the show, after the current Dio-led line-up performed their regular set. As Butler told *Vintage Guitar*, "We did something in 1992, which was allegedly Ozzy's last gig. It was supposed to be the ultimate farewell concert and he wanted to finish the whole thing with us."

A generous offer under the circumstances, but one that required a vast amount of management. Tony Iommi, the prime mover, was keen, as was Vinny Appice, Geoff Nicholls and Bill Ward, who said: "To do the reunion in Costa Mesa in 1992, I got a phone call from Gloria Butler. She told me there was going to be a gig together there in Costa Mesa. She asked if I could get down for the gig. I got that call the day before the gig. I was in northern California, about six or seven hundred miles from where the gig was! So I hopped in a car, drove madly on the freeway and I was there. I just waited there. I was backstage and I waited."

Geezer Butler was also interested, but pointed out that one key member – Ronnie James Dio – was being difficult: "It wasn't working out. Playing-wise, [the *Dehumanizer* tour] was great. But it didn't feel right. Things came to a head. Ronnie took a different attitude and refused to do the show."

Vinny confirms this, telling me that inter-band relationships were becoming strained again, just as they had back in 1982. "The same thing started happening with them getting along, and the thing that brought it to a head was the Ozzy show at Costa Mesa. Tony and Geezer wanted to do it, but Ronnie didn't want to do it. He doesn't like Ozzy, and he doesn't like Sharon, and he didn't want to open – so to speak – before Ozzy. He was also concerned that if he was on before Ozzy, that Sharon would turn his mike off or something . . . y'know, a technical difficulty! That kind of thing. So he didn't want to do it, and that was the end of the band. He said, I'm not doing it, and San Francisco is my last show."

The band, who all wanted to do the show with Ozzy, had no singer for the opening slot. Geezer tried elsewhere: "We originally asked Tony Martin to replace him, but he couldn't get a visa on such short notice." Luckily, another candidate was available: "So Rob Halford of Judas Priest offered to try. He's from Birmingham like us."

Vinny: "Now I'm in the middle again, so I talk to Tony and Geezer, I talk to Ronnie, I didn't want to leave them. If I left they'd be really screwed, because they have to get a singer and then a drummer in the two weeks before the show. I wanted to do it, so I explained to Ronnie that I couldn't leave them hanging – nothing against our relationship, unless you don't want me to do it – so I smoothed it out and they got Rob Halford to sing."

Halford, perhaps the finest heavy metal singer that the UK has ever produced after Ozzy, was a dream candidate for the job with Sabbath. As Appice recalls: "The next night we were in Arizona, and we had the next night off, so we rehearsed with Rob and went through the set-list. It was cool but there wasn't much time for rehearsal. Poor Rob – hey Rob, learn 11 songs and lyrics! And then we changed the set because we didn't want to do so much Dio stuff. So now we're doing 'Symptom Of The Universe' and all these other songs that I never really played – so now I gotta learn new songs too!"

And so, on November 15, 1992, the unbelievable actually happened. A set of Sabbath standards was executed by Halford despite nightmarish difficulties (Appice: "We played the show and we pulled it off, everybody said we sounded great, even though Rob had a teleprompter to read the lyrics and the thing broke! And he's not 20 any more so he can't see his lyric sheets – so he gets down on one knee to get closer to the sheets! He's doing that move onstage but really he's just trying to read the lyrics . . .") and then, to vast applause, Ozzy joined the band for four songs. Ward was ecstatic: "Ozzy just . . . came in! And I absolutely had a blast there. I couldn't find anything more pleasurable than to get up there with my friends and play. I absolutely had a blast . . . you know, we had a great time there. A wonderful time."

The set concluded, Ozzy said his farewells to the crowd, walked offstage and the lights went up. Those in attendance believed that an era had closed.

Plans flew around for further activity, with Appice even saying: "There was even talk of continuing with Rob. Tony liked it and said it was really good with Rob, and I thought they might ask him to stay and do an album. Nothing materialised, though!"

On the other hand, Dio and Appice were set to continue as members of Sabbath. But as Vinny recalls, there were other factors at hand: "That was the last show, and they wanted me to continue on and do another album with them. Ronnie and I were both going to continue. But the problem was, they owed me some money, and that left a bad taste in my mouth. I had a contract with different escalations and stuff, and they didn't pay, so I was like, OK, I'm not going to deal with that stuff, you pay what was agreed. So that's why I didn't do another album. No, I didn't sue them – suing them costs almost as much as you're owed anyway. Actually I did get the money from them in the end, but not voluntarily. When I saw them again, there wasn't any problem – it was a long time ago and anyway my problem was with the management, not them."

Not everyone was pleased with the Costa Mesa reunion. Cozy Powell told *Aardschok*: "I was too busy with Brian May's tour to notice what happened in Costa Mesa. Later I heard about it and I think it was all rather pathetic and embarrassing. It seemed as if all the oldies were dug up again. I saw pictures on MTV of Ozzy Osbourne, Bill Ward, Geezer Butler, Ronnie James Dio and even Rob Halford who replaced Dio. Black Sabbath just looked like a travelling circus and everyone behind the scenes tried not to laugh. After all the changes in the line-up, especially the last five years, it isn't possible to build up or keep any creditworthiness as a band. If Black Sabbath wants to keep any right to exist, it should keep [one] line-up for a few years."

What was really going on behind the scenes, according to all involved – despite Ozzy's 'retirement' protests – were plans for a full-scale Osbourne/Iommi/Butler/Ward reunion. This was for a tour, though, rather than a new album, as Butler said, "We were never going to do an album because the record companies we're all signed to wouldn't allow it. The tour was definite – we spent six months signing contracts. Last June we signed the agreements and the next day Ozzy backed out via fax. We'd already been through this before in 1985 when Ozzy said he was just kidding after talking about a reunion when we played at Live Aid together." By now, it should be noted, doctors had cleared Ozzy of any possible multiple sclerosis, stating that he had been misdiagnosed.

Iommi in particular said in many interviews at the time that actual contracts were drawn up and exchanged between the rival camp's managers (Sharon Osbourne for Ozzy, her father Don Arden's people for Sabbath), but the final step – a signature from Ozzy – failed to materialise. As he said: "At the time, I feel Ozzy let a lot of people down. It was Ozzy that put the idea in everybody's head to do it. And it went on for eight months of negotiations between managers and lawyers and everybody else. We signed our agreements, Bill Ward, Geezer and myself, and it was Ozzy that pulled out in the end. He's the one who let everybody down, not anybody else . . . The easiest thing to do, you would think, would be to just walk onstage and just play. But all the bullshit gets involved and that really does throw it. It stops everything from happening. There's a lot of jealousy goes on in this business. Unfortunately that's what happened between Ozzy and Geezer, Bill, and myself. There's a lot of bad stuff, things that just get thrown around. There's no need for it really. At our age now, you shouldn't be trying to outdo each other. It's ridiculous."

He added: "As far as I'm concerned, I just want to get on with my life, instead of going backwards all the time. It's all right doing these reunions and stuff, but in some ways it's a step back. It doesn't always work. It might work on paper. But when you go to start playing, that team doesn't work any more."

The principal victim was Bill, for whom Ozzy's presence was so crucial psychologically and who had cancelled other jobs in preparation for the supposed Ozzy tour. As Iommi said, "It just took so much effort. What was more disappointing was, I felt sorry for Bill Ward, it really stopped him. He was doing a project and put it on the shelf, and he waited around for months, thinking it was all going to work. And that was a sad thing because Bill didn't deserve that treatment."

Ward himself said: "We worked for nine months in this project. After the Costa Mesa shows, we had our mind on this for at least for nine months . . . We had conversations with [Ozzy] by phone, and our managers were in touch. Many dates had already been scheduled before Ozzy decided not to carry on with the project. We had already signed contracts, so he had to tell us so by fax. We were very disappointed. Two months later, he got in touch with those people. My staff and I spent two months sending letters to everybody. The public was angry and disappointed, but we couldn't do anything about that. We spent those two months trying to apologise to those hurt, sad people . . . after what happened he only called me twice, and that is unusual, because he is someone who can call you five or six times per day, and since then he's done so only twice in 10 months. At the beginning I was a bit angry, but now I have no problem with talking to him and sharing things."

Geezer said, pragmatically: "All the hard work was done, getting back together. It was easy after that, but at the last minute, Ozzy changed his mind and that was it. It won't happen now." Asked if he had any regrets, he mused: "Since you ask, yes. It would have been great for the young fans who never saw us; great for the older ones who remember us, and great for us, because we'd have got a couple of million dollars."

Finally, Ozzy himself said in an AOL online chat in November 1995 about a possible future reunion: "Absolutely 100 per cent no."

And so the classic reunion failed, for the second time in seven years. The fans wanted it to happen, most of the band wanted it to happen, but sufficient managers, promoters, lawyers, agents, accountants and other associated music-industry detritus didn't want it to happen badly enough to ensure that it happened.

Where did this leave the characters of the story? Well, Ozzy was retired, supposedly. Tony Iommi and Geezer Butler were still in a variant of Black Sabbath. Bill Ward was uncertain what he wanted to do. Vinny Appice and Ronnie James Dio returned to Dio. The latter, however, was not unwilling to consider the idea of a future involving work with Iommi at some stage, as he said, "With Tony I'd consider it. I wouldn't consider it with anybody else, because we got along great musically and we certainly got along probably better than anyone else in the band . . . You know, I tried not to say too many bad things about people, but sometimes you get hurt and say things that are foolish. I've taken the high road with most of this . . . I have tried to compliment Tony when he deserves it and not tear him down, even though he does deserve it or even though I deserve it as well, and he's done the same. I think he's been fine . . . I know that the working relationship we had and the songs we wrote are something that Tony can be proud of. That's quite a legacy he has in his hands with *Heaven And Hell*, let alone *Mob Rules* and *Dehumanizer,* which I thought was a great album."

As Ozzy shuffled into supposed retirement from the road, he was asked how he felt about his 'father of metal' status at the start of the Nineties, aeons since the early days of Sabbath. He replied, somewhat tartly: "I really don't feel like the father of metal or rock, more like a big brother. And, of course, I'm really not proud of everybody who claims to be a fan and thinks I influenced them. I remember some terrible Eighties pop bands who considered me their inspiration. One of them wanted me to sign all his Black Sabbath albums. By chance we were playing the same festival and that guy Limahl [from Kajagoogoo] wanted me to sign all his albums. I told him to get lost and that I wanted no part of his music and no responsibility for his taste in music. Well, you can pick your nose, but you can't pick your fans, unfortunately."

He added: "A lot of the bands just take themselves too seriously. There are so many idiots in the music business and they all think their shit doesn't stink, but smells of roses. You just can't take yourself too seriously. I don't take myself all that seriously. A little bit of comedy is healthy. You need to be able to laugh about yourself."

In 1992, three key albums had reshaped heavy music. Nirvana's *Nevermind* introduced grunge, a solid, alternative metal/rock hybrid, to the world. Metallica's self-titled fifth album had shown that straight ahead no-frills heavy metal could rule the world. And the Red Hot Chili Peppers' awe-inspiring *Blood Sugar Sex Magik* made it clear that the world liked a dose of funk and sweet balladry with its riffs. With all this amorphous uncertainty introduced by the mass media into the previously black-and-white world of rock, it was little wonder that categories began to seem meaningless. Ozzy himself was tired of genre tags, as he told MTV: "I've always had a beer up my rear end about the words 'heavy metal' because, in the Seventies, you'd have bands like Black Sabbath, The Eagles and Yes on the same bill, so if you like the Eagles, Black Sabbath and Yes, you'd see what you like. But being categorised as hard rock, heavy metal, punk, grunge, industrial, alternative, Seattle, whatever it is, I hate being pigeon-holed. What happened was, in the Eighties, as far as I was concerned, I didn't go, OK, I've got to start wearing pink clothes and all this junk . . . I just went along with what my wife says, 'I want you to look like this.' I wake up in the morning, she says, 'You're not going to wear that, are you? Wear this.' And she virtually tells me what to do and say, because she's kind of shown this to me all of her life and she kind of knows what goes on out there. I just live a very private life. I don't go to clubs, I don't go to bars, and when I did, I was out of it. I don't even know what I was listening to."

He added: "However, in the mid Eighties, metal got very confusing because it went from Poison to Metallica, Motörhead, Ozzy, Mötley Crüe, right across the board. And anyone with a single blonde hair or a single black hair and a bass guitar and the heavy eye make-up and singing the rock ballad, and, you know, looking sweet and pretty, was called heavy metal . . . you know, we're an industry which is called variety, but there's no variety. It's either all or nothing. And I think too much of anything, too much cream cake, gives you a sore belly. You know what I mean? I'm in the middle. I can remember being in the middle of that and going, 'Jesus Christ, Bon Jovi are selling 30 million albums.' Metallica's selling all those millions of albums, I was selling, Def Leppard, Mötley Crüe . . . It's like a snail in a hare race [sic], you know? I just got through it, and, I don't know the answer. I don't really *want* to know the answer. I'm just glad I survived."

Glad indeed. The Eighties had been something of a lost decade for Black Sabbath, and a series of triumphs for Ozzy. But nothing was certain for either. What might the future hold?

PART THREE

Resurrecting The Beast: 1993–2006

CHAPTER NINETEEN

1993–1994

THE controversial Costa Mesa gig came and went – and Sabbath regrouped at the start of 1993, after seeing Ronnie James Dio and Vinny Appice depart to re-form Dio. The search was on for a new line-up that wouldn't splinter and undo the good work of restoring the band's credibility after *Headless Cross*, *Tyr* and *Dehumanizer*.

Finding a singer was the first priority, and Tony Martin, who was working on his solo project, received a call from Tony Iommi. "It was pretty soon after I started my solo album I had a call to go join up again," he recalled, "but I decided to carry on with the solo thing. Then I had another call a few months later, and decided to give it a try. I met the guys at a concert in Birmingham NEC and they were great towards me, so in I went. Tony only said it had been hard working with Ronnie and didn't really expand on it, so I didn't ask . . ."

In February a new drummer, Bobby Rondinelli – whose singer had been Ray Gillen back in 1986 – was recruited. As he told me, "I played with Doro Pesch for a while, and her tour manager, Robert Gambino, used to work for Sabbath." Rondinelli had heard that Appice had returned to Dio and was keen to find out if the drummer's position might become available: "So I told him I really liked them, and it would be something I'd really like to do, and one day I get a call from Gambino telling me that Sabbath was looking for a drummer. So I said, can you call them up and put in a good word? And he says, I can't, because I had a falling out with Iommi or something . . . maybe it was with Tony's missus at the time. So he gave me Tony's number and I called him. His wife Val answered the phone and I introduced myself. I said, I heard Sabbath is looking for a drummer and I'd love to check it out. About 10 minutes later Iommi calls and says, actually your name was on our list, I was gonna get in touch with you. We talked for about an hour."

The rest went smoothly, as he remembers: "He had a few more conversations and he said, do you wanna join the band? You know, with them you're either in the band or you're not! He said, do you like to jam? Cause

231

Tony likes to play off the cuff, and I love that stuff. I was weaned on that kind of music – Cream and freeform bands like that. We hit it off and that was it. The first time we jammed was in a house in Henley-on-Arden, near Birmingham. There was a house that the band rehearsed at, and I stayed there."

As Tony Martin laughed: "We were without a drummer for some time. Bobby called us up and said, 'I'm your new drummer.' We thought, boy, he's got some nerve for saying that! So we called him over to try him out and he turned out to be really good. He's played with Rainbow and is a very good drummer."

Once the full band – Martin, Iommi, Butler, Nicholls and Rondinelli – were installed in their Henley house, rehearsals for new material began, although the previous year's mooted Ozzy reunion was slowing things down. In fact, rumour has it that Iommi and his team began work on the new album anticipating that when the expected Ozzy tour eventually finished, new material would be ready for Sabbath to play, but this has not been confirmed. Either way, a new batch of songs were ready by summer 1993, although no one could think of a suitable title: Geezer eventually came up with *Cross Purposes*, a reference to the crucifix logo which, one way or another, had been part of the Sabbath image for so long.

As Rondinelli recalled, some of the new songs were even in the can before his arrival in February, indicating that the band had been jamming since the winter: "Some of the songs on *Cross Purposes* were written, and some were in progress, and some were done later after I arrived. It was amazing to play with those guys, it sounded right from the get-go. Geezer and I played well together. He's a great player: he's totally spontaneous and a real musician. Tony's very easy-going and he's got a good sense of humour. I would say, Tony, I can play it like this or I can play it like this? And he would say, it's up to you man, they both sound good! Geezer was quieter, drier, but a very funny guy when you get him going. A good guy. Tony Martin, too, I got on with him very well."

Iommi was clearly no victim of writer's block, saying: "I will probably cut my own throat by saying this but I have never had any problem coming up with riffs and the other stuff. It seems to be easier than ever now. I don't know what it is . . . I must have written some horrible ones; I'm sure I have. I have thousands and thousands of riffs here at home that will never see the light of day. I may just play something and tape it into the box and it never sees the light of day for years."

Martin, despite being glad to be back in the band, had doubts about the work that Sabbath had done with Ronnie the second time around. Of

Dehumanizer, he told the press later on: "I think there's some good stuff on that release. Overall I don't have a problem with the album, but I do have one with the concept that was surrounding it. I just felt it was like taking a big step backwards. But there's nothing particularly wrong with the record. It sounds a little stiff, however. You see with that recording, the band made up the music together, but they had no idea what the vocals were going to be until they all got into the studio. Ronnie really wasn't at rehearsals a great deal, so they had no idea how it was going to turn out."

This time around, recording was done at speed, as Geezer said: "I like the new album because we didn't mess around. We recorded the whole thing in six weeks. But of course, if you'd told me 25 years ago that we'd spend *six weeks* recording an album, I'd have laughed. Our first one was done in two days. You try telling an engineer you want to do it in two days today, and he'll think you mean threading the tape . . . Even the teaboys don't move *that* fast!"

The delays with Ozzy meant that Sabbath was effectively on hold for the remainder of 1993, and it wasn't until February 12, 1994 that *Cross Purposes* was released, inside a sleeve with an image of an angel with burning wings. Perhaps a step in a more philosophical direction after the vile *Dehumanizer* artwork – in parallel with Ozzy's own, more subtle move on *No More Tears* – the album art seemed to offer the promise of a full-rounded, sophisticated Sabbath.

Or was it? The first track, 'I Witness', was a pacey, moderately uplifting rock tune – less heavyweight than the nostalgic Seventies-style riffage of *Dehumanizer* but much 'bigger' in sound than the dismal *Eternal Idol*-era material. In fact, it was just the right combination of both. Martin's vocals hit a satisfying point between the irritating over-improvisation of some earlier songs and the slightly artificial-sounding growl that Dio and others had brought to the Sabbath sound. The song marked a religious theme which extended through the album, as Martin explained: "'I Witness' was about something I saw on TV about the Amish people . . . They live in total seclusion. They have nothing to do with the outside world. Jehovah's Witnesses are a little strange as well."

It sounded as if the band were addressing medieval themes with lines like "We're still waiting, losing patience, with all the lies of four hundred years" on 'Cross Of Thorns', loaded with keyboard choirs and bombastic drums (Rondinelli is on no-holds-barred form). Sabbath might be construed as straying in sensitive political territory here, as Martin said: "'Cross Of Thorns' was about the situation in Northern Ireland. The young people over there are very frustrated and angry. I was talking with one young chap about religion and he said, 'Religion over here is like holding a cross of thorns.' I took that and turned it into a song about their anger and frustrations."

'Psychophobia' is a heavy blues-rock workout on which Martin does his best Steven Tyler impression: as he said, the song had roots in grim reality: "'Psychophobia' was written about Waco, Texas. The word 'psychophobia' actually means the fear of the mind. People in England would say that bloke [David Koresh] was a complete and utter nutter. He thought he was the second Messiah or something. You just have to be aware of people like that. They come out of the woodwork every now and then."

'Virtual Death' is the most obvious throwback to the style of the glory days that Sabbath had executed since those far-off times: leading in with an ice-cold bass riff – evidently Geezer was using a pick for precision on this occasion, abandoning his trademark rubbery fingerstyle – the song bursts into a huge, sludgy riff that doom metal bands such as Cathedral were now making their trademark. And yet there's plenty of Nineties-style studio precision, with Martin's multilayered, melodic vocals a producer's dream. Plenty of atmospheric subtleties (the song decays down into a wash of echoed ambience from time to time) make 'Virtual Death' the best Sabbath tune in years.

'Immaculate Deception' is fascinating, layering a slow, sugary keyboard texture and vocal on top of an unusual, weighty guitar riff that also features tempo changes – one of the first signs that Iommi et al. were on their way back towards writing the semi-progressive songs that had characterised their early to mid-Seventies work. 'Dying For Love' is more conventional, sitting over a clean picked backing from Iommi and the usual synth sheen, but it works well as a pause for breath, even if some of the lyrics are a little twee: "There's someone out there holding candles to the sun", and so on.

'Back To Eden' may have more nonsensical lyrics, referring to 'star demons' and whatnot, but the central riff is funky and heavy enough to satisfy most listeners. A slightly weird harmony section leads into one of Iommi's finest traditional solos, and it's apparent that the band aren't short of musical ideas. The depressing 'The Hand That Rocks The Cradle' – "The oath you take is sacred, to save not steal the life" – is about a real-life tragedy. Martin explained: "That one's about a mass murder that we had in England. It was a lady that worked in the hospital and killed infants. That's sick enough. You can see by the way this is going that all of our songs deal with current events, problems of today. That is the main difference from how I wrote the other albums. The others were from a historical point of view. *Headless Cross* was the name of the village that I lived in, in England." With its mellow sections, the song is one of the better, intentionally lightweight Sabbath tunes.

Apparently a generic tale of demonic threat like 'Iron Man', for example, with its lyrics of "How are your dreams? Do they claw at your sleep?", 'Cardinal Sin' was actually another song inspired by real-life events. Martin: " 'Cardinal Sin' was originally titled 'Sin Cardinal Sin' but it didn't get printed properly. That song is about a Catholic bishop in Ireland that had a love child and hid the fact for 21 years. When his kid grew up, the kid went out and told everyone. Consequently, he was fired from the Church." Of religion, the singer said: "So much of it is so two-faced. They'll say one thing and do another. You can really pinpoint religion as being responsible for quite a few wars. It's difficult to be optimistic about religion, but I do have my own personal beliefs. I'm not totally disregarding it." Interestingly, the song is – in certain sections at least – so similar to Led Zeppelin's 'Kashmir' as to raise a few eyebrows among fans of both bands.

The album finishes with 'Evil Eye', another vintage song with a brontosaurus riff that could have come from the Aston days, if it weren't for the melodic vocals. A song of paranoia – the evil eye is watching the subject – it's a perfect ending, dark and mysterious as it is, even if it ends up faster and less threatening than its beginning.

Cross Purposes was another step up, then, and one that needed to be taken if it were to consolidate the work done by Sabbath in previous years. The next step was the obvious enormo-tour, by now an indelible Sabbath tradition and one that wasn't hampered by a poor-selling album that only made number 41. Ticket sales stayed strong, perhaps because of the superb effort the live unit put into the shows. Support slots came from Motörhead (it's interesting to note that only Sabbath and Judas Priest have been making metal longer than Lemmy's crew) and, in an astounding move, the brutal Florida act Morbid Angel, who were themselves at the forefront of a brand new genre at the time: commercially viable death metal.

In recruiting these two acts to support them, Sabbath and their management showed themselves capable of canny judgement. Just as Ozzy masked his average voice and basic stage moves with a variety of amazing guitarists and onstage spectacles, so Sabbath minimised the fact that they were a group of men far from their creative peak by touring with bands whose fanbase would swell their own. Cynical? Not a bit of it – it was a win-win situation all round, as Motörhead needed the exposure (they were in the critical and commercial doldrums at the time) and Morbid Angel, despite their fearsome attack and aggression, required a major-league act to provide more exposure than the relatively confined death metal scene could bring.

Genre-spanning as the tour might have been, it was something of an oddity to witness the warp-speed blastbeats and Satanic/Lovercraftian blasphemies of Morbid Angel (not to mention the guttural vocal style of their frontman David Vincent) juxtaposed on the good-time biker-metal of Lemmy and the melodic, synth-laden show of Sabbath. However, it went well: as Appice recalled, "The band was incredibly good live. We taped almost every night and we would listen to it on the bus afterwards. Very consistent, very heavy. I don't really like death metal, but Morbid Angel were fun. I love Motörhead, though. It was a long tour, and a good one. I enjoyed it a lot."

Martin later recalled the tour with affection, saying how at one show: "I decided to jump into the pit near the end of the show and ran along the front row grabbing hands and stuff, but there was the mother of all security guards waiting for me at the other end who hadn't been watching the show. This guy was huge and, when I reached his end of the pit, he grabbed me round the neck and tried to throw me out! As it happened, one of the other security guards (who had been watching the show), saw him and peeled him off me . . . I climbed back on the stage and carried on."

The tour passed through the US East Coast and Canada in February, before passing through the US heartlands and then to the West Coast in March, with some dates in Tokyo. A UK and European jaunt in April – now supported by doom specialists Cathedral, in a rather bizarre case of the disciples out-dooming the masters – took the band through Germany and into Eastern Europe. After a final date in Finland, Sabbath took off for three shows in Sao Paulo in Brazil.

For these three shows Sabbath replaced Rondinelli with none other than Bill Ward, who had asked if he could rejoin. As Tony recalled, Ward was a little rusty in comparison with his younger, stronger and more road-fit predecessor: "We took him out for three shows in Brazil to play and he thoroughly enjoyed it. It was a bit strange for us because we had just come off from a really tight tour and then did three shows with Bill, which you have to get yourself used to. It was good for him to be able to get out and play, because he hadn't done a gig with us in 13 years." Iommi was clearly not including the 15-minute Live Aid set in his calculations.

Ward himself laughed: "The circumstance that led me there was an angry reaction. What happened was Sabbath – when I say 'Sabbath' I mean the original members of Black Sabbath – had been looking to put some things together in respect of a tour. And at that time we were all about to sign off basically, sign contracts, which is what we do. But then Ozzy didn't sign off. I was really really upset and disappointed. I was really hoping that we were all going to get together and just kick ass. So there was this offer on the table: the Tonys [Martin and Iommi] had an opportunity to go to South America to tour. I hadn't played for a long, long time. I knew some of the Sabbath songs, but I didn't know all the other songs on which Tony Martin and Tony Iommi had been working. So there were some songs on which I had absolutely no clue. I worked real hard to study them and get them into shape for that tour."

He added: "I think I failed pretty miserably in getting the songs the way that Cozy had played them . . . I play like Bill, I can't play like anybody else! And that was an unexpected opportunity. I wasn't able to put all my things together in time for those first gigs, so I really had to feel my way through those songs. I tried to learn them with the amount of time that we had. I tried to learn them to the best of my ability."

The shows – at which Sabbath played third from top, before Slayer and headliners Kiss – were a raging success, as so many South American concerts are, thanks to the metal-friendly population hungry for Western music. As you might expect, Rondinelli was less than enthralled to be ejected from the band in favour of Ward, and even less so because – in time-honoured fashion – Iommi (as he'd done with Glenn Hughes) refused to confront the drummer personally with the news of his replacement. As Bobby told me, "No, there was no single moment when I found out. That would have been fine. You know you're out of Sabbath when you hear on MTV that the original line-up has re-formed! Oh really? Oh, OK! I was speaking to Tony two days ago and nobody mentioned it then . . . They never told me that was happening! They were never very communicative with information . . . I was in and out a few times. I honestly don't remember the dates. Whenever it would fall apart, it would be because they had some offer they couldn't refuse – and I understand that – but I never understood why they wouldn't tell people what was going on. You know? I'm a big boy, tell me and I'll get on with my life. . . . but you know, I've always been lucky to work. I like Tony, there are no hard feelings at all. Life goes on. I thought *Cross Purposes* was a great record. I enjoyed being involved in the band and playing on that record. Music don't get heavier than Black Sabbath, after all."

As the tour gathered momentum, Martin told the press: "*Cross Purposes* is a new album for Black Sabbath, which is cool. It has a different sound.

Black Sabbath, all through their history, experimented with different sounds, styles, tempos and that sort of thing. Right from the Ozzy days, Tony would put classical guitar sections in between tracks and they would have orchestras, harmonicas and all sort of different things. It's not uncommon for Sabbath to do something slightly unusual . . . Unfortunately I'm not going to be able to play some of our older songs on the road. Because we're pretty much concentrating on the newer material and we're also pulling out of the bag some of the older Ozzy Sabbath songs that have never been played live before."

The Martin line-up was now the most prolific of all Sabbath line-ups apart from the original four-piece, something of which the singer could justifiably be proud. He explained: "One of the things I have to get across here is [that] Black Sabbath is not concentrating on one part of its history, it's a band with a phenomenal history spanning 25 years. Ozzy's been out of the band for 15 years. And that's a long time. In the span there have been many different people involved in Black Sabbath. Without people like Ronnie James Dio, you wouldn't have had *Heaven And Hell* and that sort of stuff. Without myself there wouldn't have been *Headless Cross* or *Tyr*. All those different eras have sections in the show, we don't concentrate on just one part, we put across Sabbath's entire history. If you're only interested in hearing Ozzy stuff, go to an Ozzy show, if you only want to hear Ronnie's stuff, go to one of his shows. But if you want to see Black Sabbath, you've got to be prepared to listen to the whole history of the band and not just part of it."

It also seemed at last that IRS was giving Sabbath the support they needed. Martin: "It's really good because we also have MTV support in Europe with spots every half-hour. We're doing a video for 'The Hand That Rocks The Cradle' . . . IRS is giving us much more support than they did with either *Headless Cross* or *Tyr*. If they'd given those two albums the same support that they're giving us now, maybe it wouldn't have been necessary for Ronnie to return to the band."

As he told *Psychedelic* magazine, some of the venues hadn't exactly been oversized – especially not given the gear belonging to the Sabbath/Motörhead/Morbid Angel camps: "The places that we've played have been really small. We could just barely get the equipment of all three bands onstage. Motörhead's and Morbid Angel's drum kits were side by side. The front of the bass drum was at the front of the stage. There was nowhere for anyone to stand on the stage. But even under all that adversity, both bands played incredibly. The audience was absolutely wild, they were stage diving, slam dancing and all that sort of crap."

All seemed well in the Sabbath camp, with Geezer buoyed up by the new line-up. Of Martin, he said: "He's great! He has no ego and considers himself an ordinary person. He's open to criticism where a lot of people – no names mentioned – aren't. If you don't like something, he'll go away and change it. He's open to help with the lyrics, too. When you get to my age, the last thing you want is an egomaniac. He's a refreshing change."

Iommi, too, was enjoying life, planning to spend time when the tour finished working with the amplification manufacturer Laney and the respected luthier Patrick Eggle on a signature range of gear. "I've started designing my own amplifier and guitar," he said. "The amplifiers are done by a company in England called Laney, whom I originally started out with on the first albums we did. They started off much the same way as us 25 years ago. We were like the first ones to use their amps then. We used to use them on tours. I thought it was a good idea to get together with them and re-develop a more up-to-date amplifier that I need now. Through the years of working with different amps, I knew exactly what I wanted. So, I got together with their technicians and I think we've come up with a really good amplifier . . . Patrick Eggle [is] a relatively new company. It's only been going about two years, but they make some good instruments. I was quite impressed with the way they work and the quality of workmanship that comes from them. So I went to London and we started working on this guitar."

Asked how he saw the *Cross Purposes* tour progressing, he mused: "You can still learn a lot more . . . Some of those big places you can play at, it becomes more difficult, in some cases, because you can't see half the people you're playing to. The first two clubs were probably about 1,500 to 2,000 I suppose, but they were really good. You can't fool yourself in this day and age. We couldn't go into a 20,000 seater over here. It's stupid, the way things are at the moment. There's not many who can do that sort of thing. I actually enjoy playing onstage. If there's 3,000 or 20,000, as long as it's not 3,000 in a 20,000 seater. Then, it looks horrible. If you're playing a 3,000 seat place, it's a great atmosphere. You can actually bloody talk to people as well!"

As for the future, he said: "We're extremely popular in Europe. For the next few months I'll certainly be busy. Then after that, who knows? We might come back to do some summer dates or another album. You just don't know."

Bill Ward said, at the time of his brief tenure with Sabbath again, that he felt good about the shows: "I am still learning the new material. I do feel like the 'new kid on the block', even though I have played drums since I was a boy. That was then and this is now. I do feel fine and am doing better than I [could have] believed." Of the new songs, he said: "It's good rock'n'roll. I think they are fine songs. I wasn't concerned about the new material for a long time – there are some songs which I do like; there are others I do not, but not because I think they are bad songs. They simply didn't capture my attention, maybe because I didn't play on them. I sometimes think that 10 years have come and gone and it will be very interesting to see how everything will work."

He also stated quite clearly that new material might be forthcoming, when asked if he was interested in writing with Sabbath: "Yes, I wish we were. After this show in Buenos Aires, we will have four weeks and then we will start writing new songs for the next album."

In October 1994 an album of Black Sabbath covers entitled *Nativity In Black* was scheduled to be released by Sony, featuring songs from Biohazard, Sepultura, Faith No More (their trademark 'War Pigs'), White Zombie and other mid-Nineties metal acts. Ward revealed that he, in fact, appeared on it: "I believe there are 10 to 12 bands on it," he said, "including Tony, Geezer, myself and Rob Halford performing 'The Wizard' [under the name Bullring Brummies]." He added, optimistically: "The magic is starting to come back, but it's going to take some time. We've known each other since long ago, but I feel I'm re-learning who they are because they've grown up, they have changed. I want to feel fine with myself, and I ask if I'm fine every night before going to bed. I always answer yes, which means it's working well. I'm not in a hurry – I'd rather wait and see which things can work and which cannot. It's just like a joyride."

Of the tribute album, Iommi reasoned: "I'm very honoured that bands have actually done tributes to us and mentioned Sabbath as their influence. It's great, I feel a great achievement inside because many years ago, 24 years ago even, when we'd only been going a couple of years, and we were doing interviews in England, they were saying, 'What are you thinking? You must be finished by now!' – trying to wrap us up after a couple of years! We didn't think this was going to go on. And now here we are, 20-odd years later. Maybe it's because – well, it's hard for me to say why, because I'm just the player, you know? I just go on and enjoy what I do and believe in what I do. To analyse it is very difficult when it's your own thing. We should ask the fans that. It's great. It's great, though. I'm very pleased. And it's things like that that really do keep you going. I mean, I get fan mail, and to read some of the mail, it really is great what people say or what the kids say. People really love what we do and they say 'Without

240

you our lives would be dull . . .
great to me."

All this optimism seemed ra
and Bill left the band – agai
   In Ward's case it was
without Ozzy. Ironically
Paulo weren't as enjoya
gigs, as much as I like
happened again," he
And just as had happ
the same. [South A.
did it because I learned son.
ing experience. I got to see the n.
poverty . . ."
   Still in the grip of his recovery – and the inte
therapy has to bring – he mused: "You know, if I look bac.
I could have reacted differently. I could have stayed within my bou.
What I had granted at that time was that I would never rejoin Tony o.
Geezer without Ozzy. Those were my boundaries, and they had been in
place for a long, long time. That's probably why a lot of people might not
have heard of me or seen me. I made the decision back in 1984 to never
play with Black Sabbath unless it was the original line-up. And I stuck to it
for quite a long time. A lot of that was about honouring Ozzy. I had to
amend a lot with Ozzy and the only way that I knew to make a decent
amend was to never try to do Sabbath without Ozz. That's how I feel
about that."
   But this time was different, he explained. Ozzy himself had got in the
way of the promised reunion: "When the opportunity finally came for us
to tour and Ozz didn't want to do it, for a few months I thought that if
Ozzy didn't want to do it, then it was OK for me to go out and be with
another singer. Now I can see that feeling in some ways was wrong. I did
cross the boundaries that I had in place. Through those 10 years [1984–
1994], there were lots of times where I really missed playing with Tony
and Geez. And with Ozz of course. Lots of times where I would have
dearly loved to pick up the phone and say: 'I would love to come back and
play.' I missed them, absolutely horribly and terribly. But I tried to do the
right thing. I'd done the wrong thing when I was drinking and all, so I
tried to do the right thing for a change."
   As for Geezer, various theories abound as to why he left Sabbath when

ack to a position of successful respectability,
ony Iommi said in July the following year that:
things I wasn't really happy with. I had sort of a dis-
eezer's wife [Gloria], and you know how that one
Geezer himself indicated that he left because he wanted
band, saying: "I was finding it difficult to work with the
n Black Sabbath, I wasn't satisfied any more with the music
re creating, it wasn't going in the direction I wanted to. I
was the best time for me to leave Sabbath, forget all that, and
rate on my own stuff . . . It was a heavy load when I was in Black
th, because the version of Sabbath I was in just couldn't ever
pare to the original Sabbath. That's one of the reasons why I left, it
as just impossible to live up to the legend. I see this as a fresh start, away
from all that. It gives me the freedom to do whatever I want to do, instead
of having 'Paranoid' and 'Iron Man' and 'War Pigs' looking down at me.
Now I don't have to compare . . . It just doesn't bear any resemblance
whatsoever to the original concept of Black Sabbath any more."

In the place of the old stagers came, surprise surprise, none other than
Neil Murray and Cozy Powell, back to the fold after personal invitations
from Iommi. Powell told one interviewer: "I have to admit that I have
respect for Iommi, and the fact that he asked me back himself made me
feel good. He said he liked my playing and he thought that I could do
something again for Sabbath. Everything had to do with the band, nothing
was personal. The same goes for Neil. We worked together for years and
that was the sound Sabbath could use again. This line-up has made some
of the better albums of the past years. If you ask Tony I think he will admit
that he wasn't too happy with *Dehumanizer* and *Cross Purposes*."

Powell went on something of a rant about the industry which had
served him so ill in recent times, saying: "The music business is a big
cesspit. A few young bands are given a chance by the record companies. In
the early days they signed up a lot more bands, but nowadays they only
want to invest in bands who will make a profit. The popular bands of
today are mostly prefab bands, developed by the record companies. The
bands are put together in the studio and by using a lot of equipment and
expensive producers they record a hit song. Nowadays there aren't many
songs that really affect me – perhaps it's my age."

However, he reasoned: "It's good to see that a lot of bands are still influenced by Black Sabbath. The grunge period was just a weak infusion of
[their] songs from the early Seventies. To be honest, we were surprised by
the sudden success of the tribute album *Nativity In Black* in the States. The

last 10 years almost no one was interested in the band and suddenly we were famous again. Especially the press was kindly disposed towards us. In spite of my criticism I cannot deny that I am proud to be a member of this band."

And so – in the space of 1992 and 1993 – Black Sabbath took one giant leap forward towards the actuality of a full-blown reunion with Ozzy, fell back again, recorded and toured a solid album with new and old players, reshuffled again and wound up back where they started. Would the rest of the Nineties be solely about reunions and revisionism?

CHAPTER TWENTY

1995

DELIGHTED with the performance of the Martin/Iommi/Butler/Nicholls/Rondinelli line-up the previous year, in March 1995 Sabbath released a CD/VHS package entitled *Cross Purposes Live*. With songs from a show recorded at Hammersmith the previous December, the collection – it's debatable whether it qualifies as a Sabbath 'album' as such, a fact borne out by its reissue on DVD by an unrelated company in 2003 – shows off Martin's remarkable voice, despite the fact that he had been suffering from a throat infection that particular night. In fact, the gig is all Martin's, with his crowd interaction a lesson in the frontman's art. The setlist – 'Time Machine', 'Children Of The Grave', 'I Witness', 'Mob Rules', 'Into The Void', 'Anno Mundi', 'Black Sabbath', 'Neon Knights', 'Psychophobia', 'The Wizard', 'Cross Of Thorns', 'Symptom Of The Universe', 'Headless Cross', 'Paranoid', 'Iron Man' and 'Sabbath Bloody Sabbath' – was skewed in favour of the current album, of course (some might say overly so), but seemed to please the obvious old-school followers and those who had enjoyed the Dio and earlier Martin eras.

The real Sabbath release of 1995 came on June 17 in the form of a new album, *Forbidden*. Any new release at this point in Sabbath's career was inevitably regarded as a make-or-break move on their part: by now the nu-metal movement spearheaded by Korn was gathering pace, and its antecedents – by definition and implication, old metal – were starting to look a little jaded.

Looking back, it seemed that Sabbath and their management seemed to view the changes in the metal scene as a opportunity to gain some new-found credibility among younger fans, and as a result had looked to a non-traditional source for inspiration. The nu-metal scene, which made its name by incorporating hip-hop, funk and other influences into the standard riffs and barks of the metal recipe, was turning heads outside the standard metal fanbase and had simultaneously become more inclusive. In turn, metal audiences had become a little more open to new and different bands: one sign of this was the emergence from Los Angeles of a band called Body Count, led by the charismatic rapper, actor and media personality Ice-T (real name Tracey Marrow). Peddling a mixture of traditional metal and hardcore punk with a dose of thrash metal, Ice-T and his band – uniquely in metal, all black musicians – had gained a measure of notoriety thanks to one of their songs, 'Cop Killer', which had appeared on their self-titled debut album in 1992. At the time America was in a temporary froth over the issue of police brutality in ethnic communities – with media attention focused on the LA districts of Compton and South Central – and had been rocked by widespread anti-police riots in that and other cities in April '92. Ice-T and his band, therefore, were receiving maximum attention – a chief shareholder in their US record company, Warner Brothers, was none other than the veteran actor Charlton Heston, who helped fuel the debate by speaking at length on the 'Cop Killer' issue in public.

Body Count's guitarist and producer, Ernie C (who had written 'Cop Killer' and produced demos for seminal acts such as Rage Against The Machine and Stone Temple Pilots) was asked by Iommi and Sabbath's management if he was interested in working with Sabbath on a potential album. He agreed – as a long-time Sabbath fan – and duly flew to the UK to work with the band.

Iommi said afterwards, "I met Ernie at a hotel and we were talking about the music. They're big fans of Sabbath. Then when it came up to naming a producer for the album, somebody suggested, 'What about Ernie C? He's really interested in doing it.' The more we thought about it, the more it seemed like a good idea to try it. We were originally going to just work with him on four or five tracks."

The tracks, one of which, 'Illusion Of Power', featured the first ever guest appearance on a Sabbath song – from Ice-T himself – worked so well that Sabbath asked Ernie to produce the whole of the new album. Iommi went on: "He worked well as far as motivating us for writing the new album. And he's enthusiastic about it and all. And, of course, while using him, we managed not to get self-indulgent. We barely ever are really satisfied. But it sort of stopped us from overdoing things and taking more time than necessary . . . It was a little strange because normally, I'd talk to [producers] and pick them. Anybody who worked on the album, engineers or producers, I'd decide on after a lot of interviewing. It was one of the few times we went with a shot in the dark, but it worked really well. We just plugged in and off we went. It was all done really quickly. We were in the studio for 10 days and recorded it in eight days. And we left a couple of the other days for other dribs and drabs."

The album, recorded far more rapidly than any Sabbath release since the

Seventies, was deliberately designed to sound organic and not over-produced, as Martin confirmed: "I just wanted to match the rawness that the guys had captured with the music. If I'd tried to lay a lot of harmonies, it wouldn't have worked. And I approached the lyrics in a very different way this time, where I didn't actually write anything down on paper. It all sort of came out from heart and soul. We set up a microphone and sang. So what you're hearing is very much how I sang it. The first time the lyrics were actually written on paper was on the album cover. Then I had to listen to the tapes to find out what the words were . . . See, the thing is we knew before we went in that we were going to go back to basics. That meant really setting up and playing. And to do that, I didn't want to sit and write everything out. The method, to get something spontaneous to go with the music, which was also spontaneous, was to just sing. So that's what I did. Basically we just set up a microphone with no lyric sheets."

Iommi was careful, as always, with his comments, saying of Body Count – inferior on all levels to Sabbath, despite their recent heightened profile – "I wouldn't say I listened to them a lot, no. I only listened to them when it was mentioned about them doing it. I wasn't that familiar with them. But, yeah, there's some good stuff on it." In fact, he was being typically polite: Body Count have always been regarded as a pretty workaday metal band at best, with many of their songs ('KKK Bitch', 'Evil Dick', 'Momma's Gotta Die Tonight') deliberately puerile.

Ice-T has always maintained that the band was merely an outlet for his rock fantasies: as he told me in 2006, "I think everybody wants to be in a rock band. Even though hip-hop is wild, and it's another form of rock, you can't fall down on your back and just totally go crazy." With this approach, and the fact that their music was neither technically dazzling nor particularly heavy, Body Count simply weren't that good and fell from critical and commercial favour soon after, as the career of Ice-T itself went from stratospheric to merely respectable.

But at the time it all seemed highly progressive, and Iommi and the others were optimistic about the band's future, especially as the Powell/Murray rhythm section was both powerful and stable. Iommi: "All of us are really enjoying it. We can't wait to get out on tour. It's great to have that feeling. You're on top before you start. If you go out with the attitude of 'Oh, I don't want to go out,' then it could be a problem. And we've had that in the past, somebody doesn't want to do this, somebody doesn't want to do that. If you can just go out with the attitude of really enjoying it and making the best show, it's great."

Of the departed Geezer Butler, the guitarist said: "There was obviously some kind of barrier there that obviously split us up, and it's a lot freer now. Everybody now, we're all looking forward to getting out because nobody's saying 'I don't want to do it' or 'I don't want to play there' or 'I don't want to travel like that.' We haven't had really big problems popping up like it was in the past. We don't have to deal with people over silly things. Everybody's getting on these days, and that's the great part even before you start . . . I've always believed in what we do. I was the one who used to sit there all night in the studio and everybody would go home and go on holiday, and I'd be left there. So it's just the way it's been, and it's always been the biggest part of my life, from day one."

When the album appeared, warning bells rang in the minds of many fans, who disliked the self-consciously 'funny' artwork – a cartoon of the Grim Reaper (in as unattractive an incarnation as we'd seen him on the front of *Dehumanizer* just a couple of years before) in a cemetery with various caricatures of the band-members and others motorbiking out of graves. Iomi defended it staunchly, explaining that a change in vibe had been necessary: "That's exactly what we wanted. We got fed up with, as soon as you mentioned Sabbath, the gloom and doom. I just wanted a lighter side of it to be looked on. When I saw the rough drawings . . . I thought, 'That's great, that's just up our street, what we want to do.'"

However, the opening song 'Illusion Of Power' was good – a heavy, riff-laden monster with suitably spooky treated vocals and laughter, plus Ice-T's guest vocals in the form of a semi-sung, semi-spoken rant. "You're caught in a complex catacomb of your own inadequacies and pitiful weaknesses!" he spits with unexpected eloquence, before adding a few more lines and fading out amid a tangle of demonic screams and guitar feedback. Of the song, Ice-T informed me: "Sabbath admired Body Count – they could listen to our songs like 'There Goes The Neighborhood' and hear Sabbath in it – so they reached out to Ernie and they produced 'Illusion Of Power'." Working with Iommi et al. had left its mark on him: "When they come walking through the door, you're like, holy shit, I've been really fortunate to have worked with some very cool people!"

'Get A Grip' was less impressive, a very standard Sabbath track that featured the usual, middle-of-the-road riffage that more or less every album since the Seventies had featured. Ernie C's production, despite later criticism, is perfectly useful on this and the other tracks, with stacks of presence applied to Murray's bass and a slick drum sound. 'Can't Get Close Enough' is much better, with the ominous quiet sections alternating with louder parts a tried and tested Sabbath trick that keeps the tension solid behind Martin's song of frustration and alienation.

'Shaking Off The Chains' suffers from an annoying unison vocal and guitar harmony that doesn't really serve any purpose, even if the rest of the song is functionally adequate. "I'm shaking off the chains, I'm tired of all the pain" barks Martin as the guitars become meshed in a technically impressive spaghetti junction.

The expected big ballad comes with 'I Won't Cry For You', which begins with the by-now trademark acoustic guitar plus slushy keyboard. "It feels like you're drowning in your tears" announces Martin before a layered phalanx of guitars burst inwards – no mean achievement in a recording time of only eight days. The song works well, but isn't really any different from the many other lighters-aloft moments that have punctuated every Sabbath album since the Ozzy era.

'Guilty As Hell' revisits some melodically threatening chords from the old days, but otherwise isn't much to shout about, and nor is 'Sick And Tired', an unacceptably sugary ballad that relies too much on Cozy's intrusively busy drums and too many solos from Iommi.

'Rusty Angels' has more cheerful melodies draped all over it – beginning like a testosterone-assisted MOR radio hit – but Iommi's deft upper-register rhythm playing ensures that the song remains better than the two songs before it, as well as the wistful, descending chorus in which Martin warbles, "Rusty angels, they can't fly".

In 'Forbidden' itself, Martin asks "How the hell am I supposed to please everyone?" – an apt question, as some critics gathered to destroy the album and others decided to cut the long-suffering band a break this time around. It's a moderately workable tune, granted, but once again – and this criticism was beginning to apply once too often – nothing particularly distinguishable from the mid-tempo, strolling content of so many of Sabbath's recent albums. Fortunately for *Forbidden*, Iommi's final fling – 'Kiss Of Death' – is an epic workout laden with slow riffs and fills that display, once and for all, how much of a virtuoso he had now become.

As *Forbidden* slips away in a gentle wash of atmospheric, chorused guitar picking and the echoed ticking of a giant clock, the listener is left with mixed emotions. Ernie C had done a competent, if unremarkable, job of producing the album, and the songs were mostly acceptable in quality – but something was missing, a quality which would make the album stand out. This was confirmed when the album only reached number 71, Sabbath's worst UK chart performance ever.

Iommi, by now a master of understated optimism, said: "I hope that this album does well, and I hope that people do like the album. I don't know what's 'in' or 'out' because I don't follow that, I just go on and do what I do. If I start following trends, it's like I'm putting a gun to my head. I just want to go out and enjoy playing and quite honestly, I've enjoyed playing more the last few years than I ever have. Particularly now, with this new line-up. It's great because we don't have any problems. There are no bad vibes ... When you've got somebody in the band that's causing a problem, it makes it very difficult when you have to go on tour."

He went on: "Maintaining a freshness is the key to maintaining a career in music, and a belief in what I do, of course, is essential as well. I've always believed in what I do. Black Sabbath has been together for the last 26 or 27 years, and making an album was my original goal! Actually, before that, it was to get gigs, really. And then, of course, to play in London, and then play in the States."

Of managing the gruelling touring lifestyle, Iommi explained: "As far as life on the road, I've been doing it for so many years, but I still think you need to adjust to it. Because when you're at home, you do things differently; you're not living out of a suitcase all the time or shoving off on buses or planes or whatever it may be. For me sometimes, it really gets me organised to go on the road, because I get into a routine and I function quite well in a routine." Did this routine make him a difficult man to work with? "No, it's just the way things are," he said. "You see with Ronnie, he's had his own band for so long now. You become set in your own ways, really, same as Ozzy, same as a lot of people who've had their own bands. It's difficult to work as a team again when you get back. And that's what you've got to do when you're in a band – you've got to work as a team. You can't have one person saying 'This is the way I want it' because it doesn't work."

The band were quick to lay down as many optimistic statements as they could on the release of the album, with Martin saying: "I can only hope [that fans will] look upon it as the era that took it into the future direction. Having tried to go back with Ronnie and failing, and trying with Ozzy and failing again, you have to go forward and stop looking into the past. The only direction to go now is farther into the future and try to make this thing as big as we possibly can. It's been a long time since Ozzy left and we're still playing those old songs. But I think the new album is good and as time goes on, maybe it won't be necessary to supplement our shows with so many old songs."

Iommi went on: "I wanted to make the album more of a live feel, to get back to the thing of walking into the studio, setting up and just playing. As opposed to going in and recording drums for three days, then guitars for three days. I wanted to just walk in and play . . . It probably isn't as heavy as I anticipated." Critics had been vocal on that score, and he had apparently noted their comments, saying: "Those critics are going to be older one day. But if they're still writing good, why should anyone condemn them? I love going out and playing. I really enjoy what I do. If it was just going out purely money-making maybe it [would be] different. Even then you can't condemn it. I actually love what I do. So I think to condemn it is wrong, because there's room for everybody. Black Sabbath has always been my life. I've been involved with it since the beginning and I've always believed in the band. If I didn't, I wouldn't do it. I still feel the same way about it as when I started."

He added: "People say 'Don't you get tired of playing 'Iron Man', and 'Black Sabbath', and 'Paranoid'?' Well, no I don't. Perhaps I'm like a fish and have got a three-second memory. But I don't get fed up. I get the most out of it I can, and I really do these days. I love it more these past few years than I ever have, and it's great to be in that position."

The band then went out on tour, taking in a huge string of dates that took them through most of the rest of the year. In June 1995 they played in Denmark and Sweden before heading off to the USA once again (in July they were supported once again by old stagers Motörhead and the progressive death metal band Tiamat), travelling through the States and Canada before winding up on August 3 in California. At this point Iommi had to undergo a brief operation for a carpal-tunnel problem which had been troubling him, flying back to the UK for this.

More seriously, when the US tour ended, Cozy Powell elected to leave the band citing exhaustion after years on the road. His replacement was Bobby Rondinelli, flown in at short notice but able to pick up the sticks once again with ease – it had been only a year since he had been replaced by Bill Ward.

Sabbath then regrouped for a European tour, with the focus on Germany, Poland, Hungary, Italy, Switzerland and Austria. Dates in Scandinavia, the UK and the Far East brought them through to December, when the band broke for a rest.

It was interesting to note how the band's perspectives on *Forbidden* had changed as time passed – the departed Cozy, for instance, was less than delighted with it, saying: "Of course Ernie C has a different outlook on the Sabbath material. He is used to different music, but he was the one who suggested the co-operation. We recorded a few songs with him and it worked out. He is a musician and a fan of Black Sabbath and he was hired on these facts. In the studio we worked harder because we wanted to prove ourselves to him. Nevertheless the CD sounds a lot like an Ernie C album so I didn't always agree with his decisions. The music remains Black Sabbath's, of course, but because of the production it sounds less polished but more rough. Of course he didn't always get things his way. He preferred to use his own style more, but luckily these four old musicians had something to say."

Asked what specifically troubled him about the album, Powell said: "I think the drum sound has changed the most, it just sounds different. He is a guitarist and knows all about guitar sounds and I think he doesn't know much about drum sounds. I would never have chosen this kind of drum sound . . . often he didn't understand how I wanted the drum sound to be. I was more involved with the production of *Headless Cross* than I was with this CD. I had to take a step back because of my sudden return and the choice of the record company to hire an objective person for the production. Even Tony wasn't allowed to interfere in the production because the record company thought he wouldn't be objective with his own product. We did the pre-production ourselves and my drum sound was still on its feet at that time. I knew I had to be prepared to let someone else decide what course to take, but it's difficult to let it go when your special sound is concerned. Sometimes changes are for the better, but if I was the producer *Forbidden* would have sounded different. Maybe this change is an improvement, who knows. Time will tell."

Sadly, Powell – who at this stage had clear plans for the future ("I've closed a Japanese deal and together with Neil Murray, Glenn Tipton and John West I perhaps have a future band to fall back on") – was destined for an early death less than three years later, when his car was involved in a crash on the M4 near Bristol on April 5, 1998. British rock fans were shocked, and his absence on the scene – as one of the few British rock drummers of international repute – has been considerable.

And so Sabbath wound down at the end of 1995.

Meanwhile, two of the three departed founder members were also keeping themselves busy. Geezer Butler, who had been working on solo material since late 1994, recruited a band – which he called G/Z/R – and released an album, *Plastic Planet*, on October 10. The band comprised Fear Factory singer Burton C Bell, a fantastic singer with a full melodic and aggressive style, Ozzy's new drummer Dean Castronovo and an unknown guitarist, Pedro Howse. Of Bell's recruitment – quite a coup, as Fear Factory were riding high with their *Demanufacture* album, a now-classic metal and electronica blend – he said: "*Plastic Planet* was always gonna be a one-off with Burton Bell, because his main commitment is Fear Factory

. . . [this] was the first album under my own name, or my band, and I didn't really know how it was going to be accepted. I wanted to give it its own particular sound. A lot of people thought that *Plastic Planet* was actually a Fear Factory album, 'cause they hadn't heard of G/Z/R at the time."

Although the music was heavier than anything Sabbath had done in some time, this was just a part of his natural songwriting, he explained: "Some of the riffs have been around for a few years. It's something that I've always wanted to do – especially in the past 10 years, I've been writing lots of stuff. Some of it ended up on the last two Sabbath albums I did [*Dehumanizer* and *Cross Purposes*] . . . Musically, it's the way I've always written. I always thought Sabbath should have remained a heavy band, instead of lightening up and becoming Deep Purple Mark 10. I've always wanted to do a really heavy album."

Geezer also revealed that Ozzy's new album – not a studio-only project, despite the singer's supposed 'no tours' philosophy – featured his bass playing, which had been his way of finding Castronovo. "Once we got most of the music written, we started auditioning drummers and singers in England, but I couldn't find the right players anywhere. Then Ozzy asked me to play on his album, and that's how I met Dean, the drummer. I played him some of the stuff I was writing – he loved it, and he asked me if he could be on the album. Then I came back to England to audition more singers, but couldn't get anywhere. So I asked Scott Koenig, who manages Biohazard and Fear Factory, if he knew any good singers in New York or wherever. Scott sent me some tapes, and he also sent me an advance copy of the Fear Factory CD [*Demanufacture*]. I listened to the tapes, and then I listened to the Fear Factory CD, and I knew that Burton's voice was exactly what I was looking for: someone who could sing aggressively, but melodically as well. I asked Scott if he knew anyone who sounded like Burton, and he told me that Fear Factory weren't going on the road for six weeks, and Burton himself was available. So Burton came over to England, listened to the material and really liked it, so he agreed to participate in the project."

As for Howse, whom no one had heard of before: "Pedro used to have a band called Crazy Angel in England, one of the first thrash bands, back in 1982. They were incredibly heavy, perhaps too heavy for the things that were going on back then. He's also been in a few other bands in the Birmingham area, but hasn't really done anything big before . . . I've been working with Pedro for about 10 years. He's great to work with, because I write a lot of the material on the bass, and he can perfectly transpose the bass riffs on the guitar without losing any of the heaviness."

Thematically, *Plastic Planet* explores many of the same sci-fi 'cyber' obsessions that Fear Factory themselves had adopted as their stock-in-trade, as he said: "A couple of years ago, I was writing this comic book about a guy who tries to find out who God and the Devil are through his computer, and he programs himself into the computer. He becomes an evil spirit that lives inside the machine, a human computer virus. I ended up taking a lot of the material I was writing for the comic book, and adding it to the lyrics for this album . . . I guess all this stuff comes from having two kids that are growing up in a totally different way than I did, everything they do is on a computer, from playing games to communicating with each other on the internet. Computers are a totally different world to me, it's fascinating but sort of frightening at the same time . . . I really want to publish a comic book one day, and I'm thinking of writing a fiction book as well. The problem is, every time I get an idea for a book, somebody else does it! They always beat me to it! I guess that's why all this stuff ends up in my lyrics instead."

Geezer described his band as a long-term project, saying: "I don't know if the line-up will remain the same for future albums, however. It's going to be difficult for Burton, since he has Fear Factory. But I will be writing more material with Pedro Howse in the future, definitely. I would love this line-up to be the band in the future, but we'll have to wait and see."

Finally, the bassist revealed that he would be playing bass in Ozzy's touring following the release of his old bandmate's new album, this despite the fact that Ozzy played his 'farewell shows' just two years previously. Ozzy himself was on fine form in late 1995, having lost the final excess weight that had dogged his final attempts to get sober and – typically – "switching his addiction to exercise", as he put it to the *Independent On Sunday*. "The natural endorphins kick in and I could go on forever," he said. Of the AA meetings which he had sporadically attended, he explained: "If you've had one of your limbs amputated," he explains, "you don't want to sit in a room with a lot of one-legged men talking about it."

Newly on Prozac ("You still get the feelings of insecurity, but it sort of nips them in the bud"), Ozzy had been through therapy, and realised that the source of his addiction was an unending well of background insecurity. "If I didn't wake up in the morning worrying," he said, "I'd worry because I didn't have a worry, then it would escalate into this great monster sitting on my shoulder . . . My therapist said, 'You're like a man in front of two doorways. You open one and there's a guy standing behind it with a baseball bat who smacks you round the head. Every time you open that door he smacks you, then one day you walk through the other door and nobody's there and you're feeling weird that you didn't get a smack, so you go back through the first door, because it's what you're used to.'"

All this profound stuff hadn't kept the Ozzy industry from working, however, and he had issued a US-only album called *Live And Loud* in the summer to keep fans happy while he worked on his new release, *Ozzmosis*. The latter was released on November 4, 1995 and was a little slow to make an impact, thanks largely to the fact that among its 10 tracks lurked no fewer than six songs which could be classified as ballads or at least ballad-esque. Still, in the nu-metal era – with Metallica reduced to alternative-rock status, Iron Maiden and Judas Priest lacking a real singer, Motörhead failing to make much headway and a whole rise of snotty, big-shorted rap-metallers on the way – the fact that *Ozzmosis* made number 22 in the UK is a real achievement.

It begins with a career classic, 'Perry Mason', on which Ozzy sings a hymn to the fictional detective in clear tones with a glittering digital production. 'I Just Want You' is a big-budget love song against a waterfall of electronic tones, while 'Ghost Behind My Eyes' is another soft-centred Beatles homage, 'Dear Prudence'-style chorused guitar and all. 'Thunder Underground' is an echo-laden metal anthem with some expert open spaces, and 'See You On The Other Side', while a moderately affecting rock composition, is basically a cheesy Eighties power ballad by any other name.

'Tomorrow' is a strange, semi-experimental studio effects workout, followed by 'Denial' – perfect post-therapy material – another riff-free slice of the atmospherics that typify this unusual album. 'My Little Man' – "I must teach you wrong from right!" – is a pleasant, dad's-club love song, although 'My Jekyll Doesn't Hide' is a return to Ozzy and Zakk form, all twisted harmonic squeals. Finally, 'Old LA Tonight' (many fans thought sourly that 'Old Aston Tonight' might have been more appropriate) was a soupy paean to his roots.

Ozzmosis, high sugar quotient and all, did the trick for Ozzy, keeping his name in lights in sufficient quantities. Not that the mainstream rock scene was impressed: by the dawn of 1996, alternative rock and nu-metal were the new genre tags to drop, bandied about by the snootiest of industry personnel.

Into 1996, and an eerie silence hung about the Sabbath camp . . .

CHAPTER TWENTY-ONE

1996

FOR the first time in Black Sabbath's history, Geezer Butler – perhaps encouraged by the critical reviews that *Plastic Planet* had been receiving – went on the record with some anti-Sabbath (and specifically anti-Iommi) comments in the wake of his departure from the band. As he told *Bass Frontiers* magazine, "I was so frustrated in Sabbath after the last few albums. I just didn't like the musical direction Sabbath was going in. I was writing lots and lots of stuff and I felt that it was more fulfilling than the stuff we were doing in Sabbath, so I thought, well, Sabbath's finished now so I'm just going to do me own thing . . . I've felt that a lot of the newer bands are doing what Sabbath should be doing. I've always wanted to go back to the heavy stuff. That's where we started and that's what people like us for, and we were getting further and further away from it. Nobody seemed to understand that. I was writing heavy stuff and they were like, you can't do that . . . Tony Martin – who hates all heavy music – came in and said, you can't do that, it sounds like Pantera!"*

However, Butler had only positive things to say about Ronnie James Dio, adding: "I thought that *Dehumanizer* was a particularly brutal album, because Ronnie came in. You see, Tony wouldn't do any of the stuff that I was writing, but Ronnie came in and listened to all of the stuff I was doing and he insisted on doing my stuff as well as Tony's stuff. It was like a breakthrough! Then *Cross Purposes* came . . . I probably did about two songs, but I wasn't happy with the way it came out at all.

"The *Dehumanizer* thing was a whole concept I had for that album, but unfortunately only a bit of it was used. Dehumanizer is this character, again, like Catatonic Eclipse [a character from *Plastic Planet*], who programmed God and Satan into this computer and the whole thing took over the world . . . I have millions of riffs from over the years and we just basically played a few tapes and turned riffs into songs. We had over 30

---

* Martin later dismissed this in an online chat, stating that the Pantera comment was a joke.

songs written by the time Burton came along . . . As far as comparing it to Sabbath or Ozzy; on this one I'm in total control."

He also paid his respects to Bill Ward and the other Sabbath drummers, adding: "Nobody's ever gonna replace Bill on the old stuff, because we just sort of grew together. I never even played bass until I met Bill. I never picked a bass up before Sabbath started. So, I just played bass to whatever he was drumming, and it just locked in perfectly. Vinnie [Appice] was really good as well for locking in with the bass."

As well as recording with his own band, Geezer was playing gigs with Ozzy Osbourne's *Ozzmosis* tour, and loving every minute of it, it seemed: "The only reason I did the Ozzy album was because all I had to do was go in, put me bass down and that was it. He wasn't even in the studio when I cut my bass tracks. Ozzy is great to work with. He's always encouraged me to make my own album – sort of even nagged at me to do it. He said there's nothing in the world like it – you don't have to deal with all these egos. I say, do what you feel like. It's the greatest feeling of all time! Now that I've done it, it's all I want to do. After I'm finished with the Ozzy tour that's what I'm going to do. It's what I'm gonna do until I get fed up with it!"

Geezer was apparently a consummate session man when he chose, even modifying his bass playing style to suit Ozzy's material: "With the Ozzy stuff I use the pick quite a lot, because I'm doing all of Bob Daisley's bass lines, and he plays permanently with a pick, and I think it sounds better with a pick. Plus it's easier to play! If you want a more attacking sound or a faster one, if you're playing with your fingers it gets too muffly if you go too fast, so I like to get more definition by using a pick. Because I practise a lot on guitar now, I'm getting used to using a pick. Before I couldn't do it."

With all the positive comments he made about Ozzy, Bill and Ronnie, it seems that the real target of Geezer's ire was Tony Iommi, who had emerged by this point in the band's career as a leader devoted to keeping his band afloat at all costs, whatever the obstacles. Geezer talked of this, indirectly, when he compared his new band with Sabbath: "There was the enthusiasm that had been missing for years. When Ronnie came back [we said] 'Why don't you sing this?', and he was like, 'What the fuck do you know about singing?' Now it's like, 'Oh yeah, we'll try that.' Doing stuff with Tony, for instance, I was writing a riff and he'd do something to it and I really couldn't say, 'That's crap, try something else.' You couldn't confront anybody in case it would hurt their ego. It was a ridiculous situation to be in. That's why the band wasn't getting anywhere in the end. I could do something on bass that was terrible and nobody told me . . . We just couldn't talk about it any more in Sabbath. The easiest possible way without upsetting anybody, was to just go along with it."

Iommi, whom the author interviewed in 2004, is an affable and polite man, but when in songwriting and recording mode is obviously most easily defined by three things: his slow, meticulous work rate (punctuated by visits to local bars, as Vinny Appice recalled); his iron devotion; and his unwillingness to confront people on contentious issues or whose presence is not required. For the last point, witness the on-the-record testimony of Glenn Hughes and Bobby Rondinelli, who were fired 'remotely' via intermediaries or otherwise indirectly. And yet, however difficult it might be to deal with him, it's his drive that made Sabbath what it was and remains.

1996 was a rare year in which Iommi, now (as before) the last original man standing, seemed to dispense with the band, at least temporarily. After the *Forbidden* tour ended in December 1995 – and the consensus came after a while that, like Body Count, the album wasn't really that good – Sabbath seem to have been put out to grass. The conclusion of the record deal with IRS came with a compilation, *The Sabbath Stones*, which summed up the post-Ozzy years moderately well. The tracklisting of 'Headless Cross', 'When Death Calls', 'Devil And Daughter', 'Sabbath Stones', 'Battle Of Tyr', 'Odin's Court', 'Valhalla', 'TV Crimes', 'Virtual Death', 'Evil Eye', 'Kiss Of Death', 'Guilty As Hell', 'Loser Gets It All', 'Disturbing The Priest', 'Heart Like A Wheel' and 'Shining' provided obvious highlights of the Gillan and Dio era, and proved to those who had given up on Sabbath post-Ozzy that, buried deep among the rest of the AOR nonsense, lay a very good album of songs.

Iommi spent most of the year working on material for a solo album, perhaps an overdue project given the misfire of *Seventh Star* and the cynical response it had received as a Sabbath album. He let it be known that several vocalists had been invited to sing on the record, including Rob Halford and Glenn Hughes, and laid down the tracks accordingly – but then elected not to release it. Inevitably, a tape leaked out and was made available shortly afterwards on the internet, although in 1996 few people had access to the web, and fewer still the broadband connection needed to make downloading an entire album worthwhile. Nonetheless, Iommi was annoyed by its availability, and even swore later that he knew who was responsible for its escape into the public domain. Fans dubbed the unreleased album *Eighth Star* and it remained the stuff of Sabbath folklore for the next four years.

Of the solo album, he explained: "I have to do that. In fact, that's one of my things – to make an actual solo album like Geezer's made a solo album, but not have it become a Black Sabbath record. I may even do that as the next album. And if not the next one, then certainly after the end of the next Sabbath tour, towards the end of the year. I'm not talking about breaking Sabbath up – but I'd just do a different project so that I can do a bit more musically than what I do in Sabbath. It will probably knock on some parts of Sabbath, but I can't help that, that's who I am. But I would like to do some more jazz stuff, blues, and instrumental stuff. I'd bring other people in. I'm not that self-indulgent to think I can play drums and all the rest of it. I'd probably have to use different people than in the past so it gets away from Sabbath, maybe just bring in a drummer and a bass player."

Despite the solo activity, Iommi still seemed optimistic about Sabbath and its current line-up, saying in March: "The *Forbidden* combination works well, and we all get on well. With other bands I've had, we'd never get out all the troubles so that we could get on with playing, which is really ridiculous. The thing I like about this one is that I can go on and say 'We're doing this, we're doing that' and they say 'Right, OK' because everybody wants to play, and really enjoys playing. With some of the last line-ups – without mentioning names – some of them went on about things like 'Where are we staying?' or 'I don't want to do this' before we ever actually got to the playing. There was this big rigmarole of sorting it out and getting involved with everybody. My feeling is simple in those regards. I say, 'This is what we want to do. If you don't want to do it, then get out.' I've gone through so many problems in my own personal life because of Sabbath, because I'm the one sitting there night and day in a studio, working on this stuff. And you know, it's taken up a major part of my life, and consequently it's upset my married life."

Iommi evidently enjoying running Sabbath – always his band – his own way. It's also apparent that Iommi, who had undergone two divorces thanks to his commitment to Sabbath, felt that he had finally earned the right to this sovereignty, as he added, "It's been annoying when people in the band called up and said, 'Right, I'm going off on holiday,' leaving me in the studio while they're going and sunning themselves. Then they'd come back and ask 'How's it going?' which I didn't particularly like very much. But now everybody's involved with it, they love what they're doing and I'm enjoying it more. If there are any problems now, everybody's going to share those problems . . . everybody appreciates what we've got, especially after breaking this line-up to do the Dio thing with *Dehumanizer*. Because you don't realise what you've got until you lose it.

With Geezer and Dio, the old problems started again. Now we've got something that's a working team, and you don't have those problems because everybody's got a different attitude."

It's interesting to compare Iommi with his contemporaries. In the great pantheon of British rock guitarists, Iommi is comparable to another maverick genius – Ritchie Blackmore – in more ways than one. Both have mastered their instrument to unprecedented levels, and expanded rock's horizons in doing so (Blackmore with his classical influences, Iommi with his heavyweight riffs); both were deemed 'difficult' by many of their colleagues; and both presented an unsmiling, 'man in black' front to the world that only added to their anti-hero allure. Furthermore, both tapped into the same pool of talent, as Iommi mused: "There's Cozy Powell, of course, and Glenn Hughes and Ian Gillan, and we even used the first bass player from Rainbow for a bit, Craig Gruber. And we almost used David Coverdale, too. I called Coverdale up when Ronnie first left, and I called Cozy up at the same time, and Coverdale said, 'Right, OK,' and then something happened, somebody came back or something and it didn't happen. Some time later I saw Coverdale again, when we were ready for another singer, and he said, 'Ah, if you had only called me two days ago, I'd be able to do it! But I just signed this deal . . .', and then he did Whitesnake. So that almost happened." Keyboard player Don Airey (who later joined Blackmore's old band Deep Purple), Rainbow drummer Bobby Rondinelli and producer Martin Birch all fall into the 'Black Purple' category, too.

In purely instrumental terms, the similarities between Iommi and Ritchie Blackmore became obvious once again when I interviewed both in 2004. Blackmore told me, "When I started the guitar, my father insisted I learn to read music and play classical stuff by Segovia and Bach, which I failed miserably at. But the melodies and the discipline stuck with me, and once I'd got the feeling of the guitar I went back into that area. Not as a purist, though: I couldn't really sit down to play and I'd forgotten how to read music. I couldn't play the preludes and things any more, but they were still there, at the back of my subconscious, I think."

Like Iommi, Blackmore was a Django Reinhardt fan – even if, as he retained all his fingertips, the gypsy guitarist hadn't turned his life around to quite the same degree as Iommi: "But when I started playing guitar, the people you listened to were the Hank Marvins and Django Reinhardts of this world. I also went through a Wes Montgomery period of about six months. Les Paul and Chet Atkins were heroes of mine too. I was never a big blues fan. I liked BB King, but I was either more into pop or classical. I like to play the blues now and again, but I find it a little bit limiting. I loved some of Eric Clapton's stuff with Cream – I think the solo on 'I Feel Free' is brilliant – but other than him I just didn't get it. Although with Hendrix, I could see what the fuss was about. Then again, he would have made it had he not even played the guitar, I think – he just had that ambience around him. The man was from the moon."

The similarities are obvious. Iommi told me in turn: "I admired Hank Marvin, absolutely. Then later on it was Clapton and Hendrix. I enjoyed some of the jazz guitarists like Wes Montgomery, but I didn't listen to the folk guitarists, I preferred the guys who made a louder racket than that."

Early 1996 was marked by a spate of reissues of Sabbath albums, as if Iommi's solo demos and the *Sabbath Stones* compilation weren't sufficient to keep fans' attention off any future band activity. The Castle Communications label, which had established a reputation as a reissues company specialising in releasing brushed-up CD versions of old vinyl classics, licensed *Black Sabbath*, *Sabbath Bloody Sabbath*, *Sabotage*, *Technical Ecstasy* and others, remastering them for release in the spring. Bizarrely, even *The Eternal Idol* was reissued, although why another version was needed was uncertain.

All this retro-focused activity turned up the fact that Iommi was unwilling to play the lucrative reissue game to its limit, to his credit. Asked if older material such as the Ray Gillen-fronted version of *The Eternal Idol* would be issued, he shrugged: "If we were going to release it, we would have released it without . . . before Tony Martin. At that point we were involved with my old management and Ray had some disagreements, and I think Ray was just about fed up with it . . . It was a mutual thing . . . I liked Ray, I liked him a lot, but he just went off and we brought in Tony Martin . . . we wouldn't release anything we weren't proud of. I've got stuff at home, 24 multi-tracks donkey's years old. There's some tracks we did with Gillan that have never been released. I don't think there's really a need; you release the stuff you think at that time is the best for that album. It would probably have collector's value . . . We've done a lot of good stuff in the studio over the years related to Sabbath . . . just jamming around. I'm not going to start releasing stuff just to make money out of it."

He added: "You don't always have the rights to certain things. In a lot of cases I do have an influence, but there's certain cases with the old stuff that I can't have a say because it's all been signed away. Although a lot of stuff has come back to us now, and we've re-signed with Castle so they can release box sets and stuff."

Despite his unwillingness to exploit the band's back catalogue unnecessarily, Iommi knew exactly what he was doing when he signed up with Castle, who were later absorbed by the large Sanctuary label (launched by Iron Maiden manager Rod Smallwood and named after an early Maiden song). By the end of the century a huge amount of revenue was coming into the record industry on the back of repackaged versions of existing product, especially as new audio and video formats such as DVD-Video and DVD-Audio established a foothold.

As well as taking care of Sabbath's fortunes (he owned the band name, at least until the early Noughties), Iommi had sunk money into various projects over the years, notably a booking agency. He recently said of the project: "It folded up many years ago. It was myself and the guy from Ten Years After [Ric Lee]. Alvin [Lee] wanted to get involved for a while, but we didn't have enough time to stay with the agency, 'cause we were both out working on tours. When you're away you can't see what goes on. We built up a few acts there. I supplied equipment and Ric gave them stuff."

In the very early days, Iommi also invested in a guitar model that had an interesting spin on sound technology: "I put money into a company because I couldn't get guitars built the way I wanted them. I had to prove it to the manufacturers. So I put money into John Birch guitars, and he built my guitars. I had to prove it worked. All of this was done by experimenting and trial and error. I paid for that myself in the early days to show it could be done. And I paid for all these companies to get the benefits nowadays. Back then they all said it couldn't be done. I also used locking nuts years and years ago without a tremolo, before locking nuts were the norm . . . I also came up with a guitar with interchangeable pickups you could slot in from the back. It was a John Birch guitar. We only sold one, and Roy Orbison bought it. I came up with that years ago and the first one was made for me to use in the studio. At the time I had a lot of problems tuning guitars because of the neck and the light strings on the Gibson. I decided to come up with a guitar that I could use in the studio with different sounds so that I didn't have to keep changing guitars. You could slot a pickup in it and get a Fender sound, then slot a different pickup in it and get a Gibson sound. That was the idea. I did use it for a while, but they were too expensive to mass-produce."

While he was looking back at those early days, Iommi mused to *Rip* magazine: "My advice to other musicians just starting out: get a lawyer! It's all changed since I started. The music business is a big business, and you've got to be very careful, as you always have to be when you go in knowing nothing. You just have to tread carefully as well as legally, even if you get a manager. I think as far as the music side of things, just believe in what you do, and don't follow trends and such. I know it's difficult these days. The public can jump from one to another thing . . . and it's so easy, I think, to fall into that and to try to please. When I started out it was much simpler. You had to make it to create the sound. It was a lot more involved that way then. Nowadays you can go out and buy things and gadgets that make a certain sound, and you can sound like Jimi Hendrix or you can sound like this or like that. In those days, you had to make your own sound, and the band became the sound of what you made. That was a difficult thing then. There wasn't much as far as airplay as well, certainly in England there wasn't. It was all very 'underground' if you like, and word of mouth more than anything else. And you managed to get on with the business, with word of mouth. There wasn't TV or videos."

He admitted that certain periods in Sabbath's history hadn't matched up to others, too, drawing a perspective that only decades in the business can bring. "I think everybody's gone through a sort of writer's block or burnout; everybody's probably gone through that stage," he pondered. "It's a catchy thing! I haven't for many years now, but years ago I went through a stage, and it was really funny, actually. But it was probably – actually, a lot of it – due to drugs and everything else I was doing at the time. More than likely I'd put it down to that, and the stress of the business and everything else that was going on. Now my life's a lot easier, and I find it a lot more pleasant to live . . . To stay fresh, you have to get people in the band who have the energy, who really want to do it. I find that if you get somebody in the band who's not so eager to do it any more, who's lost the fight for it, I think it becomes very difficult. But if you've got everybody there in the band that's right behind the band's goals, that really helps to keep the music fresh and to keep the ideas going. I like all sorts of music, really. From Frank Sinatra to Soundgarden. It's a wide variety of music. I like anything that's musically good. I don't like electronic-sounding sort of stuff. So if it's musically good, I'm there!"

As with so many bands who reach a certain level after many years in the music business, a useful source of exposure when mainstream media were no longer interested was the musicians' magazines, who tend to be interested in virtuoso instrumentalists no matter what their supposed cool quotient. Tony Iommi has always had guitar magazines breathing down his neck, a much-undervalued way for getting Sabbath some column inches. But he deserves their attention: as we've consistently seen, he has always been an incredible player – and a humble one. As he told one interviewer, he hadn't been hailed as a guitar hero despite his obvious skills

OLDER AND WISER: BLACK SABBATH, MONMOUTH STUDIOS, WALES, JUNE 2005. *(Ross Halfin/Idols)*

BLACK SABBATH IN HOLLYWOOD, 1992. *(Robert Knight/Redferns)*

OZZY, TONY AND GEEZER AT THE HOLLYWOOD BOULEVARD ROCK WALK IN NOVEMBER, 1992. *(Ron Galella/Redferns)*

BLACK SABBATH IN 2001. *(Ross Halfin/Idols)*

GEEZER AT ROSKILDE, DENMARK, 2005. *(Ross Halfin/Idols)*

BILL AT MONMOUTH STUDIOS, WALES, 2005. *(Ross Halfin/Idols)*

TONY & OZZY. *(Ross Halfin/Idols)*

THE OSBOURNE FAMILY WITH THEIR DOGS IN BEVERLY HILLS, 2002, LEFT TO RIGHT: KELLY, OZZY, SHARON & JACK. *(Stewart Volland/Retna)*

OZZY, GEEZER AND TONY AT ROSKILDE, DENMARK, JUNE 2005. *(Ross Halfin/Idols)*

THE BAND AT THE UK HALL OF FAME, LONDON, NOVEMBER 2005 AND AT THE US HALL OF FAME AWARDS,
NEW YORK, MARCH 2006. *(LFI)*

"probably because I've been more a part of the band than an actual individual . . . it's funny because there's a lot more people in the last couple of years that have said much more about [my skills]. I'm not blowing my own trumpet here, but yeah, it's spoken about a lot more. But I don't care. I don't mind. If I'd actually done a Tony Iommi album, which I was intending on doing, then maybe more people would know me as that . . . I took a lot of criticism over the years for keeping Black Sabbath going, even though I was the only one left and we had all those different line-ups. You know, you don't close the bloody factory if a worker quits, do you? No, you carry on. I carried on because it was important to me and I believed in Black Sabbath. And I'm glad that in recent years, some of those later Sabbath records, particularly the ones with Tony Martin, have started to gain some appreciation. But even then, it's nice to work outside of Black Sabbath. How certain songs come out or how you go about writing them always depends on who you're working with. Writing songs with Ozzy or Dio or Tony Martin or Glenn Hughes – it's all different."

Finally, there's a side of Iommi which would surprise most people. The guitarist, often viewed as the most practical and unpretentious member of Sabbath, has admitted to a taste for spiritual literature on more than one occasion: "I don't read science fiction – well, some people may call it science fiction," he told *Circus* in 1975, "but I believe it . . . Lobsang Rampa's writings about astral travelling and the next life. I believe there is a next life. It's easy to be sceptical but I understand a lot and get a lot out of reading his books. Geezer, who wrote most of the songs in the past, was into this kind of thing long before me and I think the influence is in some of those songs."

All this looking back by Iommi was timely, as a major watershed in Black Sabbath's career lay just around the corner. Not the product of the media of 1996, it should be noted, who were mostly far too snooty to acknowledge the band's presence.

Thank God for that very snootiness: for without it, both Ozzy and Sabbath might have disappeared into oblivion within a few years, footnotes in the rock ledger alongside successful but long-outmoded acts such as Purple and Def Leppard, both of whom were much reduced at this point from their Eighties high points. This fate would not await Ozzy, Tony and their colleagues, thanks to one perceptive woman and her reaction to a conversation she had with certain, rather stuck-up, business-people . . .

CHAPTER TWENTY-TWO

1996–1997

IN early 1996 Sharon Osbourne, looking for a gig for Ozzy, approached the organisers of the coolest, most envied rock tour available – the Lollapalooza tour, an institution since 1991. Launched by Jane's Addiction/Porno For Pyros singer Perry Farrell as a travelling vehicle for the then-new grunge and alternative rock movements, in the early Eighties Lollapalooza was *the* tour to be seen on, appealing as it did to all cultural substrata for its recruitment of metal, punk and hip-hop acts outside the grunge genre.

"They laughed at the idea," said Sharon later. "They all thought Ozzy was so uncool. So I thought, 'Right, I'll organise my own fucking festival.'"

The idea she hit upon was called the Ozzfest, and took the form of a two-stage travelling festival – like Lollapalooza itself – with multiple bands, over which Ozzy would headline. In summer and autumn 1996, Ozzy duly carried out the 20-date tour, supported by Slayer, Danzig, Biohazard, Sepultura and Fear Factory on the main stage alongside a second stage featuring Earth Crisis, Powerman 5000, Neurosis, Coal Chamber and Cellophane. The shows were a massive success, thanks largely to the judicious choice of acts on the bill. In a macrocosm of Ozzy's strategy of using a powerhouse guitarist in his own band, Sharon had recruited the most cutting-edge bands of the day to the Ozzfest stage, crucially retaining credibility by inviting unknowns (Cellophane and the then-new goth-metallers Coal Chamber, who she managed) onto the bill.

The main stage in particular was a veteran bill, with Slayer riding high after a career-best tour with Machine Head in support, and Danzig and Biohazard settling into middle-career respectability after recording a series of much-praised (if also identical-sounding) albums. Meanwhile, the remarkable Brazilian thrash metal act Sepultura was on a career high, having established a crushing template with their *Roots* album (produced by the nu-metal genre's future spokesman, Ross Robinson). Fear Factory (whose frontman Burton C. Bell had made Geezer Butler's recent solo album rather special) were in a similar position.

Ironically, as the 1996 Ozzfest ground to a halt, with organisers, musicians and fans giving witness that it had by and large been a success, Lollapalooza was in decline. Its final fling would come the following year, as by the end of '97 the grunge-based politics on which Farrell had founded it were being superseded. The inclusion of Metallica on the bill in '96 had been viewed by many as a sign that Farrell was selling out to the big record companies, and music fans were looking elsewhere for their headbanging kicks. Sharon and Ozzy saw no reason to back down, and Ozzfest dates were booked in 1997, reinforcing their dominance of the US rock festival circuit.

This all filtered through to Iommi et al. By the end of 1996 rumours were rife about the Sabbath camp. It was thought in October that Tony Martin was about to leave, but he quashed such ideas in interviews. Even in December that year, it was obvious that Iommi was still keen to use Martin in Sabbath, although the singer was clearly uncertain of his future, saying: "I was never really comfortable with the shoes that were given to me, but for a while I thought I was wearing them in. Y'know, *Headless Cross, Tyr.* But then the first break came, and it was a shock. So after that, I was always reading between the lines to try and figure out what came next. Luckily I had my manager Albert, who knew them very well, and was able to throw light on a lot of things. *Cross Purposes* felt good, but then *Forbidden* was awful, so it was a very unsure time for me, really."

He was right to be so unsure. In early 1997 Sharon Osbourne called Tony Iommi and asked him if he was interested in re-forming the classic Seventies Black Sabbath line-up. You can imagine what his reply was.

In true Iommi fashion, Martin was out of the band – although no one bothered to inform him of the fact. As he said: "Tony decided it was the right time to do a reunion with Ozzy and so I guess I got fired, although nobody ever called me to tell me. I didn't want anything to do with the industry for a while, and took time out to raise a family and build a house . . . and get divorced in the end!" But he's not bitter, reasoning: "It was probably the only way Sabbath could move forward. We took it as far as we could, with all the interference we had making albums with rap artists, so I think it was designed to get out of the deal we had and move the band on. It certainly sold tickets!"

Martin added: "I'm absolutely certain that the band wasn't able to go any further up with me or anyone else other than Ozzy. The reunion with Ronnie didn't do it, there wasn't any other singer that could have joined without another line up change, and style that could do what a reunion did . . . It wasn't happening to the extent we would have liked it to be when I was there. But if you re-unite any original line up, The Beatles or Black Sabbath, it draws attention."

Of course, this meant that Neil Murray and Bobby Rondinelli were also out of the band, but as they'd been hardened session men before (and this was not the first time they'd been asked to leave Sabbath) the impact on them was less. Murray duly teamed up with Cozy Powell in Peter Green's Splinter Group, and Rondinelli moved through various bands, Blue Oyster Cult and The Lizards among them. Geoff Nicholls, however, joined Iommi for the Sabbath reunion.

Geezer Butler, who had spent much of 1996 slagging off the rest of the band – or at least Iommi – was also quick to sign up with the new Ozzy line-up, telling me ruefully: "I always remember, I'd just done my first solo project, *Plastic Planet*, and I was doing press for that and they asked me if Sabbath would ever get back together. And I said, no way! Never in a month of Sundays. And then the very next week, Ozzy phoned up and said, do you want to do Ozzfest this year as Sabbath? And we were like, yeah."

He added: "Sharon called and asked me if I wanted to do it. She wanted to have us as the headliners with Ozzy at this year's Ozzfest because of the festival's success last year. I said yes, then it had to be put together quickly because there were only two months to rehearse."

Sharon and Ozzy's brainwave was to invite Black Sabbath to close the show at the Ozzfest 97 events, after Ozzy had performed his own songs with his own band. The idea of bringing the band back in such triumphant style might have seemed like genius, had it not been for one small thing: Bill Ward was not asked to play, making the 'reunion' concept slightly redundant. His place on the Ozzfest would be taken by Mike Bordin, sometime Faith No More drummer and Ozzy's own sticksman from time to time.

Ward told me: "I got passed over, and I didn't like that. It was a very, *very* bitter pill. I felt totally betrayed. I've never completely known the reason for being passed over, but I have a feeling that there might have been some Sharon influence going on there. Maybe I was regarded as a loose cannon, or that I wasn't really up for it, but I have the feeling that maybe some decisions were made without me being consulted in the first place. I was ready to fuckin' go out there and kick ass."

However, Bill reflects that he had hardly been the most reliable player in previous years, first sacrificing his fitness to booze and then joining and rejoining Sabbath sporadically: "To go out and play drums in Black

Sabbath, you've got to be pretty together, you can't just show up and play. It takes me a while to get everything back into the groove and get everything working."

The idea of the Ozzfest as a viable commercial institution – and vehicle for Sabbath – no doubt played a strong part in the reunion. After all, without their own festival, where would Ozzy and Sabbath have played? Not on Lollapalooza, that's for sure. As Ozzy told MTV, the original concept had sounded odd in theory – but worked perfectly in practice: "My wife first came up with the idea last year when I was doing the *Ozzmosis* tour: right at the end of the tour she said, 'I want to do an Ozzfest,' and it sounded kind of like a German beer tent with loads of people getting drunk. And I said, 'What is an Ozzfest?' She explained it, and I said go ahead. So we did four or maybe five shows that were immediately sold out. Then she said to me, 'What do you want to do with this Ozzfest?' And I said, 'We hardly made a dent last year. We only had five shows, we better do a few this year.' We started off at 10, then it went to 15, then it went to 20, and then I said, 'Hey, I'm gonna end up doing a full tour again,' you know."

Crazy man of rock or not, Ozzy knew the value of building a brand: "With the Ozzfest, what I wanted to achieve was, instead of going out and doing like 5,000 shows or whatever and selling one out and the rest die on their rear ends, I just wanted to do it slowly and progressively get a following for it. I'm a strong believer in word of mouth. It was really good, not only in front of the stage, but backstage the atmosphere was really good, you know. We all got along. Nobody had any beefs."

Iommi mused on the fact that the reunion had taken so long to organise: "It had to have time to heal everything. And just for us all to venture on to our own things and realise what we had. We were really lucky to have what we had. And you don't realise it until you haven't got it . . . It was great to get back together. We were all in the right frame of mind to appreciate what we've got. It's taken years to sit back and look at it and go, 'Bloody hell! We're lucky we're able to get back together and be able to go out and play.' And the greatest thing for me was to be able to walk onstage with the guys again and do shows, because we never thought that was gonna happen . . . You never know with this line-up. Things happen just like that, so I never would close the door on it. Unless we all drop dead, and then I would."

And so, on May 24, 1997, the Ozzfest headlined by Black Sabbath began its run. The first date was in Bristow, Virginia, and featured on its main stage (from bottom of the bill), Powerman 5000, Machine Head,

Fear Factory, Type O Negative and Pantera, before the two-band Ozzy extravaganza. The second stage featured Vision Of Disorder, Drain STH, Coal Chamber, Slo-Burn and Neurosis before headliners Downset, making the event a must for hardcore punk, stoner-rock, goth-metal and trad heavy metal fans.

Ozzy's set-list included career classics such as 'Mr. Crowley', 'Suicide Solution', 'I Don't Wanna Change The World', 'Crazy Train', 'Mama I'm Coming Home' and 'Bark At The Moon' – as well as a cheeky snippet of 'Symptom Of The Universe' during the solos – before a 15-minute pause for him to change and rehydrate for the Sabbath set. Typically, he hadn't thought beforehand how exhausting the two-show routine would be, saying: "I mean, I'm king of the mountain. I can do everything. I can't do anything in moderation, so my wife says to me, 'What do you think about doing your set and Sabbath's set?' Piece of cake. Three shows into it I felt like somebody had beaten me up. I didn't realise . . . I thought all music is music, you know. It's two separate emotions. You've got to save yourself for the next show, then you've got to go off, get changed, and do it 10 minutes later. You're running around being the man from Satan's village going, 'Agh' and all this stuff. It was a good experience. I mean I had a few problems in my voice . . . I don't want to smoke cigars any more. They killed me. I started smoking cigars because I was smoking too many cigarettes, and then I started to inhale the cigars and I liked it and so I started smoking more cigars, and ended up with a chest like a barrel organ with a hole in the side. It nearly killed me, so all my thousands of dollars' worth of Cuban cigars went out the window, you know. I mean, I stopped big time. Killed me. I had a hell of a time on that Ozzfest."

Iommi recalled: "Funnily enough, when we got back together we realised how different things were in between. Nobody plays those songs like the original line-up. You can't replace anybody, you just carry on. And that's what happened. It was only when we all played together again that we realised how those songs should sound and we went back to the way we played them. It just felt nice having the songs sound the way they should. It's funny, playing the solos again and all those particular riffs. We had it sounding much the same as it was when we'd originally done it. All through the years we had done different albums where there was more solo stuff going on, but there's probably less solo stuff in this, and more riffs."

Sabbath's set typically ran through 'War Pigs', 'Into The Void', 'Sweet Leaf', 'Iron Man', 'Children Of The Grave', 'Black Sabbath', 'Fairies Wear Boots' and 'Paranoid' – a relatively brief one-hour set to top off the night. Ozzy excelled himself, running around the stage and flinging buckets of water on the musicians and into the crowd: for the latter he had also installed enormous water guns ('Supersoakers') that pointed far out into the crowd – welcome relief for the audience on the hottest days. He said in a later webchat, "It started off with a bottle of water one time, then a bucket, and then somebody came up with the Supersoakers. It's just good fun, you know. It's kind of become the new Ozzy trademark, now. Next year it'll be firehoses . . . then the one after that I'll probably do an underwater concert. Promoted by Jacques Cousteau . . ."

The tour played in stadiums in Florida, North Carolina, Texas, Illinois, Pennsylvania, New Jersey, Missouri, Michigan, Minnesota, Wisconsin, Colorado, Nevada and Arizona before rolling to a halt on June 29 in San Bernardino, California. The Ozzy/Sabbath section of one gig, scheduled for June 17 at the Polaris Amphitheater in Columbus, Ohio, had to be cancelled when Ozzy's throat gave him problems: he was advised to miss the show or seriously jeopardise the rest of the tour. Unfortunately the venue was full of fans by the time the news broke, some of whom were angered by the announcement that Ozzy would not be appearing. However, they were treated to the sight and sound of a quickly assembled tribute band made up of members of Pantera, Type O Negative, Fear Factory and others, who played 'I Don't Know', 'Mr. Crowley', 'Suicide Solution', 'Crazy Train' and 'Bark At The Moon'. The crowd didn't disperse for some time after the lights went up, half-believing that Ozzy might come on after all: only the announcement by Pantera frontman Phil Anselmo that the show was genuinely over persuaded them to leave.

MTV News reported: "The capacity crowd of 20,000 was less than thrilled with the news, and about 1,000 of them took their anger out on the venue. Fans smashed box-office windows, ripped down panels from a wooden fence, and lit small fires around the amphitheatre ground. According to the *Columbus Dispatch* the crowd also seriously damaged at least one car and destroyed trees and fences on neighbouring property. This riot resulted in the arrest of 23 attendees. 'When one of the band members announced that Ozzy wasn't here, the guys ran to the fence and started tearing it down,' one fan told a local news crew of the situation. 'All of a sudden bonfires broke out on the lawn and people were setting seats on fire, setting the wall on fire . . .' Five fans were treated for minor injuries, one was charged by police with disorderly conduct, and the venue hopes to announce refund information in a few days."

The Ozzfest returned to the venue on July 1 to play a make-up show, this time with Ozzy back in the saddle. Mike Bordin was unavailable for that date and so Ozzy and Sabbath used drummer Shannon Larkin of Ugly Kid Joe and Godsmack for the occasion.

Ozzy, exhausted after the tour, told the press that he had no energy for thinking about a possible 1998 Ozzfest line-up, placing the decision-making responsibility squarely on Sharon's shoulders: "You know, in all fairness I don't look at the bands. I don't run out and buy the latest *Billboard* magazine, or find out who's happening this week and whatever. All I do is get my things together and go on. My wife manages me. She manages Coal Chamber. I'll be on an Ozzfest somewhere in the world probably next year, and no doubt Coal Chamber will be somewhere, either here, or over there, or wherever. But as far as the picking of the bands, that's purely my wife. I mean, behind me there's my wife. I work hard, but she works 20,000 times harder than me."

He also explained that some inspiration for the lesser-known bands on the Ozzfest came from his son Jack, a mere 12 years old in 1997. He and his sister, Kelly, were accustomed to travelling with their parents when Ozzy was on tour, and had been aware of the legions of fans that followed Ozzy and Sabbath since their pre-teen years. Sharon and Ozzy often spoke to the press about the conflicts between family commitments and the life on the road, with the former once reporting: "I caught the kids giggling once at some Ozzy fans. I was so angry. I said to them, 'Don't you ever laugh at those people, because they're the reason we live in the house we do, drive the car we do, and you go to the schools you do. Show some respect.'"

Jack and Kelly – the two youngest of Ozzy's six children, and the ones who would become best-known to the public thanks to subsequent events – had become sophisticated by their environment at a young age. As Ozzy said, "My father never set me down and told me the facts of life, sex, the dangers of alcohol, tobacco, whatever. And I've survived a lot of alcohol and drug abuse, so it's my duty to sit my son down and say things like, 'If you're going to have sex, don't go out in the rain without a raincoat. Wear protection. Don't be stupid.' I mean, sex is as natural as breathing. But I'll tell you, I wouldn't want to be a teenager these days with the HIV virus going around. A lot of people think these things will never happen to their kid. 'Oh, my kid won't get caught behind the wheel drunk,' and so on. But at the end of every show I ever do, I say, 'If you've been drinking or using dope, please make sure you get somebody around to drive you home, or leave your car and get a cab, because I want to come back next year and do this again.' And that's the last message I leave the kids with, because some of these kids really go over the edge – at any concert – it's a party atmosphere."

Amid the winding-down shenanigans of the enormous Ozzfest, Geezer Butler's new solo album, *Black Science*, was somewhat ignored. Perhaps this was just as well: the album, recorded with his ally Pedro Howse on guitar and loaded with electronic sounds from Geezer himself, was not one of his best. Even he didn't regard it with much fondness after a couple of years, saying: "*Black Science* had a lot of keyboards, and it didn't work. It sounded great in my studio but when I took it into another studio I realised it was going to take months to do. When I go into the studio it has to be raw and to the point. I like to do things quickly because I don't have much patience . . . if you polish things too much then it loses the feeling, I think. Towards the later days of Sabbath, instead of going in and knocking out what songs we did in rehearsal, we would polish them to death."

In autumn 1997 the band-members all took time out to work on their own projects. Bill and his self-titled band played a show at the Roxy in LA. Iommi went back to the solo recording sessions he had put on ice since the previous summer. Geezer played some low-key club dates to promote *Black Science*. And Ozzy put together a double-CD greatest-hits package entitled *The Ozzman Cometh*, scheduled for release in November. He told MTV: "I look back and all I see from those days is just a hangover, man. I used to go onstage hungover so bad. I look and look and it's a miracle that I'm here to do this best-of, or whatever they call this album. *The Ozzman Cometh* . . . it was nearly *The Ozzman Wenteth*, you know I mean I was OD-ing all over the place in the Eighties. It was crazy. It was like *Caligula* on the road, you know."

Of the early Sabbath recordings that he had dug out for the new collection – including demo versions of 'Black Sabbath' and 'War Pigs' – he commented: "You look back at old photographs at school or whatever, and you go, 'Did I look that geeky?' or 'I'm glad that period went.' But saying that, I mean talking about these Black Sabbath [songs], I'm one of these people that never wants to throw anything away, right? So, in the Seventies, it was the platform boot era. We used to walk around like Herman Munster onstage with these great big platforms, and my wife said, 'I'm not looking at them any more.' She said, 'Throw the damn things out.' So, I threw 30 or more pairs in the trash can. Now they're all coming back. I could have sold them, you know? I mean, Kiss went on the road and kept all their memorabilia, and there is an interest there to how crazy we really were. I mean, Elton John used to wear great big platforms, you know. Then I went into a shop in Toronto yesterday to do some TV work, and the shops . . . I go, 'God, they aren't back, are they, these platforms?' And they said, 'Yeah they are.' With me, nothing is in any chronological order. It's all thrown in a heap, and my wife is always . . . she's very clean and very tidy. I'm not. I'm a slob, you know? So, I have my dump room and the rest of it. She locks that when I'm not there to keep the flies out of the rest of the house. There's an old pizza up in the corner and old drunken friends still lying under the pool table . . ."

The album bombed – making a mere number 68 – but its purpose, keeping Ozzy's profile up in the wake of the renewed Sabbath activity, and providing record stores with product should the Ozzfests take off – was assured. The wheels of industry behind both camps were turning, and turning fast . . .

CHAPTER TWENTY-THREE

1997–1999

BUT 1997 wasn't over for the new (or rather old) line-up of Black Sabbath yet.

A live album was scheduled for recording in December, and this time Bill Ward was asked to participate. As he told me, this was just as well – the Sabbath fanbase had been close to rebellion when Mike Bordin had taken Bill's place on that summer's Ozzfest: "The fans didn't let it go. A lot of them were pissed. Those that knew the original band were like, what the *fuck* is going on, you know? It was a real uncomfortable thing to go through. I just watched it happen. I mean, I know Mike Bordin, he's a buddy of mine, and he's often referred to me and my chops in certain songs, and he asks, how does this work in certain songs?"

But it didn't take Bill long to calm down and see the bigger picture: "Eventually all that got worked out. After they finished doing the first Ozzfest with Mike Bordin, Tony was the first to call me. I felt really lucky that I was allowed to take part in the reunion, when it finally happened . . . Ozzy coming back in 1997 opened the door for me. It released me from my own self-made exile, you know, because that was what it felt like. It was so hard not to pick up the phone. One of the things that encouraged me to try and work out things for myself was knowing that I couldn't just sit around on my ass . . . it was sweet and sour. I'd started to move ahead and try to create some of my own things, but I missed them all the time. I missed them spiritually and I missed them physically, all the fuckin' time. Especially when I'd hear their new music, and I'd hear Tony's stuff, and I'd see Geezer hanging out with Ozz and whatever."

Tony Iommi offered a reason for Bill's exclusion a couple of years later when he told writer Doug Roemer: "I got a call from Ozzy and Sharon saying, 'Would you fancy doing a couple of songs onstage?' I said, 'Yeah. Why don't we invite Geezer as well?' That would be great, we'll just come up and play a few songs, you know? But the reaction was just really good, and we ended up playing more than a couple of songs. So we thought, 'The next time, let's get Bill.' And that's what we did . . ."

Ward had also released his own work – a debut album in 1990 entitled *Along The Way* (which rapidly went out of print) and a more fully rounded work in 1997 called *When The Bough Breaks*. Both records featured Bill's competent vocals, a professional production and useful performances from lesser-known musicians, but both vanished more or less without trace despite being released by a reasonably well-known label, Cleopatra. Still, as 1997 wore on, both Geezer's and Bill's solo work was eclipsed by the forthcoming Sabbath live album, which would be titled (with stunning originality) *Reunion* and released by Epic, the label to which Ozzy had been signed for many years.

Two shows took place with Fear Factory in support on December 4 and 5, 1997. The venue, in true coming-home style, was the giant NEC venue in Birmingham. Media coverage was extensive, with writer Sylvie Simmons chuckling in *Rolling Stone*, "The arena looks like a fringed-jacket sales showroom. A quick glimpse around the arena shows metal celebrities (Henry Rollins, Cozy Powell, Neil Murray) dotted among the crowd. Video screens at the side of the stage tease us with footage of the Sabs in their heyday, then here they are in the flesh . . ."

The shows were a mighty success: Ozzy, with the live album doubtless in mind, described the second night as "one of the best shows I ever did". Iommi, too, was delighted with the results, saying: "It's too late to say I shouldn't have done it, but I can say that nobody sounds like this band with the four of us. This is like coming home." Geezer was very pleased, telling me: "When Ozzy came back it was great. We said, let's bury all the past, all the bad blood and everything, and start again. It was as if we were on a different level. We recorded the *Reunion* live album because there'd been loads of bootleg live albums, so we thought, let's do a proper one."

The set was mostly the obvious standards, with a couple of less-played songs thrown in as surprises – 'War Pigs', 'Behind The Wall Of Sleep', 'N.I.B.', 'Fairies Wear Boots', 'Electric Funeral', 'Sweet Leaf', 'Spiral Architect', 'Into The Void', 'Snowblind', 'Sabbath Bloody Sabbath', 'Orchid/Lord Of This World', 'Dirty Women', 'Black Sabbath', 'Iron Man', 'Children Of The Grave' and 'Paranoid'. While 'Dirty Women' is far from a classic Sabbath track, 'Spiral Architect' and 'Electric Funeral' are out-and-out musical monoliths and long overdue for a legitimate live recording.

Those who were at the show remember Ozzy leaping onstage with the shout "We love you all!" and, conveniently forgetting Live Aid, adding "It's been about 17 years since I did a gig with these guys, and I miss them," all of which was part of the ambience and mid-song exhortations to "go fucking crazy" captured on tape.

The gigs were recorded on a mobile studio facility and produced by Bob Marlette at Rockfield Studios and elsewhere. Marlette had also been asked to record two new studio tracks to add to the *Reunion* album, saying: "Tony and Ozzy called me and I came in just to do the studio tracks. Then, once we were in there working on the studio tracks, they asked me to do the remix on [the live tracks] . . . It was mostly a combination of adding and subtracting frequencies. I always start out by removing what I don't like first and then I build up the quality of the big picture."

The band were delighted with their performance and didn't want the album made too perfect in the studio, with Bill saying, "I think there's two snare drum hits I missed. Nobody's going in there and overdubbing or anything else. This is a raw live album."

Iommi added, "We've left some of the clunks on it. We tried to keep it how it was, so if the tuning was a little bit off, it was off. We didn't want to go in and polish it all up. You can hear that."

"I wanted to keep it as pure as possible," Marlette said. "I wanted the audience to feel like they were seeing a show, not a sort of edited, shined up, overdubbed thing. Anyone in the audience who would buy that record would know better. I wanted them to feel like 'I was in the 27th row and I was watching a great Sabbath show.' Actually, I did use some stereo-enhancing boxes. There's certain places where you feel that some of the audience is coming from behind you as well."

The two new songs, 'Psycho-Man' and 'Selling My Soul', were duly laid down. As Geezer told me, the songs were valid enough but not quite as meaningful as whole-band sessions: "I don't really count those two bonus tracks – Tony and Ozzy wrote them and I just came in and played the bass on them, then pissed off home!" In the sessions Ozzy was introduced to Pro-Tools, the revolutionary recording program, saying: "It's a lot easier, to be honest with you, but I couldn't fucking turn the thing on! You can chop things around, no missing, and it's so easy. We wrote the two songs in no time at all."

Iommi added: "It was Ozzy and myself there. It enabled us to put down the ideas quick, and if that didn't work, then to scrap 'em and put something else down . . . then Bill would come in and play the drums. You've got to be careful with using click tracks because of the feel."

Of the new songs, Iommi said: "When we went in to do the mix they asked us if we could come up with two new tracks as a bonus for the album. It was totally out of the blue while we were in the middle of doing the mix. It had to be done quickly, so we didn't really have any time to think about it. We just came up with some ideas and put them down. Then Ozzy came up with a melody line and we all played it and it was as simple as that, really. They wanted it that quick and it was done in just a couple of days . . . I'd come up with a riff, then Ozzy would come up with the melody line and we'd just build it up. The new songs were done just like we had always did them. We wrote just those two songs in the studio and, overall, it took about four days in the studio to write and record them from start to finish."

Once the tracks were laid down, plans were announced for a Black Sabbath tour in 1998, and speculation mounted apropos a complete new album by the re-formed band. Geezer, for one, wasn't giving anything away: "There might be. It just depends, but we're not going to force it. It's got to be marvellous — it either happens or it doesn't."

Iommi added: "There is a possibility. I'd just rather think that when we're ready to do that, we will. We'd love to do it, but until that happens, we stand to whatever else we're going to be doing."

In one final development, Ozzy was seen on a few TV shows at about this time. He had not been invited to sit in the interviewee's chair very often before this, but something was clearly afoot. Might there be forces at work pushing him towards mass media exposure outside the rock world?

On December 22, Ozzy was a special guest on the huge-rating US show *Late Night With Conan O'Brien*. Audiences could scarcely believe their eyes when they witnessed him, clad in black and wearing purple John Lennon sunglasses, stuttering and shaking his way through the interview, plagued either by nerves or by some post-addiction palsy, it was hard to tell.

And yet he was charismatic. Host, studio audience and TV millions chuckled as he related war story after war story, in a tremulous Brummie monotone that must have seemed like some sort of alien patois in Hicksville, Middle America. Of the Sabbath re-formation, he stumbled: "Well . . . I'm one of these people that, that, that, that always says things that I'll later regret. You know, and those people? And people — now it's like people say to me, 'Is it really going to be a re-formation of the original Black Sabbath?' and I go, 'Let's wait and see,' because I, if I go, 'Yeah,' it won't happen, if I go, 'No,' it will happen . . . I thought, 'Great.' I'm still, I got breath in my lungs, I can still see, I don't need a walking stick yet, and I don't need . . . I haven't got — what — a colostomy bag quite yet."

How they laughed across the pond at the poor, wasted, English wild man of metal. And yet someone high up in media circles was watching, and the spark of an idea was beginning to flare.

Now that the band was back together – smoothly massaged into place by Sharon and her associates – things moved quickly. A Sabbath tour was booked for June 1998 and the *Reunion* live album was scheduled for release, but not until October, presumably in order to avoid a conflict of interests with *The Ozzman Cometh* and then the Ozzfest itself, on which Sabbath would not appear this year.

Unfortunately, the first half of the year was marked with misfortune. On April 4 Cozy Powell died in the car accident near Bristol, casting a pall over the year for many of his associates and fans, some of whom got together to plan a tribute concert: this eventually took place on January 5, 1999, with Tony Martin, Neil Murray and Bobby Rondinelli playing together.

Two months later Sabbath began their rehearsals for the summer tour in the old house in Monmouth which they had been using since the early days – only to be rocked when Bill Ward suffered a heart attack. The episode, on May 19, was serious enough for Bill to be sidelined for major treatment and surgery (he underwent angioplasty on June 3) but manageable enough so that a full recovery was forecast by doctors as long as Ward maintained a healthy lifestyle.

In an interview with *Vintage Guitar* magazine, Tony and Geezer recalled the run-up to that fateful day, with Iommi recalling that, "We went back and it was like going back to the beginning, to the same place we started. It was really good. We took time and all lived together in the house and just got familiar again. We had a laugh, joked, and had food. Then we started playing again and it was great because it all fit in."

Geezer added: "It was all natural, really. We hadn't played together with Bill on a full set for 18 or 20 years from the original days. He had the most difficult job, so we had to go over stuff with Bill again just to make sure that he was all right with it."

Rehearsals were going unexpectedly well, as Iommi explained: "We were due to headline some European festivals. So we got back together in the house in Monmouth and started rehearsing . . . I'll tell you, we were all shocked! Then we opened our mouths and said, 'Oh, blimey. It's going quicker than we expected!' And of course, the next thing, Bill had a bloody heart attack. We thought it was all going too good."

With only three weeks to go before a major European tour, Bill was informed that after his operation he would not be permitted to fly for another six weeks. Hearing this, Iommi phoned the old stalwart Vinny Appice and invited him to fill in for the band for that period.

Vinny told me: "Bill had his heart attack, and Tony left a message at my house when I was touring with Dio. So I called him back and he said, 'Bill's had a heart attack, can you call Sharon? We want you to play.' I called Sharon and she wanted me to leave like, that afternoon! Dio were playing that night, so I explained to her that I needed a couple of days to get somebody else in: I couldn't just leave the tour. It took me about four days to get Simon Wright in – he came to a couple of Dio shows, and we rehearsed."

Presumably Ronnie Dio wasn't exactly delighted to have his drummer taken away from him mid-tour, I ask, mindful of the less-than-amicable split before the Costa Mesa reunion shows five years earlier? Appice laughs: "Well, he was as cool as he could be . . . he wasn't that cool! But I said, it's only for six weeks – it's a good opportunity and it could be good press for the band, you know? But it didn't sit that well with him.

"Anyway, I flew out and rehearsed with the band in Wales at Monnow Valley. I was there for about a week. Ozzy showed up but he was only there for a day, so we never really played with him. He knows the songs already, he doesn't need to rehearse! So then I did six weeks with them, which was really cool as I'd never played with Ozzy before. Playing 'Paranoid' and looking out front and seeing Ozzy was amazing."

The shows, mainly European festival dates, were a blast for all concerned (although Ward, recuperating in England, must have felt a little rueful, having waited so long for a full Ozzy-led reunion but only enjoying it for the two dates at the Birmingham NEC before his health failed him). Early June gigs supported by Pantera, Helloween and Coal Chamber in Hungary and Austria set the tone for the tour, followed by a slot at the Gods Of Metal festival in Milan and further large-scale events in the Czech Republic, Poland, Sweden and Finland. The last of these was a typically quirky Finnish bill, at which Sabbath appeared alongside mainstream rock act Garbage, old-school punk band the Misfits and symphonic black metallers Dimmu Borgir, of whom Geezer said: "I didn't understand [them] . . . They're German or Swedish or something. I just didn't get that at all!"

On June 20, Ozzy and Sabbath appeared consecutively once again above a major bill comprising Foo Fighters, Therapy?, Pantera, Slayer, Soulfly and Fear Factory. The second stage featured regulars Coal Chamber plus Life Of Agony, the brand-new Limp Bizkit (whose commercial fortunes would wax and wane spectacularly in the next five years),

Neurosis, Human Waste Project, Entombed and Pitchshifter. The gig, at the Milton Keynes Bowl in Buckinghamshire, was the latest in a long line of rock shows at the venue (the site had seen an infamous date with Metallica and Megadeth back in 1993).

The tour finished off with dates in Spain, Denmark (the legendary Roskilde event), Switzerland, Belgium (a truly comprehensive bill including the cream of the modern metal crop – In Flames, Moonspell, Paradise Lost, Primus, Spiritual Beggars, Obituary, Soulfly, Deftones, Dream Theater and others) and Oslo. As a vehicle for reintroducing Sabbath to a new generation of music fans, the tour couldn't have been better: by this stage metal had diversified several times over and each subgenre attracted its own set of fans, all of whom were potential new customers at the Sabbath store.

When the *Reunion* album appeared in October, it may not have made much impact on the charts but it did make the headlines thanks to a record-signing 'tour' which the band (now with the recovered Ward) executed in eight US cities. Kicking off at the Virgin Megastore in Times Square, the signings – predictably – were a complete disaster, with thousands of fans denied entry into the relatively small stores, traffic disruptions, arrests, vandalism, fights and the usual 'angry crowd' consequences. None of this was helped by some stores' policy of issuing a pass to each buyer of the album which promised a signature, reportedly failing to deliver in some cases.

In the end, a signing due to take place three days later in Vancouver was cancelled after an event at Toronto's Phoenix Club saw security officers being rough with fans. A band statement ran, "Ozzy especially felt that the security was getting much too heavy-handed with the fans. Ozzy, Tony, Geezer and Bill would like to apologise to the fans in Toronto that they didn't get to meet, but felt that for the safety of everyone it was best to stop the festivities early. The experience in Toronto left the band feeling very uneasy going into another meet and greet situation without proper security being in place. Unfortunately, they could not confirm that this could be achieved in time for the fan event on Monday so the band cancelled their appearance, which was to be the last stop of their gruelling six-week promotional tour . . . Ozzy, Tony, Geezer and Bill feel badly about not getting to meet their fans in Vancouver, but feel that they have an obligation to have a safe environment for everyone."

However, the band continued on the promotional trail for the rest of the year, putting in a notable performance of 'Paranoid' on the hugely popular *David Letterman Show* on October 29. A world tour was set to commence on New Year's Eve, with more or less the only concern whether or not Bill Ward would be fit enough to play.

Just for safekeeping, Sharon contacted Vinny Appice again and asked him to accompany Sabbath for the tour in case Bill was forced to withdraw. Although it was a rather unusual arrangement – Appice was literally required to stand by the stage, ready to play on a second drum kit if Bill should begin to feel unwell – the drummer agreed readily, happy just to be with the Sabbath family again. As he recalls: "Sharon said, well, I want you there just in case something happens. Bill's had a mild heart attack, no one knows what could happen with the guy. So for the first 10 days or two weeks of the tour I was on the side of the stage, hands taped up, dressed, ready to jump on if he fell over or something crazy like that happened. Funnily enough, because I was on the side of the stage, Ozzy would always try to dump a bucket of water on me. He never got me though, I always got out of the way in time!"

The December 31 show in Phoenix, Arizona, was supported by the heavyweight bill of Pantera, Megadeth, Slayer and Soulfly and went without a hitch. Clearly Ward was up to the task of executing a Sabbath gig: the question was if he was fit enough to play drums for two hours a night for months on end. However, as time passed Appice recalled: "It became obvious that Bill wasn't having any problems, so I started walking into the audience a little to check out the show. Actually I started taking digital pictures for Sony, and posting them on my website so that fans could check out the shows from the night before, because I was able to go anywhere – the dressing rooms, places you'd never see. So then I started taking pictures from the audience. After three weeks I was out by the soundboard and thinking, if anything happens to Bill I'll just run! But as time went on I just became more loose with where I was going. In fact, everybody else got sick – Tony got a bad flu, Ozzy had a cold, but Bill was rocking!"

The fact that Appice was being paid to do very little might make the tour seem like the easiest gig ever, but in fact he found it frustrating to have to stay in shape in case he was needed, but never actually be asked to play: "It was the weirdest tour ever. Yes, it was a good gig, and I got paid of course, but for a musician it's a little frustrating being at the show but not being able to play – after a while you start to get a little stiff and out of shape for playing. But it was fun, I'd rather do it than not do it. Plus I got to hang out with everybody, it was pretty funny."

Did Bill find it strange to have a replacement standing by in case he wasn't up to the job? Apparently not: "Me and Bill get along great. At first, when I went along to rehearse with them in Wales, they put me in a hotel and Bill in the house they were staying in, because they thought, oh, we can't have those two staying together. But there aren't many hotels in Monnow Valley, and it was freezing because it was the middle of winter, so when Ozzy didn't show up I stayed at the house in Ozzy's room. And me and Bill hung out – we were talking and it was great. Bill's a great guy."

And so the reunion tour – supported by Pantera once again, plus other bands such as Incubus, Deftones and System Of A Down – wound its way across America into the spring of 1999. Some cancellations were inevitable due to a variety of malevolent viruses that attacked the Sabbath camp, with the first date to fall by the wayside being the January 14 stop at Salt Lake City's Delta Center. Iommi had been laid low by flu, and Ozzy was battling a head cold. The show was eventually played on February 23.

Another stop in Denver was rescheduled not once but twice when Ozzy's throat refused to improve sufficiently. Eventually the band gave up on the city, with local newspaper the *Rocky Mountain News* reporting: "Heavy metal pioneers Black Sabbath announced on Wednesday that the group will not reschedule its show at McNichols Sports Arena. It was supposed to be the first Denver concert in two decades to feature the four original Black Sabbath members, but bad health kept dogging the group, and the show was postponed twice."

The tour rolled to a halt in March, a little earlier than planned, as MTV put it: "Black Sabbath was forced to postpone the final four dates of its reunion tour this week when doctors ordered frontman Ozzy Osbourne to rest his throat. Because of the move, fans in Denver, Salt Lake City, Peoria, and Ames, Iowa will have to wait a bit longer to catch the band. Ozzy and his fellow Sabs (Tony Iommi, Geezer Butler and Bill Ward) are hoping to reschedule the shows near the end of May. A spokesperson for Sabbath said that Ozzy's throat is not expected to be a factor in the band's upcoming tour plans."

This was just as well – because April 1999 bought an announcement that after headlining the forthcoming Ozzfest, with Ozzy performing double duties as he had done back in 1997, more dates would follow in December, building up to a final extravaganza which would be billed as 'The Last Supper' – Sabbath's last ever gig. Appropriately, the final show would take place at the Birmingham NEC, where the classic line-up's re-formation had taken place in December '97.

Reactions to the statement were mixed. Catcalls of sarcastic disbelief were heard among press and fans, who summarily dismissed the idea that as profitable a brand as Black Sabbath would ever voluntarily retire – or be permitted to by its management, when the income it brought in was so consistent. On the other hand, many believed that it all might be true – guaranteeing a healthy uptake on the Last Supper tour tickets when they went on sale.

While fans attended the Ozzfest with furrowed brows, wondering what exactly would become of their band, Sabbath put on a spectacular show. With the main stage featuring Rob Zombie, Deftones, Slayer, Primus, Godsmack and System Of A Down, and the second stage featuring Fear Factory, Static-X, Slipknot, Puya, Drain STH, Hed(pe), Apartment 26, Flashpoint and Pushmonkey (the last three acts were virtually unknown), the Ozzfest debuted at Florida's West Palm Beach and worked its way down through Georgia, Tennessee, North Carolina, Virginia, New Jersey and back down across the continent's southern and western states, winding up after two long sweeps across the USA in New York in August.

After four months of rest and recuperation, Sabbath regrouped on December 5 for the Last Supper tour. After playing London, German, Dutch, Finnish, Swedish and German dates, the final stage was set for December 21 and 22 in Birmingham, which Sabbath were still maintaining would be their final fling. Although a DVD and VHS entitled *The Last Supper* would be released in June 2000, comprising footage and interviews recorded on the tour, this, it seemed, would be the last chance for anyone to see them play live.

The last show was appropriately emotional, and tied in somehow with the pre-millennial fever that was temporarily gripping the nation at the time. It all seemed rather apocalyptic as the band strode onstage that final night: the Sabs swept through their usual greatest hits, Ozzy told the crowd that he loved them – and let out a mock-tragic cry of sadness as he left the stage – before the lights went up.

And that, it seemed, was the end. Then again, as events have proved, the end of Black Sabbath had a strange habit of being postponed indefinitely.

CHAPTER TWENTY-FOUR

2000

AND so Ozzy Osbourne began his supposed 'retirement' for the second time.

With six children, a huge fortune and various properties in his portfolio – and all at the relatively youthful age of 51 – you might think that he would have no difficulty finding things to do with his time. And indeed he did devote himself to his family, as he has always done: after all, three of his offspring (Aimee, Kelly and Jack – whose mother was his second wife Sharon) were still teenagers at this point, with all that implies.

The passing years had allowed the popular perception of the 'Ozzy' concept to mellow and develop, especially when the idea of retirement was applied to the equation: "I have a saying: 'Never judge a book by its cover.' I say that because I don't even know who Ozzy is; I wake up a new person every day. But if you've got a fantasy of Ozzy, who am I to say? I mean, if you think I sleep upside-down in the rafters and fly around at night and bite people's throats out, then that's your thing. But I can tell you now, all I ever wanted was for people to come to my concerts and have a great time. I don't want anyone to harm themselves in any way, shape, or form – and my intentions are good whether people want to believe it or not. I'm not going to suddenly become a Jesus freak or anything. But I do have my beliefs and my beliefs are certainly not satanic."

It was odd that a man who loved the live adrenaline rush as much as Ozzy would choose to give it up, especially now that he was clean and sober and no such rush was available to him elsewhere. As he said, nostalgically, "If you got a gig that's going great, there's no sex, drug, drink or award that can beat that feeling . . . And you know what? That is God given. That is the nearest thing to spirituality that I've ever come across. So many frontmen now just stand there like dorks. My job is to get up on that stage and get that crowd jumping out of their fucking seats, and I will do absolutely anything I can to accomplish that. I don't rehearse; I just go for it. Some nights I suck, some nights I'm OK; but every now and again I have one that really is a ballbuster. I don't drink or take drugs any more, but I can quite understand why people want to get fucked up after a gig . . . the adrenaline rush I get is like a mega-amphetamine. I'm whizzin' around the fuckin' hotel room all night. I don't want it to stop . . . we're all out there to do one job, and that's to give them kids the best day of their fucking lives."

But Ozzy recognises his responsibilities as a father, too, and has been vocal about them in the past. He told *Cornerstone*: "I'm into rock'n'roll because rock'n'roll, to me, means freedom. Most guys my age are boring human beings. They sit in bars, get drunk, and then go home to tell their kids the way to rule their lives, while they're absolutely stewed out of their brains. I don't forget what I used to do and so I can't justifiably say to my kid, 'Don't you do that,' when I used to do it myself." This more human side of the Ozzy-monster myth may be what made him so palatable for mass consumption a few years later . . .

While we're on the subject of family, it's worth noting that it obviously takes something special to be related to Ozzy Osbourne. Even at school, Ozzy's family is not immune to the anti-Ozzy virus, as he recalled to *Guitar World*: "I enrolled my kids in a Christian school in LA. The other day my son comes home from school and says, 'Dad, is it true what my teacher said to me today? He said he went to one of your concerts a few years back, and that you handed round a big bowl and made all the audience spit into the bowl, and that you wouldn't perform until you drank all their spit.' I said to my son, 'Jack, do you think I would do that? Do you think that's true?' And he said, 'No, it sounds like bollocks. It's bullshit.' I haven't had my kids baptised or christened or any of that. I haven't made them any religion. I think it should be their choice. But a teacher at this same school told my daughter, 'Well you know, if you're not christened, you're not going to go heaven.' It's just a bunch of fucking bullshit, as far as I'm concerned. I don't believe there's a heaven upstairs and a hell downstairs. I think we've got both hell and heaven here on earth. It's all here for us."

He told one interviewer, intent on unmasking his dark side, that "I'll always be an outrageous character . . . But let me tell you a story to show you I'm not such a bad guy. I once did a phone-in show like where the kids call and ask me anything . . . this kid called in and I said, 'Are you coming to the show tonight?' And he says, 'No, my mother won't let me.' I said, 'Put your mother on,' and she gets on the phone and I say, 'I understand you won't let your son go to the concert,' and she says, 'You're a despicable human being! How dare you get on the phone!' I said, 'He phoned me.' She says, 'You shouldn't be allowed on the streets.' I said, 'I'll tell you what I'll do. I'll give your children the best seats in the hall, my people will take care of you, and then after seeing and meeting me, if you still have the same opinion, you'll have every justifiable reason to think so.' She said, 'Don't try to put that one on me, I know what you're trying to do to the children of America. It doesn't work in this house, so get off the phone!' I thought, 'Well, what do you do?'"

Family looms large in the Osbourne myth, far more so than in the case of either Tony Iommi, Geezer Butler or Bill Ward, all of whom have wives and children of their own but do not expose them to the limelight. In fact, much of Ozzy's emotional make-up seems to come from his own parents and siblings. Over the years he has been both positive and otherwise about them, saying at one point in 1982, "My whole family's fucking nuts; my sister's been committed twice. For real – she's like fucking over the top. My other sister's an absolute neurotic wreck. My whole family has this fucking thing of lunacy, you know? I use my lunacy for better ends.

"My neurotic sister Iris . . . one day, it was a Sunday. Once she'd cleaned the house, you couldn't move. You couldn't breathe, you couldn't touch a thing, you couldn't eat . . . And I got up and beat the shit out of her. Beat the fuck – blacked both her eyes and fucking pounded her around the room. I thought I'd better go and see my father when he gets thrown off the bus, 'cause he's going to kill me when he comes back and sees the sight of her face. I sat on a wall, and sure enough the bus comes, fucking off the bus, he's singing his fucking lungs off on the bus and getting the bus revved up . . . I said, Daddy, I've just beaten Iris up. He says, 'Good job. Fucking 'bout time you fucking whacked her. He knew, my old man . . . very aware of the situation, 'cause we lived on fuck-all, man. We lived on nothing."

Despite this grim childhood memory, Ozzy seems full of respect for his parents, adding: "My father was one of the greatest guys that ever lived in this fucking world . . . My father always told me, 'I don't believe in fucking God, I don't believe in fucking hell – I believe in me.' You've got to believe in yourself, because you're the only person who can believe in yourself, because you feel what you feel. That's what I fucking have taken from my father."

In 2000 Ozzy made vague statements, as he had done previously, to the effect that he might write down his memories in the form of an autobiography. But this would be no easy task – not least because so many of his memories have been sacrificed to the booze-fuelled lifestyle he had once lived. And history was moving fast, not least musically.

Times had changed irrevocably – artistically as well as personally – for

Ozzy. After all, once the heavy metal template had been established, literally hundreds of bands had adopted the style, and by the Nineties the original ethos had been lost. Ozzy couldn't help but sound a little lost as he mourned in an MTV interview, "I've never felt comfortable about this term 'metal', because when I started in 1970, what you now call metal has changed so much from the Seventies to the Eighties to the Nineties that it's not the same music, but they still call it this wretched name, metal. It's just loud rock or hard rock, you know. To me words like heavy metal or grunge metal or thrash metal have never had any musical connotations. I much preferred it when they used to call it hard rock or heavy rock, you know. At least that's got some musical connotation.

"That's the beauty of the Seventies. You weren't all kind of put on one show. I can remember Black Sabbath and James Taylor doing shows. You wouldn't get that today because it's like all the rap music or what they call heavy metal music or whatever music, it is all on one. And I defy anybody to sit through 12 hours of the same music and say, 'Well, the last band or the third band were the greatest,' because you don't know. There's no variety any more."

The 'there's no variety' spiel he outlined is not uncommon among musicians of a certain age, especially those newly contemplating retirement – although perhaps it was a little odd coming from Ozzy, who had just spent three years on the highly variegated Ozzfest bill. Ozzy's fellow Sixties survivor Rick Wakeman, the renowned keyboard player with Yes and other progressive acts and only six months Ozzy's junior, also looked back fondly on the Sabbath/Yes bill, saying: "I did some [session keyboard playing] with them originally way back in 1973 on the *Sabbath Bloody Sabbath* album, which I really enjoyed, and then I did the *Ozzmosis* album."

Just the previous year, Wakeman had asked Ozzy to provide vocals for his recent album, a sequel to his 1974 album *Journey To The Centre Of The Earth*: "I phoned Ozzy when I was doing *Return To The Centre Of The Earth* and said, 'Ozzy, I've written this sort of heavy song which I would like you to sing,' and he said, 'Yeah, OK, can I hear it?' I said, 'Of course, but what I'm going to do is take most of the heavy riffs that I played on guitar off [the song] after you do the vocal and then I'm going to stick them all back on, played by the London Symphony Orchestra.' He loved it! It was great what he did. I know that he loves the track ['Buried Alive'] dearly and we had great fun doing it."

Wakeman, a garrulous and slightly eccentric genius who has endured his fair share of alcoholic misadventures himself, went on to say: "You know, I've sat down and had dinners with Ozzy and had talks over a cup

286

of coffee, a glass of wine or whatever, and I have just had some great conversations with him. You can have fun conversations with Ozzy, you can have deep conversations with Ozzy and you know, he is a bright boy . . . When he arrives at the Pearly Gates – and strangely enough I think that he will get there – St Peter will probably say, 'Oh boy, where do we start?' But they'll have to let him in!'"

With the comfortable approval of his peers and the constant support of his family, Ozzy could be forgiven for preferring to look back rather than forward. Of the book project, he said: "I've just started – I've been dictating to my son who's been helping me on his computer. He's the brains of the family. I can't remember anything. Every now and then I'll meet someone I haven't seen for 10 years and they'll go, 'Remember the night you came round to my house and did so and so?' and I go, 'Oh fuck, yeah. I forgot all about that.' If I was to drop down dead tomorrow, which I hope I don't, I'll have not had a dull life. There's the Sabbath career, the Ozzy career, then my life before I even started music; then I've got the rehab years, quitting and non-quitting drinking, the fitness and the unfitness, the groupies and the not-groupies, the coming home and the not coming home – I've got a lot of research to do. Right now, I've just got up to 1971 when I went crazy and dived through the window . . . One time I bought a pound of grass and took four tablets of mescaline, a quarter of an ounce of cocaine and a bottle of tequila and I was out of my tree for a week. I had the worst fucking time of my entire life. I thought, 'That's it, I've done it now, I'm going to be here forever.' I was talking to horses – and the weird thing was they were talking to me back."

Further retrospection followed with *The Best Of Black Sabbath*, a 32-track double-CD collection released in June. Mostly comprising Ozzy-era tracks plus a few Gillan and Dio-led songs, it demonstrated perfectly what the fans and industry wanted and expected from Sabbath – in brief, the old stuff. What better way to draw a line under the career?

And yet Ozzy still vacillated about the real end of Sabbath, telling *Mojo*: "People keep asking, 'Is this really the end.' How can I answer that question? I already tried retiring once and that lasted about a week. I can't say whether it's the final *final* show ever unless one of us dies. I shouldn't say that. Last time I said, 'Well, at least we're all still alive,' Bill Ward dropped to the floor with a heart attack! He's doing fine now – though we do have to kick-start him before we do a show . . ."

Hints like this kept hope alive among Sabbath's fanbase, which – thanks to releases such as the *Best Of* and the ever-expanding stoner-rock/doom metal movement, was expanding, rather than diminishing.

Despite this, the remnants of the active-beyond-the-grave Sabbath – or at least their most vocal representatives, Ozzy and Sharon – weren't about to play the industry game, or if they did at least they did it on their own terms. For instance, in January 2000, Sabbath were nominated alongside Aerosmith and 13 other artists for possible inclusion into the Rock And Roll Hall of Fame, their fourth such nomination. Ozzy asked that they be removed from the nominees, saying: "Just take our name off the list. Save the ink. Forget about us. The nomination is meaningless, because it's not voted on by the fans. It's voted on by the 'supposed' elite of the industry and the media, who've never bought an album or concert ticket in their lives, so their vote is totally irrelevant to me. Let's face it, Black Sabbath have never been media darlings. We're a people's band and that suits us just fine."

In an ironic move, the same industry awarded Sabbath their very first Grammy (the ultimate symbol of mainstream acceptance in the American music business) the following month – for Best Metal Performance. The song in question was the live version of 'Iron Man' from 1998's *Reunion*, to many observers' puzzlement. Why this song, and why now?

Ozzy and Sharon responded to all these industry theatrics by setting up a record company, Divine Recordings, distributed by Priority and designed to handle Ozzfest-related releases (four albums have appeared to date) plus whichever bands they chose – Slaves On Dope was one early signing. But the most significant album released by Divine to date is Tony Iommi's solo record *Iommi*, which finally appeared on October 30, 2000, after years of gestation – if you take into account the fact that *Seventh Star* was a bizarre mixture of solo and Sabbath album, the *Eighth Star* tapes had been leaked in unfinished form and that Tony had been intermittently working on his record in between the activities of the reunited Sabbath.

Ozzy later said: "Tony worked on the album all last year during breaks from the Sabbath tour, so I'd been hearing bits and pieces, and I knew it was turning out great. Sharon and I realised it made perfect sense for our new label, so we approached Tony about putting it out on Divine. I'm very proud of him."

Iommi was passionate about his new record – which, considering that Geezer and Bill had both put out two albums by this point, was well overdue – and justifiably so, as it featured guest vocals from a stellar cast of guests, who had gathered to pay their respects. As he said, "I think it's kind of good to step out of the Sabbath banner, you know, and not go under the name of Black Sabbath or whatever, even though, yes, it was me involved throughout the whole time. But to be able to go and work with so many different people at one time as opposed to a set unit of one singer and a band . . . I've used a lot of different people on this album and it's been great for me. It's helped me see a lot of other things by using these different people. You know, I've learned a lot from it and it's been great fun."

It's interesting to note that the guitarist – for so long regarded as a dictator in his band, who supposedly couldn't deal with other egos – had greatly enjoyed the collaborations with the guest singers, welcoming and adapting to their creative talent. Furthermore, he had asked the singers to write their own lyrics for each song: "I think you've got to do that. They know how they want to sing it. I've noticed over the years with different singers there were certain words they can't pronounce properly. So they get a way around it [and] say a different word. It's quite funny, you know."

Perhaps the quality of the album could be attributed to the guitarist – famously, among the slowest of workers – having had plenty of time to perfect it. The project had been underway since at least 1996, he said: "Almost four years ago now, we started talking about this. I had to keep stopping and starting because we've had Sabbath tours, and I liked to do this in stages. But I've been very lucky, because all the people I wanted on it, I've got. I wanted them to put their mark on the songs. It was quite exciting, because you just don't know what they're going to do next."

The story of the album was complex, with a whole batch of early material discarded by Iommi and producer Bob Marlette as substandard. The only song that survived the cull was the Henry Rollins track which opened the album, as Tony recalled: "That was actually from the first batch of songs I was writing. And some of the other stuff was really off the wall, and we scrapped that because it was a bit too far gone. Because we were trying to see what sort of thing we could do. When I say 'we' I mean Bob Marlette [and I]. We were working at his house in the studio. And I tried just putting some musical things down. But it got too far away from where I wanted to go. And so we scrapped that. And then the Sabbath tour came up, and I had to shelve it for a while. Until I could start working with somebody . . . It's been so long in the making. It's gotten to the point where it's like, 'Bloody hell! When's it coming out?' "

As he told *Cosmik Debris*, he had wanted to use singers that people might not have expected: "When I first mentioned something about doing a solo album, everybody thought, 'Well, it's going to be Rob Halford, Bruce Dickinson . . .' I think they felt like it was all going to be people who were a bit older, but I wanted to have a variety of people. And of course with Billy Idol, that was something you'd never have thought of, that it'd be us together. And a lot of people have been really surprised by it and said they like it. It was great working with Billy Corgan. We actually wrote a couple of tracks with Billy, and we wrote three with Phil Anselmo, and two tracks with Billy, but you know, we could only use one of each."

This spirit of exploration extended as far as producer Bob Marlette, with whom he had worked on *Reunion*. Iommi went on, "What we did was started writing ideas and just see what would come up, whatever we liked, which is more or less what we had done with Sabbath in a lot of ways. But, if we liked it, we used it. So it's very much the same idea, but using different singers and a more up-to-date approach. Also working with Bob Marlette, a producer through it all, which I never normally have before . . . I like the singers' unique style. They've each got their own style and you can tell who it is when you hear the voice. That's a big part of it. And I liked what they were doing . . . by just seeing the other people, how they work, you can adjust things accordingly – if someone wants an extra long verse, or chorus, or sees a different part as a chorus, you know. So you just work it as it's going on. And I think it worked very well."

It did indeed. In fact, it was the most listenable Sabbath-related studio album in years, kicking off with 'Laughing Man (In The Devil Mask)', a sinister, skewed vehicle for the vocals of Henry Rollins, a long-time Sabbath freak since the days of his seminal punk act Black Flag and a scarily committed frontman in his own band. Iommi recalled: "I played him some of the other stuff and he said, 'I really like this track! Can I sing that one?' So I said, 'Yeah.' He came to the Sabbath rehearsals in England. He just hung with us for three weeks. When we finished the tour, we went to LA and recorded it all, and he put his vocals in."

The highly textured 'Meat', all vintage groaning Sabbath riffs, benefits immeasurably from the vocals of Skunk Anansie front-woman Deborah 'Skin' Dyer, whose elastic, melodic wail lends it unexpected weight. It emerged that the Skin collaboration had been almost impossible to co-ordinate. Iommi recalled: "I asked her to do it years ago, and she says, 'Yeah, I'd love to do it.' But then I saw her a year later and we still hadn't done it. And I saw her at the [Grammy] awards, and I said, 'You still want to do this track?' She says, 'Yeah, I really want to do it. But we better get the time to do it.' Because I was working at that time as well then. She was on tour constantly. Then I went on tour. It was the same with much of the others. We just had to try and fit in wherever we could. And I managed to get together with her eventually, in London."

Next is 'Goodbye Lament', a soft, threatening tune with the softly intoned voice of Foo Fighters singer Dave Grohl. Of Grohl, Iommi recalled: "I really liked it. He's a real nice guy. Energetic. He wanted to do everything. [He said,] 'I've got to play drums.' It turned out great. I found the whole thing very enjoyable."

'Time Is Mine', with the excellent vocals of Pantera's Phil Anselmo – executing his full range, from insinuated whisper to full-throated roar – is a highlight, although the superbly eccentric voice of System Of A Down's Serj Tankian (ululating vibrato and all) makes the next song, 'Patterns', for SOAD fans only. 'Black Oblivion', a sneering performance from Smashing Pumpkin/Zwan singer Billy Corgan (who would later be managed by Sharon Osbourne) is typical of that singer's back catalogue (to my mind, overrated generic alternative-rock). Of the Corgan song, Iommi recalled: "When we started that track, which was like an eight-minute track, we met in the studio in the morning and the drummer, I didn't even know. It was Kenny Aranoff. I mean, I know him, but I had never met him before. And it was great because we walked in and suddenly it was happening. We had to come up with an initial riff, and then from there it set the pace of that song. And there are a lot of changes in that song. It kept you alert because there are so many different things going on. And the drummer was particularly good, because he kept on top with all that. So while we were playing we would go, 'no,' and we changed this bit and go back to this bit. But it really worked. It was really great fun. It kept me on my toes for sure."

The pounding, highly atmospheric 'Flame On' is an opportunity for The Cult's Ian Astbury to introduce the 'yeahs' and 'oohs' that made his old band so ridiculously attractive back in the Eighties, but the presence of Type O Negative singer Peter Steele on 'Just Say No To Love' is much less effective, unfortunately.

Finally, the deliberately self-referential 'Who's Fooling Who' – which features Ozzy himself, as well as a cheekily old-school tolling bell and down-tuned darkness – and the perennially unhip Billy Idol on the unexpectedly good 'Into The Night' round *Iommi* off. The album received positive reviews almost across the board, with most reviewers (or at any rate, those who were familiar with recent Sabbath history) relieved that Iommi's enormous talent had been successfully exercised for the first time since, well, 1983.

And so the year 2000, the best for Iommi since the Seventies in creative terms, came to a close. On the subject of Sabbath, he parried yet more questions: "At the moment, it's on ice, so we don't know what we're going to do as yet. There's no plans. We didn't want to be under that pressure, you know, to say, 'Oh yeah, we're going to tour again.' We wanted just to leave it for now. We've done what we said we were going to do, and if anything happens, it will. If it doesn't, then we've done what we wanted to do." Asked about Sabbath's perceived status as deemed worthy of a clutch of tribute albums, he marvelled: "One that surprised me, quite honestly, out of all the people that have covered our songs, was the Swedish band [the] Cardigans. They recorded 'Sabbath Bloody Sabbath'. I heard it on a radio station in Sweden. The DJ played it for me. I couldn't believe it. I thought, 'What's this?' I thought it was a joke at first. I was amazed at the treatment they'd done to it. It's really good and different. Sang sweet and nice."

Asked if the solo project might lead to live dates, Iommi laughed and reasoned: "Well, we'd like to put a few singers together and do a selected amount of dates. Just make it a special thing as opposed to doing a tour everywhere. Just do a certain amount of dates in particular places with a select amount of singers." As for the current status of Sabbath, he insisted: "No, there's nothing planned. We've tended to put this Sabbath on hold for a while and whatever happens, happens. If we decide to do something, we'll probably call each other up and say either, yes, we'll do it, or no, we won't, and that's more or less how we work the Sabbath thing. Because we find that when you try to plan anything, it never seems to work, you know. We sort of play it by ear. I mean, if it's a Sabbath thing and someone says do you want to do a dozen shows or something, we'd get together, rehearse and click it together pretty quick. But it has to be done right, we can't put Sabbath out now and not do it right."

As ever, Tony's statement was far from conclusive, refusing to concede that Sabbath was dead and gone forever. If anything, the idea that the band was merely on an indefinite hiatus reassured many listeners that they would be back at some point in the future. So much for 'The Last Supper'.

By this point in the story, all the players were drawing together, their fates intertwined – not least that of Sharon Osbourne, who had extended her managerial reach as far as Billy Corgan. However, she only managed him for three months before quitting, saying in a sarcastic statement: "I must resign due to medical reasons. Billy Corgan is making me sick." She added: "I shouldn't have said it, but I like to be honest, and after all these years I can't be bothered being politically correct."

A Sabbath reunion had occurred in 1997. A split had taken place in 1999. And so, as 2000 ended, something was sure to happen. Nothing was ever certain in the world of Black Sabbath, and 2001 would be an eventful year.

CHAPTER TWENTY-FIVE

2001

BY 2001 the Ozzfest was the premier tour for rock and metal in America. Smaller, more punk-centred events such as Vans, Anger Management and Warped had successfully evolved in its wake, but if it was big names alongside new, breaking acts that fans wanted to see, the Ozzfest was the best bet. A whole raft of major acts can thank the Ozzfest for taking their careers to the next level, including Slipknot (who rose to the top of the metal tree in 2000 and 2001), Marilyn Manson and Soulfly. Although its reputation became inextricably associated with the nu-metal wave (Limp Bizkit, Papa Roach and a host of riffs-plus-scratching aggro-merchants), the Ozzfest remained wide enough in scope to include art-rock bands such as Tool and unclassifiables like Queens Of The Stone Age on the bill.

As the Ozzfest grew to dominate the market, so the public profiles of Ozzy and Sharon Osbourne began to transcend the confines of the music scene. The latter was sought out for management advice from artists like Limp Bizkit's Fred Durst, Guns N'Roses and Courtney Love, but she declined them all as her husband's career exploded, although she was quoted as saying: "I do like Courtney. She's hysterical." The couple's frequent battles and the domestic disasters they faced, juxtaposed against their obviously close relationship, made them highly telegenic, which – in the great tabloid tradition of celebrity couples being worth more than the sum of their parts – led even as early as 2001 to productions such as *Wayne's World* director Penelope Spheeris' *We Sold Our Souls For Rock'n' Roll* movie, a documentary of the Ozzfest named after the Sabbath compilation of 1975. One scene in the film saw Sharon confront a Christian protester outside a show, who informed her that Ozzy was "a practising cannibal" . . .

As with her husband, Sharon's outspoken character was becoming the stuff of legend, even to those who weren't familiar with her past. On May 5 in *New Musical Express* Sharon slammed the Welsh rock band Stereophonics, who had booked a show at Donington Park, thus preventing the Ozzfest from playing there. She called them "Stereo-whatever-the-fuck-they're-called" and added that the band had "a clause in their fucking contract preventing anyone else from playing there this summer". Four days later she apologised in a letter to the magazine, calling herself the "Queen of Evil" with a "big fucking mouth and a crass attitude", saying that Stereophonics were one of the "greatest bands in the world" and later commenting, "After Ozzy heard what had happened, I had to go to the hospital to have his foot taken out of my ass."

All good publicity for her, Ozzy and the Ozzfest (which had finally scheduled a UK date on May 26 at the Milton Keynes Bowl). Stereo-phonics themselves maintained a dignified silence throughout.

Good news for Black Sabbath fans came when Sharon announced that the band would be re-forming to headline the 2001 Ozzfest, travelling to the US in June after the Milton Keynes date. Few observers were surprised by the move, although eyebrows were raised in certain quarters when rumours began to spread that a new Sabbath album was underway. After all, it had been six years since the dismal *Forbidden*, even if the reunion album, the best-of and Iommi's solo album had made it clear that there was both songwriting talent and industry support around Sabbath.

Sessions took place in the first three months of the year but were shelved when Ozzy began working on a new solo album, with Bill Ward explaining: "I look to do another album with Black Sabbath if it's possible. We did three months of rehearsals [in] January, February and March of 2001. I have a good idea of my instrument, but I never know what I'm gonna play next, Tony never knows what he's gonna play next, Geezer doesn't know what he's gonna give us on any given day." Of the band's playing skills, now that they were all in their mid-fifties, he commented: "I feel very proud of what we were accomplishing onstage, there were just a few concerts in the early part of the reunion where I was mixed up a little bit because of certain complications – but in the bigger picture, I loved all the gigs and I thought we played a lot better and tighter than we did in the day. But one of the things is, I'm sober. My ears aren't exactly the best ears in the world now. But where we were at, I thought Geezer was playing unbelievably well, Ozzy was doing great, and I love working my chops with Tony. I would answer back to Tony with some off-the-wall jazz lick and just carry on with the track. And I don't know if the audience heard it, all I know is that we really connected and were that tight."

While Sabbath honed their act – the band played a set at the ESPN Sports And Action Awards at the Universal Amphitheater in Los Angeles alongside De La Soul, Rob Zombie, Busta Rhymes and B-Real on April 7

– Ozzy was engrossed in pre-production for his next album, tentatively titled *Down To Earth*. As he told MTV, he and his producer – U2 and Robert Plant console-tweaker Tim Palmer – had been absorbing sounds from the younger Ozzfest bands, although this sounded to many fans suspiciously like a way of avoiding looking unfashionable. "He's got a new set of tricks," said Palmer. "He's a big Beatles fan, and that's going to come out. But it's still going to sound like him. You can have a track that is way out there, and as soon as he lays the vocal track down, you know it's Ozzy. He has the most recognisable voice in rock music."

The album, recorded with old faithful Zakk Wylde (now gaining infamy of his own thanks to his eye-opening interview technique while promoting his band, Black Label Society), ex-Suicidal Tendencies bassist Rob Trujillo and drummer Mike Bordin, was still not fully complete when Ozzy was recalled for the Ozzfest. Palmer was relaxed about the deadline not being met, saying: "If we don't get everything done, I'm just going to stalk him on tour. With today's technology, you can record vocals in a tour bus."

After a warm-up gig for charity at the Birmingham Academy on May 22, the Ozzfest proper landed at Milton Keynes four days later. Sabbath were scheduled to perform over Slipknot, Tool, Papa Roach, Amen, Soulfly, Disturbed and Mudvayne on the main stage, while the second stage featured Black Label Society, Raging Speedhorn, Apartment 26, Planet Earth, Pure Rubbish and Union Underground. This was the perfect blend of the bands *du jour* – mainly nu-metal (Papa Roach, Disturbed, Mudvayne), punk-metal crossover (Amen, Raging Speedhorn) and all-round modern metal (Slipknot, Soulfly). Half a decade later, it's interesting to note that of the supporting acts on this bill, only Slipknot, Tool, Soulfly and BLS can truly be said to have survived the sea-change that killed nu-metal, this thanks to the unique twist they placed on their music without bowing to prevailing trends.

By now Sabbath were being regarded with a respect by the nation's metal writers that had been completely absent a decade before. As the cordoned-off press area filled up over the day with drunken journalists (your rather intoxicated correspondent among them), industry sharks and musicians (notably Slayer, whose singer Tom Araya guested onstage with Soulfly), it seemed that Sabbath had truly come home to roost, with a luxurious aura of credibility that most of the notoriously snooty British press had denied them since Ozzy's departure in 1979.

In retrospect, Sharon and the other Ozzfest organisers' decision to include a UK date that year may have been more important than they could have realised, allowing the impression to form that Sabbath were still close to their British roots.

A couple of days later the whole package upped and left for America, kicking off the summer tour in Illinois and expanding the bill enormously. Now with Marilyn Manson, Slipknot, Papa Roach, Disturbed, Black Label Society, Linkin Park and Crazytown on the main stage and Drowning Pool, Beautiful Creatures, American Head Charge, Pure Rubbish, Systematic, Hatebreed, No One, Union Underground, Nonpoint, Otep, Godhead, Taproot, Union Underground, Spineshank, Prssure 4-5 and Mudvayne on the second, the US Ozzfest was a far more weighty beast than the frankly inferior line-up that had appeared in the UK. Still, such was the pulling power of the US audience, and the tour rapidly grossed tens of millions of dollars . . . again.

The Sabbath set was notable that year for the inclusion of a new song, 'Scary Dreams', penned by Bill Ward and the only tangible result to date of the spring 2001 writing sessions. As Ward explained to Guillaume Roos at Sabbathlive.com: "I don't know about it being released, but I heard a rumour from the corporates and from the people who do these things that it was a bit too commercial . . . Tony had this very cool jazz lick that's at the beginning of the song. I threw a couple of lyrics around, a couple of melodies, and we started developing the song. Geez started putting in his parts too. I came up with a couple of drum things and ideas. The 'Scary Dreams' part – the melody and that lyric – I actually got that idea from Ozzy . . . one day he was talking about his scary head. I just stopped and went: 'Oh my God, what a great title for a song!' And then I thought of 'Scary Dreams'. He actually calls his head something else, but I'm not going to say what it is because that belongs to him . . . So I brought some ideas: Geez seemed to like it, Tony seemed to like it. When we went on from there, they put it together and we built the song. It was a band effort, unlike what was on that live album, *Reunion*. 'Scary Dreams' was actually a band effort at doing some new material since our live album."

The huge string of dates took the Ozzfest through to August 12, but while the bands dispersed, Ozzy was a busy man. A short tour with Disturbed in support was supposed to take place for the rest of August and into September in the north-east states of the US – but had to be cancelled, reportedly at the direct command of his record company Epic, who wanted *Down To Earth* to be finished in time for the planned deadline. He duly completed the record and went home to rest with his family.

It had been another exhausting year for Ozzy, as he explained: "I keep on saying to myself, 'When is it going to slow down?' I can't complain because it's not like I'm being forced to play to empty halls, I'm playing to fucking monumental crowds. For the life of me, I can't work it out." Since 1996, his life had been truly busy: "I had the Black Sabbath [reunion], then I had the Ozzfest where we played my set and Black Sabbath sets, two shows in one day. Then I did the Ozzfest with my own band and then I did Ozzfest with Black Sabbath, then I did the Black Sabbath tour after Ozzfest. In between I'm trying to fucking make an album. It was like putting on a different hat every day and then at the end of it, I've got a fuckin' album done . . . I keep saying to Sharon, 'How long is [the Ozzfest] gonna go?' And she'll go, 'We'll know when it's time to pull out.' Every year it gets bigger and bigger – what else am I gonna do?"

As the festival expanded, Ozzy explained: "When Sharon came up with the idea to do the Ozzfest, I was sceptical, more than sceptical. And I wasn't really sure that anybody would bother to come. But the kids are coming and I heard that a lot of them, in fact, do come to see me, old Ozzy. That's a great feeling and it's good to know that I'm not considered some old fossil."

Of the Ozzfest's high nu-metal quotient, he pondered: "I'm not so sure what's so new about nu-metal, but it's cool. You can't always reinvent the wheel and I've been around the block once or twice. So it's not so new to me. But I really do like some of the new bands, the guys from Iowa, Slipknot. They're really cool."

He was still sanguine about less convivial bands, to his credit, saying: "I even like Papa Roach, even if they did cause a lot of trouble for us during the last Ozzfest! Their singer [Jacoby 'Coby Dick' Shaddix] really acted like an asshole. He was getting the audience really worked up and encouraged them to cause some riots. The fans and the audience got out of hand and the cops cancelled the show. They fined him, and since it was his fault – nobody else caused the incident – we did let him pay the fine out of his own pocket. I think it was fair, but he didn't like it. So the next day he was bitching onstage about the fucking Ozzfest, even though he caused the trouble himself. We were really all pissed off about it but, hey, that's the singer and his personality doesn't make their sound and their music any worse. As a band, they are really intense and you've got to separate the music from the people. I can like somebody and hate their music. On the other hand, I can like the music and not like the people behind it. You've got to separate the art from the person."

Black Sabbath, Ozzy and his Ozzfest had by now become part of a three-headed industry institution that generated literally hundreds of millions of dollars in revenue with their every move: a far cry from the days of Henry's Blues House in Aston. Innovations were crowding round the musicians thick and fast, with Ozzy fielding one interviewer's naively technical question about his new website with the words: "That's a question for my wife. Websites are simply the way to go. Kids are so amazing with these things – my kids have got each hand on separate keyboards." As for the new downloading controversy (the prime filesharing program of 2001, Napster, was currently under legal fire from Metallica, Dr Dre and other artists), he reasoned: "The record industry should have done something to protect itself long ago. If they stop Napster there will be another one, and another one, and . . . it'll be the decline of music as we know it."

Similarly, the refocus of the record industry on reissuing veteran artists' back catalogues was a new development. As Geezer told me, "The catalogue's still selling millions. The reissues are just the way the record companies work these days – old stuff seems to be outselling the new stuff for some reason. My youngest son only discovered Jimi Hendrix when he was 14!" The bassist himself had now become rather refined in his listening tastes, adding: "I mainly listen to jazz. I love Madeleine Peyrou, and anything by Billie Holiday that comes out again. The remastered stuff does sound better. I love John Coltrane, but not really Miles Davis after *Kind Of Blue*: when he did all that fusion stuff – *Bitches Brew* and all that – I didn't like that. Nor Kenny G and all that cack. I like some Weather Report, and obviously you can't argue with Jaco Pastorius' bass playing. He was way out of my league! He did stuff that I'd never even thought about playing on bass. I really like Art Pepper, Charlie Mingus, Jimmy Cobb, Bob James and Ahmed Jamal – the old-style jazz rather than the middle of the road stuff. I can't really get into the modern rock bands, although I quite liked Linkin Park when they were on the Ozzfest with us a couple of years ago. But my kids were like, you can't like Linkin Park!"

In early autumn Ozzy was preparing for the release of his *Down To Earth* album, led off by a single called 'Gets Me Through'. However, as he was getting down to the business of doing the usual press and promotion for the album, he was profoundly shocked (as was everyone else) by the World Trade Center attacks on September 11. He later marvelled: "I was in New York when that went down. I was in the Peninsula Hotel, which is some distance from the Trade Center, and my assistant phones me up just before nine and he goes, 'Put the TV on, a plane just ran into the Twin Towers.' I saw these really bizarre pictures and I'm going, 'Fuck, man, what a dreadful, terrible accident.' I'm thinking it's a small commuter plane."

Then the second tower was hit, as he recalled: "I'm watching this thing and there's a hole in one of them and I'm thinking they must be having an action replay because there's another plane crashing into the other side. I'm going, 'This is fucking weird, man. How can there be a hole in a building and the fucking plane is still flying?' But then all of a sudden reality kicks in and I'm screaming, 'Sharon, for fuck's sake, fucking watch this shit!' When they both collapsed, fuck, I couldn't believe it, man."

Like all family men, Ozzy's first thought was for his children: "When it first happened I said, 'Oh my God, I've got to get out of here and get back to my kids!' Two of my kids are in California. I didn't know if it was the beginning of a major fucking out-and-out terrorist campaign all across America, where they were gonna fucking gas LA or drop something on LA. Nobody knew what the fuck was gonna happen."

Down To Earth was released on October 27, and was something of a career high for Ozzy, at least in that it finally rebranded him as a singer for the new millennium, Ozzfest association and all (the logo on the cover – simply 'Ozzy' for the attention-deficit-disorder generation – was written in the same typeface used for the Ozzfest). 'Gets Me Through' was an apt choice for single release, based on a huge, upwards bending riff from Zakk and a vintage Ozzy-style vocal performance. The accompanying video was both impressive and ridiculous, a glossy montage of the singer rising Nosferatu-like from an altar, black cape, eyeliner and the full range of Goth jewellery adding a thoroughly modern sheen.

'Facing Hell' was less essential, although Zakk's guitar style – heavier than on previous albums – is worth checking out. But the song is more or less a stopgap between 'Gets Me Through' and 'Dreamer', the record's big, cheesy high point – a power ballad somewhere between 'Hey Jude' (the Beatles similarities are almost painful) and an Aerosmith-style stadium anthem. "If only we could all just find serenity / It would be nice if we could live as one," he intones, later explaining: "I didn't go, 'Oh fuck it, they just blew New York up, I better write a song appropriate for the times.' I co-wrote it with Steve Jones and Marti Frederiksen about two years ago. It's just one of those songs that's hopeful. It's kind of like Ozzy's 'Imagine', if you like . . ."

The song mentioned 'Mother Earth' and the fate of the planet in a few places, as he said: "Going back to Sabbath again, I talked about [the environment] in several songs. It's always been in my mind, not so much for me, but I'd like somewhat of a life for my kids and their kids. That World Trade Center, getting back to that again, I get sad that fucking people do such crazy shit to each other. What good's gonna come out of it? A lot of people are gonna fucking die, both over here and in the Middle East by the looks of it . . . How will we know when we've won – or *if* we've won? How will we know when the last terrorist is stopped? Terrorism doesn't wear a uniform or have a flag. It's the heaviest kind of warfare that you can imagine, because these guys obviously don't give a fuck what happens to them or anybody else. When will our leaders go, 'OK, today we got the last terrorist and his name was Ali Baba and we fucking blew his eyes off. Now it's all normal, go back to normal?' Forget America pre-fucking-two weeks ago, because that ain't never gonna be again."

And yet Ozzy isn't a political singer, saying: "There are no political overtones, it's just fun all around. I don't like uniforms, I don't like fucking orders. I won't go out of my way not to conform, but I don't like rules and regulations. It's stupid, because there are rules you have to abide by, there are natural rules, but I don't like stupid fucking rules. The reason I originally got involved with music was because I didn't want to go to work every day from nine to five and die working on some machine out in some fucking factory. I couldn't conform to a regular job. When I was in school I must've had thousands of jobs, because as soon as I wanted to go to a concert or something, I'd walk off the job and tell the boss to go fuck himself. I could never do it.

"If [the army] said to me, 'We want your son to fight,' I'd tell him to go jump off a fucking cliff. I won't have it. I think it's the most barbaric thing in the world. But it scares the heck out of me. That's one of the biggest fears in this world, is fucking global war. Nobody will win. War doesn't achieve anything. My opinion is, if one gun is fired in anger, it's wrong no matter who's right or wrong. But, unfortunately, as a last resort you will always have war of some form. It's a necessity . . . you get violence everywhere you go. I go crazy at a concert when I see people being beaten. I don't like this mentality that if you're a big, six-foot fucker you gotta break somebody's head. That's not security, that's some fuckin' moron, if you ask me. If a guy gets a broken nose and has to go to the hospital, I get the blame. But it's not what I want, it's not what I represent . . . You'll never have a mass of people where everyone's thinking the same thought at the same time. You can pretend, and go along with the crowd, but out of 50,000 people you're going to get a handful that say, 'This is bullshit. I want to go this way.' We're not lemmings, otherwise you might as well jump off that cliff."

'No Easy Way Out' and 'That I Never Had' are generic melodic rock of the sort that Ozzy has been churning out for decades, but 'You Know . . .'

is better, a song for his children apologising for his mistakes. The acoustic backing and delicate instrumentation is a thing to behold compared to the slightly dull song which follows – 'Junkie' – but 'Running Out Of Time' steps up the ante again, with Ozzy's arcane wails echoing over the Sabbath-like riffs. 'Black Illusion' is more slow, Iommi-meets-McCartney melodicism – the modern Ozzy trademark, it seems – and 'Alive' is an excellent, horror-movie elegy. Finally, 'Can You Hear Them?' brings *Down To Earth* to a close with a burst of echoed guitar pyrotechnics that owe more to, say, U2 than the trad-metal of old.

Ozzy was in philosophical mood in the rundown to the album release, explaining its title with a slightly unexpected nod to his past: "I thought, 'What the fuck are we gonna call the album?' I reflected on my whole career and it started off with Black Sabbath, really, but then before there was Black Sabbath it was called Earth. I thought, 'Yeah, it was all down to Earth,' and it went 'bing'."

The album art, a composite of X-rays of Ozzy's body revealing his skeleton and reducing his face down to a vague skull-like form, was actually rather artistic. He recalled: "What they did for the actual photograph itself was X-ray my whole body; I left my jewellery and my tattoos on and you can see the skeleton of me. It's the most bizarre fuckin' thing . . . and it was not my ideal way of spending a nice Wednesday afternoon, in a fucking X-ray machine. The guy was going, 'You'll be fine, you'll be fine,' and he closes a 14-foot lead door and you're in an X-ray room being exposed to radiation, you know? But anyway, when I saw the results I was like, man, that's really so fucking incredible!"

Ozzy told Guitar Center that the writing process was as unplanned as always: "It just comes to me. For this new album I have coming out, I used ProTools. No tape whatsoever. It was unbelievable. I never thought the day would come when I'd be singing in the control room to a playback." Modern technology was not always Ozzy's bag, however, as he recalled: "The beauty about [the old] days was there was no trickery. It was just [what] you played is what you got out of it. I think a lot of technology is OK, but that it takes a lot of the spirit away. *Ozzmosis* was like pulling teeth out, making that record, and all we did to make the first Black Sabbath album was go in, plug in, play, then loaded the stuff back in the van and went on our way and that's the way we thought you make records, you know. We never thought about 24 tracks and all these different machines. We never thought . . . if there was only three tracks required, we would only use three tracks. Until we found out we could use 16, 24 and we started going nuts with it, you know . . . bag of white powder, close the door, and we're in there for about two years, you know. It's just a waste of time and money. If you got the stuff, just put it down, you know."

He added of the songwriting method that had served him so well: "My early days seem like another life . . . Very often I'll come up with a melody line or an idea. Then, I'll give it to the band that I have at the time. Sometimes Zakk will come up with a riff . . . When I did the Black Sabbath reunion tour I was thinking to myself, 'How did we ever get this [music] together?' We'd get something going and then go somewhere else. We'd change into seven different rhythms in one song. Tony Iommi, for whatever it's worth, is a really underrated guitar player. Like with 'Iron Man', a classic riff that's not that complicated, but makes you want to pick up the guitar and play . . . I'm not a studio buff. I'm not a producer. I like working with a team and every album is different. My street-level mentality has to be pretty good, because I don't understand a lot of what I'm doing, technically. But, that can be an advantage in coming up with new ideas. One thing I can say, is that I always have the last word . . . I've never solely written anything. I've either co-written with a band or with a member of the band. If you were to ask me the worst thing I'd written, I could tell you the one I like the least easier than I could tell you the one I like the best. It's fair to say you can possibly find the worst song I've written on the *Ultimate Sin* album. I don't think anyone goes into the studio with the intention of making a bad record, but it was like 'Liberace takes acid' at that point.

"I've had a very charmed career. People think I must be tired of playing 'Paranoid' because I've been playing it for 35 years. But that's one of those songs that I never get tired of playing. When I get on the road with my own band and try to do my own thing, I find out that there are still kids that want to hear the Sabbath stuff. If I don't play songs from my album that's out and some of the old stuff, then it's disappointing. I try to look at it from a fan's point of view and give them what they want. [The Ozzfest] is another wonderful surprise in my life, but it really should be called the Sharon Osbourne And Family Tour because of all the bands they come to me with. It's really amazing when the media says this music is over."

Amid the slightly saccharine post-9/11 philanthropy (Ozzy: "I hope people in the world who are suffering can get some satisfaction and comfort from any one of my songs. There's a lot of sad people around the world right now, people that are really sad") came a genuinely progressive bit of peacemaking between Sharon Osbourne and her father, Don Arden, who finally buried the hatchet later that year. "She later told me that it was

302

in the wake of all that that she finally started to think kindly of the old man again," wrote Arden, 78, when he published his autobiography in 2004. A meeting duly took place, with Don's son and Sharon's brother David in attendance, and the tension apparently fell away, with the pair recounting the evil things they had said about each other in the past with high merriment (for example, earlier that year Sharon had told the *Guardian*: "The best lesson I ever had was watching him fuck his business up. He taught me everything not to do. My father's never even seen any of my three kids and, as far as I'm concerned, he never will").

Ozzy backed up the *Down To Earth* album with a US tour, taking Rob Zombie with him in support, but 10 dates had to be rescheduled after he suffered a stress fracture to his leg after slipping while stepping out of the shower before a show in Tucson, Arizona. He then continued to play for a week's worth of dates before the pain became intolerable and doctors diagnosed the fracture. However, the tour – dubbed 'Merry Mayhem' – resumed on 29 November and continued until the end of the year.

The incident would be the first in a long sequence of misadventures which the public, rock lovers or not, would become intimately acquainted with the following year. The Osbourne family, and by attachment the other members of Black Sabbath, were about to enter the mainstream.

CHAPTER TWENTY-SIX

2002

BLACK Sabbath were pleasantly surprised on January 15, 2002, when they were nominated for their second Grammy in two years – this time for 'The Wizard' – and competing against songs by Tool (who won the award), Slayer, System Of A Down and Slipknot. Although they didn't win the award, the nomination itself said something for the industry and how it viewed the band after so many years.

But the mood among the band's admirers turned a little sour in March, when Ozzy's first four albums – digitally remastered versions of *Blizzard Of Ozz*, *Diary Of A Madman*, *Tribute* and *No More Tears* – were reissued, each with bonus tracks. The decision to revamp and reissue the albums was not what annoyed some fans: it was the fact that Mike Bordin and Rob Trujillo had been brought in to re-record the original drum and bass tracks laid down by Lee Kerslake, Bob Daisley and the other original players. Randy Rhoads' guitar tracks and obviously Ozzy's vocals were left untouched, although the remastering meant that relative levels were different in the final mix to the original versions, a fact most fans noticed.

The story behind the re-recorded rhythm section tracks was a little complex, revolving around the efforts by Daisley and Kerslake to get their songwriting contributions acknowledged – a struggle made more complex by the shifting business relationships between Jet Records, Don Arden and Sharon Osbourne. Sharon said in a press conference before the reissues that "because of Daisley and Kerslake's abusive and unjust behaviour, Ozzy wanted to remove them from these recordings. We turned a negative into a positive by adding a fresh sound to the original albums."

Bob Daisley has been publicly outspoken about the issue to many interviewers, telling *Cosmik Debris* reporter DJ Johnson: "Oh yeah, that was Sharon's statement. It was like, 'Kerslake and Daisley have been harassing us and our family for years, and so Ozzy decided to take them off these recordings.' That is absolute bullshit because we've had no contact with them. How can you harass someone when you've had no contact with them? The only contact we've had with them is our lawyers contacting their lawyers trying to get us paid. And if asking to be paid is harassing, then yes, we've harassed them."

He added that buyers would not necessarily know that the new albums were made by a different line-up until they heard them: "Well, it's about time the truth is known, and the gloves are off as far as I'm concerned because to me that was the ultimate sin, taking our performances off those two records. Not just for our sake, but what an insult to Randy and what an insult to the record-buying public. You know they put all these little stickers on the front of those records saying 'Ozzy's blistering first recording of his solo career' without saying, 'Hey, if you're going to buy this record, know it's not the original recording, and it's not the original band.' That's what they should have said, and they didn't."

Issues alongside the re-recorded sections of the remasters included the fact that Daisley's songwriting contributions, and those of the other Blizzard Of Ozz members, were not reflected in the band's profile: "It wasn't a solo project. He was a bigger name than anyone because he'd come from Black Sabbath, but I remember we'd had many meetings about how we wanted this called a band name, not The Ozzy Osbourne Band. It's got to be a band name. That's why we settled on The Blizzard Of Ozz; because it sounds like a band."

All this made the reissues controversial, although Daisley's voice was not heard much outside the confines of the metal and hard rock community and for most people, the new albums remain simply a fresh opportunity to explore Ozzy's early catalogue.

In any case, in early 2002 Ozzy's fanbase – or at any rate the sheer number of people who knew his name – suddenly increased by a factor of 10 times or more, as he was suddenly to be seen in every home in the land. Alongside his family, Ozzy was to become the latest star of reality TV.

The Osbournes, filmed and initially broadcast in America by MTV, was a masterstroke. Someone at the world's most successful music-TV network had seen Ozzy on TV, noted his on-screen charisma (apparently, genuinely unforced), his wife's propensity for a soundbite and the renewed success of the Ozzy and Black Sabbath brands and proposed to Sharon the idea of turning the family's daily lives together into a live-action sitcom. Soundtracked by a cheeky, Brat Pack-style lounge version of 'Crazy Train', the series – filmed and edited in the glossy, jump-cut style which MTV had made their own – followed Ozzy, Sharon, Kelly and Jack (their elder sister Aimee had opted out, and moved out accordingly) around their house in Beverly Hills and, to a degree, on tour and elsewhere.

Filming started in November 2001, with 12 cameras installed in the Osbournes' house (a palatial residence with the usual LA features – a sculpted pool, huge gardens, dozens of rooms) and a roving camera crew capturing the family doing their thing. Three months of filming produced an endlessly watchable parade of fights (verbal and physical, at least between Jack and Kelly), screamed arguments and an endless tirade of dreadful language. In the centre of it all was Ozzy, who shuffled around the house in a strange, almost elderly, gait dressed in leisurewear, constantly fumbling with the giant TV and other state-of-the-art domestic technology (in an early episode he famously took three minutes to replace a bin-liner) like some deranged inmate of an institution. Some objected to this: as John Lydon told me, "Ozzy's hilarious, but I felt sorry for him when his wife orchestrated that terrible, *terrible* MTV production, because I thought it was humiliating for him. It was like a Victorian mental asylum where you pay a penny to prod the loony with a stick."

Terrible or not, *The Osbournes* was addictive, as viewers pondered how anyone could live in this way. Sharon came across as the matriarch with slightly sinister edge, trying to bring her kids up properly, manage her utterly dependent husband and deal with annoying neighbours (at one point she throws rotten meat into an adjacent garden after the spoilt-brat teenagers there party too late and too loud, incurring a visit from the LAPD). Jack and Kelly come across as fairly typical teenagers with attitude, albeit teenagers with vast amounts of cash and playthings, and far more informed about the rock'n'roll life than most kids their age. Other dramatis personae include the teenagers' nanny/minder, Ozzy's personal assistant, his fitness trainer and the family's huge number of cats and dogs, whose urine and faeces (invariably deposited on the carpets and furniture) became as much a feature of the show as the animals themselves.

Within weeks, the show was attracting six million viewers a week in America – making it MTV's most-watched programme ever – and it made a proportionally similar impact when it debuted in the UK on Channel Four in March 2002. Ozzy always protested that he had no idea why it was so successful: "I didn't know we were doing the series until I came back from playing gigs in Asia and found Sharon had got a camera crew in the house. I don't know why everyone thinks the programme's so funny. I don't play to the camera. I just wander round scratching my arse, same as usual."

The success of *The Osbournes* relied on the voyeuristic thrill of snooping inside someone else's house, especially one as lavishly – and eccentrically – appointed as this one. The family – inevitably labelled 'dysfunctional' by many observers, although in fact they are obviously very close – seem to be in permanent conflict, making the show, with its atmosphere of constant tension and release, highly watchable. Ozzy, the obvious focal point, hooked people in with his strange gait, his thousand-yard stare (just one of many post-recovery traits he exhibited alongside a tremor and a permanently stoned appearance) and his apparent inability to deal with everyday life – and yet he was in good physical condition, telling *Mojo*: "At one time, I was a happy guy when I had a few drinks or dope or whatever, and then I just got miserable and depressed. So I thought, 'What the fuck am I doing this for?' My biggest addiction these days is exercise. I run every day. I'll probably be next to Jimmy Savile next year, running the fucking [London] marathon! I only take pills now for clinical reasons, not to get stoned any more. All the stuff I did left me with some neurological problems – I'm a manic depressive, a nutter. Sharon says she'll second that."

The other fascinating element of *The Osbournes* is the way that Ozzy and Sharon are reduced down to embarrassing parental clichés when viewed through the eyes of Jack and Kelly. Ozzy added: "With three teenage kids it's hard to have sex – they say, 'We know what you're doing in there, you dirty pair of old bastards,' or 'We can't go in there, Dad's dry-humping mum again.' If I'd dared to say what they say to my dad, I'd be lying in the garden with a pitch-fork stuck in my fucking chest."

At the heart of the show, perhaps its strongest asset, is the dark core of experience that Ozzy has endured as America's most wanted satanic hard rocker. Although he may be clean and sober now, those who know what he has endured found the show even more revealing: this is, all jokes and dog-turd jokes aside, the life of a man who has been through hell, barely surviving to tell the tale. And Ozzy has always been gloriously inconsistent, meaning that it's never possible to know what he'll do next; as he once said, "When I was a drug addict, I used to write things like 'Flying High Again', 'Snowblind', all this shit. And the other night, I thought, 'Fucking hell, I sing one song for it and then straight after I sing one song against it.' But the thing is, that's OK. Because that was where I was when I wrote that, so why shouldn't I do it? It's part of my life. It's a part of what I am and what I will be."

His struggle against substances was unending, it seemed, and was now approaching two decades in duration. Ozzy once told Sylvie Simmons at *Creem* as far back as 1986 that the drugs and booze had to go: "I was fighting my drug addiction. Now I don't take drugs, apart from the occasional drink of alcohol, and I'm trying to beat that one as well. I was miserable! Because I was drugged out of my head all the time, I didn't know what the fuck was going on. It was a physical and mental torture . . . In the past, if I had a day off like this I'd get up and go straight to the drinks cupboard and get smashed all day . . . I'm training hard now most days, when I can get around to it. All last week I was running three miles a day, and I've got this karate expert on the road with me.

"Everything becomes a pain in the arse when you're suffering from yesterday's drunk. So now after a show I'll have a couple of beers and that's about it. I want to quit drinking entirely. Part of the problem is that just as in Jacques Cousteau's business, where water comes with the territory, ditto for rock'n'roll and drink. It's *my* excuse anyway.

"I know a lot of people who've taken cocaine, including myself, a lot of people who've smoked dope, including myself, a lot of people who've taken a lot of things – but I've never really taken heroin, only once or twice. Everybody that I know that's taken heroin is either a mental case or dead. Or they end up zombies. Even if you stop taking it, you never return to the person you were before; you end up screwed up for the rest of your life. I think it's terrible that young kids at school are getting junked out. I did Hammersmith the other night, and they were carrying these kids out who were sniffing glue! It's getting ridiculous. I'm not trying to be a goody-goody two-shoes. I suppose since I've got a family, I wake up to the fact that it ain't clever. And if Chief Inspector Jones gets up there and says, 'You shouldn't take heroin' they'd go, 'Oh fuck you!' And I thought, if *I* did it maybe I could save someone's life. Heroin *is* awful. Look what happened to poor old Phil Lynott. So many rock stars have died now, look at them! I'm not saying I'm any better than Phil Lynott or Keith Moon – I'm luckier, that's all . . . You don't have to take a drug to be a monster! It's pathetic what I was like. On that *Bark At The Moon* tour I was insane. I didn't know what I was doing. I couldn't remember anything.

"It's all no good really, none of it, not even booze. I'm going to go back to the AA meetings and stop for about a month and then keep slipping back in, but eventually I know I'll come to terms with it one way or another. But it ain't an easy battle. When I first got involved with rock'n' roll, I thought the equipment was a bag of drugs, a crazy attitude and a wild party at the end of the gig. That's honestly what I believed rock'n'roll was." And it's not? "And it's not. I don't blame rock'n'roll for my addiction – it's my fault, and I've got to fight it. But it'd be good if we could all do just one gig, like the Band Aid thing, and build a proper clinic for them, like the Betty Ford Center. That place really opened my eyes. I was so embarrassed to go and get help. I said, 'Me? Ozzy International blah-blah? I've got to tell them I'm sick?' But I couldn't fight it any more. I did my 15 rounds and I couldn't go out for a 16th. It was killing me, and I didn't want to die."

Back in the new century, Ozzy fell off the wagon once or twice during the filming of the *Osbournes* show. As he said: "I hate watching myself at the best of times, and I can't bear to see myself pissed. But it was the show that made me do it! Some days I couldn't bear the fucking pressure of a camera crew all day long. I had to find some way to escape, and I ended up knocking back a bottle of wine . . . I'm somebody who always worries about things. I worry how the programme might change the kids. They're 17 and 18, and getting this sort of attention's got to fucking affect them. It might be a good idea to send them to a therapist when it's all over, to get some of this shit out of their heads." He marvelled at the public reaction, saying: "I walk down the street in LA, and it's like Beatlemania! And I'm just some daft fucking 53-year-old bloke from Birmingham!"

The press latched on to the phenomenon with alacrity, with *USA Today* asking, "How did an ageing, drug-battered monster of rock morph into the nation's newest teddy bear?" and a second series of the show – worth $20 million dollars to the family – signed in early 2002. "It's great to get a shitload of money," remarked Ozzy warily, "but if this show starts to disintegrate my family, I'll throw the towel in. I won't see my son turn into a smack addict because of the pressure . . . People keep telling me I'm like Homer Simpson. Am I? I don't know. I just wonder why Middle America is so keen on me when 20 years ago they thought I was the fucking Antichrist."

Despite his past, it was probably Ozzy's 'safe' status as a reformed family man that hooked most people in. After all, he satisfied the right criteria, avoiding extremes and appealing to all generations. His musical tastes were universal and unthreatening. He remained a Beatles fan: "I went to see McCartney last year at the LA Forum – I never got to see the Beatles, though; tickets were always sold out like 10 minutes after going on sale – and he was playing Beatles classics, and I was just melting in the audience."

All this new-found publicity made Ozzy's February to May 2002 world tour a great success: he was even asked to play for US servicemen stationed in Japan and Korea. While in Japan, a Tokyo show was filmed for later release on a DVD titled *Live At Budokan*, before he signed autographs on a visit to the US base in the same city. At both the Tokyo and Seoul shows, his live set was the same as usual, although he was asked not "to perform anything that would be degrading in any way to the troops or the organisation" according to a USO entertainment spokesperson. That ruled 'War Pigs' out, presumably.

The tour would be a chance for Ozzy to refine his onstage act since the MTV show had been cramping his style slightly: "Ever since *The Osbournes* took off with the filming and all that shit, it took a lot of time up, but I'm really looking forward to getting out to some big arenas. I've played in fucking pubs, outdoors, indoors, as long as it's fun . . . I don't drink, I don't smoke, I haven't become a fucking evangelist . . . I don't worship the devil. I don't thump a bible. I'm just a guy, you know? . . . I mean, I'm still fucking crazy . . . there was this one time I was so hungover from the night before and I'd taken some deadly stuff, some deadly fucking potion and I was like 25 minutes late . . . I almost drank some [urine] once! I picked up a half-empty fucking bottle up from the stage and I started to drink it and everyone in the band just stopped the show and went, 'Nooo . . .!' "

As Ozzy's life became documented on TV, so the sequence of events that followed in 2002 started to resemble the up-and-down episodes of a real-life soap opera. It began with a tragedy, as Ozzy's former drummer Randy Castillo succumbed to squamous cell cancer in March at the age of 51. Also a veteran of Mötley Crüe and Lita Ford's band, Castillo had been fighting the disease for two years and was on the point of forming a new band when the cancer returned, this time fatally. His bass-playing bandmate with Ozzy, Phil Soussan, said: "He had a flair for playing the drums. He had a heavy right foot that was incredibly fast and his whole unique approach to drumming was just really powerful. He wasn't really good at copying other people, but he was really good at being himself, and it was very difficult for other people to copy him. He was the kind of guy that made a great friend wherever he went. If he showed up to someone's house, everyone wanted to see him. It wasn't like he took over a conversation, he just had a really good vibe." Ozzy said: "I am heartbroken about the passing of one of my dearest friends. I will see you on the other side, Randy. I love you."

On May 6, Ozzy and Sharon found themselves unexpected recipients of an invitation to the 88th Annual White House Correspondents' Association Dinner at the Hilton in Washington DC, hosted by President George W. Bush himself. Bush even mentioned Ozzy in his speech, saying: "The thing about Ozzy is he's made a lot of big hit recordings – 'Party With Animals', 'Sabbath Bloody Sabbath', 'Facing Hell', 'Black Skies' and 'Bloodbath In Paradise'. Ozzy . . . Mom loves your stuff." Clearly the White House speechwriter had done his research (although he'd failed to quote from 'Sweet Leaf' . . .)

A Presidential notice in front of some of the world's most powerful people – surely the absolute limit of establishment acceptance – showed how important the wave of publicity around *The Osbournes* had been for Ozzy's career. Of course, the fact that Bush heaped such obviously fake fawning on him doesn't say much for the President's taste in popular culture – merely that his staff noticed a new and cool reference for him to drop, and exploited it. Ozzy's delight at the speech (he stood up and threw his hands in the air in jubilation) left many fans with a nasty taste in their mouths as well. But then, what else was he supposed to do . . .

Ozzfest 2002 didn't feature Black Sabbath, probably because Sharon and Ozzy rightly felt that the double-set trick that had worked well in previous years wasn't worth repeating on every festival. But this didn't make much difference to the tens of thousands of music fans who turned up in droves to see an array of hard-hitting acts such as Slayer and Cradle Of Filth take the stage, first in Europe until mid-June and thereafter in the US.

However, the festival was plagued with difficulties, first when Ozzy's guitarist, Zakk Wylde, was struck down with exhaustion, requiring the last seven dates of the European jaunt to be cancelled. The iron man of rock, who had been playing with his own band, Black Label Society, as well as Ozzy's band for every show, had reached his limit at last. After all, he had endured a busy two years – since 2001 he had recorded and toured a BLS album, *1919 Eternal*, recorded guitar for Ozzy's *Down To Earth* album, toured with Ozzy for the Merry Mayhem tour and made a cameo appearance in the movie *Rock Star*, as well living the life of a veritable modern caveman (beer, weight training and rock music seemed to be the key ingredients of his day-to-day existence).

Ozzy himself had been experiencing some difficulties on the European tour, suffering a throat infection that required the May 26 date in Dublin to be cancelled. However, on June 3 he put in an appearance before the only audience that might be said to top President Bush, stepping onstage at Queen Elizabeth II's Golden Jubilee celebration in the garden at Buckingham Palace. What HM The Queen, 77 at the time, thought when the so-called Prince Of Darkness fronted a band of Tony Iommi (also drafted in to provide a 'Sabbath' flavour) and the most inappropriate rhythm section ever (fretless bass slidemaster Pino Palladino and the cheeky Swiss-exile chappie Phil Collins himself on drums) is not recorded, especially when they ran through a rendition of 'Paranoid'. The lesson from the Jubilee gig was that Ozzy had somehow, against all expectations, been elevated to the level of respectability enjoyed by the rest of the bill – the great and the good of superannuated rock stars including Paul McCartney, Cliff Richard, Eric Clapton, Rod Stewart, Ray Davies, Brian

Ferry, and (just about the only guest who could boast as many wasted brain cells as Ozzy) Brian Wilson.

July 6 marked the scheduled start of the American Ozzfest, an event on the usual massive scale which looked set to utterly dominate the summer rock circuit. Zakk Wylde had fully recovered and returned to level the audiences, but despite all the omens the festival was in serious jeopardy. Five days before the first show, the Osbourne family was stunned by the news that Sharon was suffering from colorectal cancer. Two days later she underwent surgery to remove a foot of her colon. Ozzy was devastated, telling *People*: "I've always had a plan that I'd get sick before she did, that I'd die before she did, but my plan didn't work out. Life has a way of kicking you in the nuts."

Sharon, maintaining a level head, convinced Ozzy to play the Ozzfest dates after the first two shows were cancelled: "It was not the best news," she told *People*. "You think nothing will ever happen to you. You're invincible. Then after you get over the shock and panic, you realise how lucky you are to be alive. That's where I am right now. I simply have to take care of this thing. [Ozzy] was hysterical, just terrified. The doctor had to come over and sedate him."

In mid-July Sharon was told that chemotherapy would be necessary as the surgery had failed to remove all the cancerous cells, which had been found in her lymph nodes. Three months of treatment were scheduled to begin at the end of the month and would continue during the filming of the second series of *The Osbournes*.

Sharon said in the same interview that her prognosis for recovery was "very, very good" and added, "Why'd they have to find it in my bum of all places?" Of the clinic where she would be receiving chemotherapy, she added: "We need to get a different vibe going. I think I'll bring some music, introduce myself, maybe we can sing some songs and cheer the place up." She would be joined for the first few weeks of therapy by Ozzy, who temporarily left the tour to run without him. He told MTV, "I'm putting on a brave face here, guys, but I'm burning up inside. I have to go home . . . This is one of the hardest decisions I've ever had to make in my life, but I'm sure that everyone out there will understand . . . The Ozzfest is my baby, and no one is going to take my baby away from me. Keep Ozzfest going. We're going to get over this hurdle. We've gotten over worse before. Stick it out with me. I need you now more than ever. I'm sure my fans will understand. Anyone in this position would do the same thing. I relish seeing you people. You're my life, you're my air, you're my breath, you're everything to me."

Most of the Ozzfest's August dates would be headlined by System Of A Down over Rob Zombie, POD, Drowning Pool, Adema and Zakk Wylde's Black Label Society: fans missing Ozzy's band would be consoled with an appropriate discount on site, a last-minute move instigated by Sharon. "As sick as she is, she's still organising shit," said Ozzy.

Meanwhile, Jack Osbourne was making headlines, albeit understated ones. He'd slightly injured an arm by climbing an empty building in Malibu to dive into the ocean . . . hardly world-shattering stuff, but indicative of the strength of *Osbournes* fever. A few observers predicted tough times ahead for Jack based on the whirlwind he was currently trying to navigate, and soon their predictions would be proven right.

Two summer releases kept the Ozzy and Sabbath flag flying in 2002 – the former's by-the-numbers *Live At Budokan* DVD in June (fine for fans who needed a modern-day Ozzy memento) and the slightly more interesting *Past Lives* Sabbath album, released in August. A double album comprising the *Live At Last* album from 1980, remixed and bolstered with added songs, *Past Lives* was supposed to provide the US market with songs that had previously only been available as an import. Bill Ward surmised in a *Shockwaves* interview at the time that the album had probably been released simply because Sabbath had been touring again in recent years, but it has to be a moot point as to how many fans actually bought it, bearing in mind that the excellent (and sonically superior) *Reunion* collection had appeared a mere three and a half years before.

On the other hand, Sabbath was coming to the forefront of people's minds again in late 2002 – even though they hadn't done any touring – thanks to another nomination for the Rock And Roll Hall Of Fame (the nominating committee had evidently not been put off by Ozzy's dismissal of the last such event), and a genuinely impressive double-video set, *The Black Sabbath Story Volumes 1 & 2*, covering 1970–1978 and then the post-Ozzy era as far as 1992 (as with this book, the Costa Mesa shows in that year form a natural breaking point between sections of the band's history). Although neither Ozzy nor Bill Ward were interviewed for the videos (later reissued as DVDs), Tony, Geezer and other personnel such as Jim Simpson provided invaluable commentary over the live footage which made up the bulk of the content.

As '02 closed with news that Iommi and Geezer were both recording more solo albums, Bill released a limited-edition single called 'Straws'. He pressed 2,200 copies of the CD and sent the first 1,200 to various political and charitable leaders worldwide, as he explained to Jeb Wright of *Classic Rock Revisited*: "I hope it is a message of some kind . . . We sent a copy of the song to the President of the United States as well as senators, actors, the Queen's grandchildren and the Prime Minister of England. We had some great response from it, especially from 10 Downing street and Tony Blair. I was worried that I might get in trouble sending them out to these people. I worried that I was crossing the line. I decided I would do it whether I was crossing the line or not. I started getting some great responses back from people, and that made me feel a lot better about the whole thing."

Inspired by 9/11, the song is a pro-peace work that avoids being maudlin or earnest by simply setting out the fears of a person caught in a bomb explosion: "I felt very helpless, like many other people, during the 9/11 terrorist attack," said Ward. "I wondered why I was feeling like cannon fodder, waiting for something to happen. Everyone involved felt really good because they were giving some positive energy with a hopeful positive end. The positive end would be that we are raising money for five different charities. We hope we can be helpful to the men and women in uniform. It felt like I should not be part of the problem, instead I should bring something to the table."

In true Sabbath style, the remaining 1,000 copies of the single (which Bill sold via his website) were available for a reasonably low donation to the charities that Bill had selected, apart from numbers 666 and 911, which were on sale for $1,000. All were autographed by Bill.

Elsewhere, Kelly Osbourne took the not-unexpected step into a career of her own. The 18-year-old formed a band, signed to Epic alongside her father and recorded an album, *Shut Up*, which failed to sell well despite a well-received cover version of Madonna's 'Papa Don't Preach' and the title track, which both received reasonable amounts of airplay when released as singles. The singer, whose heavier than average frame for a pop singer made her something of an icon for girls of similar age and proportions, possesses a decent enough voice and stage act but the general conception that she had established her career on the back of her father and the *Osbournes* TV show threatened to be an insurmountable problem for her.

With all this low-level activity, 2003 looked like it could be another successful year for Ozzy. Would the same apply to Black Sabbath the band, whose return to form had now been five years in evolution?

CHAPTER TWENTY-SEVEN

2003

NOW that the Osbournes brand had been established at mass-media level, the industry made sure that a constant feed of product was supplied to the by-now-massive fanbase. The first obvious step was to supply brand-new Ozzy fans with a reminder of his pre-MTV career, and so a best-of entitled *The Essential Ozzy Osbourne* was issued by Epic on March 15. At this stage in internet history, of course, anyone could have downloaded a collection of Ozzy tunes and made their own bespoke compilation, but the official version did well nonetheless.

Asked by MTV how much of a hand he'd had in putting *The Essential Ozzy Osbourne* together, Ozzy said: "Well, I'm not good with these kind of projects, because it's an old record for me. I mean, I'm not good with making a new record, and I'm trying to pick out the best ones of my previous music. My list is endless, and I go, 'You can only put so many on the album.' I made a list, and Sharon says, 'There's too many off *Blizzard of Ozz*. There's too much off *Diary Of A Madman*.' I said, 'OK, you do it.' So she made a list, she went insane, she gave it to the record company and I just say, 'Whatever you want to do.' And it's not my greatest hits, because I've never sat down and written or co-written a hit single. I haven't specifically gone, 'Oh yeah, I'm going to write a single.' I have plenty of hit albums, you know, so where do you begin with a catalogue like I have? It's trying to cram 30 years into 14 tracks or whatever it is. I know somebody out there is going to go, 'I wouldn't have picked that, I would have picked that one instead of this one.' I mean, that's what I was doing. I was changing the list every five minutes, and then I thought, 'You know what, I haven't got 'Suicide Solution' on the thing.' And then there's so much stuff to pick from. I didn't think that it was going to be as difficult as it was, you know."

What did the future hold? No one was prepared to comment. As Ozzy said, he had learned the value of caution: "Well, I've made a lot of grandiose statements throughout my career, and then something happens, somebody sees an apparition, and you wake up and he ain't there, so I don't want to say too much. Let's see how we get on, you know . . . I'm just gonna take it stage by stage because too much can happen, and I'm still pursuing my own solo career. I still want to do a solo album when I get off this [next Ozzfest] tour and they let me go home and start writing."

Of Mike Bordin's involvement here and there, Ozzy said: "Michael Bordin from Faith No More did a tremendous job, but Michael Bordin is not Bill Ward and Bill Ward is not Michael Bordin. Mike is a great friend of mine and a great drummer, but every night onstage I would miss Bill, you know, but what do you do?"

The Sabbath reunion, now some years along the line, had turned out to be the right decision, he concluded: "I was fed up with saying over the years, 'Yes, there is going to be a reunion,' and something else happens . . . and I said to the guys, the other two guys, 'Look, if we're gonna do it, just don't mess around any more. Get up there and do it, because I'm fed up with saying to people why we never did it.' This is not the first time we ever tried to get it together. It's been 10 years now, and my wife said to me at the beginning of the year, 'What do you think about this Sabbath situation?' I said, 'All I'm gonna say to you, Sharon, is you're my manager, I'll say to you, yes. Now the ball's in your court. You carry on with it, because I'm damned if I'm going to start sending lawyer's letters. Everybody's got a lawyer, everybody's got an accountant, everybody's got a business manager. That ain't my rock'n'roll, babe . . . I'm more than thrilled, I'm over the moon about it. Thirty years ago if I would of [sic] known when we wrote 'Paranoid' and the likes of *Master Of Reality*, and if we had a crystal ball and we could go, 'Yeah . . . we'll be looked upon as gods for our time,' I mean, it's an extra bonus. This business never ceases to amaze me . . .'"

A yearly routine was emerging for Ozzy: the TV show (the third series of *The Osbournes* wrapped in February 2003), the Ozzfest and regular record releases, interspersed with occasional projects (of which Sabbath was, it seemed, merely one of many) with his family and extended acquaintances. Now his wife and children were celebrities, the pressure on the family must have been intense. Nonetheless, the brand stayed afloat, with the announcement of another Ozzfest for the summer emerging in February 2003. And no, Black Sabbath would not be playing, although why – or why not – is not known.

In any case, Ozzy was overseeing his own band at the time, with a remarkable shift in personnel taking place the following month. The biggest metal band in the world, San Francisco quartet Metallica – the seventh-biggest-selling band in history since the millennium – had undergone a couple of troubled years, with their bass player, Jason Newsted, leaving in

2001 amid a flurry of resentment and frustration over not being allowed by Metallica singer James Hetfield to work on side projects. After two years of struggle and group therapy sessions (filmed by a camera crew for eventual release as the *Some Kind Of Monster* documentary film in 2004), Metallica invited Ozzy's usual bassist, Rob Trujillo (who had re-recorded Bob Daisley's bass parts on the reissues of the previous year), to join them, with a million dollar fee on arrival recoupable against future tour income.

Trujillo, a veteran of the hardcore band Suicidal Tendencies and his own funk-metal side project Infectious Grooves (in which he exercised his miraculous slap-and-pop playing) was torn between loyalty to Sharon and Ozzy, with whom he had toured the world, and wanting to join the biggest metal band on earth. He approached the Osbournes for their approval and was given it freely, leaving him – highly relieved – to join up with Hetfield et al. for a career in the limelight as a full band-member rather than just a hired hand.

In a stroke of coincidence that has never been seen before, the vacant bass position in Ozzy's band was given to Jason Newsted, also a powerful player – if less flamboyant than the funk-master Trujillo. Fans of both bands were open-mouthed at the exchange, but the vibes seemed good on all sides. Ozzy gushed, "I'm the happiest man in the world today. I'm a strong believer that it was destiny that I end up playing with Jason . . . He reminds me of a young Geezer Butler." Newsted, blown away by this comment, replied: "There could not be a bigger compliment. [If someone said], 'Here's a million dollars' or 'Here's this compliment,' I'll take this! That's it. Butler is my number one teacher in life. And only [Ozzy] gets the right to say that. He's the only one!"

Metallica fans, who had by and large warmed to Newsted in his 15-year tenure in Metallica (he was drafted in from thrash metal act Flotsam And Jetsam in 1986 after the death of Cliff Burton) were delighted with the news that he had joined a band of serious stature. He had performed in a small-selling rock band called Echobrain and the cult progressive metal act Voivod since leaving Metallica, but there was a definite feeling that he was not achieving his full potential in either outfit. Ozzy even dropped hints about writing new music alongside Jason, leading the new recruit to froth: "Dude, if he's telling me the truth right now, if he really wants to write . . . songs, it's going to be fucking crazy! I'm telling you right now, it's gonna be out of this world. If I get an opportunity to write bass behind his vocals? Working with Zakk? It's just going to be sick, man, that's all I can say."

It emerged that Sharon had first considered Newsted for the post after Jack had recommended Voivod to play on the second stage of the Ozzfest:

she asked him to audition shortly afterwards and the deal was struck smoothly. Just as he had done with Metallica back in '86 (famously, he had learned every single one of their songs before the audition), Jason had made sure his command of the Ozzy back catalogue was honed before the event, saying: "I really wanted to be prepared for Oz, so when he walked in the room he could call out whatever song and I would be able to hit it."

Bizarrely, Jason's first rehearsal with Ozzy was executed alongside Trujillo, who was still on board in order to ensure a smooth change-over. By the end of the day, Newsted found himself advising Trujillo on how to play Metallica classics like 'Battery' and 'Damage, Inc.'

Ozzy went on: "I don't believe in tarot cards or crystal balls, but I believe that somebody, before you're born, maps out your life. And it was destiny that Metallica end up playing with Robert Trujillo. I'm not pissed off with anybody . . . It's so nice to end a relationship nicely for a change." Of his replacement in Metallica, Newsted said, accurately: "I'm not sure that anybody else could have worked for Metallica, because he has the girth, as it were – that strength, mentally and physically, to deal with what has to be dealt with in that band. He's familiar with this calibre of an operation. I think it worked out the best for everybody involved . . . This is a huge opportunity for both [Metallica and Ozzy] to prove themselves again. It can be a cool thing for the next era of both of the biggest metal bands America has seen . . . It's going to be an incredible summer."

And so the Ozzfest prepared itself to roll, amid a swathe of extracurricular activities such as Sharon entering the news in less-than-demure circumstances. April saw a public spat with an entertainment agent named Renee Tab spill over into public farce when the two were involved in a physical fight in a West Hollywood restaurant. MTV reported that "officers arrived at the Japanese restaurant Koi on La Cienega Boulevard at 10:45pm, after Osbourne and Renee Tab, an entertainment agent for International Creative Management, were involved in an altercation, an LAPD spokesperson said. No one was arrested, though police took reports and photographed each woman. It's unclear how the argument started, but it escalated into a physical altercation that found Tab hitting Osbourne in the face, according to the report given by Ozzy's wife. Tab, however, maintains that Osbourne spit on her, a claim Osbourne's publicist denied."

The argument was the culmination of a feud that had been brewing since a New Year's Eve party which the Osbournes had hosted, and at which Tab had won a $15,000 diamond necklace as a door prize. However, Sharon contended on the *Celebrity Justice* TV show and elsewhere that the win was invalid as Tab was an uninvited guest.

This pointless aggro was put into perspective just weeks later when on April 23 Jack Osbourne entered a rehab facility at Las Encinas Hospital in Pasadena, California to battle an addiction to OxyContin, a powerful painkiller. A popular drug among a certain demographic of American teenagers, OxyContin has been described by America's Food & Drug Administration as 'as addictive as morphine', thanks to its all-powerful tranquillising effect. According to *People* magazine, Jack had been using alcohol and marijuana until a break in January, but had relapsed, leading to the stint in rehab.

When Jack came out he was open about the pressures that had caused him to seek solace in the drug, saying: "There was the Jack Osbourne my parents knew, the Jack Osbourne my friends knew and the Jack Osbourne that the public knew. The one my parents knew was the funny, facetious, nice, loving son who's truly caring. To my friends I was a crazy, insane, drinking, using party animal who knew how to have a good time. And the public one was, well, the one they wanted to vote out of the house."

Ozzy and Sharon were devastated, with the former saying of their 17-year-old son: "The mistake that Sharon and I both made, and we both agree on this, is we never set any boundaries. We never said, 'You must be in the house by a certain time.' We just let them have the freedom. Sharon and I are still learning. We're not the parents that say, 'We're always right,' because we're not."

Ozzy added: "One thing I noticed is that he never cried. He never showed. He just locked it in, you know. I think what families should do more often is have family meetings and talk: get around the table and say, 'What's up? How you doing?' Every day I say to my family, 'I love you,' you know. And I do love my family. People forget to say 'I love you. I care for you. Are you OK? Is there anything you need?' . . . It takes a lot of courage and strength to admit you need help, and both Sharon and I are proud Jack is facing his problems head-on."

Perhaps swayed by his son's trauma, Ozzy told MTV: "I used to think they should legalise pot, but you know what? They should ban the lot. One thing leads to another. Coffee leads to Red Bull, Red Bull leads to crank [speed]. When I found out the full depth of him getting into OxyContin, which is like hillbilly heroin, I was shocked and stunned. The thing that's amazing was how rapidly he went from smoking pot to doing hillbilly heroin."

It didn't take him long to refer to the subject of his own drug history, of course, saying: "When I started doing drugs years ago, they were hard to get, but today it's everywhere. It's not just America. It's not just

California. It's not just Beverly Hills. It's not just downtown New York. It's not just London. It's all over the world . . . I'm 55 years old, and I didn't get off scot-free. I have to take medication for the rest of my life because I've done so much neurological damage to my body" (although the last sentence was a little physiologically confused).

The pressure on Jack was actually a composite of forces, as he told reporter Gideon Yago. Firstly there was his self-perceived unpopularity in the Osbournes house, and then there was his mother's struggle with cancer, as he said: "I'd read things, like people criticising me. 'You're the least favourite Osbourne. Can we vote you out of the house?' Shit like that . . . But no one likes to read stuff about that, and I know you should probably never read shit like that. And probably the main thing that was getting to me was my mum's illness. When my mum first told me she got sick, I didn't cry. I probably cried over my mum's illness twice. And that shit hurt a lot, you know? I was constantly just drowning it out. Drinking and using . . . a lot of opiate-based drugs. OxyContin. I had smoked pot and drank every day for two years. I was taking Vicodin by the handful. Valium, Xanax, Dilaudid, Lorcet, Lortab, Perocet, you name it . . . It's LA, you know? You just get it from people."

On top of this was the celebrity status that had been suddenly thrust upon him – and which Ozzy had worried might affect his children: "It's been real weird. It wasn't how I expected my life to turn out, specially, mainly pertaining to the show. It never crossed my mind that one day I'm gonna be big and famous and have my own TV show, you know? All of a sudden we're meeting with MTV, saying, 'You are gonna be doing a show, and you are gonna be followed around.' When we were filming I never thought once about it coming out. And then when it came out, it was just such a . . . it was like a shock to the body. Because . . . I wanted to go one way, I was interning at a record label – OK, cool. I'm gonna do what my mom did, you know, work her way up in the music industry, the business side of things. I was comfortable with that. That was what I wanted to do. And then just suddenly I am thrown from that . . . There's people outside our house; you get followed by photographers; you can't go out and have a cup of coffee with a friend without someone coming up to you with a picture and [saying] 'Sign this.' I'm totally grateful for the fans my family has and I have; they gave me a lot of support when I was in treatment. But it was just odd, you know? It's stressful. Just the whole fact of being someone in the public eye."

All this led to a need to play up a fake party-boy reputation, he explained: "The party guy was just, you know, drunk Jack. It was just fun.

I would do things I never thought I would do. Just stupid shit, you know? Drunk Jack wound up in, like, parties with insane celebrities, hanging out with them. If I was sober they'd be like, 'You are boring.' I always had that. If I was sober, people wouldn't like me." This led to a lifestyle where: "My own thing was, you know, wake up at five in the afternoon, it's dark out, hang out, maybe take a shower, then start drinking, start smoking pot, go out with friends, get wasted."

Some of this went with the territory of living in Malibu, he explained: "Malibu's just a totally different place. It's like a mountain town right next to a city, so if you can imagine some of the weird shit that goes on in a 15,000-population mountain town, it goes on there, you know? There's a lot of drugs, a lot of alcohol, a lot of sex. It's like debauchery's paradise . . . I could remember being 13 and at a bar and people were like, 'What's this 13-year-old doing here?' and I would proceed to drink them under the table. I started taking Vicodin occasionally when I was like 14, and from about 14 onward it was just picking up, so another one here and there. It started maybe once every two months and [got] shorter and shorter and it really started picking up April of last year."

By the time Jack's addiction was in full flow, his mother was at her lowest point in the fight to survive and wasn't able to help him through his now-suicidal frame of mind: "I tried . . . I took a bottle of pills. I'd been in Europe and I had a lot of absinthe and I was just drinking and drinking, trying to, you know, just shut my body down . . . I'd run out of OxyContin, I was doing a lot of Dilaudid. Dilaudid is like a millimetre down from OxyContin. I was doing a lot of those, and life just got super stressful for me, and I just sat in a hotel room [thinking], 'I want it to end, I want it to end.' And I'd actually gone up to my mum one morning, just sitting on her bed, and I started crying. Mum was like, 'What's wrong? What's wrong?' I said, 'I need help. Something's wrong. I need help.' And she was really sick at the time, and she was like, 'What can I do? What can I do?' And I said, 'I don't know, I need a lot of help,' and she goes, 'Is it the drinking? Is it the using?' I said, 'Yeah.' She said, 'OK, I'll get you help,' and then I went in my room and I got high and I convinced her I was OK and that I was just tired, and she was like, 'No, you just told . . .' And I just said, 'No,' and I kind of went on with it saying I was fine.

"Mum had her cancer, so she had to really focus on herself, you know – she was surviving. And dad was just an emotional wreck. He was drinking a lot of the time, he was smoking a lot of pot. And because he takes certain medications, the drinking was making him . . . you know, he wasn't even present, really."

In due course, however, it was Sharon – as ever – who saved the day when her health had recovered somewhat. "My parents approached me to go to rehab," Jack explained. "They came up to me and they were like . . . mom threw a bag down and was like, 'You're going to rehab,' and I was like, 'No. How dare you say that to me? I'm fine.' A friend had called my mom and said, 'Jack's hooked on OxyContin. He's in a pretty bad way.' At this point [Sharon] had been cancer-free [and] she was starting to regain her strength, her awareness of what was going on around the house. She was trying to mend things. Dad she smacked down to shape, and my dad started getting back on track when my mom said, 'You're going to rehab or you're dead.' So I ran away. I just took off running. I went to a friend's house and I went pretty buck wild. I was snorting Demerol, OxyContin. I'd gotten a hotel room and just . . . I don't really remember much . . . I went to a friend's house and we just started using. I took myself out of the picture for a second and I looked around at every single person in the room . . . it was like, 'I don't want to be like that.' I don't want my life to be controlled by a drug. I want to be in control of my life. I was really loaded and I came home and just sat on my mom's bed, and I said, 'I'm going to go pack my bags. I'm ready to go. And you know, I want to go – I need to go.'"

When rehab cleared Jack's body and mind and left him a wiser kid, he realised that he and his father understood each other better as a result. "It's brought me and my dad a lot closer. In a way, we're doing this together this time around. He'll openly admit he's been trying to get clean for some 18-odd years or so. When I was younger I was like 'What the fuck? Why can't you get this right? What's so hard about it?' And now I can understand how hard it is . . . Sobriety can't be forced upon you; you're gonna have to want to do it."

With Jack's coming of age, Sharon's apparent recovery from cancer (she remains free of the disease at the time of writing in spring 2006) and 2003 shaping up with a new band and new opportunities, Ozzy must have felt as the Ozzfest swung into action that at last things would go better. The third season of *The Osbournes* was aired in June and the touring season was in full flow: ironically, one of the main competitors for the hard-earned buck of the rock festival-goer was his old ally Robert Trujillo and his new band Metallica, who were embarking on the vast 'Summer Sanitarium' tour with Limp Bizkit and Linkin Park (both of whom would fall spectacularly from grace in commercial terms the following year). A new Lollapalooza, headed up once again by Perry Farrell, had been launched too. But Ozzy said, with supreme nonchalance: "My thing is that there's enough room for everybody, the more the better." Sharon added: "Each tour stands for something different, and if you want alternative music, you don't come to our festival."

She said it herself – the Ozzfest had now become the mainstream, with Ozzy and the big-selling nu-metal and rock acts on its bill a safe haven for big-label, big-budget bands. One such was Korn, the Bakersfield nu-metal pioneers with whom Sharon endured a brief falling-out, having labelled them "has-beens" and "just too fucking gay from the word go" in *Rolling Stone* the previous autumn.

Fortunately, Korn singer Jonathan Davis chose to rise above it all, saying at a pre-Ozzfest press conference: "She started rumours about us, but that is just how she is. She is a shit talker and it doesn't bother me. I mean, with negative press, they are still talking about me, so I don't give a fuck . . . We are all in this thing together. We all want to do a good show, and I can look [past] that. Who cares?"

Sharon herself apologised (as she had for the Stereophonics incident two years previously), saying: "I had cancer. I was sick and I didn't know what I was saying. Now that's a good sympathy card . . . Being a manager, it's not right to knock on the bands, and I did it because I am such a bitch and I did it because I don't like his manager."

At the time, Jack theorised, the future of the Ozzfest was less secure – America was gripped by post-9/11 paranoia and the economy was suffering as a result, plus Sharon was ill – which contributed to her outburst. But none other than Marilyn Manson stepped up with encouragement, saying: "I think that entertainment and theatre were created back in the day to distract people and get their minds off the shit that is going on in the world and make them think about something else, and Ozzfest is a great escape. It's more than just a day. It sticks with you, especially if you make yourself a real part of it."

The show would go on for the long term, Sharon added, saying: "With our genre of music, with Korn, Disturbed or Ozzy, the industry always, always says, 'It's over, it's over, it's over,' and it's not for us to determine. It's for the kids to determine. So if kids don't show up this year, then we know it's dead, but it's not for the media to say that it's dead."

A couple of weeks into the tour, Ozzy came down with laryngitis and was forced to miss a show in Maysville, California as a result: Korn took the headline spot. "After struggling through his performance in San Francisco, Ozzy Osbourne was examined by his personal physician this morning and was diagnosed with having severe laryngitis," a spokesperson said. "Ozzy's doctor has ordered him to rest his vocal cords for the next few days."

But nothing remained tranquil for long in the lives of the Osbournes, and even after Ozzy rejoined the tour he was rocked by the death of his long-time tour manager, Robert 'Bobby' Thomson, who succumbed to throat cancer in his bed at the Townsend Hotel in Birmingham, Michigan. "We are devastated by the loss of our dear friend Bobby," Ozzy said. "He has been a part of our family for 23 years and loved very much. He will be greatly missed by all of us. Our sincerest sympathies go out to the Thomson family." Thomson had, like so many others in the family's circuit, become known to the public after appearing in *The Osbournes* on a few occasions.

Ozzy's laryngitis struck on two more occasions on the 2003 Ozzfest, forcing him to miss dates at the PNC Bank Arts Center in Holmdel, New Jersey and a Washington show a few days later. Hints that all was not well with his voice came when he put in a truly atrocious mangling of 'Take Me Out To The Ballgame' at Chicago's Wrigley Field during a baseball game. Still, despite the slip-ups, the Ozzfest became one of the summer's highest-grossing tours, according to *Billboard*, and wound up on August 28 with its organisers generally feeling that a good job had been done in the circumstances.

One rather bizarre turn of events was the sudden departure of Jason Newsted from Ozzy's band at the end of the Ozzfest. Strangely, neither he nor anyone in the Osbourne camp could provide a convincing reason for this: he himself hinted that he had returned to work with Voivod, and vanished from the public eye for a while. Something was clearly going on behind the scenes . . .

As the annual hype around the festival died down and fans began to think again about the other Black Sabbath members, it emerged that only Bill Ward was up to much, although Geezer and Iommi were reported to be still slaving away at new solo albums. As Ward told *Classic Rock Revisited*, "I'm trying to finish the never-ending album I am making called *Beyond Aston*. There have been a lot of starts and stops. It is the most interrupted album of all time. All the songs are finally done and it is in the mixing stage. We are mixing it in a home studio, and when we get them to where we want them, then we will go into a big studio and do the final mixes. I always like to do the final mixes in what would be considered a normal studio. My priority is to get this album done by hook or by crook. It is almost like I am getting obsessed with it. There have been genuine things that have come up. I am hoping that the next album won't be like this."

Of the album's projected title, Bill mused: "All of the guys in Sabbath are from Aston. The album represents the difference to where we used to be to where we are now. The title track was written when I was thinking about Ozzy. It is about how we are both in safer houses today, spiritually speaking. Many of the songs have to do with Black Sabbath. I guess it is a very personal album . . . Most of the tracks are pretty hard edged. The album has been a bit of a struggle. It started in the analogue era and has now moved to the digital age. The song I wrote with Ozzy in mind is nearly 10 years old."

His own band were still active: "I have been invited to drop in on a few gigs but I am busy with the band rehearsing. If this album does fly, then I want to be able to make sure we can make it fly live in concert . . . I would love to go out on tour. I'm 56 years old and the body is starting to stiffen up! I would really love to go out and do something. The body is going to disintegrate."

Crucially, he admitted that the 2001 Sabbath sessions were at an advanced stage – news to most fans: "The tapes were made in early 2001 before we went on tour. We were in England and we just recorded a bunch of stuff . . . I have 60 cassette tapes right here in my house and we have everything else on file . . . Some of the tracks are finished with lyrics."

Asked what the status of Sabbath was, he replied: "I wish we could record an album. Things have just stopped. I never push on it. I don't know how each – all of us try to be respectful of where each of us are at. It is that kind of a deal . . . A lot of it would depend on Ozzy wanting to do it. I think all of us want to be OK with doing it as well. We would all have to believe it was the right thing to do. I have reservations about it. There is some scrutiny in there. I can't quote Tony and Geezer but I think they would have to consider it very carefully."

Finally – and revealingly – Bill explained: "It is frustrating. On the last tour we did, we all worked so hard. I became frustrated and a little bit angry and disappointed at the end of the touring period because the band was sounding so hot. It made no sense to me to stop at the last gig. My chops were tight with Geezer and Tony. I was just learning what I had forgotten! I felt that I could go on for years, but we had to stop and pull the plug. That is where commercialism comes in over music-ism. However, we still sounded great and we were having a blast, and I just wanted to go on. We could have gone around the world. Those were just my expectations, and I could understand things from a business point of view, but it was kind of sad . . . By no means has Sabbath broken up. If they have, nobody told me. I am still in a place where I want to go on tour. I don't have any fear any more."

But Sabbath was now primarily under the control of Ozzy and Sharon, although Iommi still wielded some decision-making power as he always had. Ozzy had other things on his mind, including a Broadway musical based on the life of Rasputin, the Russian monk. More seriously, he and his daughter Kelly had both been dropped by their record label, Epic, and then re-signed to Sanctuary, the new contender for major-label status which had grown up in the Nineties. The first move by Sanctuary would be a high-profile collaboration between Ozzy and Kelly on a cover of the classic Sabbath ballad 'Changes', which would re-establish audience awareness of the Sabbath back catalogue (conveniently owned by Sanctuary imprint Castle) and boost both musicians' profile. Coincidentally, Aimee Osbourne was also now finding her way into the limelight, acting the role of Raquelle in a modernised musical production of Emily Brontë's *Wuthering Heights*, a film released on September 4.

When 'Changes' was released, it was better than expected. Brushed up with a modern production and the vocals split between Kelly and Ozzy, the melancholy melody found a home in the public's affections and the single received plenty of airplay, assisted by a gothic video featuring the two singers seated back to back on a revolving throne. "It was really fun," said Kelly after the video shoot, while Ozzy explained a little more eruditely, "I'm not good with videos . . . To be perfectly truthful, I don't see why it takes all of this fuss to make a three-and-a-half, four minute video and you're flying crews of people to Prague, and you're getting all the local people out of their houses in the freezing cold and saying, 'Stand there and look medieval. You don't look that medieval. Put this loincloth over your head and stand there and shiver, and we'll set this one on fire.' It's a bit like a mini-Monty Python sketch to me. I mean, I proved that. I'll always remember on the *No More Tears* album, when I did 'Mama, I'm Coming Home', we had one with all this hi-tech, standing around, hurry up and do nothing, you know. And I said, 'That sucks.' That cost a hell of a lot of money, the first one, and then I just said, 'I don't like it. I'm gonna do my own.' So, then I made another which cost me about $25–35,000 when the other cost $500,000 or something. I mean, it was one cameraman in this little studio and it was just as good. I mean, we're not making an Arnold Schwarzenegger film . . . It's getting out of control, you know? . . . I like to have a little bit of tongue in cheek with my videos. I don't want to be this serious guy. You know, there is so much hammy acting going on. I mean, I'm not an actor. I'm just Ozzy, you know."

Of the old Sabbath videos, he laughed: "My hair's gone and changed. Tommy Iommi's hair has gone a bit weirder. I mean, you gotta understand that MTV wasn't around then, so you're doing television and you sit there thinking you're gonna get shot. Getting over the camera shyness takes a while, you know. And we were just kids of 19, 21, scared out of our pants to do a TV thing. It was all live then, every bit of it was live. There was none of this lip-synching. What you saw was what you got . . . When I did the Black Sabbath 'Iron Man' thing, we had to turn up at the studio and this guy had . . . this projector which he'd squirt oil into it on this big white screen. We went in, played it, and went home. Now you have to get there at six o'clock in the morning, and there's like tea breaks, coffee breaks, lunch breaks and everything and you do nothing . . . It's a necessary evil, but I have to do them. But I don't have to say that I enjoy doing them."

The 'Changes' single, billed jointly to Ozzy and Kelly, won them some new fans – but not everyone was an Ozzy fan in late 2003, it emerged. The Midlands news outlet IC Birmingham reported that the city's council members had blocked a proposal that would allow him the freedom of the city. One councillor, John Hemmingway, was quoted as saying, "If we want to give the honour to musicians, UB40 would be a far better vote . . . Frankly the idea of Osbourne as a role model is laughable."

Something of a David versus the Goliath of the Osbourne empire, the issue faded into insignificance as America continued to welcome the Ozzy brand with open arms. Sharon was even given her own syndicated TV programme, *The Sharon Osbourne Show*, in September, on which she interviewed the great and the good of current entertainment. Although the show didn't possess enough staying power to last long (Sharon's website refers to her "taking a stab" at the talk-show host's job) it gave her valuable screen time and set a chain of events in motion that would bring her to TV screens again, this time in the UK the following year.

Unfortunately, a fairly grisly few months lay ahead of the Osbourne family. The end of 2003 was marked by controversy, as Ozzy cancelled autumn dates in Ireland and Europe due to illness – for the second time. Initially he had pulled out of the shows due to surgery he was undergoing on a damaged foot, rescheduling the tour for the autumn, but had to move them again due to the side-effects of a new medication he had been prescribed to counteract a tremor which he had been suffering since his late twenties – and which had contributed to his unhinged appearance on *The Osbournes*. The shaking of his hands gave rise to rumours that he had Parkinson's disease, which he denied: "I swear on my wife and my children's lives that I do not have Parkinson's [and] I am not covering anything up. It's just a thing that's been with me throughout my life. And as I've gotten older, it's degenerated. There is treatment for it. When this guy put this medication in my vein, it was like someone had turned this machine off in me. It was like instant, man!"

In fact, Ozzy had suspected Parkinson's himself after noticing how bad his tremor had become while watching a playback of his recent appearance on *The Tonight Show With Jay Leno*. "I wasn't aware that it was so obvious that I had a tremor," he said. "I said to Sharon, 'I ain't going to do any more TV because I look like a fucking lunatic!'"

His personal physician, Dr Allan H. Ropper, chief of neurology at Caritas St Elizabeth's Medical Center, stated: "Ozzy Osbourne does not have Parkinson's disease. However, he does have a tremor which is coming under control with medication. Unfortunately, one of the side-effects of the medication is dry mouth, which greatly impairs the voice. This problem usually subsides after three to four weeks, but the downside is that this will definitely affect Mr Osbourne's ability to sing at this time."

The tremor, which had been eating away at Ozzy's self-esteem, the singer said, needed to be addressed in order for him to lead a normal life. "It turns out that it's a hereditary thing that I have from my mother's side of the family. This guy in Boston fixed me great. He's taken me off all the medication that I was on. I'm taking one medication now for this tremor. I'm being selfish here . . . I can't tell you how wonderful I feel . . . it was like somebody turned the bad switch off. I feel good again. I phoned my sister up and I said, 'I've got this hereditary tremor,' and she goes, 'Not you as well?' And I go, 'What do you mean? Don't you think it would have been a good thing when I was around 15 to say, 'See Auntie Edna? She's got the tremor!' Nobody ever told me anything!"

Another mystery – his strange, shuffling gait – was explained away by the foot injury he had sustained: "Why do people limp when they've got an injured foot? Because it hurts and you limp because you want to put more weight on your undamaged foot. But if you have that all your life, you learn to manoeuvre. It doesn't mean to say you're crazy or that you're a cripple."

"I've done a fair amount of self-abuse and self-medication for years, but I've got no choice any more," he said. "If I drink alcohol or do any recreational drugs – like smoke pot – it will affect the medication I'm taking for this tremor and it'll probably make it worse.

"I feel like I keep letting you all down, which breaks my heart," he added, "but you have my word that I will be over in the new year to complete my European tour."

Rash words. An unnervingly close encounter appointment with death lay round the corner . . .

CHAPTER TWENTY-EIGHT

2004

E IGHT broken ribs, a punctured lung, a smashed collarbone, severe concussion and a crushed neck vertebra were the net result of a quad-bike accident on December 8, 2003, which left Ozzy with no memory of 11 days of his life. Eight of those days were spent in a coma after the accident – which occurred at the Osbournes' country estate in Buckinghamshire, fortunately not far from a major hospital, Slough's Wexham Park facility.

The accident happened when Ozzy was showing an MTV film crew some land he had bought next to his Chalfont St Peter estate. He took his ATV (all-terrain vehicle, or quad-bike) and was flanked by his bodyguard, a retired policeman called Sam Ruston, who borrowed Sharon's own vehicle. As Ruston told the *Daily Mirror*: "Ozzy was keen to show the crew his new land. I took Sharon's bike, he took his and we set off into the fields. I somehow felt I should go along with him in case someone got hurt. I remember him warning the crew to be careful of the bulls in the field. He was being the usual, caring Ozzy. I flanked him the whole way. We were riding over a large area and there were some very steep hills and a lower valley area. Overall, the terrain is very uneven. There are also some craters left by World War Two bombs.

"Ozzy came to the top of a hill and left the crew filming some cattle. He then rode down the hill. Suddenly, he hit a pothole and the front of the bike buried itself in the ground. The back end of the bike shot up, throwing Ozzy over the handlebars. I was horrified. He landed head first and started rolling, followed by the bike. Eventually he stopped and the bike landed on his back. Ozzy was face down in the dirt, his arm and leg twisted. I rode down to him and turned him on to his side as fast as I could."

The bodyguard recalled that on turning Ozzy over, he saw that the singer's face was purple and his eyes had rolled back. "I stuck my fingers in his mouth because he had swallowed his tongue. Then I pinched his nose and gave four good breaths into his mouth. I watched his chest rise, then thankfully Ozzy started to cough. He was vomiting and spluttering. I noticed blood in his saliva which told me he had a punctured lung.

"Ozzy lay back down and it was clear he was failing again. I followed the same routine as before and gave him CPR. Although he was breathing he went into seizure and started convulsing. Every now and then he would say, 'I'm all right,' before having another seizure. He was in shock and totally unaware of his surroundings, but was trying to get up off the ground and stand up. I told him to lie down, but he was shouting and cursing, saying, 'Get the fuck off me.' I was worried he would injure himself by moving. At one point he managed to stand up – I am certain he was having an adrenaline-fuelled reaction."

Told by the MTV crew, who had called for an ambulance, that the rescue vehicle couldn't reach the field, Ruston carried Ozzy to his own bike and drove him back to the house, holding on to his client's limp body as best he could. Ozzy was then driven to hospital and taken immediately into surgery – an artery had been blocked by his broken collarbone and needed to be freed before the lack of blood to Ozzy's arm caused permanent damage.

After the operation, Ozzy was sedated and put on a ventilator to permit him to breathe, a feat which would have been agony with eight broken ribs, had he attempted it unassisted. Sharon was called in from America, leaving her son Jack and other stand-ins such as Lance Bass from the boy-band 'N Sync to host the show in her place. Ozzy was also visited by Kelly, in the UK to promote her new album *Changes* (Sanctuary's reissued version of *Shut Up*).

Thoughts of suicide haunted Sharon, as she said: "If Ozzy had gone, I would have gone with him. I wouldn't want to, or be able to, spend the rest of my years without Ozzy. I couldn't go on without him. He is not just the love of my life, he *is* my life . . . I would have taken the cowards' way out and taken pills or something. I am not a gun person, that is far too frightening. It would have been pills and alcohol . . . The children are at a stage where they are all grown up and have got their own lives with a good bunch of people around them. They could make their own way in life and go on without me. But I couldn't survive without Ozzy."

Once Ozzy regained consciousness, he was still too weak to move, and the medication had left him confused. As Sharon recalled, "After eight days Ozzy came out of his coma and we were all so relieved. I was terrified he would never wake up, particularly when I played his favourite Beatles tracks and nothing stirred. When he woke they took him off the ventilator and he started to breathe on his own. I just thanked God. He would wake

330

up periodically and go back into a coma. At first he was only with us for a couple of hours a day."

When Ozzy began talking, it was apparent that his memory was playing tricks: "He was terribly confused for the first couple of days he was awake," said Sharon. "He was dreadfully paranoid and his mind was all jumbled up. He just did not know what had happened and could not make out what was reality and what he had dreamt . . . he kept telling me there had been a bomb blast in Wales. I have to patiently tell him what is real and what is not. He has even told me that we met Prince Edward at Buckingham Palace. He keeps saying that Edward was too frightened to come up to speak to him and kept hiding behind his brother Charles. When I tell him we have not met either of them, he won't believe me."

When Ozzy looked back on the incident, he was equally nonplussed: "I didn't know where I was or how long I'd been there. It felt like months or years. I was so confused you could have told me I was lying upside down in a kilt and I'd have believed you! Or you could have told me I was stark bollock naked talking to the Queen, and I wouldn't know any better. It's all patchy. I would drift in and out of consciousness. One minute I would be walking down Beaconsfield High Street and the next I would be in Auckland, New Zealand. Other times I could step from Monmouthshire to fucking California. I went everywhere: Switzerland, Amsterdam . . . At one point I was convinced I was with a group of Asian fisherman off the coast of Wales. How mad is that? Other times there would be a white light shining through the darkness, but no fucking angels, no one blowing trumpets and no man with a white beard."

On December 24, Ozzy defied doctors' advice by checking himself out of hospital in order to spend Christmas at home. Initially he slept in a hospital bed in his bedroom, and Sharon, so recently free of cancer, noted: "It used to be me, but now it is Ozzy in the [hospital] bed. We seem to have a thing about them in our house. We have had feast, famine and the plague in this family. The only positive is that we have been through so much as a couple that Ozzy's injuries are just the latest little hurdle."

As Ozzy recovered, he looked back on the near-death experience with renewed gratitude, saying: "I'll never go near one of those damn bikes again. I've finally grown up. The bloody thing nearly killed me. I am lucky to be here today and not paralysed . . . If it wasn't for Sam I probably wouldn't be here. He had to bring me back to life twice. I hurt myself so badly I'm lucky to be alive and lucky I can walk. But if I don't wear a neck-brace at the moment, doctors have warned me I could be paralysed for life.

"Maybe this accident has been a blessing in disguise, because I'd have never fucking slowed down if it was up to me. All my life I have worked, worked and worked. I just have to face the fact that I'm bloody 55."

He later admitted that he had been driving the quad-bike without a helmet, and regretted it: "Those bikes are for kids and fools – and I'm a fool. Those bikes are like putting a powerful motorbike engine on a Flymo. They are competition bikes and can easily do more than 70mph. They are bloody dangerous and I should have known better. There's a sticker on them that says always wear a crash helmet, which I ignored . . . My head knows I'm 55 but my arse still thinks I'm bloody 21. I probably forgot when to slow down and when to speed up. So if there is anybody out there who has got a quad-bike, always use the equipment . . . or burn the bloody thing."

In the meantime, hospital life was grim: "I hated feeling like I was going to the bathroom in the middle of Brent Cross shopping centre. I wanted to be at home. I got sick of having nurses, doctors, students and sick people around me all the time. I tried to make everyone laugh – except the ones who died on me! But seriously, I wasn't sleeping well. I'd been in a coma, woken up and couldn't stand the pain and noise. I was fed through a tube at first. But when I could eat I wouldn't touch hospital food. I lost my sense of taste and smell, which was just as well I suppose. The TV was the size of a postage stamp and that annoyed me too. The doctors and nurses did a really great job repairing me, but I just wanted to get home to my family for Christmas."

Sharon added: "I didn't want him to check out, and neither did the doctors. They were devastated when he said he was walking out the door. There was nothing anyone could do. He just wouldn't stay there. I was panicking that he would fall over at home or choke in his sleep. I am not trained to deal with such things. It's all right with a small child, but with a grown man it is much more difficult."

With all this, it was little wonder that the forthcoming 20-date tour, already cancelled twice thanks to Ozzy's foot surgery and dry mouth in late 2003, had to be cancelled a third time. As he told MTV, "I am deeply disappointed, but it's out of my control. Right now I need to concentrate on my recovery, and unfortunately this is something I cannot rush." The accident also cost Kelly some much-needed exposure: she had been scheduled to open the dates.

2004 could only get better.

Fortunately, by March and April things were moving not just for Ozzy but for Black Sabbath, who were announced later as the headliners for Ozzfest '04. The two years out of the live arena – during which Tony Iommi, Geezer Butler and Bill Ward had all been working on solo albums and spending time with their families – had been a long wait for Sabbath fans.

In what was becoming a routine process, the Ozzfest was prefaced by a classic-era release for the fans – in this case an American box set from Warner Brothers' reissue division Rhino, who manufactured *Black Box 1970–1978*, containing the eight Ozzy-era studio albums. Remastered and repackaged – but only boosted by four video tracks on a bonus DVD – the box came in at a cool £85.99 as an import in the UK.

Iommi, who had spent two years out of the public eye, resurfaced to promote *Black Box*, saying: "If you want to hear what Black Sabbath was about with Ozzy, this is it . . . No, really, without a doubt. This is it. For those years." In the interim since the last Ozzfest, he had seen Ozzy become an international TV celebrity, and laughed: "I don't know how he does it. He's had people living in his house for four years. It's funny, though . . . finally people are seeing what we have for 35 years. Now they know what we've been moaning about."

Some unspecified hindrances to the re-formation of Black Sabbath were hinted at by Bill Ward on his website on May 18, when he wrote via webmaster Joe Siegler (who also runs www.black-sabbath.com): "This morning I received the very sad news that Mike Bordin is to play drums with Black Sabbath on Ozzfest '04. Black Sabbath is, and always will be an important priority in my life. I support Geezer's, Tony's and Ozzy's decisions to move ahead into Ozzfest '04 without me. I can appreciate they may not be overjoyed with the decision, and I'd really like to be with them. Nothing would please me more than to be a part of the show.

"Last week I did receive a proposal which allowed no room for negotiation. It was a cul-de-sac proposal, in my opinion, where the only answer was yes or no. I was asked to respond by Friday, May 14. I wrote a brief letter of decline on Thursday, May 13. I answered directly at the proposal, and left out any personal comments, other than I was sad to have to decline . . . I understand and believe in a united front when it comes to Sabbath. I can appreciate the fallout from such a decision will upset some people, and I am so sorry. I'm more than willing to support Ozzfest in any way I can.

"I've walked down this street before when Sabbath did the first reunion without me and had Mike Bordin play instead. I want you to know, I'm not being the bad guy here. I'm not trying to hold anyone to ransom. And

I'm not trying to reverse my decision to decline in hope of a positive managerial response to this letter.

"I'm ready, willing and able to rock. There are some details on the proposal that don't work for me. I guess it's a case of the importance of things on both sides and I think that's all I can say for now."

Note that Bill wrote, "I support Geezer's, Tony's and Ozzy's decisions to move ahead into Ozzfest '04 without me. I can appreciate they may not be overjoyed with the decision . . ." This seems to imply that the decision was not theirs. In that case, it can only have come from Ozzy, Sharon or a related manager. However, as with the Jason Newsted case the year before, the issue was resolved behind the scenes without either party explaining exactly what had happened, because Ward then posted some days later: "I have communicated to Sharon that I will accept the proposal of 5/11/04 regarding me playing Ozzfest, and today I received a very positive response from her. At this time, I am taking this response as a move forward. This announcement is for the benefit of all those who these past few days have been so outspoken favouring and supporting me as a member of Sabbath. I personally thank all of you."

Finally, he added the cryptic words: "I have read the new Ozzfest statement that it's going to be an original member line-up for Ozzfest '04. In the immortal words of Buddy Holly, 'Well all right.' And while maintaining some disagreement with the Ozzfest statement verbiage, all I can say is 'God Bless Black Sabbath. Let's Fxxx-in' Rock.'"

Just another wiring-beneath-the-boards manoeuvre in the Black Sabbath scheme of things . . .

Ozzfest 2004 kicked off on July 10 in Hartford, Connecticut, with Ozzy now fully recovered: he had even spent time before the tour working on his Rasputin musical. "He's very territorial about his studio," Sharon said. ". . . he's like, 'Never buy anything for my studio. That's my studio!' So he's very territorial. He has a lock on it with a code, so I can't get in there and the kids can't get in there. It's his thing."

The road to fitness had been a tough one, said Ozzy: "The whole thing is just a blur. When I went into the coma, everything got jumbled up. It's like the year starts now and I have to work backwards. Nothing makes sense . . . You think you are going crazy and seeing people that you haven't. I say to Sharon, 'Do you remember going to so and so.' Then she'll say we never went there. I don't know the difference between dreams and reality . . . It's all a bloody jumble." As he had said at the time: "I haven't made any plans for the future because something else may go wrong. They have to do more X-rays and scans. You can't rush. I have to take things one step at a time now. Still, I'm pretty optimistic. I don't want to give a date but I'll be back. I don't want to let my fans down. I'll be ready when I'm ready. But it's down to me – I've got to fight but sometimes I fight too hard. One day I will walk to the field gate and the next day I'll walk further. On the third day I'm back in bed because I've done too much. As Annie Lennox said, 'Dying is easy but living is hard.' Now I'm walking around I want to run a marathon, I wanna do gigs, but if this crack in my vertebra gets worse I could end up crippled."

But he had quipped: "I'm getting fitter by the minute, because I have to keep running away from Sharon fussing all over me. I'm in constant pain from the minute I wake up until I go to bed, but I'm determined to get better no matter what it takes. The old Ozzy Osbourne will be back. But I ain't gonna go rock and rolling and until I get the all-clear from the doctors. I ain't got no plans. Before the accident I was a keep-fit fanatic. But the thing about keeping fit is, if you miss one week at keeping fit you have to start from scratch. I will be starting from scratch now."

Clearly the slow-and-steady approach had worked: Ozzy had become well enough to top a world-class bill. The Ozzfest line-up was phenomenal, although this time Ozzy wasn't performing his own songs, he was sticking to the Sabbath catalogue – which allowed fans the opportunity to see a full set for the first time in years, the 2001 show excluded. Unusually, Ozzy's solo band keyboard player, Adam Wakeman (son of the venerable Rick), would be playing keyboards – the long-serving Geoff Nicholls was not coming along for the ride, for reasons which (yet again) remain unclear.

The main stage began with Zakk Wylde's perennial Black Label Society and continued with ex-Pantera singer Phil Anselmo's new hardcore band Superjoint Ritual, and Norwegian black metal big-sellers Dimmu Borgir. The veteran thrash metal band Slayer followed before a remarkable special guest, old stagers Judas Priest, who had followed in Sabbath's footsteps by reuniting their classic line-up (drummer aside), which featured singer Rob Halford. The big three acts on the second stage were Slipknot, Lamb Of God (a New Wave Of American Heavy Metal – or NWOAHM – scene-leader) and Hatebreed, the punk crossover band that had won many recent converts. They were supported by a batch of new bands such as Bleeding Through, Lacuna Coil and God Forbid, themselves big enough in their own right to fill medium-sized venues.

The tour made its usual huge-selling stops right across America, passing from the east to the west and back again, before going south to Florida, in three enormous steps. One show on August 26 in Camden, New Jersey, saw Ozzy struck down with bronchitis, making it necessary for Priest's Rob Halford to step in and take his place. This combination – a dream for many, with Halford's extraordinary voice teamed up with the heavy riffs of Sabbath – worked well, even if some fans felt cheated. Sharon stepped in to quell any ill-feeling with a statement, which ran: "To those who attended the Ozzfest show in Camden on August 26, I would like to address the few complaints that have arisen from Black Sabbath's performance with Rob Halford . . . The situation quite clearly was that Ozzy was suffering from bronchitis. He was hoping from the morning of the show until the afternoon that he would have some sort of voice so that he could perform that evening. Unfortunately by late afternoon he was advised by doctors that that just wouldn't be possible. So, our options were: (1) have Black Sabbath not to perform at all and inform the crowd at 4 p.m., which might have led to a riot; or (2) ask one of the legends of the genre, Rob Halford, if he would step in for Ozzy that evening so that people wouldn't leave feeling disappointed not seeing Black Sabbath perform at all. Of course Ozzy's more disappointed than the fans and he feels incredibly guilty that he let everyone down."

A show on September 4 at the Sound Advice Amphitheatre in West Palm Beach, Florida, was cancelled when a hurricane threatened to hit the state, with rock website Blabbermouth reporting: "According to local media reports and Ticketmaster.com, the September 4 Ozzfest show has been officially cancelled. The concert, which was scheduled to be held Saturday in West Palm Beach, FL, was called off because Hurricane Frances is expected to hit the area around the weekend."

Otherwise, the Ozzfest, now on its ninth outing, performed as expected – that is, more hugely than any other equivalent tour. The industry and press were now united in their acceptance that the Ozzfest and its associated brands were the most powerful force on the scene, even if they didn't like it.

Back in the real, non-touring, world, Tony Iommi had another project cooking – this time the official release of the solo sessions which he had first recorded back in 1996 with Glenn Hughes on vocals. The album – labelled *The DEP Sessions* after the Birmingham studios where they were laid down – received an official release from Sanctuary on September 28 and, like the *Iommi* album issued four years before, was much praised. The original drum tracks had been recorded by ex-Judas Priest drummer Dave Holland – who seven months before had been sentenced to eight years in prison for the attempted rape of a male student – and for this reason and the fact that the tracks needed cleaning up, new drums were recorded by Jimmy Copley, who said: "I can't tell you how great it is to work with Tony and Glenn. I was blown away with the power and energy they produce. I went to Tony's studio on a Wednesday and it went so well we finished the whole thing by lunchtime on Friday. Which was just as well as I left for Russia on Saturday . . . Tony would come in and say 'Yeah' or 'Can you try this?' or 'Do you fancy a bit of pork pie?' We had so much stilton and pork pie that I called it the Pork Pie Project. All in all great music, great people."

The album was credited to 'Tony Iommi Featuring Glenn Hughes': as Glenn told me, it was a recording that suited his new, drug-free life perfectly: "Tony and I are really great friends and we make great music together. Tony's been around rock'n'roll behaviour his entire life, and when we get old and we get married . . . well, I don't hang around with anybody who's negative or dark. You know, when I work with Tony, we have a cup of tea. That's who he is. I don't want my epitaph to be, that guy who did coke and got into fights. I want to be remembered for my music and my voice, which is so much more important. Every band has had these terrible things – Def Leppard, The Who, Deep Purple – look at Tommy Bolin – Led Zeppelin . . . mine have made me a very strong person. People actually call me from all over, asking my advice. You know, I'm godfather to Red Hot Chili Peppers drummer Chad Smith's kids: people weren't asking me to be godfather to their kids when I was whacked out of my brain on coke. I surround myself with loving, nurturing people."

Iommi explained to writer Jeb Wright that the original 1996 recordings had come about quite by chance: "I bumped into Glenn on a couple of occasions beforehand. I then heard he was coming to England and I told him to come by the house when he was here. He came by and we had a play. We really enjoyed it and it went into another day and then another day. Before we knew it, we had these eight tracks written. We decided to get a drummer involved and we put the songs down on tape. It was never supposed to be released; it was for our own enjoyment . . . If it was intended to be released then, believe me, it would have been released, then and there."

The bootleg then came out – dubbed *Eighth Star* by fans – causing much anger for Iommi: "These things have a way of doing that, don't they? I try to have control of anything that I do. First of all, we started in my studio and then we went to another studio, finally we ended up in DEP Studios. I think it was after all that the bootleg came out. All it takes is for one of the

players in the band to play it for somebody and they make a copy of it."
(Iommi was more specific when he told me in 2004: "I have a vague idea
of who did it, but how do you prove it? The quality of the bootlegged
version was terrible, so I redid it and now it sounds great.")

Once the album tracks were cleaned up, Hughes' remarkable voice
came through with great impact, as the guitarist marvelled: "He never
ceases to amaze me, actually. I never know what he is going to come up
with next. I often wondered, 'What is he going to sing to this riff?' He
always comes up with something. He is very talented and he is very underrated as well . . . For some reason, we really gel. We get into a room and
we start coming up with ideas and we bounce them off of each other very
quickly."

Why had the bootleg been allowed to remain so long as the sole source
for the *DEP Sessions* material, then? Iommi: "The songs came together
very quickly, and we were almost like, 'Oh, what do we do with them
now?' We were knocking out these tracks, which we really liked, but we
didn't do anything with them. Then the Sabbath reunion came up and I
was due to go on tour, and Glenn went off to do his own things, and we
just sort of abandoned these tracks. In the meantime, I was in the States,
and I started putting another album together, which became the *Iommi*
record in 2000. The time just sort of flew by with it, really. Glenn and I
would see each other from time to time, and we'd always get to talking
about, 'Hey, what are we gonna do with those tracks?' But I've always just
been too busy to get back to them . . . I went back and listened to the
tracks again. And I thought, 'These are really good. I gotta do something
with them,' so I had Jimmy Copley redo the drum tracks. We polished up
some things here and there, since the tracks never really were finished . . .
I did want a better drum sound, because the initial versions of the songs
were only demos, but yes, Dave's problems [i.e. his crimes] were a big
factor in Jimmy coming in to redo the drums."

Sadly, he added that Copley had used a drum kit that had once belonged
to the late Cozy Powell: "I've got Cozy's drum kit at my house. He was a
very, very close friend of mine. He's sadly missed. We went back a long
way, Cozy and me."

As Iommi and Glenn Hughes promoted their album and Geezer and Bill
rested on their laurels after another exhausting Ozzfest, the Osbournes
were plunged once more into their own particular brand of activity. The
Osbournes TV series itself was set to close after the fourth series, which
aired in the US from 13 September: in the wake of the dozens of inferior

reality-TV programmes that had followed it (a show following the lifestyle of the troubled model Anna Nicole Smith was a case in point), Ozzy and Sharon realised that it was time to pull the plug. As Sharon marvelled, "Now, without the camera crews, soundmen, directors and technicians roaming the house all day, the dogs are all we have left. And, with our schedules this summer, it's positively quiet. But we Osbournes always have something up our sleeves."

Indeed. Hints at a co-hosted Ozzy and Sharon talk show were being dropped here and there, but this has yet to materialise. What was much more imminent was Sharon's arrival on the board of judges on the top-rating UK entertainment show *The X Factor*, a three-month weekly programme that occupied a prime-time TV slot and grossed extremely high audience figures.

Since early 2001 Britain had been in the grip of cheesy but addictive TV programmes which ostensibly searched for new musical talent. The first show of this type was *Pop Stars* in which hopefuls audition before a more or less spiteful panel of judges. If they pass they move up to another audition and ultimately a record deal; if they fail they are humiliated in public. *Pop Idol* was next, featuring on the panel the BMG A&R exec. Simon Cowell, who spun off a US version called *American Idol*. Then Cowell co-produced a new show, *The X Factor*, through his Syco company and asked Westlife manager Louis Walsh and Sharon to be his fellow judges. "I'm slapping him around a bit, keeping him in line. You know, that's what you have to do with him," said Sharon of the notoriously critical Cowell.

It wasn't long before Sharon and Simon established a highly media-friendly 'warring' format for the benefit of the screen: Cowell would play the role of merciless industry mogul to the hilt, dismissing candidates with a disgusted sneer, while Sharon adopted the caring-mother part, letting even the most ridiculous of applicants (of which there were no fewer than 50,000 for the first series) down with a polite word of encouragement. It was all highly viewable, and the series finally established her as a celebrity on a par with, or some would say above, her husband.

Commercially, *The X Factor* was a smash hit, attracting top fees for its advertising slots and attracting three million phone calls from the public.

Meanwhile, Kelly Osbourne had put her underperforming pop career on hold, taking an acting part in a ABC TV series called *Life As We Know It*. The teen drama was the story of three teenage males and their high-school rites of passage: Kelly played one of their girlfriends, a character with weight issues. "My character is an overweight teen, who is a little insecure and nervous when it comes to boys, but at the same time is really confident and really doesn't take any shit," she said.

The experience seemed to suit her, as she added: "I have to be on set at 6 a.m. every day, which was a little bit hard to get used to. But it's great. I work with really great people and I like doing it because it's really controversial and I think it's going to push a lot of buttons. It's a show that's in kids' language, so they'll be able to get it. I'm excited."

As if cancer and the quad-bike accident weren't enough for the Osbournes to deal with, on November 22 their house was burgled. At 4 a.m. Ozzy and Sharon – who had lately returned from the birthday party of Sir Elton John's partner David Furnish – were awoken by the noise of an intruder entering the window of Sharon's first-floor dressing-room via a ladder. Ozzy was reported to have 'grabbed' the burglar – described as well-built and wearing a ski-mask – but his opponent escaped by a miraculous leap from the window, landing 30 feet below and fleeing in an accomplice's car. Unfortunately, the burglar took about two million pounds' worth of jewellery with him – which turned out to be uninsured as Sharon had not stored it in a safe. The couple offered a reward for its return.

2004 ended with more crime, this time with the indirect reappearance of a character from long ago – Patrick Meehan, who was now working in the movie business. The BBC reported in early December that outbuildings of his house in Edenbridge, Kent, had recently been burgled, with the loss of a 12-string Fender guitar and gold and silver Black Sabbath discs. Two discs were subsequently advertised on eBay and then bought at a second-hand record fair in Essex, where the police recovered them.

After an appeal for information, an anonymous phone call to Crimestoppers led to the recovery of the remaining discs. They were left in plastic bags behind recycling bins near Longmead Stadium in the Kent town of Tonbridge. The guitar remained missing, however, but Meehan was quoted as being 'very pleased' to hear that the discs were being returned.

Clearly more people placed value on Black Sabbath's early career than had been expected of late. This was borne out by the events of 2005.

CHAPTER TWENTY-NINE

2005

OZZY had stated many times that following the quad-bike accident of late 2003, he wasn't sure if he would ever be able to perform live again, leading his fans and Sabbath's to wonder if, at last, the band was finished. After all, in 2008 and 2009 – just around the corner – Ozzy, Tony, Geezer and Bill would be 60 years old, and Iommi and Butler (arguably the bandmembers with the least exhausting tasks to do onstage) were the only ones who had escaped serious illness or injury.

As fans looked forward, the industry looked back once again, with Sanctuary releasing an equivalent to Rhino's *Black Box* of the previous year in *Prince Of Darkness*, a 4-CD Ozzy box set issued on March 22 that covered his entire career from the *Blizzard Of Ozz* era through to 'Psycho Man' and beyond. With live and remixed versions of his own and Black Sabbath tunes, the set offered a slightly unusual take on the back catalogue, with rarely heard takes on standards such as 'Iron Man' recorded with Irish rock band Therapy? A stack of covers finished off the third and fourth discs, with Ozzy's recordings – including the Stones' 'Sympathy For The Devil', Bowie/Mott The Hoople's 'All The Young Dudes', The Beatles' 'In My Life' and John Lennon's 'Working Class Hero' – ranging from mundane (the first two) to excellent (the latter two).

Despite the box set's varying quality, it did show that someone in the Osbourne camp was feeling adventurous, at least. For instance, Ozzy had collaborated with the premier hip-hop collective the Wu-Tang Clan, that group's rapper Ol' Dirty Bastard and another hip-hop star, DMX, as well as the techno crew the Crystal Method. A previously recorded version of The Bee Gees' 'Stayin' Alive' with Dweezil Zappa and 'Shake Your Head (Let's Go To Bed)' with Was Not Was and Kim Basinger were thrown in too, as was a version of Steppenwolf's 'Born To Be Wild' with the Muppets' Miss Piggy. More conventional rock and metal musicians such as Jerry Cantrell (ex-Alice in Chains) and Leslie West (Mountain) had worked with Ozzy on other covers.

Of the various other collaborations Ozzy had recorded, he commented:

"With Lita Ford, I had a song idea, what became 'Close My Eyes Forever', with a melody and a few scratchy words. Lita liked the song and asked me to finish it. So, I flew to England and finished writing it. Then she asked that I sing it with her, and I had to fly there again. Then, I had to come back from a holiday to do the video. That's the downside of side projects; all the promotion. Busta Rhymes is a trip. The rap world is totally different, not very rock'n'roll. But Busta Rhymes was nothing but a gentleman, a really good guy to be around."

Of the ridiculous but persuasive 'Staying Alive' with Frank Zappa's son Dweezil, Ozzy recalled that the song was previously unissued: "Dweezil, who is a good friend of mine, asked me if I would do this as a spoof, and I said sure. He wanted to put it out, and it was quite funny, but the record company didn't want to put it out because they thought it would be detrimental to my career, I just thought it would be a good laugh. Apparently when I left they replaced me with Donny Osmond. I thought it was funny. The problem is that everyone is too serious now."

He had also recorded a song with the songwriter Holly Knight – a track which only made it to demo stage and thus not to the album: "I've recorded a song, but it'll never get released. It's very dated. It is called 'Slow Burn', and it's kind of a rock ballad, but it never really worked out at the end. We tried several times to record it, but it never worked out."

The new year was destined to bring the Osbournes yet another domestic disaster, this time in the form of a serious fire at the Chalfont St Peter house that was caused by a fireplace igniting some wooden panelling. There were no injuries, but Ozzy and Sharon – who managed to save their pets from the blaze – were both treated for smoke inhalation by firefighters, along with two house staff. Jack and Kelly were not at home, and so the results of the fire – although a section of the house was effectively ruined – were far less serious than they might otherwise have been.

Better news came with the announcement that Black Sabbath were to play again, with a tour lined up in Europe for the spring. Even better, Sabbath were tagged to headline Ozzfest 2005, an unexpected move – they had not appeared on the festival in two consecutive years before. Iommi looked back fondly on the previous year's jaunt with the mighty Judas Priest, saying: "I really enjoyed having them on the bill. We are all from the same town. They are a good band and they are nice guys . . . Like most things that happen with Sabbath, it happened all of a sudden. I was intending on doing some recording, but out of the blue, Sharon called up and said she wanted us to do these gigs with Ozzy. I said that if everybody else was up to it then I would love to do it . . . With this band, you never know what is going to happen. One minute we are broken up and the next minute we are back together doing an album. You just never know what is going to happen."

Of Rob Halford's set with Sabbath the previous year, Iommi recalled: "One thing that sticks in my mind was the day in New Jersey when Ozzy couldn't perform, so we had Rob Halford sing, which was the second time he'd saved the day for us." He was referring here to the Costa Mesa dates in 1992 when Halford stepped in for Ronnie James Dio, who had refused to play before Ozzy.

"At first we were worried, because people expect Ozzy," he added, "but if Rob hadn't helped us out, there wouldn't have been a show at all. When our manager told me Ozzy had bronchitis and couldn't sing, he asked me what I thought about Rob doing it. I said, 'I think it's a good idea as long as you tell everybody beforehand so they know.' Of course, they told the audience right before we went onstage, so I thought, 'Oh, no.' But the crowd received him really well."

By now a veteran of dozens of musical collaborators, Iommi was still full of praise for the original Sabbath line-up and the now-sober Glenn Hughes, saying: "It is great with Bill, though. Bill is the ultimate drummer for Sabbath. It is that combination that makes that sort of sound . . . I think you just feel it. Working with Glenn, you can just feel that it is bloody good. It depends on how people see it but I look at it like, if I like it and I am enjoying it, then it is good. I don't need the aggravation any more of having anyone who is out of their brains and falling about the place. It is nice to work with someone who enjoys what they do. I get a lot of pleasure out of that."

Of Sabbath's future plans – and whether a new album might be on its way or not – Iommi said: "There are no plans. We talk about it as we always do. I think everyone in Sabbath is into making another album. We are certainly into doing another tour, for sure, if we could. I would like to make another album but, as has been the case for a long time, it's hard to get everyone together to do it. We've got quite a few tracks that we did. We had a writing period where we wrote about seven tracks that are very good. Do you think they are going to end up on a bootleg as well? We better do something before anybody else does!"

After a near-silence for a couple of years, Geezer Butler resurfaced with a new G/Z//R album entitled *Ohmwork*, another enthusiastically received record released on May 9 by the Mayan label. He was in great spirits when I asked him how he felt about the new record, saying: "Very pleased. It took ages to write but really quick to record. It started off with loads of keyboards and effects, but I stripped it all down. I wrote some of the songs on a piano, which I've done across the years. I have to be in the mood to compose, I go into my studio at home and just start playing, record everything and stay there all day. Then I just pick out the bits that work. For lyrics, I gave Clark the directions and the titles and he came up with the words."

Singer Clark Brown, whose performance on *Black Science* had been somewhat overshadowed (as was the entire album) by the original Black Sabbath reunion in 1997, made more of an impact this time around, as Geezer said: "*Plastic Planet* was always gonna be a one-off with Burton Bell, because his main commitment is Fear Factory. And [it] was the first album under my own name, or my band, and I didn't really know how it was going to be accepted. And, because of how well it was received, it gave me the confidence to just go on and do another album, and so on and so forth. But I wanted to give it its own particular sound. A lot of people thought that *Plastic Planet* was actually a Fear Factory album, 'cause they hadn't heard of G/Z//R at the time. So to give it its own sound, I had to get a permanent singer just for G/Z//R. And I did lots of auditions, and Clark got the job."

Always a fast worker, Geezer revealed that he had recorded the new album in a matter of days: "All the albums under the G/Z//R title have been recorded in between 10 to 12 days, 'cause everybody has other commitments, so we have a very limited timeline in which to do it. And I prefer working fast anyway, 'cause people concentrate more when they know they have to get down and do it, whereas if you've got like six weeks or something, everybody disappears down to the pub for days on end. So this way, we can all get down to it and do what we're there to do. And as far as how it stands up today, well, I don't really think about it. We do what appeals to the band . . . what pleases us first . . . I can't possibly compete with a lot of the younger bands or anything like that, and I don't want to. I just like to do whatever I fancy at any particular time."

All this sounded cheerful enough, but Geezer had made his thoughts clear on a variety of grim subjects this time round, adding that his inspirations were: "Just the world we live in. Depression, the war in Iraq, being ruled by a bunch of pissing business idiots. I wouldn't want to write something about something I do not think about."

Because Geezer's last album, *Black Science*, had been more mellow than its predecessor *Plastic Planet*, he felt that *Ohmwork* was more similar to *Planet*, saying: "I feel that this is the sequel to it, it has the anger back . . . [the song 'Dogs Of Whore'] is about George Bush [and] the other pissing mad warmongers . . . I cannot believe in this day and age [that he's] going to war over these things. He could have solved all of this diplomatically . . . or sent someone in to assassinate [Saddam Hussein]. He didn't have to kill hundreds of thousands of innocent people and thousands of young American soldiers . . . his companies own all of the oil interests out there. He doesn't get what Iraq is all about, all of the mad factions there. There are six different factions there that all hate each other and it was like opening a Pandora's box . . . this is going to end up like the Vietnam War. There will be no end to it, and all it will do is make the world a worse place with all of these loony terrorists."

G/Z//R the band, he said, might well have a future after Sabbath's dates and the Ozzfest. The new band ("There is me, Pedro Howse on guitar, Clark Brown on vocals, who was on the last record *Black Science* and Chad Smith from St Louis. Not the Chad Smith from the Chili Peppers . . .") was vital and enthusiastic enough to run for the long term alongside his day-job band. "The Ozzfest came up well after the album was done, and when I was in the middle of putting together my own tour. I would love to take the band out on tour after the Ozzfest is over . . . It was a surprise because we just did it last year and I don't know if this will be Ozzy's last year or not. It was out of the blue that Sharon called up and asked me if I would do it . . . I just have fun doing what I do. I'm certainly not doing it for the money, because there's certainly not any money in it. It is good that I can go out for the music again . . . I make all of my money from Sabbath, so that lets me go out and do G/Z//R."

Geezer's was not the only Sabbath-related release in the summer of 2005: Kelly Osbourne's debut album for Sanctuary, *Sleeping In The Nothing*, was released on June 7 and (rather more significantly) Tony Iommi issued another collaboration with Glenn Hughes, titled *Fused*, the following month. Like *The DEP Sessions*, the album was mostly a successful fusion of Iommi's Sabbath-like riffage and the soaring vocals of Hughes, whose star had risen in recent years to the point where current acts such as the Red Hot Chili Peppers were asking him to collaborate with them. As the guitarist said, "Glenn came over to England about five weeks ago and we went into a rehearsal situation. It has been great fun, and we have been coming up with some really good stuff. Glenn will come back in a week and we will keep writing and then we will go in the studio and record them . . . We are really pleased with how the new songs are going. Glenn is even more enthusiastic than he was last time; I can't stop him. I'm trying to slow him down. He will sit there and do it all night. I have to say, 'Glenn, that's it for now. Let's start again tomorrow.'"

On the eve of departure on a Black Sabbath tour, Iommi seemed to be well pleased with the current activities of his main band – but pointed out to *Revolver* magazine that there was one downside to being reunited with the Ozzy line-up: "The only unfortunate thing about the Sabbath reunion is that it squashed a lot of the stuff that went on for years after that. The first 10 years with Ozzy were great, but I think we did plenty of stuff afterward that was also really good." This was a point that needed to be made, even if received wisdom is that the Ozzy years were the best ones.

Iommi looked back on the long and arduous career of Sabbath and its many members, saying: "I've never left, it's everyone else that's left – some twice! I own the name. It's not only that, it's because I believe in what I'm doing – I always have done. I've laid my life down in this band . . . marriages, everything's gone by the wayside over the years for the band. I believe in what we do and I do feel justified . . . I've liked to have a band, I like to have other people's input – because I think as soon as you become the one, then the music becomes very stale; I like the input. It's very difficult for me because you can't really make somebody stay – if something isn't working you have to replace them. I'll always go for the best band I can get – be a band and stick together. If you've got somebody who isn't 100 per cent into it, or it's somebody who's not right, what's the point of carrying on? Although I still remain friends with them . . . You want people to be like yourself, you want people to believe like you do. It's hard, in a lot of cases, because they don't understand that – to believe in it – they just think they're coming in to sing . . . it's a job, at the end of the day it's a job for them. Where with me, it's a belief. I like people to have that same belief."

And so Sabbath departed once more, taking in a string of festival headliners on the European festival circuit, now a regular and vastly commercial industry that booked its main acts in two or three years in advance. A warm-up show at the Aylesbury Civic Centre in Buckinghamshire was followed by the gargantuan Download festival at Donington Racecourse, for many years the scene of the legendary Monsters Of Rock festival. With two extra stages (the Napster stage and the Snickers stage) alongside the main attraction, the event was enormous, running from the amazingly early time of 11 a.m. Sabbath themselves were supported by the cream of the rock and metal scene, including Velvet Revolver, HIM, Anthrax, Alter Bridge and others, while the other stages featured among their 25 bands renowned acts such as In Flames, Chimaira, Lamb Of God, Meshuggah, Helmet and Panic Cell.

Of the forthcoming Download show, Ozzy recalled some old memories of the Donington festival: "Everyone's had good gigs . . . everyone's had bad gigs. I'm not trying to blow anyone off the fucking stage. This isn't no contest for me. Just give them kids the best fucking show they can fucking get . . . I'm an old-timer and back in the day people didn't worry about that. There were all kind of fucking stunts, like pulling the plugs out, or fucking their guitars up, or their booze, or amps. But I can honestly say that I've never done that, because the bottom line is that those kids out there work at fucking gas stations, pizza delivery, whatever fucking job they need to buy tickets for the show. And if I find out the fucker who's responsible, they're getting their butts kicked big time."

The Donington show had an honourable tradition, but the 1988 show (at which Iron Maiden headlined over Kiss, David Lee Roth, Megadeth, the brand-new Guns N'Roses and Helloween) had blotted its copybook after two fans had died in the crush at the front of the stage. This meant that subsequent shows had seen a large barrier erected between stage and crowd, which Ozzy disliked as it made the gig impersonal: "Donington is something that holds a lot of great memories for me from those Monsters Of Rock days. The only thing I really remember is this fucking ridiculous barrier at the front of the stage. Your audience is in fucking Coventry. But if the weather's great, there's nothing like Donington. [Last time] it was fucking raining, it was fucking miserable, the barrier was . . . I understand there were people who died one year, but it's gone from the fucking sublime to the ridiculous. Let me see the audience! I'm just playing to fucking blackness otherwise. I mean . . . I couldn't see the audience last time!"

The method of approaching a huge show such as this, he said, was psychological: "It's like a lot of festivals. It's hard to get into it and the crowd can't see you getting into it because you're so far away, so I kind of got pissed up a bit and then I just fucking went for it and it turned out OK. The weather made it fucking miserable, mind. I mean, just pray for a good fucking day, people. If you've got a good sunny day, there's no place like Donington."

More festival dates followed, interspersed with individual shows supported by Soulfly and Black Label Society, including the Fields Of Rock Festival in Nijmegen, Holland (an even huger event than Download, at which Rammstein co-headlined) and – in typical European fashion, dates at which Sabbath played above or alongside non-metal acts such as Garbage, Moby, Sonic Youth and British Sea Power.

Perhaps the oddest bill was that of the famed Roskilde event in Denmark, where Ozzy et al. played with bands including Duran Duran, Foo

Fighters, Green Day, Snoop Dogg, Brian Wilson, Chic, Carl Cox, John Digweed, Armand Van Helden, Junior Senior, Femi Kuti & Positive Force, Royksöpp, The Tears and Ali Farka Toure – a mixture of house, world, surf, punk, disco and even old New Romantic music. But all this fell to one side when the Ozzfest rolled around, although Sabbath ended up playing the same (or similar) set as they had done since 1997: as Geezer told *Metal Sludge*, "You'll have to ask Mr Osbourne. We're always trying to get him to sing something different, but it's always a losing battle!"

This time, the Ozzfest bill over which Sabbath played was the most prestigious yet. Fans of classic British metal were treated to the sight of the most visually entertaining metal band ever – Iron Maiden – playing before the headliners. The two great bands, on one bill, was something of a dream combination for many Ozzfest visitors and the potential for drama was great.

And so it turned out. For over a month (July 15 to August 20) the tour did its usual rolling-monster act through America, starting in Boston with a plethora of great bands on its two stages – Shadows Fall, In Flames, Killswitch Engage, Mastodon, The Haunted, Arch Enemy and Soilwork among them. On certain dates it was noted that Iron Maiden singer Bruce Dickinson appeared to be slightly unhappy with the way the tour was progressing, dropping some anti-Ozzy comments from the stage. Ozzy and Sabbath had been obliged to miss some dates in mid-August, as Ozzy had – once again – contracted an illness that left him unable to sing, but whether this had anything to do with Dickinson's attitude is not known.

Matters came to a head on Maiden's final scheduled date with the Ozzfest on August 20 in Devore, California. During their set, the band were pelted with eggs and other items from the front of the stage, and the power was cut on some occasions, interrupting their set repeatedly. Festival goers also reported that the words 'Ozzy, Ozzy' had been shouted through the PA system during Maiden's performance. After the set Sharon Osbourne took the stage and in a statement to the crowd called Dickinson a 'prick'.

The mystery as to who was responsible was cleared up when Sharon released a statement admitting that she had been behind the power cuts, although she did not claim responsibility for the egg-throwing. It read, in part: "For 20 shows we were forced to hear Dickinson's nightly outbursts from the stage: 'When we come back to America, we'll be back with a proper sound system' or 'We won't be playing the same old songs every night (like Sabbath),' 'We don't need a teleprompter (like Ozzy)' and 'We don't need a reality show to be legit (again, like Ozzy)' . . . Was Dickinson so naive to think that I was going to let him get away with talking shit about my family night after night? I don't think he realises who he's dealing with." She signed the statement as the "real Iron Maiden".

A massive row blew up, with Maiden manager Rod Smallwood claiming that he had "never seen anything anywhere near as disgusting and unprofessional as what went on that night" and press officers for the two camps feeding emailed updates to the press on an almost daily basis at one point.

Of course, all this publicity for Sharon simply added fuel to her rapidly rising profile across all media, which was about to be enhanced still further by her appearance for the next four months on *The X-Factor 2*, which slithered glossily across the nation's TV screens from August until December. The programme even won the award for Best Comedy Entertainment at the British Comedy Awards that year, even though it wasn't actually supposed to be funny . . .

The nation, it seemed, could not get enough of Sharon, proving it still more when her autobiography, *Extreme*, appeared through Time Warner Books (publisher of high-profile biogs by Gene Simmons and others) in October. Remarkably, the book and the paperback version which followed six months later have sold over 600,000 copies in the UK alone to date. Perhaps this is a just testimony to her remarkable life story – which, when the Arden family background, the 'drunk Ozzy' years, the 'sober Ozzy' years and the MTV and Ozzfest eras are taken into account, almost matches Ozzy's life for eventfulness.

Ozzy also tapped into the lucrative but undemanding ITV market when he appeared alongside Cliff Richard, Charlotte Church and Shirley Bassey at the annual Royal Variety Performance, two years after he had sung for the Queen for the first time at her Golden Jubilee. As he told *The Scotsman*, "She looked at me and she goes, 'Oh, so this is what they call variety now, is it?' One thing about her, she's got great skin on her face. She's still a very good-looking woman, I think . . . You know what, I've met her twice now, and each time I don't know what I've said to her. I can remember my first wife's mother's telephone number, but I can't remember what I said to you 10 minutes ago."

Of the occasional rumour that Ozzy was beginning to resent his wife's success, he laughed: "She has her own life and her own career. After she's gone through chemotherapy for seven months and kissed death on the lips a few fucking times, I'm just so happy for her that she's having fun. It said in one of the papers, 'Ozzy's extremely jealous of his wife's success.' How much more success can I have? I'm really grateful and happy that she didn't die . . . She'd stop to sign autographs for a fucking dead body in the road because it's all new to her."

He added that he hadn't read *Extreme* because: "It just fucks me up. I've done some pretty bad things and some pretty good things, but I haven't done it all at the same time. If you just read the extracts they put in the paper, you'd think I was Charles Manson ... My image is fucking bat-biting, Alamo-urinating, drunken, drugged-out, fucking one-brain-cell freak. I suppose when people saw *The Osbournes* they realised that I am human, that I don't go bat-hunting every night ... I've overdosed regularly and I'm not proud of it, but if I changed any of the amazing things and the dumb things I've done, I wouldn't be here now. When I think about it, you couldn't have written my life. It's incredible. I can honestly say, all the bad things that ever happened to me were directly, directly attributed to drugs and alcohol. I mean, I would never urinate at the Alamo at nine o'clock in the morning dressed in a woman's evening dress sober."

He wound up with the pithy self-evaluation that: "I'm not proud of everything I've done. I'm not proud of having a poor education. I'm not proud of being dyslexic. I'm not proud of being an alcoholic drug addict. I'm not proud of biting the head off a bat. I'm not proud of having attention deficit disorder. But I'm a real guy. To be Ozzy Osbourne, it could be worse. I could be Sting."

And all this from a man whose early life was hardly blessed with good fortune. Looking back at his early years, he commented: "When I was in school, it really wasn't school. I suffered from ADD [attention deficit disorder] and dyslexia, as do my children. So, looking at the blackboard was like reading Chinese for me. It was very embarrassing. I used humour and singing to get by. I left school, went to get a trade. For an apprenticeship, I wrote down 'plumber'. When I thought about it, I realised the only time a plumber works in England is when the pipes burst in the winter. Well, I hate the cold, so that didn't last too long ... When I got into a band, it was just my idea of fun. Lo and behold, we made our first record and I haven't looked back since ... The biggest break in my life came when The Beatles hit. They totally sucked me in and I thought, 'That's my way out, my music.' I used to fantasise, as all kids do, about Paul McCartney marrying my sister and all that crazy stuff. That set me off into music and my first gig ever."

In November, Ozzy released another covers album – in the wake of the cover versions he had included on the *Prince Of Darkness* set earlier in the year – entitled *Under Cover*. He had taken a step towards his wife's career by recruiting, as the album's musical director, Mark Hudson, the vocal coach who appeared alongside Sharon on *The X Factor*.

The album was reviewed fairly disparagingly by most critics – the fate of 99 per cent of covers albums, although people keep making them anyway – who noted that Ozzy's last album of original songs had appeared a whole four years before, despite the plethora of reissues, box sets, live albums and other projects that had littered the recent pathways of Sabbath and his solo band. But it's unlikely that their words bothered Ozzy, who had plenty of ideas on his agenda. The *Osbournes* show was now over (its fourth and last season had just wrapped shooting, leading Ozzy to comment: "People in Hollywood do rehearsed reality. Our [TV show] was real reality. It's about having the bottle to let your ugly side be shown as well as your good side . . . it felt like your kid was leaving home. I did miss it. You're damned if you do and you're damned if you don't") and next up was the still rather implausible Rasputin musical. As he mused: "I do identify with him. He lived the lifestyle of a rock'n'roller without the guitars. It's all written and there are a lot of people interested, but it's my wife's and my business manager's job to get me the best deal. We're looking for a top-class producer, not some marblehead."

At the time of writing there have been no more releases from Ozzy Osbourne, Kelly Osbourne, Tony Iommi, Geezer Butler, Bill Ward or Black Sabbath. But that doesn't mean the tale is finished . . .

CHAPTER THIRTY

2006 And Beyond

INTO 2006, and it seemed that the story of Ozzy and Black Sabbath might plateau at last. Long-time relationships were showing signs of faltering, and old age was clearly setting in to a number of people and events.

Heavy metal fans – and those keen on the new generation of guitar shredders in particular – were astounded when the announcement came in January that Ozzy Osbourne was looking for a new guitarist. Zakk Wylde, it seemed, was either out or on his way out. The Osbourne offices were flooded with applications from young, nimble-fingered guitarists who fancied themselves as the new Randy Rhoads, or the new Jake E Lee, or indeed the next Zakk.

However, within a matter of weeks a statement came from the Ozzy camp which read: "Ozzy would like to thank everyone who took the time to send in submissions to be his new guitar player. At the time we announced the search, Zakk Wylde's itinerary with Black Label Society was quite overwhelming. Fortunately, Zakk has now been able to go back and rearrange his schedule to make sure that he would be available to write, record and tour with Ozzy in 2006 and beyond. Therefore, the search for a new axe man has been called off. We sincerely apologise to all of the talented musicians (and there were lots of them) who were excited by this incredible opportunity and we wish you the best of luck with all of your future musical endeavours."

Disaster averted, it seemed.

Next, Ozzy's old bassist Rudy Sarzo went public in *Rock Eyez* magazine with a claim that Sharon Osbourne had tried to block the publication of his autobiography, as follows: "I have a book called *Off The Rails* and the publisher at the time, Cherry Lane, suggested a subtitle *Off The Rails – My Adventures In The Land Of Ozz*. One of the reasons why I chose Cherry Lane was not only because my relationship with John Sticks, the publisher, but also his relationship with Randy [Rhoads]. He was the editor of *Guitar World* and he knew Randy pretty well. I knew the book was going to be a labour of love. But it happened that Cherry Lane also has the sheet music for the Ozzy/Randy catalogue. So when Sharon Osbourne found out the book was going to be hitting the street on September 14, they put a 'cease and desist' order and applied pressure. After many communications between Cherry Lane's lawyers and the Osbourne lawyers, it finally came down to Sharon writing me a very nasty letter and putting an ultimatum on Cherry Lane that if the book was published, she (Sharon Osbourne) was going to pull the catalogue. So the contract was released . . . right now I have another deal in the works and it's still going to come out – thank God! Also, the Editor in Chief at *Guitar World* contacted me because they are putting together a tribute to Randy. It's the whole issue and they will be using some excerpts from the book."

Why would Sharon want Rudy's book not to appear? You'll have to read it and see.

Then, Ozzy raised a few eyebrows by agreeing to appear in a UK TV advertising spot for a butter substitute called I Can't Believe It's Not Butter, which had recently been relaunched. The brand owner, Unilever, had spent £7 million on the ad, which featured Ozzy and a TV impressionist called Jon Culshaw in a kitchen shambling around like fools and getting butter (or the oily alternative version) out of the fridge in a state of high confusion.

Brand manager Noam Buchalter was quoted as saying: "The aim of the activity is to communicate the improvements made to the spread and to highlight the new packaging . . . I Can't Believe It's Not Butter now tastes so much like butter that the two Ozzys can't tell the difference . . . [our product] has always been a great impersonator of butter and proud of it. Who better to star in the ads than the UK's best impersonator? Jon and Ozzy make a great double act and their infectious personalities will have a great impact on consumers."

More than a few fans asked themselves how Ozzy could stoop so low.

But it wasn't all bad news. Much was made in late 2005 and early 2006 of our heroes' long-awaited induction into the Rock And Roll Hall Of Fame, a distinction they had turned down on several occasions but which Ozzy now felt would be worth enduring for the sake of his bandmates. As he put it, "You build yourself up, then you get knocked down, then you build yourself up, then you get knocked down, and I'm thinking in one of my interviews I said something about the fact that, why should the Hall of Fame be judged by people in the industry? But I was just saying that because I was pissed off . . . the fans should vote, the people or whatever. I can't really remember."

On March 13, 2006, the ceremony took place at the Waldorf-Astoria Hotel in New York City. The celebrities who would welcome Black Sabbath into the hallowed elite were none other than Metallica, the biggest-selling metal band ever, who were in so many ways the inheritors of Sabbath's legacy. The San Franciscans also performed a medley of 'Hole In The Sky' and 'Iron Man' before a star-studded audience. Metallica drummer Lars Ulrich, the band's usual spokesman, began his speech with the arch words, "Oh, by the way, Sharon, if I fuck this up in any way, please no eggs. This is my finest leather, this is my finest leather."

He went on, "Anyway, I wonder how many times on this very night in the last 20 years that the words 'If it weren't for you, we wouldn't be here' have been uttered. Well, here we go once more. Bill, Geezer, Ozzy and Tony, if it weren't for you, we wouldn't be here. Obviously if there was no Black Sabbath, there would be no Metallica. If there was no Black Sabbath, hard rock and heavy metal as we know it today would look, sound and be shaped very, very differently. So if there was no Black Sabbath, I could possibly still be a morning newspaper delivery boy – no fun, no fun. So thank you for meeting, thank you for knowing each other, and thank you for forming a band so I would have something relevant and important to do on this Monday night in 2006."

Lars then went into quite a historical essay about the family tree of metal, before concluding it with the words: "All the metal bands and all the so-called subgenres of metal still trace their lineage to one place: four kids in their late teens from the Black Country of Birmingham who named their band after a 1963 Italian horror movie starring Boris Karloff. Subsequently they changed hard rock and by doing so the entire family tree of metal and everything that metal, for better or worse, stands for, was and will be forever both invigorated and elevated."

He then recounted an amazing anecdote from the early days, when Metallica were supporting Ozzy on tour in America in 1986. "Are they taking the piss? The question 'Are they taking the piss?' still rumbles in my mind. It's 1986 and we're fortunate enough to land the much-coveted support slot on Ozzy's *Ultimate Sin* tour. We would, when given the chance to soundcheck, often start jamming on any number of Sabbath songs – be it 'Symptom Of The Universe', 'Fairies Wear Boots', 'Sweet Leaf', or what have you. Apparently, as the hallowed sounds of our meek attempt at Sabbath music reached into Ozzy's dressing room, his first reaction – so I was told – was, 'Are they taking the piss?' And as we were later threatened with, if indeed we were 'taking the piss', we would be at the receiving end of – something I was unfamiliar with at the time –

namely, a 'Birmingham handshake', of which I could only imagine the horrors. So I can now answer Ozzy's question in person face to face. No, Ozzy, we weren't taking the piss. We were just four snot-nosed kids on our first go-around in the big leagues hoping [you'd join] us onstage . . . And with that, Bill, Geezer, Ozzy and Tony, I salute you with much love, respect, appreciation and gratitude. Thank you."

Metallica guitarist James Hetfield gave a shorter, emotional speech, coming close to tears as he recalled his nine-year-old self playing Black Sabbath LPs in his bedroom: "And now, as the former nine-year-old speaks to you here, as an adult musician – I know those two words really don't go together – I realise that without their defining sound, as my friend Lars has said, there would be no Metallica, especially with one James Hetfield. Never have I known a more timeless and influential band. They have spread their wonderful disease through generations of musicians. They are always listed as an influence by heavy bands to this day. They are loved and highly respected as the fathers of heavy music. It truly is a dream come true and an extreme honour for me, and the nine-year-old still inside of me, to induct into the Rock And Roll Hall Of Fame such a significant group of musicians. And in the words of our fearless leader Ozzy Osbourne, 'Let's go fucking crazy!' "

Later, Hetfield told *Rolling Stone*, "It was like, 'Oh, no, I'm going to start crying' . . . I'd never known it until I had to access all those emotions in front of that crowd, but it just goes to show how much Sabbath mean."

Although Sabbath didn't perform themselves (rumours flew about, inevitably), the band were more than generous in their thanks to the Hall Of Fame itself and Metallica for the honour they had been paid. Ozzy said of Metallica's performance, "They did fucking better than great!" and added, "What I did was wrong. I read an interview where Bill said, 'I'd like to have gotten inducted, but I respect Ozzy's decision.' I went, 'Fuck me! I'm not Black Sabbath. The four of us are Black Sabbath.' And in the end, I'm also honoured to be in. It's something to leave my family when I go."

Endless press followed the event, with Iommi telling *Billboard*: "I'm really thrilled with it, to be honest. I mean, you can't say you're not thrilled for any award, especially something like that . . . I mean, I feel we should be in there, because without blowing our own trumpet, I think we've done a hell of a lot for the music, for what we've offered to the music industry . . . we've probably heard that from day one, you know, that 'You're never gonna be any good, you're never gonna last' and all this stuff. But it has, and it's stood the test of time, 38 years now."

Ozzy added: "All through the early days of Black Sabbath we never got a good review for a concert, we never got a good review for an album, and we kind of liked it that way back then, because we didn't want to be liked by the fucking media or anybody because we were a people's kind of band. After my departure in '79 from Black Sabbath I thought, 'That's it, I'll probably be back on the fucking unemployment line.' Then they go and do two great albums with Ronnie James Dio, and then at the end of that, people come up to me when I started the Ozzfest, I hear all the time, 'I'm not worthy,' and all this fucking stuff, you know. And at first I was going, 'Are you joking? You're pulling my leg.' They would say Sabbath was their biggest influence, and I must say, I do believe that Tony's been underestimated for coming out with the riffs."

Iommi explained of the music's strength that: "It's from inside, it's from the heart. It's something that a lot of kids can associate with because it's not technical, you don't have to be a genius to play it. It's a very straightforward power . . . the riffs are fairly simple and they're catchy, and the melodies on top are the same, so I think you can associate with that more easily than something that's very technical, because we're not technical."

The future of metal seemed to be in good hands, as Geezer admitted when asked who the successors to Sabbath might be: "Metallica. It's hard to say because it's so faddish now. It depends on what they do. *Metallica* is one of the best albums I ever heard. That's a classic album. That's the sort of music I really like listening to; something that is heavy but has got melody at the same time. It's still in the Sabbath sort of vein. It's not too extreme, where you are going 'What the hell is he doing on the bass?' or the singing sounds like he is puking. I like bands. Metallica has strong songs. That's what's missing from a lot of bands – they've got the riffs but the songs aren't going to stand up as songs. I like to hear an actual song, great riff, good vocal line and good lyrics. I'm too old–fashioned really, but it still works. Metallica sold big around the world, so if you're into metal that's probably what a lot of people want to hear. To me it's just got really strong songs on it . . . Metallica admitted they were influenced by Black Sabbath. In fact, Lars Ulrich, Metallica's drummer, said he never heard of Led Zeppelin when he was a kid. He was brought up on Black Sabbath albums.

"Iron Maiden were probably the first band I read about who admitted to the press that we had influenced them. Anthrax was one of the first bands I heard cover Sabbath. It was great to hear somebody else cut 'Sabbath, Bloody Sabbath'. I think Cathedral are very Sabbath-like. Soundgarden are one of the bands I've heard closest to the original Sabbath sound. Even the way Chris Cornell sings reminds me of Ozzy. Usually it's just the music a lot of people go for; they even seem to go for the vocal approach as well. I think they are a great band. They are not like clones or ripoffs; they have taken that sort of Sabbath feel and spirit . . . it's good that we've had that much influence the way Hendrix or Cream influenced me; that I'm like that to them instead of some old has-been band from the Sixties or Seventies. People keep us alive in their music."

More mysteries were cleared up when Ozzy and Sharon appeared on a March 10 broadcast of *The Howard Stern Show*, whose website reported afterwards that: "When Ozzy and Sharon Osbourne came into the studio, Howard commented that Sharon looked better than ever to him. Sharon responded that she recently spent $200,000 on plastic surgery and that part of her procedure involved doctors taking fat from her stomach and inject- ing it into the lines around her eyes. Sharon went on to mention that, like getting a new car, she spaces out her time under the knife to about once every three years."

The conversation had started well.

It went on: "Howard then pointed out that he has always respected Ozzy because of his commitment to Sharon, even when she wasn't at her most attractive physically. Ozzy replied that he's been attracted to Sharon since being introduced to her, but that they rarely have sex any more because of his inability to get an erection, a condition, he said, that has been caused by his dependence on antidepressants.

"Since Ozzy is about to embark on another tour this summer as a part of Ozzfest, Howard asked if he was doing it because the family needs money. Sharon insisted to Howard that she and Ozzy are doing well financially and that an autobiography she wrote brought in $10 million last year alone. Since Sharon mentioned her book, Howard wondered if one of its stories – namely, the time Sharon claimed Ozzy drugged her food – actu- ally happened. Sharon said it did and recalled that Ozzy put pot in a stew he had prepared for her while they were dating. However, Ozzy claimed that the drug in question was actually acid and that two of his friends were the ones responsible for the incident."

Two more questions needed clearing up – firstly the Iron Maiden 'problem' from the previous year, to which Sharon explained that she had "personally asked Bruce and his band to join the last Ozzfest tour and, despite the fact that Iron Maiden was being paid $185,000 per show, Bruce, out of what she called jealousy, bad-mouthed Ozzy onstage every night. Because of this, Sharon reported that she hired 200 'Hispanic kids', some of whom had worked at the hospital where she recovered from her bout with cancer, to throw eggs at Bruce during the final night of the tour. Sharon noted that the plan went off without a hitch and that Bruce had a difficult time looking serious onstage that show because of the 'eggshells in his mouth'."

More surprisingly, Sharon revealed that "the family lost all of the $10 million it received from MTV's *The Osbournes* on legal fees. Sharon explained that, after the show became such a hit, people started coming out of the woodwork demanding credit for coming up with its concept and that all of the family's earnings from it went into defending itself."

After all this, it was some indication of Sharon's stock in her home country that the UK's Freemans organisation voted her Freemans Celebrity Mum Of The Year over Katie 'Jordan' Price, Kate Moss and the Duchess of Cornwall. She gushed, "I'm absolutely delighted to be voted Freemans Celebrity Mum Of The Year and the fact that this is a public vote makes it extra special. It has been a very tough few years and the British public have been so supportive of me and the family, and seen that I am a real old-fashioned British girl at heart."

The resolutely traditional Freemans company, which produces catalogues for mail order clothes and goods, may have been prompted to award Sharon the title because she had also become the face of Asda, the low-price supermarket chain that epitomised the English shopping experience in the new century (even though it is owned by the giant US firm Wal-Mart). For a year or so Sharon had been popping up in TV ad breaks promoting Asda stores and in doing so, had re-established herself as a recognisably British celebrity.

In fact, recent headlines have been more or less all about Sharon Osbourne rather than Ozzy, thanks to a couple of extracurricular activities. After signing up to act in the play *The Vagina Monologues* in 2005 – but pulling out when her daughter Aimee went through a breast cancer scare – Sharon performed in the play at the Mayflower Theatre in Southampton. One night was slightly spoiled when some thugs threw a cup of hot soup at her, outside the venue (they missed). A witness said: "She was about to go after them when her security men held her back. Luckily, she saw the funny side and stayed on to sign autographs."

While Sharon, a manager and TV presenter, dabbled with acting, and her singing daughter Kelly became a TV actress, her other daughter Aimee – a journalist – recently embarked on a singing career. The Osbournes are clearly a family with many strings to their bow, so much so that it was reported at this time that a film company wanted to buy the rights from

Sharon for the movie of *Extreme*. However, she responded: "The book was hard to write. And I feel the book covered it all."

Back on rock'n'roll turf, the line-up for Ozzfest 2006 was announced – with the obvious difference to previous years' line-ups being that Ozzy was only playing 10 dates of the tour's run, which would commence on June 29. Of the reduced burden, Ozzy remarked: "I'd like to do more recording and less touring for about a year or so. All I've done throughout my life, you can't say I'm doing that much touring now, but I just take it as it comes . . . I'm not as young as I used to be. It's disappointing when I get fucking sick on the road, it's disappointing when I can't deliver what I want to, and I'm fed up of having fucking B12 shots up my arse."

While discussions were underway of how much involvement Ozzy would have in the Ozzfest, it became apparent that he was still slightly nervous about performing live. Did this mean that the nail in the coffin of Ozzy's live career had been planted that fateful day?

After all, this wouldn't be the first time that Ozzy had downsized his live schedule. Back in 1992, you will recall, he had supposedly retired from touring altogether. However, of that ill-judged decision he later said: "You know I'm one of these people that if you catch me on the wrong day, I'm like, 'Fuck you, get away from me.' I go crazy. I told Sharon, 'I've been doing this for so long. I've never been able to reap the benefits of my hard work. I want to retire.' She said, 'OK.' So we made *No More Tears* and we announced the retirement tour, which was a huge success. I retired and I went home and I suddenly discovered: now what? One thing I found is that you have to have something to retire to. It's not like I'm retiring from a job that I hate for someone that I've hated for years and years and I can't wait to quit. At the end of the *No More Tears* tour, I got home and I was so bored! I'd get up, open the fridge, close it, sit down, get up, open it . . . Sharon said, 'What's going on? I said, 'I'm bored.' She said, 'You drove me crazy about retirement! . . . You can't retire then un-retire!' I'm one of these people that when I'm on the road I want to be home, and when I'm at home I want to be on the road, so I'm always jumping over the fence. You've got to have something to retire to – if you're sitting and looking out the window every day then you'll die."

Ozzy seems to have a love-hate relationship with touring – perhaps unsurprisingly, bearing in mind the fearsome physical load it demands and the temptations it offers. As he explained as early as 1991, when he was first considering the idea of retirement: "I smile when I'm onstage; I'm having a good time, you know? When it's not working, I get pissed off, but when it's working I get this feeling . . . It's like everyone is part of my band and we're all having this great big party. There's nothing to beat this type of feeling. When I get that vibe, that magic that comes out of me onstage, there's not a woman, there's not a drug, there's nothing in this world that can compare to it. It's like, the fucking thrill of the audience is better than Ecstasy. Believe me, if you could sit down and mathematically figure it out, everyone would be a rock star . . . When you've got the crowd in your hands, believe me, it's beyond any thought you could ever imagine. And when it goes the other way, it's beyond any bad feeling. And when I can't make it work for one reason or another I become extremely miserable. There are people that have got this power and people that haven't. I like people working for me that I don't know how they can play what they do, because I haven't got an ounce of fucking rhythm. I saw Aerosmith and Mötley Crüe, and they've got this magic.

"But what often happens to people is that ego gets in the way, their ego starts telling them what they should be doing. And if you start listening to your ego, it's out the window because you lose the natural feeling. I've been doing this for 24 years and I still get the horrible feeling that it's going to be a failure. I still get stage fright. I'm fucking terrible to be around until the show. When I played at Long Beach recently, I was screaming on the phone, 'It's going to be a total disaster. I haven't done a gig since Russia. I'm gonna go to a doctor, my throat doesn't feel good . . .' That's the way I am. I'm a fucking brat before I go onstage. Then suddenly I'm onstage and I'm all better. But, if I didn't do that, I wouldn't have this thrust inside of me. I admire people who can go play in a tennis championship. Imagine the stress! It's one against one. I'm panic-stricken for the first song; it takes me a song and a half just to settle."

Back to the 2006 Ozzfest – and it was announced that Black Sabbath would not appear at all. As Iommi commented: "We couldn't possibly do Ozzfest again this time, because we've done it two years running now and there's only so much you can do, and I think we need a break from that. And Ozzy, he doesn't particularly want to perform on them anyway this year, so yeah, we take a break, and if things happen again we do it, and that's how we seem to play it. We play it by ear now. If everybody wants to tour and people want to rehearse we usually get together and do it."

The tour schedule was set to run until August 13, with Ozzy on the main stage (for the 10 dates he had specified) over System Of A Down, Disturbed, Hatebreed, Lacuna Coil and a further unspecified act at the time of writing. The second stage was set to feature a grab-bag of respectable B-league acts including Black Label Society, Bleeding Through, Strapping Young Lad and The Red Chord.

Of course, with Ozzy's partial involvement, rumours soon had it that the Ozzfest was on its way out. These were fuelled by reports that Korn had been offered a slot but had turned it down: as guitarist James 'Munky' Shaffer told *Launch*, "We did get an offer to do Ozzfest, but I don't remember, it fell through fast because we're wanting to do our own festival. You know, I think it's time for us to start making those plans for the future and it would've been just settling. It's just too easy just to – I mean, it's still cool, but for us right now, it's important for us to establish ourselves and our own fans." Korn had previously run a successful tour called Family Values in 1998 with Rammstein, Limp Bizkit and Ice Cube.

With this development – the first inklings that the mighty Ozzfest might have run its course – came more musings on the subject of the state of modern metal from Ozzy and Iommi. The guitarist pondered, "Things are very, very different nowadays, of course, from when we started, and . . . we're one of the very first, for doing what we're doing. But there's been so many bands since then, of course, and there's some really good bands, there really is. Some of those we've had on Ozzfest have been good. But as far as who [could be as influential as Sabbath], I wouldn't know . . . There's been so many, but I think it'll find a way at the end of the day, it always does. It goes round in circles and somebody pops out. But whether it's got the longevity, I don't know. I don't know if that happens these days now. Things seem to be moving a lot quicker, and people are in and out, you know. To be able to hold for 30 years or 40 years is a bit of a miracle now, I should think."

Ozzy staunchly defended the tour, saying: "The Ozzfest is kind of like a mania fucking circus on the road, you know. That's one of the things I'm proud of. There's nowhere for these fucking kids to play, so we've given them a place to play their music . . . System Of A Down came from there, a lot of bands made it from the Ozzfest. Limp Bizkit, the fucking list goes on and on. Korn, they made it."

The legacy of the Ozzfest, if there is to be one, will be the inspiration to play music, Ozzy mused: "I like to feel that if I pass the torch around, if I've given any kid out there the inspiration to pick up the guitar or pick up a microphone or get a band and want to have some fun, then that's great, but it certainly wasn't my personal intention to have this thing happen, you know. I mean, I'm not saying I don't like it. I love it, you know. I'd be an idiot to say I didn't like it. I mean, I love every minute of it, but I don't really know how to handle it to be honest to you."

So what of a new Sabbath album? After all, it would be a genuine shame if this fantastic band ended their studio career with 1994's *Forbidden*.

Asked years later why *Forbidden* had been such a weak album in a Sabbath fan-club chat, Iommi explained: "I'm not happy with that album. I was at first, but when you sit back . . . you get involved in it and you can't see what's wrong. We brought in Ernie C. to do production; which was a bit difficult really because I had to leave him to it, because he was brought in to do that job. One of the problems was we weren't all there at the same time – when we were writing it. Cozy and Neil were still contracted to do other stuff, so it ended up with just Tony Martin, Geoff Nicholls and myself just jamming around and putting ideas down. It all came together very quickly and we didn't really have time to reflect, make sure it was the right songs and the right way of doing it . . . because we had no drummer, Cozy was away doing other stuff."

It seemed, though, that Black Sabbath's much-desired new album might never come to pass, with Ozzy reasoning: "I love the guys and we had fun and all became friendly again. But it's time to move on. I don't want to make another Sabbath album, not if it's not up to scratch. I could put any old bollocks out and it would probably sell. But what's the point in demolishing such a great thing?"

Iommi told *Billboard*: "We talked about an album and we've talked a couple of times on and off, you know, but I just now go with the flow. If it looks [good] I'd love to do another album, but it's got to be right and you can't just do an album for the sake of it. We wouldn't do that. It's got to be a very good album. But we haven't gotten any further with it, and it seems to have gone very quiet on that side."

Funnily enough, when Iommi says that things have gone quite 'quiet' he seems to be ignoring the fact that he, along with Ozzy and Sharon, is the key instigator of any new movement in that direction. But this points to a simple fact: perhaps he feels that he has done everything he wants to do. Prevous statements bear this out, as he once said, "I don't think I've got any other greatest achievements. I mean, through Sabbath I've been allowed to achieve quite a lot of what I've wanted to achieve. That's not financial – it's more being recognised for what I do. When this Hall Of Fame thing came up it was a great honour . . . there is nothing I can think of that I really want to do. I'm quite happy with the way things are, I'm very happy with my life at the moment."

It's not as if Iommi is short of musical inspiration, as he said, "I've got tapes at home . . . boxes and boxes of tapes full of riffs. For one, it's hard to label a riff – you might have 200 riffs on a tape; unless there's a song you can't remember what the riff is. You know, tape one, riff number 25 –

what is it? How do you describe it? It's so bloody confusing! If somebody's got an idea for sorting that out it'll be welcome!"

Ozzy added: "Well, we have tried. I guess it will happen or it won't happen. I mean, I could probably go in the studio tomorrow with 'em and come out with an album written by Tony Iommi, Bill Ward, Geezer Butler and myself, but if it wasn't up to the standard where we used to be, what's the fucking point in doing it? Because it's called 'Black Sabbath', because it'll be Ozzy, Tony, Geezer and Bill. It's a pretty heavy thing to take on, because we're all different people now; we've all gone our own ways and got our own families, we're not four angry guys any more. But I'm sure we could do one, but if it's not up to the standard, then I wouldn't do it. We did try to write, some of it's OK . . . I've read a few things in some of these magazines that say, 'Hey guys, you should get rid of Ozzy; you got no intention of doing an album.' You've gotta be fucking mad. If you think that I wouldn't do a Black Sabbath album if the material was great, you gotta be stoned."

Pressure has recently been on Sabbath not just for a new album, but also for a full box set of rarities and live classics. Iommi, nominally in charge of the catalogue, reasoned of the many available bootlegs: "I've had copies – tapes – given to me. I can't really go into a store because they know me, and if I go, 'Have you got any Black Sabbath bootlegs?' They go, 'Oh no, we don't do them!' I don't buy bootlegs but if I get sent them I'll listen to them and see what they're like. The one thing I do dislike about them is, if there's going to be a bootleg, at least let it be good quality so people who are buying that album can have a good sound, as opposed to the poor, crappy sound of all those bootlegs . . . I like to hear them . . . I also like to hear the set we done at that time. Although I have kept tapes over the years; I used to get a tape of every show we played, I had thousands and thousands of tapes! I like to hear them, it's just the sound quality."

Ozzy told MTV that he had discovered an archive of Sabbath material: "I found more of them . . . I looked around and I threw about 50,000 old cheeseburger packages out, and I found another box full of tapes, and I've got to send them to a lab up here in New York that can repair them. It's amazing what they can do with these things now. I mean they bring it all back to life, you know. I don't know what they must do. It's really good . . . They were in a big heap all knotted. It took me about a half a day to unravel them, but I knew it was old, because on the box it said . . . in the beginning, when we changed the name to 'Black Sabbath', as kids we used to try and write it in different ways . . . in different cool styles, you know, and I knew we were still kids then. So I opened this box, and this musty, musty old tape in there, and I thought, 'Wow.' It was like finding the lost Ark or something. I was like, 'What's this?' I love it. We were all so out of it all the time. I'm more out of it. I've forgotten albums. So, we just found recently another box full of bits of tape which I'm going to send to a laboratory to see what's on it. It will probably be a lot of interviews or something, you know."

But there's no way of knowing what will happen in this area. Do we even know who holds the purse strings any more?

The future of the individual musicians, even if there is to be no more 'real' Black Sabbath, is interesting to predict. For example, Bill Ward is certainly a man with potential. He seems to be a renewed person, as he told *Shockwaves*: "I feel like I've got a bit more confidence. I'm also trying to learn other instruments and I'm allowing my melodies to come out a lot more. I have no restrictions upon myself – whatever is gonna come out of me I let it come out of me. Lyrically, I'm turning new corners all the time, because I'm in the process of self-discovery and so wherever I was at 19 years ago, I'm not that person now. I'm 19 years sober, but I feel I've grown just a little bit, enough to be able to identify myself a little bit more . . . It's easy to blame and criticise . . . that was me. It's easy to covet and to blame somebody else's messes. It's easy to look at somebody and go, 'Look at that asshole, shame on them.' All these ingredients in a person are quite negative, and they tear the body to pieces . . . I know Henry Rollins is a big Sabbath fan, and he talks sometimes about the lows and highs for himself as well. If the music that I write can help other people in some way, then that's great. If I judge what I'm doing . . . it's not up to me to allow judgements of myself, I had to stop doing that because I drove myself crazy."

Like so many recovering alcoholics, Bill appears almost to have lived life as two separate people – pre- and post-booze. "I used to kill the pain. And now I'm facing the pain. I'm not pain-free every single day – I'm just an ordinary drunk. I'm just a sober drunk. I couldn't stand the pain for a long time, man. All that what was reflected in Sabbath for me was all past life. I can't live 100 per cent of whatever I was then. And it all meant something – all those songs like 'War Pigs' – were so precious to the history of art. When I came in to do the reunion – as a sober person – for a moment I had to question myself and say, 'How in the hell can I play in a reunion when the songs emulated me in my drunk life?' Then I stopped for a second and said, 'Fuck it, that is me . . . that was me.' All you got to do is get back in touch with yourself as you are and as soon as I tied that together, it was no problem."

He's lucky: he retained enough of his faculties to recall his whole career. Ozzy, it seems, can't do the same. As Ward said: "I have some very fond memories. Now, getting to be an older man, I look back and think, 'My God, these guys are just beautiful.' We were on a plane coming back from Texas the other day, and I looked into the clouds and just started to think about Geezer for some reason, and then I saw Ozzy and I saw Tony and they just looked really well and young, and this is the God's honest truth . . . I just started to cry a little bit. I was crying because it was just such a good vision. That might sound a bit old-fashioned, but I can see that now . . . when I was drinking I had those feelings, but it was a distorted feeling, now there is no distortion. It was distorted because high highs were really high, so laughter lasted over an hour, and low lows were really low – so if I was really angry . . . I was really angry! Now, high highs are still there, I just don't laugh for an hour – if I did I would probably have another heart attack!"

Healthwise, Bill is in good shape, as he told me in 2005: "I had a heart problem seven years ago, so I try to look after myself. I walk a lot and I do a lot of rigorous exercise, so I try to keep myself really active." He added: "I'll leave counselling to the counsellors, those who know something! In my private life I spend a lot of time with other alcoholics. I talk about it all the time. I help them, and by helping them I help myself. If they want to get sober, I help them. I've been on the 12-step programme for a long time. I went through nine hospitals all told, which is not unusual. But I got cleaned up Stateside, eventually. I'm in my 22nd year now. Yes, I've been through therapy – after I got sober I realised there were a lot of things going on with me that I didn't know about. But I went to therapy for certain things. But you know, I don't think drink: I don't, um, I don't do my recovery every day because I'm craving for a drink, it's nothing to do with that. I do my recovery every day in order to have a really decent life, and what I mean by a decent life is the way that I feel on the inside. I don't mean, I'm going to be a fuckin' millionaire or anything like that: in fact, it's quite the opposite of material possessions, you know. It's about your own strength . . . It's made it easier to be everything. I've been really discovering myself as a musician in the last 22 years. I didn't even know who the hell I was until I started getting sober. I'm still discovering all kinds of things about me, and I push myself as far as I can push myself. As a drummer, I've got so much to learn. And I push myself as a musician and a dad. I feel like I'm at the beginning of my life, most days."

Bill is still attempting to get his album, *Beyond Aston*, completed. He told me: "I'm still trying to get that done. I do it piecemeal because I finance it myself, you know. I do have a record company but it's not too healthy at the moment, you know! I've got a few mixes still to do but then it'll be almost done. I've got another two albums behind it so I want it out, because it's driving me crazy."

He, too, wants a new Sabbath album to be recorded: "From my perspective, Tony is more than keen to move forward on a Sabbath album, and as far as I know everybody's still keen to do it. I'm straining at the bit to get it done. We're trying to find a time to get the songwriting process done. We did some writing a few years ago and it dwindled and fell off the shelf. Since then we've been touring, but the talking about getting a new one done hasn't died out. We've all said that we want to finish it up . . . How it works is, if Oz is OK and up for it, then we get a call from Sharon or a manager. That's the engine that moves it along. If you asked me if I'd be up for it, I'd say, yeah, you're fuckin' right I am! But Sharon and Ozzy have agreed to it. The last thing Sharon said to me in September on the Ozzfest was, we'll have to make time for this new album. It's been out in the open for ages. I'd love to go onstage with some new stuff, some new music that kicks ass and moves along. We still play tight and I don't see why we can't put some good stuff together."

Of the band-members, it's Bill who is most in touch with the current metal scene, thanks to an internet radio show in LA on which he guests every week. (Iommi has a similar show − called *Black Sunday* − which focuses more on classic rock.) As Ward told me: "I think what modern extreme metal lacks in soul it makes up in energy and technique. Look at In Flames, Shadows Fall, Killswitch Engage − just three bands off the top of my head − their energy is incredible. I would have a tough time to match it, to be honest, with the energy that goes into the bass drum. These kids are playing 32nd beats! I've done that with Black Sabbath and what would have been regarded as the real fast bass drums of the day, but the way these guys are playing it . . . they have special foot plates now which are unorthodox and not the ones we've been using for the last 50 years. I've spent some time with these drummers, and I'm like, what the fuck did you do there? It's almost like they're dancing on the foot-pedals. Some of these guys are pretty overweight, though! Gene Hoglan of Strapping Young Lad is an example of a guy who may not be as fit as a fiddle, but he kicks ass because he dances."

He went on: "I have a radio show here every month, which I do every month in Los Angeles. I've been playing Grave, In Flames, Soilwork . . . my favourite band right now is Mnemnic, who are signed to Nuclear Blast. They're great, I fuckin' love 'em! Kind of like a more refined

366

Slipknot. I love the Knot, I've got some buddies in that band. They're one of the bands that kicked this off. Going back, look at Slayer and Metallica: you can see where this groove started. I also love The Mars Volta, Machine Head, American Head Charge, Pantera of course . . . I felt a bit weird about playing Pantera on the radio, with Dimebag dying. Pantera were a great band. So those are some of the bands they play regularly. I love new music."

Geezer, too, is a reformed character since his statue-headbutting days, although he does, however, have clinical depression to deal with, as he told me: "We talked about it regularly, once we'd all admitted it! Ozzy and Bill helped each other out with their alcoholism, too: Bill became an alcoholism counsellor, so him and Ozzy have got really close on all sorts of aspects over the years. But because I wasn't an alcoholic I wasn't in on that." With all this under control, a solo career seems highly likely for Butler.

Musically, Geezer is a much improved player since the early days, saying: "I have definitely improved since then. Though sometimes I hear the first album and think, 'How the bloody hell did I do that?' Not technically, but the way I used to bend the notes in certain things. I've gotten to stages where I can't even look at a bass and I think I've gone as far as I can with it and I'm just not good enough to improve any more − I've got mental blocks on what to play. Tony will come up with a riff and I'll be sitting there thinking, 'What the bloody hell am I going to play to that?' It's not that it's a bad riff but I don't feel up to being musically capable of making it a better riff. It's just like writer's block − some people get used to it, some people don't. I used to get it a lot and think I was crap. I'd think, 'I've got to give up, I'm absolute rubbish.' Having someone like Tony talk to me about it helps a lot. The worst thing I can do is bottle it up and believe in it myself. Only you can get yourself out of it in the end. If somebody says, 'What about doing this?' you think, 'It's their idea, it's not mine, I'm still crap.' You have to give yourself time. I've talked it out with Tony, for instance, and maybe we'll go into something else and I'll get more time to come back and hopefully come up with something I think is up to my old standards . . . I just accept my limitations − I know my limitations now. I was trying to bloody master this thumb bass for a long time. Then you hear someone who can really play it and you know you'll never be as good as them. Plus it doesn't fit in with anything we do, so what's the point? I know my limitations and I stay within them. I don't profess to be the greatest bass player on earth. As long as it works within the band, that's all I ever want . . . I always strive for something out of the ordinary rather than just chugging along playing one note. I'll try and do anything else but that."

He also isn't short of inspiration, finding that ideas come to him at regular intervals: "With me it's always after a tour. You're doing it every day and getting the groove of the thing. You come off tour and you still think, 'It's time to go out and play now.' You've finished the tour so you go up to the recording studio and put something down. That's the only time when I get inspired to write. The only thing that really gives me inspiration is playing live on tour. Immediately after the tour is when I come out with most of my things. You are all riled up from playing every night. Your fingers are working properly. You're still thinking about the road. You're still thinking rock'n'roll."

When it comes to composing songs, Geezer still follows the old Sabbath recipe, apparently: "When we first used to write, it used to be all together. That's the way it was done. Tony would come out with a riff, then I would put the bass in and Bill Ward would drum along. Ozzy would instantly put a lyric or a vocal melody on top. You actually would hear the song the way it was going to end up. You knew immediately if it's going to work or not and where to put the bits in what songs. The collaboration was immediate and it was all there. If we got stuck, we'd do a vocal bit next or a change. Dio would like to have the riff first, then go away and come up with his side of it; whereas with Ozzy it was always instant. We always knew what it was gonna be. We could always change something and that would be it, and then I would go and put the lyrics to his melody and it would be finished . . . We were never afraid to do whatever we felt at the time. I think that's what kept us as Black Sabbath. Listen to anything past the first three albums; we do soul stuff, not what everybody else would do, but there's funky bass lines in there or funky guitar in bits, some synthesisers and straight-ahead ballads. Anything. We thought it would kill the band if we weren't allowed to grow up within it . . . You get known for the original stuff. Obviously everything that you ever write isn't 100 per cent original. It can't be."

Geezer looks back with justifiable pride, saying: "It is nice because when we first started people put us down, said we were not relevant, said our music was not real music, totally put us down. It is nice all these years later to be still playing it and be acclaimed for doing it. When you see all of these bands citing you as influences, it makes you feel relevant . . . back when we first started I was 18, and we thought 25-year-old people were old people – and pop groups would last a few years and couldn't go on because they were too old. We grew up in an era when you just could not be old. It was like The Who song, 'I hope I die before I get old', but now it seems like the older bands are bigger than ever. Now we get a mixed crowd where you have kids and up to old blokes like me.

"I think the Eighties were the worst period . . . Because you had these horrible pop bands growing their hair and calling themselves metal. Bands like Poison and Warrant and all that, it was horrible, all of those horrible ballads and all of that sickly crap. It was not furthering anything as far as I am concerned. Then you have good bands like Anthrax and Metallica that took it back to where it should be . . . If you're a pop band, don't say you're a metal band. Poison and Warrant were about as metal as the Backstreet Boys. People can see through that easily and that is why none of them are not really around much any more."

There's evidently some frustration on Geezer's part – as there is on Bill's – that Sabbath is weighed down by so much inertia. "It takes so long to come up with anything!" he told me. "We still do it like we used to do it. Me with my bass guitar, Tony with a guitar, and when we try and write something together it's all down to Tony, really. When I come up with a guitar riff, people don't really take me seriously. It's like, oh, you're not the guitarist, and it's really weird because I can't get past that. That's why I love doing my own stuff. I can't get round it: we tried three years ago to come up with material for the new album, and I played all my stuff, and it was like, Tony hasn't played that so we can't do it. I just got really pissed off and now I've told them that Tony and Ozzy can go off and write the album, and I'll play bass on it when they've written it. I've got so used to doing my own stuff, and I like working really fast, where they like to take their time.

"We came up with about eight songs, two or maybe three could be workable – but they're not brilliant. The tapes are all there, but I didn't think they came anywhere near the old Sabbath stuff. I don't think we should record something just for the sake of putting it out: it has to come up to the old Sabbath stuff, especially after all these years. It has to be something incredible. That's why I like doing my own music, you know – there's no pressure to sell millions or anything, or to make sure it's radio-friendly and all this crap. It would be great if we could do it, you know, because Tony played me some incredible riffs. I think they might get together eventually. I played them the riff from my new song, 'Aural Sects', but there was absolutely no reaction. It's hard, you know, it's really frustrating for me. It's just as well I've got my own band, or I'd go mental . . . again!

"I'd love Tony and Ozzy to come with something together. It's still there. Tony's just finished his new solo album and he's still writing great riffs, but it's so hard to get the band together and nail a song. Getting the four of us to go, yes, it's a great riff, is difficult, because what I think is a great riff, maybe Ozzy doesn't. The way we've always worked in the past is that we all jam together and then we pick out the riff that we like collectively, and work on that. Even right back at the start it was like that, it's what Sabbath was founded on. We all had to like the song we were working on, or it just wasn't us."

Tony, now acknowledged as the master of his craft, remains typically modest about his achievements. He once said, in a way that epitomised his relaxed attitude to fame and fortune: "I think everybody has a unique style – it's just that certain way you play. I imagine people try to sound like somebody else, but it's hard to do because you have a unique way of playing and how you create that sound. You should try to develop your own style and go from there. We're players from the heart, we play from within . . . It's amazing to me as well. It just happens particularly now. Everything seems to have worked well and fallen into place. In the past, I've done riffs where it's just gone past everybody. They might think, 'Oh, that's a good riff', but nobody else has taken a notice even way back with Ozzy. I've done some riffs that I thought were good and nobody's sort of picked up on it. I think a lot of stuff in the past has gone down the drain because nobody's picked up on it."

Even manufacturers take note of what Iommi and Butler want nowadays, whereas they were hardly falling over themselves to provide equipment for them when Sabbath were in their Eighties doldrums. Iommi told me: "I use the signature Gibson SG that they've made for me, the Iommi series. It has smaller fretwire and 24 frets and crosses on it. They also do an Epiphone model, which I've played onstage and I really like. It's great for how little it costs. Gibson also made me a custom Les Paul, which was absolutely beautiful, but I like the double cutaways on the SG and the fact that it's really light. I've got a lot of Gibsons, but I honestly don't know how many. There are loads in storage, and I have about 30 at home.

"And Laney do an Iommi amp which I like a lot. I only use a wah-wah pedal and a chorus pedal onstage, the distortion comes out of the amp. It doesn't bother me if it doesn't sound exactly like the old Sabbath distorted sound, I just play me! In the old days I used to use a pedal which boosted the guitar sound before it went into the amp, that was how it distorted. I suggested putting one in the amp to a few manufacturers, but of course they didn't listen. They all said that amps had to be clean. And nowadays all the amps have got it built in."

As for the status of Sabbath, he trotted out the party line: "I'd like to do a new album. We did some tracks two years ago which I think sounded really good, and Ozzy was up for it – but everyone's so busy. To be honest, I don't want to stick my neck out in case they take me up on it . . . Well, I lived the *Osbournes* show for 35 years. It's just Ozzy, isn't it? They possibly edit it a tiny bit to look more extreme than it is, but basically it's a true representation of what his life is – chaos!"

And Geezer, of course, is a respected bass player across the industry, even if he seems to think that his playing could be better. His gear list is impressive, as he told me: "I'm using Lakland basses and Ampeg SVT amps . . . you can't beat them for my sound. They're modelled on Fender Precision and Jazz basses. The sound is like an old Fender, because I don't really like the new Fender stuff. I collect Fender basses, so I sort of know which sound I'm looking for – that old Sixties sound. It has that nice edge to it. I used to always play the wide Precision neck but now I've started to like the Jazz neck as well. I vary it onstage because a lot of the songs we tune to different keys. We tune down three semitones for some songs, some are two and some are one. It depends on what I'm tuned down to, what neck I use."

Elsewhere, he said that certain manufacturers took their time to appreciate his requirements: "I love Spector basses but then they went bust so I can't get any custom ones. I went on to Vigier and they were really helpful. Fender asked me to use a Fender Precision. I said it's got to be 24 frets to start. 'Oh no – this is what you get.' Bollocks. Vigier said, 'What do you want?' I said, 'This is the basic thing – redesign it for me.'"

There will be a new Iommi album at some point, it's safe to predict. Iommi thoroughly enjoyed doing his solo record of 2000. The style of *Iommi* had evolved by chance, Iommi explained to *Cosmik Debris'* DJ Johnson: "When I first started putting stuff together, I wrote about 15 or 20 songs trying to find a direction where I was going with it, because I wrote a lot of different sort of stuff. Then, of course, I went back to the riff again. Then I started putting some stuff down, but then, of course, the Black Sabbath reunion tour came up, and so I had to shelve what I was doing. There wasn't time to work on it because we were working a lot with the reunion around the world. So I could only work on this project in between and/or after we'd finished the tour . . . it was really good. When you take a project on, obviously you wonder, 'Oh, God, what's it going to be like working with these people,' you know, which could be anybody. You could know them for as long as you like, but until you actually work with them, you never know. But they were absolutely great. I really, thoroughly enjoyed it. They were really nice people, real gentlemen, real polite. We had a great time and real fun making it, and I think that comes over in it. We were all pretty excited about working with each other." And why shouldn't the exact same approach apply next time?

Sharon, it seems, will continue to reap the enormous success that she has earned in recent years. Still only 48 at the time of writing, she is in the prime of her life as a businesswoman, and has learned vast amounts about the industry she works (and lives) in. As she once explained before resolving the rift with her father, Don Arden, she had a fairly early education in showbusiness: "I learned everything from him, and I saw what it did. It doesn't work. Because every artist he ever, ever managed left him – from Gene Vincent onwards. It doesn't work! I mean, I lived through it as a child, I saw . . . I can remember the arguments with Gene Vincent. But, you can't get away with that shit any more, you just can't. It works to the point that you will find that one vulnerable kid that's talented, and you can get them for a while, two to three years, but after that they're gone. They wise up real quick . . . It's like the old form of management! . . . My father was one of the main fucking culprits from the Fifties on. He'd get these people and turn them into stars, but then everything went to him. He would put them in a house and give them a car, he would give them money for clothes and whatever, but then nothing more. They basically worked for him."

And Ozzy? Ozzy will do what's he's always done, which is oscillate between madman in public and family man in private. He has always discussed his children with great affection, once explaining: "I have one daughter, one son, and an adopted son, from that first marriage . . . On the *Diary Of A Madman* album cover, the kid in the background – that's my son. He's my double. His name's Louis, but I call him Bombins. It's just a name I thought of for him, because I don't like regular names. I wanted to call my daughter Burt Reynolds, but my wife wouldn't have it."

He once added of Louis: "I turned my 15-year-old on to fucking marijuana. I said to him, 'Son, I'd prefer you to smoke this than tobacco.' He says, 'Why, Daddy?' I says, 'Because you can't physically smoke as many cigarettes of marijuana as you can of tobacco, because tobacco is the [most] subtle drug of all. Because you don't realise. You smoke a big fat joint and you're dead – you're crashed."

But he seems to know who he is and what he represents – a true sign of wisdom. As he told *Launch*: "I'm about caring, I'm about people, and I'm

372

about entertaining people. I'm a family man. A husband. A father. I've been a lot of other things over the years, which we don't really want to talk about. I'm always working on trying to better myself, you know? I think that that is an ongoing thing with me. I think I'll do that for the rest of my life. I'm always thinking of what I can do today to better my life. Like quitting smoking . . . Whenever I meet someone who doesn't know me, they say, 'Oh you're the guy who bites the heads off everything.' I get kind of cheesed off with it, but at least they remember. The thing that pisses me off is that that's not what I'm about. If that's what you think Ozzy Osbourne's about, then you're way off."

Nonetheless, the life he's led is not something he chooses to deny: "You know, I've had every known chemical – cocaine, booze – and tobacco is the hardest one in the world for me to quit . . . somebody said to me this morning, 'To what do you attribute your longevity?' I don't know. I mean, I couldn't have planned my life out better. By all accounts I should be dead! The abuse I put my body through: the drugs, the alcohol, the life-style I've lived the last 30 years! Now, some rare fly will fly over me, crap on my shoulder, and I'll drop dead, you know? My life story is a real-life story. If I have people I've admired from a distance and have the occasion to meet them, I've been very disappointed. I've had this picture in my mind, and when I meet them, it's never right. I'm a big Beatles fan; I was on the Concorde with Paul and Linda McCartney. I could have met them but I didn't because I didn't want to shatter my fantasy. I would have loved to meet Lennon."

His biggest recent achievement, as he recalled, was the Ozzfest: "The real story of the Ozzfest: 10 years ago, a friend of mine in the music business who does TV and radio in England said to me, 'God willing you survive, I could see you in the future having a rock'n'roll circus – you being the ringmaster.' All of a sudden, in 1996, Sharon, my wife, said, 'What do you want to do?' and I said, 'I wonder if it would work – what Jonathan King said. Could I work my nuts off for two and a half hours?' She said, 'Give it a whirl!' I did four Ozzfests in 1996. They sold out right away. In 1996, I launched Ozz Records. I wanted to sign new bands. We never said we were looking for strictly metal bands – I wanted folk, jazz, poetry, just to give someone a break. The one mistake I made was calling it Ozz Records, so people said, 'I'm not sending my record in because it's not metal and he won't listen to it anyway.' Our office was full of mail of new kinds of metal bands. Which was okay. But then Ozzfest took off and the label went to the back burner. So in 1997, Sharon asked me if I wanted to do it again, and we did 22 more shows and word-of-mouth spread like wildfire. We were the second highest-grossing tour . . . But we're not fools. I'm not taking it for granted that this will last forever. It will peter out eventually. And I'll move on. It's all exciting. Usually you write, record, tour. Write, record, tour. But you have to let the mouse off the wheel after a while and do something with a different approach, you know?"

Of the state of health of modern heavy metal, Ozzy told *Mojo*: "People keep saying, 'I bet you're glad it's been revived,' but it's never gone away. In 32 years I've never been out of work. What happens is whenever the music industry gets boring they'd bring out 'Smoke On The Water' and 'Paranoid'. Over here, in the States, they're all getting rhinestone fucking Ozzy T-shirts and studding up old clothes." Of his old stagewear, he complained: "I should have kept them – they'll sell for a fortune at Sotheby's. Some of them I've given away to be auctioned for charity – then this guy, Tony, who's now working for me, bought one of them at an auction so the fucking thing's ended up back in my house! Remember when I used to wear that stupid chain-mail suit? Or that dumb glitter outfit in the Eighties? I looked like Liberace on fucking beer."

As for his stage act, he laughed: "I've dressed in women's clothes, I've dressed as a Nazi. I've gone onstage naked. I've gone on so drunk I didn't even know I did a show. I've done so many stupid things, but it's all part of Ozzy. I never pre-planned 99.9 per cent of the things I've done. Some were drastically wrong, some were drastically right. I don't know if you saw [VH1's *Behind The Music* documentary] recently. In one hour, it's impossible to write my life down. I come from a rather large family, three older sisters and two younger brothers. On the documentary, they interviewed my sister and it was the first time I'd seen her in years. I've had a very, very unique life. I often sit back and remember when I had no money – when you're in the middle of it, you get depressed thinking it's going to last forever. All of a sudden, out of nowhere – a bolt of lightning – here I am! I'm very well-off; I've got property all over the place, I've had a very fruitful career. But I've never had a number one album in America. But I've lasted several generations and somebody says to me, 'Do you notice any difference in the audience?' I've been doing it now for 30 years. Some of the fans are older, but I've picked up new fans along the way. But when you listen to one of my first albums I don't sound like I'm 21, I don't sound like I'm 49. I sound like Ozzy."

He concluded: "I'm not one of these people who says, 'I'm going to plan next year out and this is going to happen.' I'm a very lucky man. I don't even play an instrument. I just sing and entertain. I don't consider myself a great singer. I have a connection with the audience. I'd like to be them, and I'd like them to be me for an hour and a half. I get criticised for being the Antichrist, causing kids to commit suicide. That's total bullshit. My intentions are not that. But every year, they have Halloween, and all I do is take Halloween night out on the road every night. It's like a Halloween party every night."

The wild man of rock is no longer the Ozzy of the Noughties. And nor is the drug and booze life for Geezer Butler, who told me: "I've had two kids, I've been there and done it. One's 24 and one's just turned 20. No, it never stops, you still call them every single day to see how they're doing. They really like my music. Biff, the oldest one, he's actually on two of the tracks, doing harmonies, and James, who's at Oxford at the moment, really likes it. He's not a musician but he loves music, I think he likes all this pissin' DJ stuff, this turntable thing – I haven't got a clue how you do it. I think he only does it to get free booze at Oxford."

It seems that Sabbath's place in history is assured.

Asked how he would like his band to be remembered, Tony Iommi reasoned with his usual reasonable manner: "Obviously for our music, and we've been there a long time, we've stuck to it, what we believe in . . . But it's nice to be remembered, and I think things like the Hall of Fame are making sure we're there and will be remembered.

Ozzy, asked the same question, replied: "Well, just the fact that we're remembered is enough for me. I know when I fucking croak, I know what they're gonna put on my fucking grave: 'The man that bit the head off the fucking bat in Des Moines, Iowa . . . whatever the fuck it was . . .'"

UK DISCOGRAPHY

Singles	Label and year	Chart
Evil Woman	Fontana, 1970	n/a
Paranoid	Vertigo, 1970	4
Never Say Die	Vertigo, 1978	21
Hard Road	Vertigo, 1978	33
Neon Knights	Vertigo, 1980	22
Die Young	Vertigo, 1980	41
Mob Rules	Vertigo, 1981	46
Turn Up The Night	Vertigo, 1982	37
Headless Cross	IRS, 1989	62
TV Crimes	IRS, 1992	33

Albums		
Black Sabbath	Vertigo, 1970	8
Paranoid	Vertigo, 1970	1
Master Of Reality	Vertigo, 1971	5
Volume 4	Vertigo, 1972	8
Sabbath Bloody Sabbath	Vertigo, 1973	4
Sabotage	NEMS, 1975	7
We Sold Our Soul For Rock 'N' Roll	NEMS, 1975	35
Technical Ecstasy	Vertigo, 1976	13
Never Say Die!	Vertigo, 1978	12
Heaven And Hell	Vertigo, 1980	9
Live At Last	NEMS, 1980	5
Mob Rules	Mercury, 1981	12
Live Evil	Vertigo, 1982	13
Born Again	Vertigo, 1983	4
Seventh Star	Vertigo, 1986	27
The Eternal Idol	Vertigo, 1987	66
Headless Cross	IRS, 1989	31
Tyr	IRS, 1990	24
Dehumanizer	IRS, 1992	28
Cross Purposes	IRS, 1994	41
Cross Purposes Live	IRS, 1994	n/a
Forbidden	IRS, 1995	71
The Sabbath Stones	IRS, 1996	n/a

Reunion	Epic, 1998	41
The Best Of Black Sabbath	Metal-Is, 2000	24
Past Lives	Sanctuary, 2002	n/a
Black Box: Black Sabbath 1970–1978 (US)	Rhino, 2004	n/a

Ozzy Osbourne Singles

Crazy Train	Jet, 1980	49
Mr Crowley	Jet, 1980	46
Bark At The Moon	Epic, 1983	21
So Tired	Epic, 1984	20
Shot In The Dark	Epic, 1986	20
The Ultimate Sin/Lightning Strikes	Epic, 1986	72
No More Tears	Epic, 1991	32
Mama I'm Coming Home	Epic, 1991	46
Perry Mason	Epic, 1995	23
I Just Want You	Epic, 1996	43
Dreamer	Epic, 2002	18
Changes (with Kelly Osbourne)	Sanctuary, 2003	1

Ozzy Osbourne Albums

Blizzard Of Ozz	Jet, 1980	7
Diary Of A Madman	Jet, 1981	14
Talk Of The Devil	Jet, 1982	21
Bark At The Moon	Epic, 1983	24
The Ultimate Sin	Epic, 1986	8
Tribute	Epic, 1987	13
No Rest For The Wicked	Epic, 1988	23
Just Say Ozzy	Epic, 1990	69
No More Tears	Epic, 1991	17
Ozzmosis	Epic, 1995	22
The Ozzman Cometh	Epic, 1997	68
Down To Earth	Epic, 2001	19
The Essential Ozzy Osbourne	Epic, 2003	21
The Prince Of Darkness	Sanctuary, 2005	n/a
Under Cover	Sanctuary, 2005	n/a

Tony Iommi Albums

Iommi	Divine, 2000	n/a
The 1996 DEP Sessions With Glenn Hughes	Mayan, 2004	n/a
Fused	Sanctuary, 2005	n/a

377

Geezer Butler Albums

Plastic Planet	Raw Power, 1995	n/a
Black Science	Sum, 1997	n/a
Ohmwork	Mayan, 2005	n/a

Bill Ward Albums

Ward One: Along The Way	Chameleon, 1990	n/a
When The Bough Breaks	Cleopatra, 1997	n/a

Kelly Osbourne Singles

Papa Don't Preach	Epic, 2002	3
Shut Up	Epic, 2003	12
Come Dig Me Out	Sanctuary, 2004	n/a
One Word	Sanctuary, 2005	9

Kelly Osbourne Albums

Shut Up	Epic, 2003	31
Changes	Sanctuary, 2004	n/a
Sleeping In The Nothing	Sanctuary, 2005	57

Ozzfest Albums

Ozzfest Live	Red Ant, 1997	n/a
Ozzfest 2001: The Second Millennium	Sony, 2001	n/a
Ozzfest: Second Stage Live	Virgin, 2001	n/a
Ozzfest 2002	Columbia, 2002	n/a

Black Sabbath's albums have been reissued on several occasions, notably by Sanctuary imprint Castle, in a variety of formats (CD, enhanced CD, miniature LP replica, you name it).

SOURCES

All quotes used come from original interviews by the author (see introduction for full list) except where stated below.

PART ONE

CHAPTER ONE

"We only had three bedrooms . . ." David Gans, January 1982
"A no-frills place . . ." Bob Nalbandian and Mark Miller of Shockwaves, 2002
"Birmingham is on a par . . ." Jeb Wright of Classic Rock Revisited, April 2003
"Two of my brothers . . ." Loudplanet, 2004
"He used to call . . ." CNN, 2004
"I'm the original clown . . ." David Gans, January 1982
"We used to have this next-door neighbour . . ." David Gans, January 1982
"If you're in a room . . ." Ben Thompson, Independent On Sunday, 1995
"Where I came from . . ." David Gans, January 1982
"We were all destined . . ." Jeb Wright of Classic Rock Revisited, April 2003
"There was some classical music . . ." Guillaume Roos, Sabbathlive
"There's something inside me . . ." Bob Nalbandian and Mark Miller of Shockwaves, 2002
"I used to steal records . . ." David Gans, January 1982
"My early influences were . . ." KNAC
"The timing couldn't have been worse . . ." Guitar World, 2002
"We started playing together . . ." Jeb Wright of Classic Rock Revisited, April 2003
"I just connected . . ." Bob Nalbandian and Mark Miller of Shockwaves, 2002

CHAPTER TWO

"I know all of us . . ." Bob Nalbandian and Mark Miller of Shockwaves, 2002
"Tony came into that band . . ." Jeb Wright of Classic Rock Revisited, April 2003
"We've had our ups . . ." CNN, 2004
"The first gig I can . . ." Jeb Wright of Classic Rock Revisited, April 2003
"Ten Years After . . ." John Stix, Guitar For The Practicing Musician, May 1994

"It seemed to . . ." CNN, 2004

"I learned quite a lot from . . ." Jeb Wright of Classic Rock Revisited, April 2003

"really used to intimidate me . . ." Sylvie Simmons of Mojo, 2000

"The stuff we had . . . " John Stix, Guitar For The Practicing Musician, May 1994

"You know what?" David Gans, January 1982

"We didn't earn a whole lot . . ." Bob Nalbandian and Mark Miller of Shockwaves, 2002

"I just thought they were . . ." Russell Tice, 1999

"When we first got . . ." CNN, 2004

CHAPTER THREE

"We came in . . ." CNN, 2004

"We found in a lot of blues clubs . . ." Knac.com

"It was fuckin' great . . ." Bob Nalbandian and Mark Miller of Shockwaves, 2002

CHAPTER FOUR

"You know, [our] very early shows . . ." Guillaume Roos, Sabbathlive

"When we first . . ." Bass Frontiers, 1996

"[It was] really . . ." John Stix, Guitar For The Practicing Musician, May 1994

"On the first LP . . ." Bass Frontiers, 1996

"Back then you had . . ." John Stix, Guitar For The Practicing Musician, May 1994

"We have a thing . . ." David Gans, 1982

CHAPTER FIVE

"Well, that's actually BS . . ." Gary James, 1994

"I think ['War Pigs'] was a little bit . . ." Bob Nalbandian and Mark Miller of Shockwaves, 2002

"Originally it was . . ." Loudplanet

CHAPTER SIX

Record Plant interview: Harold Bronson, UCLA Daily Bruin, 1972

"You know what that is?" Bob Nalbandian and Mark Miller of Shockwaves, 2002

"Frank Zappa . . ." Ben Thompson, Independent On Sunday, 1995

"We had been in America . . ." Classic Rock Revisited

"I think that was . . ." Metal Sludge

CHAPTER SEVEN

"You've got to remember the time," Mojo, 2000
"I was brought up . . ." Dave Thompson, The Rocket, 1994
"We hid our real message . . ." Guillaume Roos, Sabbathlive
"Any lyrics that . . ." Metal Sludge

CHAPTER EIGHT

"It's more of a basic rock album . . ." Circus, 1975

CHAPTER NINE

"I kind of volunteered." Bob Nalbandian and Mark Miller of Shockwaves, 2002

CHAPTER TEN

"We were potless . . ." David Gans, 1982

PART TWO

CHAPTER ELEVEN

"I'd gone to Los Angeles . . ." David Gans, 1982
"Speaking for myself . . ." Jeb Wright of Classic Rock Revisited
"When I left the band . . ." Guillaume Roos, Sabbathlive
"Ozzy had been . . ." Jeb Wright of Classic Rock Revisited
"If there's one person . . ." Ozzyhead.com
"I think I was doing . . ." Bob Lang, Boston Rock, April 1994

CHAPTER TWELVE

"All of the bands . . ." Bob Nalbandian and Mark Miller of Shockwaves, 2002
"Rock and roll is my religion . . ." David Gans, 1982
"Few people know this . . ." Electric Basement
"I eventually ended up . . ." David Gans, 1982
"What Sharon would do . . ." Ben Thompson, Independent on Sunday, 1995
"My sister [Gillian] went nuts . . ." David Gans, 1982
"It wasn't a thing to . . ." Richard Hogan, Circus, March 1983
"Our fights were legendary . . ." The Guardian, 2001
"At first, when I first come . . ." David Gans, 1982

CHAPTER THIRTEEN

"That's a load of crap . . ." Jeb Wright of Classic Rock Revisited

CHAPTER FOURTEEN

"I had been doing . . ." www.black-sabbath.com

"The biggest thing . . ." Guillaume Roos, Sabbathlive

"It was a fun group . . ." Bob Lang, Boston Rock, April 1994

CHAPTER FIFTEEN

"Ozzy was served . . ." Bob Lang, Boston Rock, April 1994

CHAPTER SIXTEEN

"They were really . . ." Metal Express Radio, 2005

CHAPTER SEVENTEEN

"We were promised . . ." Joy Williams, Novaya Yezhednevnaya Gazeta, 1991

"I go onstage now . . ." The Sunday Chronicle Examiner, San Francisco

"I'm a lot happier . . ." Beth Nussbaum, Rock Scene, 1988

"I didn't know what . . ." Bob Lang, Boston Rock, April 1994

"While Ronnie was . . ." Thomas Orwat, 1994

"For me, that . . ." Doug Roemer, Psychadelic

"I was kicked out . . ." Petra van Kasteren, Aardschok, 1995

"I really don't understand . . ." Joy Williams, Novaya Yezhednevnaya Gazeta, 1991

CHAPTER EIGHTEEN

Multiple sclerosis diagnosis: The Guardian, 2001

"Musically, it's back . . ." Toronto Sun, July 1992

"We don't even . . ." Bob Lang, Boston Rock, April 1994

"At the time . . ." Livewire

"I really don't feel . . ." NY Rock

PART THREE

CHAPTER NINETEEN

"I will probably cut . . ." Jeb Wright of Classic Rock Revisited

"I like the new . . ." Dave Thompson, The Rocket, 1994

"We took him out . . ." Livewire

"*Cross Purposes* is . . ." Thomas Orwat, February 1994

"He's great!" Bob Lang, Boston Rock, April 1994

"I've started designing . . ." Gary James, 1994

"I'm very honoured . . ." Kristina Estlund, Rip, October 1995

"Well, there was a few . . ." St Catharines Standard, July 1995

"I was finding it difficult . . ." Metaverse/www.black-sabbath.com

CHAPTER TWENTY

"I met Ernie . . ." Livewire
"I wanted to make . . ." Dave Derocco, Pulse Magazine, July 1995
"Of course Ernie . . ." Petra van Kasteren, Aardschok, 1995
"*Plastic Planet* was always . . ." Metal Sludge

CHAPTER TWENTY-ONE

"It folded up . . ." Gary James, 1994
"I put money into . . ." Vintage Guitar, 1999

CHAPTER TWENTY-TWO

"They laughed at the idea," . . . The Guardian, 2001
"My father never set . . ." Sundance 2001, Pablo Kjolseth
"*Black Science* had a lot . . ." Jeffrey Easton, 2004

CHAPTER TWENTY-THREE

"I didn't understand [them] . . ." Metal Sludge

CHAPTER TWENTY-FIVE

"I have a saying . . ." Launch
"My whole family's . . ." David Gans, 1982
"I've just started . . ." Sylvie Simmons, *Mojo*, November 2000
"Tony worked on the album . . ." Clay Marshall, Billboard, October 2000
"Just take our name . . ." Metal Edge
"I think it's kind . . ." KNAC.com
"Almost four years ago . . ." Clay Marshall, Billboard, October 2000
"I had a little list . . ." Doug Roemer, Psychedelic
"I shouldn't have said it . . ." The Guardian, 2001
"I look to do another album . . ." Bob Nalbandian and Mark Miller of Shock-
    waves, 2002
"I was in New York . . ." Greg Sorrels, Clear Channel, 2001

CHAPTER TWENTY-SIX

"I didn't know . . ." The Guardian, 2001
"I hate watching myself . . ." Ian Gittins, The Guardian, June 2002

CHAPTER TWENTY-SEVEN

"I'm the happiest man . . ." MTV
"It was really fun/I'm not good with videos . . ." MTV

CHAPTER TWENTY-EIGHT
"After eight days . . ." The Daily Mirror
"I can't tell you . . ." www.black-sabbath.com

CHAPTER TWENTY-NINE
"I really enjoyed having . . ." Jeb Wright of Classic Rock Revisited
"One thing that sticks . . ." Revolver
"I think I finally got . . ." Jeffrey Easton
"I love bluegrass! . . ." Metal Sludge
"Glenn came over . . ." Jeb Wright of Classic Rock Revisited

CHAPTER THIRTY
"The book was hard to write . . ." The Sunday Mirror
"I'd like to do . . ." Billboard
"You know I'm one . . ." Launch
"We couldn't possibly . . ." Billboard
"I love the guys . . ." contactmusic.com/Blabbermouth.net
"I learned everything . . ." Joy Williams, Novaya Yezhednevnaya Gazeta, 1991
"I have definitely . . ." Guitar For The Practicing Musician, May 1994

I highly recommend the excellent www.black-sabbath.com, www.ozzyhead.com and www.sabbathlive.com.

1 2 3 4 5 6 7 8 9